Walter Ulbricht
Whither Germany?

Speeches and Essays on the National Question

 ZEIT IM BILD PUBLISHING HOUSE, DRESDEN

Publisher: German Institute of Contemporary History in Berlin
Works from the period 1930 to January 1960 have been taken in an abridged form
from the Complete Works of Walter Ulbricht,
Zur Geschichte der Deutschen Arbeiterbewegung
(On the History of the German Workers' Movement),
published by the Dietz Verlag in Berlin

Helga Kargus and Harry Köhler
of the German Institute of Contemporary History in Berlin
were responsible for the compilation of the works included in this volume

On German soil exists the first German peace state, the German Democratic Republic.

The German Democratic Republic, in which the working people exercise political power, sees its national and social mission to be to do everything in its power to ensure that a war never again starts from German soil, and that the path is paved for Germany's rebirth as a peace-loving, democratic state which maintains good-neighbourly relations with all countries of the world. It therefore above all supports a policy of understanding with the other German state, the West German Federal Republic, the normalization of relations between the two German states and their joint efforts to guarantee European security.

In contrast the program of the West German government envisages the perpetuation of the imperialist expansionist policy of the former Reich. That means annexation of the GDR and West Berlin as well as of Polish and Soviet territories. The simultaneous demand for control over nuclear weapons and the striving to establish once more a hegemony in Western Europe have also caused deep anxiety about the fate of peace on our continent in broad circles of the West European peoples and governments.

In view of this situation it is understandable that interest in the world is growing about the conceptions which the two German states themselves have on the future of the German nation, on a German peace settlement and on Germany's contribution to European security. In particular interest is growing in objective information about the German Democratic Republic and its policy.

*

This volume, which contains excerpts from speeches and essays by Walter Ulbricht, Chairman of the Council of State of the German Democratic Republic and First Secretary of the Central

Committee of the Socialist Unity Party of Germany, is to meet this need and give information on the social and national policy of the German Democratic Republic.

A son of the German working class is head of state in the German Democratic Republic in which the working class together with the peasantry, the intelligentsia and other sections of the people exercise political power. Walter Ulbricht, who from the period of his youth has stood in the front ranks of the anti-imperialist and anti-militarist struggle, is today the first representative of the socialist German peace state.

Since the end of the First World War Walter Ulbricht has had a considerable share in working out the national and social policy of the German working class and of all democratic forces of the German people. In the years between the two world wars he resolutely sought to have the necessary lessons from German history drawn and to have the peace-loving and democratic forces determine the path of the nation.

When in 1933 German monopoly capital set up the bloody dictatorship of Hitler fascism and began to unleash a new world war and realize its aggressive lust for power, a truly national German policy demanded the unity of all anti-fascist forces against the common foe, Hitler rule. The solution of this task was all the more urgent when Hitler fascism plunged mankind into the Second World War.

The German opponents of Hitler, in the first rank the communists, made every effort to unmask the anti-national and inhuman barbaric nature of fascism, to proclaim the truth to the German people, to organize the anti-fascist resistance movement and by the speedy ending of the fascist predatory war to create the prerequisites for Germany's rebirth as a democratic, peace-loving state which is respected in the world.

After German imperialism had been defeated on German soil by the assault of the armies of the Soviet Union and its allies in May 1945 the historic opportunity arose for the German people to go a completely new path and to find their place in the community of peace-loving peoples. As a leading politician of the party of the German working class Walter Ulbricht had a considerable share in working out this path which envisaged the joining of all democratic forces of the German people in order to abolish the foundations of imperialism and militarism and thus to uproot the policy of aggression.

Of quite particular importance was the establishment of the unity of the working class which was realized in Berlin on 21 April 1946 by the merger of the Communist Party of Germany and the Social

Democratic Party of Germany (SPD) into the Socialist Unity Party of Germany (SED). As the strongest and most influential party in Germany the Socialist Unity Party of Germany indefatigably supported the implementation of the principles of the Potsdam Agreement in the whole of Germany and the creation of a united, antifascist democratic and peace-loving Germany.

After the restoration forces of German monopoly capital, supported by the Anglo-American occupation powers, had split off the three western zones from the German national community in 1949, and a separatist West German state, the Federal Republic, was founded, the democratic forces in the East of Germany created the German Democratic Republic. As a state in which power was exercised by the workers and peasants, the German Democratic Republic, in accordance with its responsibility towards the whole German nation, saw its task to be to prevent the fatal course of remilitarization which was taken in West Germany, and to make possible the reunification of Germany as a peace-loving and democratic state.

The German Democratic Republic submitted numerous proposals for the solution of the German question, which envisaged the conclusion of a German peace treaty and the reunification of Germany by way of all-German elections.

The Federal Republic, however, rejected all these proposals, which were based on the recognition of the results of the Second World War, and instead further deepened the division of Germany by joining NATO in 1955 in the hope of attaining the forcible revision of the results of the Second World War with the aid of the North Atlantic Treaty Organization. It sharpened its cold war against the GDR which was primarily expressed by an unrestricted anti-communist agitation campaign, by the organization of espionage and subversive activities, by the systematic enticement of working people and by numerous other actions which caused serious damage to the GDR's economy. This cold war was designed to increase the tensions and finally prepare the forcible conquest of the GDR. The plans of West German generals for a military annexation of the GDR compelled our Republic in August 1961 to safeguard and control its state borders with West Berlin and West Germany. The failure of the West German federal government's unrealistic policy of revenge was thus demonstrated by these measures to the whole world.

The German Democratic Republic has consistently adhered to its policy serving peace, social progress and national unity. Already in 1957 Walter Ulbricht submitted the significant proposal for the formation of a confederation of the two German states. With the aid of a confederation a national link was and is to be established between the West German Federal Republic and the German Democratic Republic, a link which takes the different development in the two German states into consideration.

In its national policy the German Democratic Republic seized upon every constructive idea for a rapprochement of the two German states and for the establishment of peaceful relations, which was proposed by West German politicians as, for instance, in the Germany plan of the Social Democratic Party of Germany in 1959. It is characteristic that the government of the West German Federal Republic did not submit a single constructive proposal as to how existing tensions can be lessened and steps initiated for Germany's reunification as a progressive, democratic state.

In the following period the international prestige of the German Democratic Republic, whose economic upsurge could be continued unhindered, has further grown. By its efforts to pave the way for international relaxation of tension, to improve relations between the two German states on the basis of the principles of peaceful coexistence and to promote the peaceful cooperation of all European peoples, the significance of the German Democratic Republic as an important factor of European peace grew.

In view of this the number of West German citizens who support a democratic alternative to Bonn's aggressive policy is also increasing. Particularly in the recent period a lively discussion is taking place in West Germany on how to find a way out of the blind alley in which the West German Federal Republic is stuck as a result of the unrealistic revanchist policy of its government. In the international public the voices which demand a fundamental change of this peace-threatening policy are increasing.

The West German people's increasing desire for peace and understanding corresponds to a great degree to the national dialogue which began on the initiative of the Central Committee of the Socialist Unity Party of Germany and its First Secretary, Walter Ulbricht, at the beginning of 1966. The matter-of-fact discussion between the two largest German parties on the basic questions of the nation, proposed by the SED in an Open Letter to the members and friends of the Social Democratic Party of Germany, had a big echo which the SPD leadership could not ignore. For the first time in the history of the relations between the SPD and SED an official reply was given by the SPD to a letter of the SED. The SPD leadership, however, was not willing to sever its close ties with the policy of the West German government and sought to exploit the dialogue for an ideological penetration of the GDR, thus proving to be a defender of a more mobile imperialist policy of revenge. These tactics of the SPD leadership showed that at present it is not ready for understanding between the two largest German parties on the vital questions of the German people. The SED is therefore making efforts to extend the dialogue into a broad discussion between the workers of the two German states and with all forces in West Germany interested in peace, democracy and understanding. The issue is to confront the Bonn policy of revenge with a policy of disarmament and understanding between the two German states.

By this national dialogue the SED once more made an important contribution towards preventing a war from starting from German soil. This policy of the SED, which corresponds to the interests of all peace-loving people, in particular also to that of the peoples of Europe, was again extensively dealt with by Walter Ulbricht in his speech on the occasion of the 20th anniversary of the founding of the SED in April 1966. This speech was new evidence of the constant endeavours of the SED to do justice to its national responsibility.

This volume, which contains the lessons of German history, conveys a picture of the continuity of the national and social policy of the German Democratic Republic and its constant efforts to make use of all—even the smallest—possibilities, to serve the welfare of the German people which is inseparably linked with the safeguarding of peace.

The constructive policy of the German Democratic Republic makes plain that, although the German question can be solved by the people of the two German states in a democratic manner, its main point, however—the lasting safeguarding of peace in Europe—affects the vital interests of all peoples in the world, because in the final analysis the aggressive policy of the West German Federal Republic threatens not only the German Democratic Republic. The recognition is therefore increasingly gaining ground that it is in the very interests of all states to maintain normal relations with the GDR, to reject the West German Federal Republic's aggressive presumption that it is the sole representative of the Germans and thus also to promote the establishment of peaceful relations between the two German states on a basis of equality.

The agreement of the basic interests of all peoples with the policy represented by the GDR is not least also expressed by the approving and active attitude which the GDR adopts towards conventional and atomic disarmament.

The active solidarity of the socialist German state with the peoples struggling for their liberty has also received general recognition. In *contrast the West German Federal Republic has up to now always taken the side of the oppressors of other peoples. It suffices to point to the support of the West German Federal Republic for the aggressive actions of the US imperialists in Vietnam and the aid to the racist regimes in South Africa and Rhodesia.*

In national as well as in international policy the opposite character of the two German states is becoming ever plainer. If the West German Federal Republic embodies the fatal past, the German Democratic Republic represents the new, the real Germany. The GDR embodies the peaceful future of the whole German nation, its social progress and its new relations with all peoples.

*

The individual works of this volume have been put in chronological order so as to give information on the development of the national policy in the sequence of events. The sole exception is the introductory contribution entitled "Way and Goal of the German People". Walter Ulbricht wrote this work in 1959, on the eve of the 10th anniversary of the founding of the German Democratic Republic. It is a concise summary of the most recent German history, primarily the development of the national question, and it seemed to be particularly suited to give the foreign reader first a survey of the concern of this volume before he turns to the numerous, extremely instructive details worked out with a profound knowledge of the subject.

Professor Dr. Stefan Doernberg

Director of the German Institute of Contemporary History

Berlin, July 1966

Contents

Way and Goal of the German People

On the occasion of the 10th anniversary
of the founding of the German Democratic Republic,
published in September 1959

The Historic Task

After ten years of the advancement of the German Democratic Republic it is time to draw up a balance. The founding of the German Democratic Republic—this has been proved in these ten significant years—was a turning-point in the development of Germany. The way was barred once and for all to German imperialism and militarism. Moreover, in ten years of construction of the German Democratic Republic the workers and peasants, intellectuals, craftsmen and tradesmen in the GDR showed the entire German people that the German people can live in peace and friendship with other peoples and in prosperity without militarism, without frontier demands and other revanchist aims, without Hitler generals and armament millionaires.

After the military defeat of Hitler Germany under the blows of the heroic Soviet army the united working class under the leadership of its revolutionary party, the Socialist Unity Party of Germany (SED), has accomplished the greatest revolution in German history in alliance with the working farmers, intellectuals and the other working sections of the population. Protected by Soviet troops, it has thoroughly eliminated German imperialism, i. e., the economic and political power positions of monopoly capital, in a democratic way. The SED has overcome and banned the barbaric ideology of German imperialism and fascism. It has set up an anti-fascist–democratic system and boldly carried out the transition to the socialist revolution.

The way led from Georgi Dimitrov's challenge in the Leipzig trial to the unification of all peace-loving, democratic forces against Hitler fascism, from the Brussels Conference of the Communist Party of Germany in which the strategy and tactics for the overthrow of Hitler fascism through the creation of a Popular Front were worked out to the struggle of the National Committee for a Free Germany, to the unification of the Communist and Social Democratic Parties of Ger-

15

many, the formation of the bloc of anti-fascist democratic parties and the founding of the first workers' and peasants' state in German history which is based on the National Front of Democratic Germany, to the great Seven Year Plan, the plan of the victory of socialism.

The historic task of uprooting rapacious German imperialism which twice precipitated Germany into catastrophe and of laying the foundations of a peace-loving, democratic Germany was fulfilled in one part of Germany. Why was this the historic task of the working class and all peace-loving, progressive forces in Germany? This requires being substantiated.

The Destiny of the German Nation

The German bourgeoisie whose leadership was in the hands of monopoly capital has twice led Germany into a war catastrophe in the course of 25 years. Now the ruling circles in West Germany are in the process, in a way similar to that of Hitler, of using the defeat of Germany in the world war to stir up chauvinism and justify revanchist demands. Ruling circles in West Germany try to persuade the population that Germany was defeated in the two world wars only because its political leaders had carried out a wrong alliance policy. But in alliance with the USA and by the formation of the Bonn–Paris axis the "new order in Europe", that means the domination of Europe by German imperialism, will be achieved the next time.

The ruling circles of the German bourgeoisie which before the First as well as before the Second World War were completely unable correctly to assess the relation of forces between the states still do not understand that since the great change in the world, since the victory of the Great October Socialist Revolution, any imperialist policy of conquest is doomed to failure. Only for a short time, when the Rapallo Treaty was concluded between Germany and the Soviet Union, did the leading circles of the German bourgeoisie seem to correctly perceive the new situation. They temporarily entered upon the road of a new foreign policy which strove for friendly relations with the Soviet Union. But to the detriment of Germany the reactionary circles got the upper hand and undermined the German-Soviet treaty.

The German bourgeoisie had tried to persuade the German people for many decades that the expansion of its domination over other peoples was the key to national power and freedom. The ruling circles maintained that the German nation would be the more powerful and free the better it was able to expand its rule over other peoples, suppress the freedom and self-determination of other peoples, subject and plunder them in predatory wars.

Thus the national question was dealt with completely within the sense of chauvinism which corresponds with the nature of imperialism. Broad sections of the German petty bourgeoisie have long followed the Junker-militarist, imperialist-fascist forces on this way without realizing that in doing so they were only forging their own fetters, that with it the abyss between the German people and the neighbouring peoples threatened by Germany was torn open and kept open, that with it the people were deprived of freedom, delivered up to the imperialist interests and finally precipitated into the gulf of war catastrophes. For the German people only strengthened the power of monopoly capitalism and the militarists when the majority of them followed the reactionary forces.

What German reaction passed off as the highest national principle, the "freedom of expansion" as it was expressed in German militarism was in reality the deepest humiliation and most wretched violation of people and nation.

The unity of Germany was not brought about by the revolutionary insurrection of the democratic forces of the German people in the democratic revolution from the Peasants' War to the bourgeois-democratic revolution of 1848, that is, not in the struggle against the feudal Junker powers. On the contrary, national unity was created as the result of the concentration of the reactionary forces in their struggle against the democratic revolution, especially against the most democratic force, the working class. This fact had a decisive influence on the entire national development, it gave and gives it a specific character.

National unity did not result from the democratic revolution. Therefore, democracy did not become the content of the developing German state and the national idea characterizing it. The alliance of the bourgeoisie with the feudal Junker forces meant the rule of bourgeois-Junker reaction over the German people. This was necessarily connected with aggressive foreign policy objectives, with efforts for expansion and domination over foreign peoples. This anti-democratic development which was directed against democracy at home (the rule of the German people) as well as against democracy abroad (respect for the freedom and self-determination of other peoples) constantly sharpened the internal and external contradictions.

Already in 1848 Marx had clearly recognized and stated that the destiny of the German nation depends on the development of democracy. He stated that not only the contradictions in Germany but also

17

the contradictions between Germany and its neighbouring states will sharpen and that there will be no peaceful Europe if the national development has an anti-democratic trend and is directed against its own people and foreign peoples. Marx wrote in the *Neue Rheinische Zeitung* in July 1848:

"If Germany's blood and money is no longer to be wasted to its own disadvantage for the suppression of other nationalities, we must struggle for a real people's government, the old building must be torn down to its foundations."

Only the German working class, educated by the great ideas of the world-changing theory of Marxism-Leninism and the experiences of its struggles, has understood the real nature of this national task. Starting from the laws of social development discovered by Marx and Engels it recognized the internal contradictions of German capitalism and the laws of its decline in the period of imperialism. This scientific theory gave Karl Liebknecht the strength to raise the banner of struggle against the war policy of German imperialism during the First World War and Ernst Thälmann the ability to call to the German people in due time: Hitler means war!

Capitalism has fulfilled its historic task. It has enormously raised the productive forces of man and brought forth that political force which is called upon to free these productive forces from the fetters of capitalist and imperialist domination, initiate and guide their systematic development, the proletariat. It is the leader of the liberation struggles of the peoples against the capitalist and imperialist yoke, the struggles for the achievement and full unfolding of democracy, the right of self-determination and the liberty of the nations.

Lenin's great prophecy that a new epoch of human history begins with the October Revolution has proved to be true. Not only the national contradictions of the old Russia broke out and were solved in the Great October Socialist Revolution. The contradictions revealed and solved by the Great October Socialist Revolution were the essential contradictions of the epoch, the contradictions between the interests in exploitation and conquest of the imperialist rulers, the masters of finance capital, and the vital interests of the people. And the solution which was attained through the setting up of Soviet power, the dictatorship of the proletariat, the formation of the first socialist state under the leadership of the great Lenin and the Communist Party of the Soviet Union, this is the solution of the fundamental contradictions of our epoch.

The victory of the peoples of the Soviet Union and the establishment of Soviet power on one-sixth of the globe led to the rapid maturing of the working-class movement in all countries of the world and also in Germany. The Communist Party of Germany (KPD) grew and strengthened as the great anti-imperialist, democratic and socialist force. It concentrated all its efforts on gathering and organizing the masses in the great anti-imperialist united front, leading them into the struggle for the overthrow of the imperialist forces and helping true democracy to break through at home. If this struggle had been successful, democracy would have been asserted in foreign relations, and Germany would have entered the family of peace-loving peoples. How much sacrifice of blood would have been spared the German people! How high could our material and cultural standard be today if all productive forces which were wasted in the war had been used for peaceful constructive work!

These great world-wide antagonisms between the proletarian-revolutionary forces on the one hand and the imperialist-reactionary forces on the other must be kept in view when we turn to our national development in Germany; for these antagonisms also went right through our people and were expressed in the great class struggles. We cannot correctly assess either the national development as a whole or its present state and its perspectives if we do not correctly recognize the contradictions of social development and the class struggles of our time.

The development of German imperialism after the First World War took place under basically different conditions than before.

The development of the Soviet Union into a world power and the most powerful state in Europe made the imperialist policy of the ruling circles in Germany still more hopeless. Whereas in the working class and elsewhere in the people sympathies for the socialist Soviet Union became increasingly stronger and the call for close economic and friendly relations with the Soviet Union ever louder, the most reactionary and aggressive circles of German monopoly capital and militarism sought a way out in fascism and war. The great economic crisis from 1929 to 1932 had deeply shaken German capitalism. The masses of the people did not want to live as before, and the ruling class was no longer able to maintain its rule with the old means.

As deep as the crisis was, the German bourgeoisie was still in a position to maintain the division of the working class and prevent the social democratic and trade union leaders from taking part in the anti-fascist united front. Whereas the bourgeoisie shifted over to active support for fascism, the right-wing social democratic leaders spoke of the possibility of "economic democracy". The extreme circles of the bourgeoisie promoted the transition to fascism through dictatorship with the help of Article 48 of the Weimar Constitution and support for the SA terror whereas the liberal circles of the bourgeoisie caused the social democratic leaders to remain inactive and saw their chief task in preventing the Social Democratic Party of Germany (SPD) from participating as a party in the anti-fascist unity of action. As a consequence of the division of the working class the heroic struggle of the Communist Party of Germany under the leadership of Ernst Thälmann together with the social democrats, trade unionists and democratic citizens who fought in the anti-fascist action was not able to prevent the seizure of power by Hitler fascism and the beginning of the war of conquest of fascist German imperialism.

The cycle of the historical development in Germany from crisis to temporary increase in economic activity to crisis to war led to the Second World War. The Communist Party of Germany not only condemned the war crime of Hitler fascism and organized the resistance but also explained to the German people from the beginning that the catastrophe of Germany will also be inevitable in this Second World War and why it will be so.

Germany which had already been defeated in the First World War also had no chance whatever to win the Second World War when it attacked the most powerful state–the Soviet Union.

The imperialist aggression of the ruling class of Germany in two world wars and the inevitable defeats which Germany suffered in them as well as the policy of the circles ruling in West Germany at present to go this way for a third time by means of atomic war armament prove that the elimination of German imperialism is the vital question of the German nation. After the ruling class of the bourgeoisie had plunged Germany into two war catastrophes the safeguarding of peace, the happiness of the people and the future of the nation demand that the working class–the only class which is not incriminated by any imperialist war policy and which consistently struggles for peace–take the destiny of the nation into its hands in alliance with the peasants and all other working strata. In view of the existence of two German states–a socialist state and a capitalist state–the safeguarding of peace is possible only in the alliance of the peace-loving forces of West Germany with the German Democratic Republic.

The Capitulation of the German Army and the Potsdam Agreement

Nazism carried through the policy of German imperialism in the most barbaric way. It attacked one capitalist state after the other in

Europe until after the invasion of the Soviet Union it suffered one defeat after the other under the heavy blows of the Soviet army and through the heroic struggle of the Soviet people.

Against the up-to-then most serious threat to the future of the whole of mankind through barbaric German nazism the peoples of the world united in the anti-Hitler coalition under the leadership of the Soviet people. It was the masses of the people of the capitalist states which forced their governments to join the anti-Hitler coalition. The attempt of the Hitler government to conclude an alliance with Great Britain and the USA during the war failed since fascist German imperialism directly threatened the British people and the direct spheres of influence of Britain and the USA. The Hitler armies were beaten to final destruction and capitulation on German soil.

Great Britain and the USA not only wanted to hit German fascism in their struggle against Hitler Germany but to weaken and beat Germany down as a competitor. At the same time they were interested in having the Hitler armies wage the chief blow against the Soviet Union so that Hitler Germany and the Soviet Union would weaken each other in mutual struggle and finally the USA and Great Britain could control the European continent. The later US President Truman expressed this in the following words: "When we see that Germany is winning we should help Russia, and when Russia wins, we should help Germany, let as many as possible kill each other in this way." (*New York Times,* 24 June 1941)

In the Great Patriotic War of the Soviet Union against German fascism the Soviet people were victorious, although Hitler Germany had available the economic reserves of all occupied European countries, and thus proved the superiority of Soviet power, the socialist economic system and the moral-political unity of the Soviet people. In order to be able to have a share in making decisions at the end of the war the USA and Great Britain were forced to form the second front in Western Europe–after long delay. The Soviet people on whom the Hitler armies had inflicted horrible suffering began the reconstruction in the hinterland already during the advance of the Soviet troops to the west. The Soviet Union, through its military, economic and political victory, was strengthened by the Great Patriotic War and won great authority throughout the world.

The three states of the anti-Hitler coalition–the Soviet Union, Great Britain and the USA–drew the conclusions from the war in the Potsdam Agreement and agreed upon measures to make a return of German fascism and militarism impossible and to guarantee a peaceful, democratic development in Germany. The Potsdam Agreement therefore not only obligated the allied occupation powers to denazify and demilitarize Germany, but also to dissolve the excessive concentration of power in the German economy. Thus the Potsdam Agreement gave the democratic German forces the express right to start the struggle to deprive nazism and militarism of power. For example, the Potsdam Agreement provided:

"It is not the intention of the Allies to destroy or enslave the German people. It is the intention of the Allies that the German people be given the opportunity to prepare for the eventual reconstruction of their life on a democratic and peaceful basis. If their own efforts are steadily directed to this end it will be possible for them in due course to take their place among the free and peaceful peoples of the world."

In their basic tenor the Potsdam decisions corresponded to the interests of the working people of Germany. This agreement envisaged the liquidation of nazism and militarism, the creation of democratic conditions, the elimination of the power position of the monopolies and made the carrying through of a democratic land reform possible. The USSR brought its entire authority to bear in the working out of the Potsdam Agreement to save Germany from dismemberment and assure an anti-fascist–democratic development.

The special aspect of the situation was that the armies of states with two different social systems acted as occupation powers. The eastern part of Germany was under the administration of the socialist Soviet Union, the western part under the administration of the three capitalist states, the USA, Great Britain and France. Whereas the Soviet occupation organs granted the anti-fascist–democratic forces all democratic freedoms and promoted the formation of democratic parties and mass organizations, the western powers prevented the democratic activity of the working people and the formation of their organizations, supporting the monopolists and their employer organizations.

The safeguarding of peace which was to be achieved through the Potsdam Agreement was only possible through the development of democracy in Germany itself.

The task was clear. It was to develop an anti-nazi, anti-militarist, democratic and peaceful state power which guaranteed democracy internally and externally, thus giving the German nation the secure ground of firm friendship with the Soviet Union and with the other peoples and at the same time opening the door to social progress. For this reason a radical breach had to be made with the reactionary, imperialist past.

The Unification of the Working Class and the Formation of the Bloc of Anti-fascist–Democratic Parties and Mass Organizations

The population of Germany was still influenced by the horror of the defeat of Hitler Germany when the class struggle broke out with full sharpness in Germany. It was the struggle between the anti-fascist and democratic forces on the one side which fought for the fundamental transformation of the old conditions by the complete liquidation of the fascist state apparatus and the deprivation of the war criminals and monopolists of economic and political power, and the reactionary forces on the other side which wanted to save the foundations of German imperialism and its state apparatus.

The necessary fundamental change in Germany could not take place within the framework of the old capitalist state or within the framework of the old formal bourgeois Weimar democracy, for precisely under the Weimar Republic had fascism been able to develop and finally seize power. The ultimate liberation of the people from nazism could only take place through the assumption of political power under the leadership of the working class and in alliance with the other working sections. Under the conditions of the Soviet occupation the assumption of political power took place in the form of the construction of new, anti-fascist–democratic administrative organs from the bottom to the top and the transfer of the largest trust enterprises to the administration of the occupation power and the taking over of the management of the enterprises of the war criminals and active nazis by the workers and the technical intelligentsia. In connection with the taking over of the control of production in the industrial enterprises, the removal of war damage and the creation of normal economic conditions the working class acquired the knowledge which enabled it to play the leading part in the new shaping of Germany.

The working class and the working people who for decades had been influenced by bourgeois and reformist propaganda and afterwards had to submit to the nazi agitation were at first clear only that fascism had to be uprooted. But there was nevertheless much unclarity about the further way because the decisions of the Brussels Conference of the KPD of 1935 were known but to a part of the officials. The Communist Party of Germany which had been an opposition party since its founding had to completely adapt itself to its new role and to assume the initiative in the construction of the new state administration and in the control of production.

The appeal of the Central Committee of the Communist Party of

Germany of June 1945 set forth the strategy and tactics clearly and simply and formed the basis for the unification of the working class and the union of all anti-fascist–democratic forces. The appeal of the Communist Party of Germany stated:

"Now it is a question of learning the lessons of the past thoroughly and for ever. We must enter upon an entirely new road!

"May every German become aware of the fact that the road taken by our people up to now was a false road which led to guilt and disgrace, war and ruin!

"Not only the rubble of the destroyed towns, but the reactionary rubble of the past must be thoroughly removed. May the reconstruction of Germany take place on a solid basis so that a third repetition of the imperialist policy of catastrophe is impossible.

"With the destruction of Hitlerism it is at the same time a question of completing the democratization of Germany, the bourgeois-democratic reformation which began in 1848, of completely removing the feudal vestiges and destroying the reactionary old Prussian militarism with all its economic and political offshoots.

"We are of the opinion that the way of forcing the Soviet system on Germany would be wrong, for this way does not correspond to the present conditions of development in Germany.

"We are rather of the opinion that the decisive interests of the German people in the present situation prescribe another way, the way of the setting up of an anti-fascist, democratic regime, a parliamentary-democratic republic with all democratic rights and liberties for the people.

"At the present historical turning-point we communists call all working people, all democratic and progressive forces of the people to this great struggle for the democratic renewal of Germany, for the rebirth of our country!"

The appeal of the Communist Party of Germany of June 1945 which showed the German people the way of the anti-fascist–democratic transformation leading to a new, democratic, peace-loving Germany became the basis for the unity of action of the SPD and KPD in the eastern part of Germany. The readiness of the communist and social democratic comrades to overcome the division was an essential prerequisite for the final elimination of the years-long quarrel between brothers. The comrades had realized that the night of fascism had been able to spread only because of the disunity of the working class.

The founding of the Socialist Unity Party of Germany was the greatest achievement in the history of the German working-class movement since the proclamation of the Communist Manifesto by Karl Marx and Friedrich Engels. The founding of the SED means the historic victory of Marxism-Leninism in the German working-class movement. The "Principles and Aims of the Socialist Unity Party of Germany", the constitution of the party and a "Manifesto to the German People" were unanimously adopted at the unification congress on 21 and 22 April 1946.

The New was that now the working class appeared as a united integrated force in one-third of Germany and was led by a party based on the Marxist theories of scientific socialism. Its consistent struggle against the political, economic and ideological restoration attempts of the trust rulers, Junkers and militarists and its close connection with all working people made it the leading force in the solution of the new tasks.

However, the unification of the working class through the founding of the SED did not suffice to liquidate nazism and uproot German imperialism. It was necessary to conclude the alliance with the working peasants and with the democratic forces of the crafts, tradesmen and also with those sections of the bourgeoisie which opposed nazism. This great ideological-political-economic process of transformation represented by the anti-fascist–democratic revolution in the eastern part of Germany could only be successful when, along with the SED, the revolutionary party of the working class, there were also other democratic parties in which members of the various sections of the working people could join. The bloc of anti-fascist–democratic parties was formed.

The struggle of the Socialist Unity Party of Germany for the setting up of an anti-fascist–democratic system served to save the German nation. For this it was necessary to win the majority of the people for this struggle. This was only possible through the creation of political conditions which corresponded to the nature of the democratic dictatorship of the workers and farmers.

The Anti-fascist–Democratic Transformation

We began to build up a new state administration and to mobilize the working people for active participation in the political, economic and cultural construction.

For the first time the masses of the people were led onto the road of the conscious shaping of the social system. The working class and the other working people learned to master the problems of new social construction only by raising questions of social development

25

with the masses, discussing them with them and involving them in the solution of these tasks.

Despite inadequate food and clothing many responsible workers appeared in their old works in the first days after the liquidation of Hitler fascism. Overcoming the disruptive manoeuvres of the monopolists, they salvaged machines and raw materials out of the rubble, cleared out the work-halls and got production going again. In doing so they had the unselfish support of the representatives of the Soviet occupation power. The Soviet Union has always distinguished between the Hitler regime and the German people—despite unheard-of sufferings and losses inflicted upon the country and its population by the criminal aggression of Hitler Germany. Immediately after the military defeat of the Hitler army it helped the German people with foodstuffs to overcome hunger and with raw materials to get economic life going.

The spirit with which the workers began to reconstruct the east of Germany inspired all the other working sections, too. Communists, social democrats, trade unionists and other anti-fascists placed themselves at the head of the masses of the people who were seeking for a way out. In the struggle against hunger and cold, in the struggle against moral decay and spiritual disorganization which fascism had brought upon Germany they were able to make vivid to the working people the great perspectives of a democratic Germany linked with the other peoples in peace and friendship. Often the workers asked if the disappointments of 1918 would not be repeated and if the power of the German monopolists would not nevertheless be restored after all their efforts and sacrifices. They received the following convincing answer from those working class officials who were familiar with the teachings of German history: Everything depends on what force is developed by the working class to strengthen the unity of its own ranks and conduct the struggle for the destruction of German imperialism and militarism together with all the other working people. The working class officials who had been instructed in Marxism had recognized that even under the conditions of a highly developed and numerically strong industrial proletariat the following words of Lenin are fully valid:

"Only the proletariat can be a consistent fighter for democracy. The proletariat can only become a victorious fighter for democracy on condition that the mass of the peasantry joins its revolutionary struggle."

In the eastern part of Germany the enterprises had to be put into operation again, the harvest had to be gathered in and at the same time the state and economic power positions of the fascists and war criminals had to be destroyed.

Such a turn in development necessitated the overcoming of the old contradiction which had arisen out of bourgeois society between the rule of the armament monopolies, the militarist Junkers and other fascists and the democratic interests of the people.

The big barrier of the old conditions opposing the development of democracy had to be torn down, as it were. Thus all political forces had to be concentrated on unfolding the creative energies of the people, educating the people to conscious cooperation in the social development and practice and organizing and developing the entire social life on this basis. The anti-fascist democracy had to be based on that class and in its development be led by that class which alone is in a position to break the resistance of the reactionary forces, to free the masses of the people from their influence and thus lead them onto the way of conscious transformation, the working class.

Its unification as well as the development of its strategy and tactics on the basis of the Marxist-Leninist theory of the role of the proletariat in the democratic revolution—that was the foundation for the gathering of all anti-fascist, democratic forces and their orientation on the great revolutionary transformation of social conditions.

From the bottom to the top, in the towns, communities and regions and later in the provinces the anti-fascist—democratic parties formed new, anti-fascist—democratic administrative organs under the leadership of the working class. The working people who for years had suffered in the concentration camps and prisons of the fascist state, the supporters of the anti-fascist resistance movement in Germany and the officials who had been banished from Germany and had struggled against the Hitler war from outside Germany jointly organized the new state power. The new administrative organs directed the normalization of economic life, they showed the masses the way of new social construction and helped them to get rid of old, reactionary conceptions.

The Democratic Land Reform

After the anti-fascist-democratic forces had taken the control of industrial production into their hands the centres of militarist-fascist reaction in the countryside had to be removed. With their big landed property the Junkers also had a "ruling position" in the village, and democratic life could not develop in the countryside. The Junkers' big landed property had therefore to be liquidated; therefore, the expropriation without compensation of the big landowners and Junkers, the carrying through of the democratic land reform was the most essential prerequisite for the democratization of life in the village and for the development of democracy at all.

The peasants and agricultural labourers had correctly understood the KPD's program of action of 11 June 1945.

Many workers and other anti-fascists answered the call of the party and went to the countryside. They convinced the agricultural labourers and small peasants that the rule of the Junkers and barons had ended for good and that the agricultural labourers, small and medium peasants now determine their destiny themselves. Together with the workers and supported by the democratic administrative organs the peasants with little land and agricultural labourers set to work.

By reason of many demands of the working rural population for the distribution of the big landed property the administrations of the five provinces issued decrees on the carrying through of the land reform which legalized the actions of the masses. Hundreds of thousands of agricultural labourers and working peasants carried out this tremendous task with the active support of the working class and the new anti-fascist–democratic administrative organs. The alliance of the working class with the working peasants received a solid basis with the democratic land reform. The working peasants were no longer forced to do statute labour. They were able to develop their farmsteads with the support of the working class and with their mutual help. The new alliance of the working class with the working peasants was the basis for the successful construction of the anti-fascist–democratic system.

The democratic organs suppressed the resistance of the Junkers and big landowners and ensured the uniform carrying out of the land reform in all Länder and provinces of the Soviet occupation zone.

Land reform commissions were elected in the villages at meetings of the agricultural labourers, peasants with little land and resettlers. The composition of these commissions reflects the active cooperation of broadest sections of the population. Thus there were 51,939 members of the land reform commissions in the entire Soviet occupation zone on 15 January 1946. Of these 24,761 were non-party, 26,649 were communists and social democrats and 529 were liberal democrats or members of the Christian Democratic Union.

The carrying through of the land reform characterized its democratic nature. The large number of non-party members of the land reform commissions clearly shows that the working people were ready to carry through the democratic transformation and eliminate the rule of the reactionary forces in the countryside.

Various forms of mutual help developed among the peasants. Committees of mutual peasant aid came into existence out of which the Peasants' Mutual Aid Asociation, the large democratic mass organization of the working farmers in the Soviet occupation zone, grew in the further development. This mutual economic aid of the peasants contributed to raising the democratic consciousness and political activity in the village.

The creation of new economic relations between town and country essentially contributed to the fact that in the east of Germany the decisive majority of our people was united in the struggle for the democratic transformation of our fatherland.

In the solution of the historic task, in the construction and the shaping of the new system the working people in the east of Germany were supported by the Soviet occupation power in every respect and always found advice and aid.

The Democratic School Reform

Another important measure on the way of the democratic transformation of social life in the Soviet occupation zone was the democratic school reform. The party of the working class was faced with the task of educating the German people, and especially German young people, in the spirit of peace, democracy, friendship among the peoples and humanism by giving intellectual and cultural life a new form.

In a joint "appeal for a democratic school reform" of the Central Committee of the KPD and the Central Committee of the SPD of 18 October 1945 the two working-class parties declared:

"... the uprooting of nazism and militarism with their reactionary foundations, the safeguarding of a lasting peace and the democratic renewal of Germany are unthinkable without a fundamental reform of the German school, without a universal democratization of the entire educational system."

In this appeal reference was made to the following problems in the reorganization of the German school system:

1) The education of the young generation in the spirit of militant democracy.
2) The purging of the entire educational and administrative personnel from nazi and militarist elements.
3) The creation of a uniform school system for all children.

4) The German school must promote and consolidate the democratic unity of the nation. The separation of church and school was fixed.
5) Instruction is the task of the public school system.
6) Creation of a democratic staff of teachers.
7) Fundamental reorganization of the curricula and the production of new textbooks.
8) Reshaping of the entire higher educational and university system.

The joint appeal of the KPD and SPD was of great significance for the preparation of the laws for the democratization of the schools which were adopted in the individual Länder in the summer of 1946.

The educational monopoly of the possessing class was broken by the democratic school reform. All working people were guaranteed the right to an education. A uniform school system was established and the level of education decisively changed and improved. Thousands of communists, social democrats and non-party workers, peasants and anti-fascist minded representatives of other sections began to work as new teachers, thus guaranteeing the democratic education of the young generation in the Soviet occupation zone.

The construction of the new school system, the opportunity to attend secondary schools for the children of workers and peasants, the later introduction of the workers' and peasants' faculties and the generous grants at the colleges and technical schools were the prerequisites which made the development of a new intelligentsia possible from the ranks of the workers and working farmers.

The democratic school reform broke the educational monopoly of the possessing class. All working people were granted the right to an education. An integrated school system was created and the standard of education decisively changed and improved.

The Expropriation of the War Criminals and Active Nazis

After the industrial enterprises had in part been set going again with the help of the working class, the technical intelligentsia and with the support of the Soviet occupation organs the workers insisted on the expropriation of the war and nazi criminals so that the material basis for a restoration of the old conditions would be taken from them.

On the initiative of the SED which had placed this important task at the head of its present demands, the democratic parties and the provincial section of the Confederation of Free German Trade Unions (FDGB) cooperating in a bloc in Saxony proposed to the

Saxon provincial administration a referendum on the taking over of the enterprises of war and nazi criminals. The Saxon provincial administration complied with the request of the democratic bloc and fixed the plebiscite on the expropriation of the war and nazi criminals for 30 June 1946. Through this referendum a basic question of Germany's future was made the subject of direct democratic decision by the population.

The idea of the plebiscite fully corresponded to the interests and thoughts of all working people and met with immediate general approval in Saxony as well as in the whole of Germany. "Advocating the referendum means avoiding the third world war", was one of the many slogans bearing witness of the will of the working people for a peaceful future for Germany.

In many meetings, rallies and declarations it was expressed that large parts of the population considered the referendum a day of judgment of the people over those guilty of the catastrophe of Germany. In this question the workers were of one mind with the working farmers, tradesmen, resettlers, intellectuals, clergymen and former ordinary members of the nazi party. The shop committee members and trade union officials in Dresden, for example, demanded:

"The general meeting of shop committee members and trade union officials of the Dresden region of the FDGB (Confederation of Free German Trade Unions) unanimously demands the transfer of the enterprises of war and nazi criminals to the democratic organs of self-administration. They demand this to ensure the peaceful development of the economy. They thereby want to pave the way for a better future of the working sections in Germany and prove to the world that in Germany the democratic forces have taken over the leadership and that those guilty of the Hitler crimes and the war are punished."

The large number of voices from all sections of the population showed that the party executive of the SED (Socialist Unity Party of Germany) assessed the situation correctly in its appeal for the referendum when it stated:

"The war criminals were always united against the people.

Now the people are uniting against the war criminals."

The population of the province of Saxony, the strongest industrial area of the Soviet occupation zone, gave the entire German people an example in this focal question of the German future.

When the votes were counted on 30 June 1946 the anti-fascist–democratic forces had won an outstanding victory; 94.1 per cent of the voters had made use of their right to vote. This high participation showed a degree of political activity which up to then was unusual in Germany; 77.7 per cent of the voters said "Yes" to the solution of the vital question for Germany, 5.8 per cent of the votes were invalid and only 16.5 per cent of the voters defended the criminals of Germany. This result was an unambiguous judgment of the majority of the population on the war criminals and war profiteers.

The poll in Saxony proved that the relation of forces in East Germany had significantly changed in favour of the anti-fascist–democratic forces. The unity of the anti-fascist–democratic forces which formed the cornerstone of the policy of the SED had won a new victory. The big participation in the referendum and the vote of 77.7 per cent in favour proved that the sympathies of the population turned to those who safeguarded the democratic and peaceful development of Germany.

Already before the plebiscite in Saxony wide sections of the population in the other Ländern and provinces of the Soviet occupation zone also declared their sympathy for the referendum and demanded the expropriation of the war criminals. Thereupon, in accordance with the will of the large majority of the population, decrees on the taking over of the enterprises of the war criminals and active nazis and their transfer to the people were enacted in Thuringia, Saxony-Anhalt, Brandenburg and Mecklenburg in July and August 1946. In the provincial administrative bodies the representatives of the working class, peasants and petty bourgeois circles agreed upon legal regulations for the expropriation of the war criminals which was afterwards carried through by the working class itself in alliance with the democratic members of the intelligentsia.

Naturally it could not be expected that the reactionary and imperialist forces would accept this decision tacitly. Therefore, the realization of the decrees required vehement, long-lasting class-struggles in the entire Soviet occupation zone. With the referendum and the expropriation of the enterprises the struggle of the workers against the monopolists which had begun in 1945 with the purge of the enterprise managements and administrations of active fascists and the dissolution of the Flick trust reached a new climax.

The anti-fascist–democratic system received a firm social-economic basis in the nationally-owned sector of the economy which now came into existence. The ground had been paved for the development of a true democracy.

New economic laws became effective in the nationally-owned sector. Where the ground had been cut from under the anarchy and competition of the capitalist mode of production, the economy could and had to be developed and managed in accordance with a forward-looking economic plan. The very expropriation of the war profiteers was very complicated, but the far more difficult tasks came only afterwards. The working people had to learn to direct the enterprises and the nationally-owned economy and overcome the old habits from the capitalist period. The great experiences of the trade union officials and those comrades who had become acquainted with the construction of socialism in the Soviet Union as well as the friendly relations with the technicians, engineers and scientists made it possible to solve the new tasks.

The new construction of a German peace economy had to be accomplished by the working people under the most difficult conditions. The German working class had taken over a terrible heritage after the catastrophe of the Hitler war. The fascist mismanagement of many years, the destruction of industry, transport, agriculture, the exhausted soil, the lack of cattle and implements created many difficult problems in getting the economy in operation again.

Many millions of resettlers had to be fitted into a normal life. The splitting of the German economy and the hampering of the goods turnover between the individual zones by the western occupation powers made the normalization of life more difficult. The economy had to be set going in the daily struggle against hunger, cold and destruction. Food rations were scanty. But the democratic administrative organs, with the help of the Soviet occupation power, saw that the food rations could be supplied regularly and to the full extent until the new harvest.

The soldiers and officers of the Soviet occupation power always were friends, protectors, helpers, advisers and teachers alike for the workers. They unselfishly made available the entire treasure of their knowledge and capability for the construction of an economy systematically managed by the working people.

The way from the anarchy of capitalist economic management and the chaos of the Hitler heritage to a systematic construction of a democratically guided economy was not easy to find. Initial successes proved that the working class will master these great tasks.

At the same time the German people had to make great efforts to repair at least a part of the damage inflicted upon other peoples by the fascist predatory war and contribute as best they could to reconstructing the destroyed countries. Honest fulfilment of the reparation obligations was not only a demand of justice and morality but at the same time of decisive significance for the re-education of the German people. Only thus could the German people regain the confidence of other peoples.

The First Free Democratic Elections

In the second half of 1946 and at the beginning of 1947 communal, regional and provincial diet elections took place in all occupation zones of Germany. In the Soviet occupation zone the population elected the communal legislative bodies from 1 to 15 September 1946. The elections for the regional and provincial diets were held on 20 October 1946. The Berlin town council was elected on the same day. The holding of the elections corresponded to the democratic way which was fixed in the program of the Socialist Unity Party of Germany and in the joint decision of the anti-fascist–democratic parties. After the state apparatus had been purged of active nazis, after the democratic land reform had created the basis for a democratic development in the countryside and after the hegemony of the trusts, big banks and armament capitalists had been liquidated by the expropriation of the war criminals, a really democratic basis for general, equal, secret and direct elections existed.

For the Socialist Unity Party of Germany the carrying through of the elections meant a further step to the realization of its program which demanded the construction of the administrative bodies on the basis of democratic elections and the unification of Germany as an anti-fascist democratic republic.

The carrying through of the elections and the formation of democratic representative bodies in the communities, regions, provinces and Länder corresponded with the Potsdam Agreement. The elections in the Soviet occupation zone in 1946 were thus the first elections in German history which took place without the pressure of monopoly capital. They could reflect the real relation of forces and show to what extent the German people had learned the lessons of the past and learned to act in a democratic manner.

The anti-fascist democratic administrative bodies which had been formed after the catastrophe of Hitler Germany were now placed on the firm basis of elected representatives of the people and could rely on the confidence of the population and the authority of parliamentary decisions.

For the SED the elections were at the same time a crucial test. Every party, the Socialist Unity Party of Germany (SED), the Christian Democratic Union (CDU) and the Liberal Democratic Party of Germany (LDPD) drew up their own lists of candidates for the elections. The democratic administrative organs which were responsible for the elections closely adhered to the provisions of the Potsdam Agreement.

In the discussion during the electoral contest new forms of democracy hitherto unknown in Germany developed and stood the test, forms which were expressed, for example, in the reports of administrative employees, in free criticism and the democratic nomination of candidates. The results of the elections proved that the vast majority of the working people of the Soviet occupation zone decided for the policy of peaceful construction and the unity of the anti-fascist–democratic forces as proposed by the SED. The heavy poll of 90 to 94 per cent showed a political activity which had scarcely been experienced in Germany before. On 20 October 1946 50.3 per cent voted for the SED in the regional elections and 47.6 per cent of all voters voted for the SED in the provincial diet elections. In the communal elections in September 58.5 per cent of all valid votes were for the SED.

The elections in the autumn of 1946 showed that the majority of the population was for the construction of the anti-fascist–democratic system in Germany which was advocated by the SED. The elections proved that the SED received by far the most votes despite the party lists. For the first time in German history the forces of peace and democracy had been victorious in free elections over the forces of fascism and reaction. The unification of the working class had made this success possible.

After the elections the new, democratic state organs were formed in the provinces, regions and communities. The provincial governments had the character of an anti-fascist–democratic coalition in which the SED as the leading workers' party and the petty bourgeois parties, like the CDU and LDPD, were represented.

Restoration in West Germany and the Role of Social Democracy

Whereas the anti-fascist–democratic forces in the east of Germany destroyed the foundations of German militarism and imperialism and waged a determined struggle to overcome the vestiges of fascism, restoration began in West Germany. After the total defeat of Hitler fascism the international relation of forces had changed in favour of the Soviet Union so that in West Germany, too, there was the possibility of uprooting fascism and militarism and of a democratic development. These possibilities could be clearly recognized since in the eastern part of Germany there was the example of the anti-fascist–democratic transformation. But in West Germany the occupation powers did not adhere to the provisions of the Potsdam Agreement but hampered the democratic development, the overcoming of nazism and the formation of anti-fascist–democratic political parties and trade unions. The monopolists and big capitalists were already able to form their organizations when the workers were still forbidden to organize their trade unions.

The occupation powers tried to prevent the democratic development in West Germany especially by measures against the Communist Party of Germany. Permission for the KPD to exist was delayed in part for weeks and months in contrast to other parties. Despite all chicanery the communists fought untiringly and under great personal sacrifices. Also in West Germany the Communist Party of Germany was the only party which looked after the true interests of the nation. It was this party which mobilized the working people for the struggle against the policy of splitting Germany.

It is indisputable that at that time the economic power of German monopoly capital was paralysed and its political power lost. The social democratic workers, too, did not want a repetition of the Weimar Republic but thorough order. Countless resolutions of enterprise employees, trade union conferences and enterprise conferences testify to the great readiness of West German workers also to follow the example of their brothers in the Soviet occupation zone, to carry through the land reform and break the rule of the trusts. Over and over again the workers demanded that mines, works and enterprises become common property. Thus, for example, the employees of the Blohm and Voss Shipyard in Hamburg demanded that the shipyard become public property.

Whereas the social democratic leaders rejected the community of action of the workers, the big capitalist forces made efforts to carry through the union of those forces which were interested in the restoration of the rule of monopoly capital and the maintenance of the reactionary state power through the formation of a new party, the Christian Democratic Union. At that time the CDU was very skilful in pretending to support many demands of the people in order first to build up an influential party and then with its help prevent the expropriation of the big monopoly capitalist undertakings.

It is interesting that in June 1946 Konrad Adenauer, in a letter to *Neues Deutschland,* the central organ of the SED, protested against the reproach that he supports big capital, the trusts and monopolies and denied that big capital called national socialism into existence. This is the text of the letter:

"I receive your issue of 18 May 1946 with the article entitled 'Political Smugglers at Work'. In this article you state in detail that I solemnly announced in a meeting in Cologne that it is not true that big capital called national socialism into existence. The quotation is correct, but incomplete because it is torn out of context. I declared at this meeting that militarism called national socialism into existence and that the economy supported it only when it had been approved to a certain extent by militarism, especially by the Reichswehr. This representation is correct. I further think that the struggle against militarism should not be postponed in favour of the struggle against trusts and monopolies or big capital. Big capital is down and out at the moment, but not so the militarist idea. By the way, I opposed big capital, the trusts and monopolies with great determination and clearness in my speech."

Adenauer's letter shows that the bourgeoisie had changed its tactics. It took a position against Hitler's policy and nazism and shifted the entire responsibility for the military defeat and catastrophe onto the Hitler government which was in fact already annihilated. It thereby tried to distract attention from the main question, namely the uprooting of German fascism the roots of which lay in the rule of monopoly capital, big landed property and militarism. Leading circles of the bourgeoisie utilized the depression of the population about the defeat of Germany and the political confusion to salvage the roots of German imperialism under the mask of the alleged abolition of Hitlerism. The imperialist occupation powers supported these deceptive manoeuvres.

The big capitalist forces and the western occupation organs exerted pressure on the leading SPD bodies which were being formed and tried to intimidate them with threats. Nevertheless, they could not prevent many social democratic groups in West Germany, too, from demanding cooperation and unification with their communist class brothers. In large enterprises of the Rhine-Ruhr district, in Hamburg, Hanover, Heidelberg, Mannheim and South Baden decisions of SPD and KPD factory groups for unification were adopted. Joint organizational committees of the SPD and KPD came into existence on the lower and middle levels. In many shop committee elections the representatives of working class unity received the majority of votes.

At the shop committee elections in twenty Munich enterprises, including the most important large enterprises, 36 candidates of the KPD, 15 of the SPD, 8 of the CDU and 10 non-party candidates were elected.

The mass demonstrations in Essen, Wuppertal, Cologne, Brunswick, etc., at which the two chairmen of the Socialist Unity Party, Wilhelm Pieck and Otto Grotewohl, spoke, were high points of the movement for the unification of the working class in West Germany.

The imperialist western powers did everything in their power to maintain the division of the working class and help their German business friends who were down and out. An intensified suppression of the unity movement by the western occupation powers began. The SED organizational committee was not allowed to travel into the western zones and appear in meetings. Nevertheless the western occupation powers were able to prevent unity only because the SPD leadership supported them and even tried to excel them in their agitation against the Soviet occupation zone and the construction of the anti-fascist–democratic system which began in the east.

To establish an alibi for themselves and further undermine the fighting will of the working people the right-wing SPD leaders often used the argument that the occupation regime hinders the German people from making their own democratic decisions on their vital questions. In an essay in the London *Star* Schumacher wrote that the tragedy of Germany lay in the fact that the victorious powers had not found a common standpoint in their policy towards Germany.

This was answered by the Socialist Unity Party of Germany as representative of the interests of the entire German nation:

"It seems to us that the tragedy of Germany has its deepest cause not in the relationship between the allies but in the disunity of the German working class and the German people. This is also the tragedy in the western areas of Germany! The allies are not to blame that in the western areas the militarist big landowners are not yet expropriated; the allies are not to blame that the trade unions do not yet have the full right of co-determination in the economic organs; the allies are not to blame that there are so little sound forces of the working people active in the organs of self-administration; solely to blame is the disunity of the working people. That is the tragedy of Germany."

The Prevention of Trade Union Unity

The establishment of trade union unity and the already advanced cooperation of the trade unions in the whole of Germany was also systematically sabotaged by the leadership of the SPD and the right-wing West German trade union leaders. The joint decisions of the interzonal trade union conferences were not carried through in West Germany.

Under the pressure of the trade union movement in the Soviet occupation zone and the West German trade unionists and with the support of the World Federation of Trade Unions interzonal conferences of the German trade unions were held from 1946 to 1948 to discuss joint tasks and the formation of a united German trade union movement. According to the will of the millions of trade unionists in all parts of Germany these interzonal conferences were to work out a clear trade union program and the foundations of a renewed, united German trade union movement.

Although the West German trade union leaders were mostly reformists they could at first not put forward their line openly at these interzonal conferences because if they had done so they would have unmasked themselves before their own members and the entire German working class. That is the explanation for the fact that at the interzonal conferences decisions were made which were suitable for forming the program of a progressive trade union policy for the whole of Germany. The most significant document adopted at the interzonal trade union conferences is the decision of the fourth conference on the new shaping of the economy. The document contains such demands as the socialization of the key industries, economic planning, land reform, etc. The first measure to be carried through was to be the socialization of the coal mines and other basic industries.

Other decisions of the interzonal conferences envisaged the creation of a uniform social insurance law for the whole of Germany and the authoritative cooperation of the trade unions in the administration of the social insurance system. The conclusion of a peace treaty was also demanded already at the Fourth Interzonal Conference whereby it was expressly stated that the German people must have the opportunity to make their voice heard by letting representatives of the trade unions have a hearing with the foreign ministers of the powers.

The World Federation of Trade Unions performed a great service concerning the coming into existence of the interzonal conferences. It repeatedly intervened with the occupation powers in the interest of the German working class and showed great interest in the development of a free all-German trade union movement.

The military governments of the western zones, however, in carrying through their policy of splitting Germany, soon shifted to hampering the work of the interzonal conferences, making the appearance in West Germany of representatives of the Confederation of Free German Trade Unions (FDGB) and progressive West German trade unionists impossible and influencing the West German delegates in the sense of the imperialist western powers.

From the middle of 1947 and to an intensified degree from the end of 1947 and the beginning of 1948 the West German opportunist trade union leaders struggled against the enforcement of the decisions adopted at the interzonal conferences. They made efforts to distract attention from the decisive questions and postpone final decisions. They also disavowed the jointly adopted resolutions and intensified their efforts to split the German trade union movement. With their participation in the conference of the trade unions of the countries taking part in the Marshall Plan in March 1948 which in fact came to terms with the restoration of the rule of monopoly capital in Europe the West German right-wing trade union leaders tore up the fundamental decisions of the interzonal conferences. At the end of 1948 they completed the break in relations with the FDGB and thus brought about the division of the German trade union movement for a long period.

None of the decisions jointly adopted at the interzonal conferences has been implemented in the western zones. These decisions which were joint resolutions of the German trade union movement were implemented only in the then Soviet occupation zone, the present German Democratic Republic. Thus the promising establishment of a united German trade union movement was thwarted for the time being by the reformist trade union leaders and the imperialist western powers.

The First Negotiations on the Cooperation of the German Organs of the Four Occupation Zones

In accordance with the provision of the Potsdam Agreement that Germany should be treated as an economic unit the SED tried to bring about the cooperation of all democratic forces in the whole of Germany and also cooperation between the existing state organs, the provincial (Länder) governments. The SED struggled for the treatment of the German question as a whole, for it was our aim to bring about anti-fascist–democratic development in the whole of Germany. A conference of the prime ministers was agreed upon between the provincial governments of the four zones. But the conference of prime ministers which was held in Munich in June 1947 already clearly showed the gap which had developed between the western zones and the eastern zone in the two years since the unconditional capitulation of Hitler Germany.

Already at the first session the prime ministers from the east of Germany were able to state that they stood before a wall of federalist and reactionary prejudice. The prime ministers of the provinces of the Soviet occupation zone were not allowed to make proposals for the agenda. The prime ministers of the western zones refused to discuss the formation of a central German administration. They even refused to give the representatives from the east of Germany the opportunity to make a declaration. Even when the prime ministers of the provinces of the Soviet occupation zone accepted the request of Prime Minister Reinhold Maier of Baden–Württemberg to deal with the question "How do we come to an All-Germany?" as the main point they were voted down. The social democratic Deputy Prime Minister Dr. Hoegner of Bavaria openly admitted that the theme and course of the conference were fixed by the American military government and that there was an instruction not to participate in any political or public law discussion. Under these circumstances there was no possibility in Munich of honest, frank talks and effective decisions for the benefit of the German people.

In Munich the way was to be prepared for the creation of a divided Germany with antagonistic particularist interests of the provinces instead of a united, democratic Germany. The western occupation powers wanted to prevent an agreement between the prime ministers of all German provinces from coming about. The prime ministers and not delegations of the individual provinces composed of all sections of the population were to be called in as representatives of Germany to the future deliberation of the peace treaty. The creation of an all-German secretariat of the prime ministers which was to work with a reactionary western majority only in the interest of the western occupation powers was therefore envisaged. The prime ministers of the Soviet occupation zone were to play the role of dummies. Their participation was only to camouflage the division of Germany.

No honest German could lend himself to such a game. The prime ministers from the eastern zone drew the only possible conclusion from this situation–they left the conference.

The Western Powers Prepare to Split Germany

The western powers resisted especially stubbornly the realization of the obligation to maintain Germany as a unit which they had assumed in the Potsdam Agreement. They repeatedly prevented the formation of central German administrations. At the meeting of the

Council of Foreign Ministers in Moscow at the beginning of 1947 the delegation of the Soviet Union had proposed the formation of five central German administrations as a first step to the treatment of Germany as a national unit, including the drafting of a provisional democratic constitution and the preparation of general, equal, direct and secret elections for an all-German parliament and a provisional all-German government. But the western powers, especially the representatives of the USA, rejected these proposals with the argument that they did not think such elections to be necessary.

At the London conference of the Council of Foreign Ministers in December 1947 the Soviet delegation again proposed the creation of an all-German government and, in addition, the formation of a German consultative council from representatives of the provinces, the democratic parties, the trade unions and other democratic organizations of the whole of Germany. The delegation of the USA, which, in the interest of its policy of division prevented the adoption of all joint decisions of the four powers concerning Germany, thought it opportune to reject these proposals, too, thus breaking up the London conference of the Council of Foreign Ministers.

Whereas the USA, Great Britain and France thus dismissed all proposals aiming at the treatment of Germany as a unit they organized in West Germany separate administrative organs for the western zones and thus broke the Potsdam Agreement. On 2 December 1946 the unification of the American and British zones was accomplished through a separate agreement. Afterwards special administrative organs were created for this area to which the French zone was later attached. Finally, on 20 June 1948, the three western powers introduced a separate currency for West Germany without informing the Soviet Union. The up-to-then uniform German currency was called in in the three western zones. Thus the economic relations between the western zones and the eastern zone and the normal relations between them were destroyed. This measure meant the beginning of the open division of Germany. It became obvious that the western occupation powers and the reactionary circles in West Germany had prepared a plan for the division of Germany for a long period. A little later the USA changed over to reducing West Germany to economic dependence on the USA by means of the Marshall Plan.

In this dangerous situation the Socialist Unity Party of Germany took the initiative of convoking the German People's Congress in which delegates from all parts of Germany took part. This first German People's Congress addressed a unanimously adopted manifesto to the London conference of foreign ministers in which it is stated: "The German people want the peace treaty to guarantee the economic and political unity of Germany or that the German people be granted the right to decide on this question themselves through a referendum."

But the British government refused an entry visa to the delegation of the German People's Congress to go to London, and shortly afterwards the American and British occupation authorities also banned the movement "For Unity and a Just Peace".

The demand for the conclusion of a peace treaty was raised by the peace-loving forces in the whole of Germany at a very early date. Thus the first German People's Congress demanded the peace treaty in December 1947. In July 1948 the German People's Council renewed the same demand, and also after the founding of the German Democratic Republic the struggle for the conclusion of a peace treaty always remained on the political agenda. The Soviet government explicitly supported these demands of the German peace forces. But the imperialist western powers which feared that a peace treaty could frustrate their systematic policy of the constant division of Germany sabotaged all these endeavours. In doing so they had the full approval of the ruling reactionary forces in West Germany.

It gradually became evident that although the western powers had temporarily postponed the division of Germany in Potsdam, they had by no means abandoned it.

The Result of the First Period of the Revolutionary Transformation in the Eastern Zone and Developments in the Western Zones

The anti-fascist–democratic transformation in the eastern zone led to a change in the socio-economic conditions and the relation of class forces. In the process of the revolutionary transformation the democratic dictatorship of the workers and peasants was created.

These are the fundamental changes which were obtained through the anti-fascist–democratic transformation:

1) As a consequence of the unification of the working class, the merger of the KPD and SPD into the Socialist Unity Party of Germany and the creation of the alliance of the working class with the working peasants, the working class was able to take over its leading role in the further historical development. In this period a vehement class struggle took place between the remains of the imperialist bourgeoisie and the working class. As a result of this struggle the socio-economic basis of the imperialist big bourgeoisie, the big landowners

and the Junkers was destroyed. With the taking over of the enterprises of the war criminals and active nazis and the property of the big landowners and Junkers by the working class, the working peasants allied with it or the Soviet socialist occupation power solid foundations were created for the leading role of the working class.

Under the leadership of the SED the working class created the new, anti-fascist–democratic administration, the first organs of the new state power, in alliance with the parties of the anti-fascist–democratic bloc.

2) Immediately after the overthrow of nazi rule the working class began to create the alliance with the working peasants. This alliance began with the cancellation of certain coercive measures of the fascist dictatorship and the establishment of normal economic relations between town and countryside on a democratic basis. In accordance with the program of the KPD and later the SED the democratic land reform was systematically prepared, adopted by the bloc of anti-fascist–democratic parties, and the peasants were helped to carry through this revolutionary transformation in the village. The rule of the big landowners, Junkers and landed proprietors was replaced by the alliance of the working class and the working peasants. The middle peasants won the strongest influence within the peasantry.

3) The anti-fascist–democratic transformation took place peacefully without civil war because the united working class succeeded in convincing the majority of the working people and because the Soviet occupation power protected the construction of the anti-fascist–democratic system against the western occupation powers' attempt to interfere. It was a special feature of the anti-fascist–democratic development in the eastern zone of Germany that petty bourgeois parties had also come into existence alongside the revolutionary party of the working class. The alliance between the working class, the working peasants and the other working sections of the people found its organized expression in the cooperation of all parties in the anti-fascist–democratic bloc.

As concerns the so-called middle classes, the liberation of the petty bourgeois sections and the middle-grade enterprisers from the pressure of finance capital formed the basis of this new relationship. After the catastrophe of the imperialist war policy of German monopoly capital these petty bourgeois circles sought the way out in a peaceful, democratic development and saw in the working class that force which is able to prevent the cycle of crises and remove the social insecurity which is caused by the capitalist law of dog eat dog.

4) The far-sighted and consistent policy of construction of the working class under the leadership of the SED led to a new relation of broad circles of intellectuals with the working class. The democratization of social life, the re-establishment of scientific work, the school and higher educational system and cultural life induced large parts of the intelligentsia to take an active part in the democratic construction. All this led to the development of friendly cooperation between the working class and broad circles of the intelligentsia and to the overcoming of the vestiges of nazi and imperialist ideology.

5) In the struggle for the construction of the anti-fascist–democratic administration, the setting of the economy in operation and the taking over of the enterprises of the war criminals and big landed property by the people the working class acquired the expert knowledge to exercise its leading role in the state and economy. The construction of the anti-fascist–democratic administration soon assumed a new quality. The democratic dictatorship of the workers and peasants came into existence. Nor could this be otherwise since the anti-fascist–democratic transformation necessitated the suppression of all restoration attempts of the overthrown reactionary forces and the protection of the democratic achievements against sabotage and subversion. The development of the state power into a firm state power of the workers and peasants was also necessary in the interest of speeding up the economic and organizational construction.

6) The anti-fascist–democratic parties of the eastern zone of Germany acted in the national interest of the German people by consistently realizing the principles of the anti-Hitler coalition and the Potsdam Agreement of the USSR, the USA and Great Britain with the help of the Soviet occupation power.

7) The SED and the other democratic parties and organizations of the Soviet occupation zone did everything for Germany to be treated as a unit and its division prevented in accordance with the Potsdam decisions. They worked for the formation of an all-German economic council, for central German administrations, for a united trade union movement in the whole of Germany, for the conclusion of a peace treaty which would safeguard the construction of a united, democratic and peace-loving Germany.

8) In West Germany the ruling big capitalist circles had decided to prevent an anti-fascist–democratic development in every way possible. For this purpose they organized the division of Germany by creating a separate currency for the three western zones to prepare for the establishment of the West German separatist state and the West German separatist government.

This national disaster, the division of Germany by the imperialist circles of the USA and the reactionary big capitalist circles of West Germany was possible only because the western occupation powers prevented the free development of the workers' organizations and because the right-wing social democratic leaders led by Schumacher and the trade union leadership headed by Tarnow prevented the unification of the working class and split the working class.

The Founding of the German Democratic Republic, the First Peace State in Germany

On 7 October 1949 the German People's Council which had been elected by the Third German People's Congress constituted itself as the Provisional People's Chamber of the German Democratic Republic and put the Constitution into force. Comrade Wilhelm Pieck was unanimously elected president of the German Democratic Republic in a session of the People's Chamber and the Länderkammer (provincial diets) on 11 October 1949. The provisional government of the German Democratic Republic headed by Comrade Otto Grotewohl as prime minister was confirmed on 12 October 1949.

The founding of the German Democratic Republic was the reply of the patriotic forces of Germany to the formation of the Bonn separatist state. Through the founding of the German Democratic Republic the way to the east was barred for ever to German militarism. A peace state was created as the basis for the struggle of the German people against the corrupters of Germany, for a peace-loving, democratic and united Germany. "We can state with satisfaction," Comrade Wilhelm Pieck declared in his speech on the occasion of his taking over the office of president of the German Democratic Republic, "that the struggle of the National Front of all Germans for the unity of Germany and a just peace treaty has reached a new phase with the founding of the German Democratic Republic. We can continue the struggle for our just cause with a greater prospect of success than before. The German Democratic Republic does not stand alone. In its struggle for peace, unity and justice it can rely on the friendship with the great powerful Soviet Union, on the friendship with the peoples' democracies and with all peace forces in the world."

The first German workers' and peasants' state is the legitimate German state because in it the principles of the anti-Hitler coalition are implemented and the roots of German militarism removed for ever. The first German workers' and peasants' state is the legitimate

German state because it has raised to the status of public law those aims for which the peace-loving, democratic and progressive forces of the German people made tremendous sacrifices in the struggle against Hitler fascism and which were fought for by the states of the anti-Hitler coalition—the Soviet Union, the USA and Great Britain.

The first German workers' and peasants' state is the legitimate German state because in it the principle "State power derives from the people" has been realized for the first time in German history and the working class exercises state power in alliance with the working farmers, intellectuals and the other working sections of the population.

The first German workers' and peasants' state is the legitimate German state because it represents the peaceful interests of the entire German people and strives for the reunification of Germany through the formation of a confederation of the two German states.

The founding of the GDR was the strongest blow after 1945 against reaction which was restored in West Germany; it created the prerequisite for the national rebirth of Germany as an anti-imperialist, peace-loving and democratic state. The founding of the German Democratic Republic was a turning-point in the history of Europe, for the safeguarding of peace in Europe depends on developments in Germany. There is but one force in Europe which can drive to war, that is German imperialism. Thus peace in Europe is safeguarded when German militarism and imperialism are successfully muzzled.

The founding of the German Democratic Republic faced the working class with new, greater tasks. Whereas up to then the functions of the local organs and the central administration were still limited and the central state administration lay in the hands of the Soviet military administration, after the founding of the GDR the working class took over the main responsibility for the central state power, for the economic, political and cultural development of the country. A special feature of the people's democratic state, which is one form of the dictatorship of the proletariat, is that the state power relies on the National Front of Democratic Germany. Although the working class bears the chief responsibility all fundamental questions are deliberated and decided in the bloc of the parties (Socialist Unity Party of Germany, Christian Democratic Union, Liberal Democratic Party of Germany, Democratic Peasants' Party of Germany and National Democratic Party of Germany).

A new stage in the development of the working class also began with the founding of the German Democratic Republic. Whereas up to then many measures were introduced by order, the working class and its leading party, the SED, now had to develop the people's democratic state power, strengthen the state positions of power of the working class and at the same time strengthen the alliance with the working farmers and the other strata, create a real relationship of confidence and unfold the active cooperation of the entire working population.

The economic basis of the young workers' and peasants' power was the nationally-owned sector of the economy. To augment this property of the people was one of the most important tasks of the working people. At the time of the founding of our Republic about two-thirds of industrial production came from the nationally-owned enterprises and the Soviet joint-stock companies. Elements of socialism had already developed in the period of the anti-fascist–democratic transformation. With the creation of the workers' and peasants' state the task of the transition to socialist planned economy and the development of the nationally-owned sector of economy into the socialist sector was on the agenda. The following words by V. I. Lenin applied to the situation at that time:

"The objective course of development is such that one cannot advance from the monopolies without going to socialism . . . There is no middle road."

After monopoly capital had been expropriated the working class faced the task of carrying through the socialist transformation and winning the allies in the bloc parties for this higher task.

The imperialist bourgeoisie of West Germany had divided Germany to safeguard its class rule in West Germany and on this basis wage the struggle to restore the rule of monopoly capital and militarism throughout the whole of Germany. The dialectics of development consisted in the fact that this class policy of the imperialist bourgeoisie of West Germany forced the working class and the progressive forces in the German Democratic Republic to carry through the transition to the socialist revolution. For the tasks of overcoming the consequences of the war, the raising of the material and cultural living conditions of the people and the removal of economic contradictions could be solved only by the socialist transformation. The Socialist Unity Party of Germany had long held back with socialist demands. The SED for a long time restricted itself to the consistent implementation of the principles of the anti-Hitler coalition until the western powers and the most reactionary circles of the West German bourgeoisie proceeded to divide Germany in the interest of safeguarding their class rule and restoring German imperialism. After the most reactionary forces of the West German bourgeoisie had set up a wall on the Elbe and Werra, thus documenting their desire to make West Germany the basis of revanchist policy and the struggle against the socialist states, the only way left to the population of the German Democratic Republic was that of the construction of socialism.

The transformation of the anti-fascist–democratic development into the socialist revolution resulted logically from the internal laws of development of the people's democratic revolution begun in 1945. When the party set the task after the defeat of Hitler fascism firstly to complete the bourgeois-democratic revolution and build up an anti-fascist–democratic system it was aware that this was the only possible and best way under the specific conditions of development in Germany to uproot German imperialism and lead the working class and its allies to the socialist revolution. The most important prerequisites for the transition to the socialist revolution were created with the destruction of the foundations of imperialism, the creation of the nationally-owned sector of the economy and the construction of the new state power from top to bottom.

The necessity of this transition was put on the agenda by the course of the class struggle in Germany. In view of the policy of the imperialist occupation powers and the Adenauer regime which was directed to the restoration of German imperialism and militarism in the western zones the working people could not stop with the introduction of general democratic transformations.

In Germany there existed the strongest concentration of industry in large monopolies, the class rule of a small group of the monopolist bourgeoisie over the majority of the people. Precisely in this Germany whose people were plunged into catastrophe in two world wars it was to be proved with the example of the first workers' and peasants' state that the working people are able to create the model of the peace-loving Germany which is in a position to solve all political, economic and cultural problems of Germany through the construction of socialism. The antagonistic contradictions which are characteristic of capitalism, the contradictions, class antagonisms and difficulties still existing in our Republic could only be overcome step by step through the transition to socialist planned economy. All exploitation of man by man was abolished and the full unfolding of the creative forces of the people guaranteed. Only through the transition to the socialist revolution could the achievements of the first stage, the anti-fascist–democratic transformation, be safeguarded and the restoration of the rule of monopoly capital and militarists made impossible once and for all.

The First Five Year Plan

At the Third Congress of the SED in July 1950 the directives for the first Five Year Plan were adopted which became the program of the National Front of Democratic Germany for the first phase of this new stage. The Five Year Plan envisaged a two-fold increase in industrial production as compared with 1936.

The Five Year Plan was to lessen the disproportions and difficulties which had come into existence in our economy as a result of the division of Germany. Above all a national metallurgical basis was to be created and by means of the raising of labour productivity the pre-war standard of living was to be achieved.

The rapid development of the productive forces which is a law of development of all socialist countries was of special significance for our Republic since it has to conduct the economic competition with the imperialist system on the territory of a nation with open frontiers with the opponent. The economic construction represented from the beginning the main front of the struggle against the imperialist forces of the west. After these had been unable to prevent the German Democratic Republic from coming into existence they tried to force our Republic to its knees and throttle it economically. They tried in every way possible (blockade of interzonal trade, economic espionage and sabotage, enticement of scientists and specialists, etc.) to prevent the economic strengthening of our Republic. As a consequence of a few objective reasons (greater war destruction than in the western zones, economic disproportions as a result of the division of Germany, the lack of hard coal, the lack of a heavy industry, etc.) our Republic had a far worse economic starting point than the western zones. The USA had not only suffered no war losses but had made gigantic profits during the war and increased its economic strength; it could therefore give capitalism in West Germany great help. The Soviet Union and the people's democracies, however, had suffered immense war damage and could therefore give our young people's democratic state but little economic support in the first years. This is the explanation of the fact that West German capitalism temporarily won a considerable advance in some fields.

The imperialist forces of the west did everything in their power to sharpen the class struggle. The ruling reactionary circles of West Germany speculated on bourgeois-parliamentary illusions in the population and tried to organize the resistance of citizens of the GDR to the workers' and peasants' power under the slogan of "freedom". But the social-economic foundation of our people's democratic state became ever more solid. The nationally-owned sector grew. The alliance between the working class and the working farmers strengthened. The result of the popular elections of October 1950 showed the population's approval of the Five Year Plan. With a participation of 98.5 per cent 99.7 per cent of the voters voted for the electoral program and the joint list of candidates of the National Front of Democratic Germany.

The fulfilment of the Five Year Plan, especially the development of heavy industry, demanded great efforts and tremendous sacrifices from the working class. The living conditions of the working class improved more slowly than those of the other sections of the population. But the mastering of these great economic tasks determined not only the destiny of the German Democratic Republic but also the future of the nation. It was the heaviest blow against the splitters of Germany, for thus the independence of our Republic was defended and consolidated. The foundations were created systematically to promote all branches of the national economy and to be able to constantly raise the material and cultural standard of living of the working people. This task could only be solved by socialism.

The Transition to the Construction of Socialism

The Second Conference of the SED which took place in July 1952 stated that the political and economic conditions as well as the consciousness of the working class and the majority of the working people are so far developed that the construction of socialism has become the basic task of the German Democratic Republic.

The Second Party Conference pointed out the multiplicity of forms and methods of the transition to socialism and emphasized the significance of the National Front of Democratic Germany for the construction of socialism. The party conference declared that there is no intention to expropriate the small private entrepreneurs but that ways and means should be found to give the members of all sections of the working people a perspective in socialism.

As the chief instrument of the construction of socialism the people's democratic state power had to solve many new tasks. It was its task to guide the socialist transformation deliberately and systematically, promote the initiative of the working people, develop socialist consciousness and at the same time protect the people's democratic system from hostile machinations.

The implementation of the Five Year Plan faced the cadres of the party, the state and economy with many new and complicated tasks.

4*

The working class did not yet have much experience in this field which had for decades been the monopoly of the bourgeoisie.

In the struggle for the implementation of the Five Year Plan the officials of the working class had to learn to master the planning and management of the national economy. This was connected with great difficulties. Many obstacles, old views, customs, ignorance and indifference had to be overcome and, not least, hostile sabotage activity had to be prevented.

The transition from capitalism to socialism takes place in the GDR under the special conditions of the existence of two German states with two different social systems. This creates a complicated situation and many additional difficulties for the overcoming of which there was no specific experience up to now.

The West German monopolists and militarists try with all their forces to utilize the inevitable, objective contradictions and difficulties of the transitional period for their purposes in order to discredit our party and undermine the workers' and peasants' power. In doing so they make use of West Berlin occupied by the imperialist western powers which was expanded by the reactionary forces into a centre of cold war in the middle of the territory of the German Democratic Republic.

When in 1953, for a number of economic and political reasons, a difficult situation temporarily arose the Bonn rulers tried with the support of the American occupation power to overthrow the workers' and peasants' power. The objective of the fascist putsch of 17 June 1953 consisted in destroying the revolutionary achievements of the working people of the GDR, setting up a counter-revolutionary regime, returning the former trust enterprises to the monopolists and the land of the working farmers to the Junkers and creating a new hotbed of war in the heart of Europe. The fascist elements suffered an ignominious failure because the overwhelming majority of the working class and the working people firmly supported the workers' and peasants' power and the Soviet troops stationed on the territory of our Republic supported the working people in putting down the fascist putsch.

In the struggle to carry through the first Five Year Plan the working class and all working people recorded performances of historic significance. The tasks set in the Five Year Plan by the Third Party Congress were overfulfilled.

The industrial production plan was fulfilled by 105 per cent; the index of production rose by 110 per cent as compared with 1936; whereas the west zone increased by only 77 per cent. This tempo of industrial development was unique in Germany and only possible under the conditions of the workers' and peasants' power and on the basis of socialist relations of production.

The working people were able to record such widely visible successes as the construction of the East Metallurgical Works, the West Iron Works in Calbe, the large coking plant in Lauchhammer–the first integrated lignite works in the world–the construction of new shipyards and large power stations.

The share of the socialist sector in the entire national economy increased to 71.9 per cent, in industry to 86.3 per cent and in trade to 77.8 per cent. The national income increased by 62 per cent, and the general standard of living, supply, health and cultural care of the population were considerably raised. These results confirmed the correctness of the policy of the party, the government and the National Front of Democratic Germany. These successes expressed most clearly and convincingly the historic role of the working class as the creator of the socialist social system which is superior to capitalism.

In the years of the first Five Year Plan the working class became the real leading force of society. The workers were no longer as before the proletariat exploited and oppressed by the reactionary state power but the working class freed from exploitation and leading the state power. It proved able under the leadership of the party to give all working people social security and made them who were once oppressed by capitalism the true creators of history. It raised them to be shapers of a happy, socialist future. The growth of the working class as the decisive force for shaping the new society was the most significant result of developments in our Republic.

One of the greatest performances of the working class in creating the foundations of socialism was the continuation of its policy of alliance and the assistance granted to the individual working peasants in their voluntary joining of cooperatives, After the working class and the state power had helped the working peasants in the previous years, especially through the creation of a broad network of machine lending stations, to strengthen their husbandry and reach peace-time yields per hectare the prerequisites for the step-by-step socialist transformation of agriculture had ripened in 1952.

This was of national and international importance. In West Germany the working peasants increasingly suffered under the pressure of bank capital and war armament. Against this it was proved in the GDR for the first time in the history of a highly developed West European country that the working peasants in alliance with the working class can create a life in peace, prosperity and happiness through the transition to socialist large-scale production. The voluntary joining of cooperatives freed the working peasants from the fetters of small-scale production in whose narrow borders their abilities and initiative could develop but to a limited extent. It is the only way to remove the centuries-old backwardness of the village, that heavy heritage of feudalism and capitalism, and gradually abolish the antagonism between town and countryside. Through the transition to the socialist transformation of agriculture the alliance of the working class with the working peasants, the class basis of our state, was increasingly strengthened and assumed a socialist character.

Through strenuous joint work the agricultural production cooperatives proved their superiority to the individual small-scale husbandry, and the strength and viability of the cooperative movement became obvious. Party and government helped the cooperative farmers through extensive measures to consolidate the agricultural production cooperatives economically and politically. By the end of the first Five Year Plan 77,392 farmsteads had joined in 6,047 agricultural production cooperatives with 196,946 members who cultivated almost 20 per cent of the GDR's agriculturally useful land (1,279,200 hectares). The consolidation of the socialist sector in the countryside made it possible for the Third Conference of Agricultural Production Cooperatives at the end of 1954 to decide that rich peasants, too, who behave loyally towards the workers' and peasants' power, fulfil their obligations towards the state and are ready to take part in socialist construction can be admitted to an agricultural production cooperative (LPG). Some of the rich peasants made use of this opportunity. Thus the rich peasants received a clear reply to the question of their future in our Republic.

Socialist construction in the GDR also opens broad perspectives to intellectuals. Freed from dependence on monopoly capital which misuses the results of science and technology for the exploitation of the masses of the people and for criminal predatory wars, intellectuals were able to unfold their forces creatively. The working class was aware that it cannot solve the great tasks of socialist construction without the active cooperation of intellectuals and it showed great respect for their work. From year to year the workers' and peasants' state made available large funds for the promotion of science and technology, art and literature and honoured the great performances of the scientific, technical and artistic intelligentsia with high state decorations and distinctions. The gap which in the past had been created between the working class and intelligentsia by the bourgeoisie was overcome step by step. Ever closer friendly relations also developed between the working class and the intelligentsia, for the objective antagonisms between them had been removed. At the same time the working class began to educate a new, socialist intelligentsia out of the ranks of the young workers and peasants after it had broken the educational privilege of the bourgeoisie. The party conducted the struggle for the further development of the anti-fascist–democratic reform of the school and higher educational system to the socialist transformation which had been hampered for years under the influence of revisionist conceptions.

The transition from capitalism to socialism also caused new problems in the policy of alliance of the working class with the urban middle sectors of society, craftsmen, tradesmen and others. Whereas imperialism and militarism ruin the middle sectors, as is proved by history and again confirmed by developments in West Germany, the crafts and trade can develop fully only under the conditions of the workers' and peasants' power. The government supported their development by means of generous laws and measures (law on the promotion of the crafts, and others). Thus the crafts were able to increase their performances from 4,424 million marks in 1950 to 8,261 million marks in 1957, i. e., by nearly 87 per cent.

The urban middle sectors of society greatly profited from the construction of socialism. Through its great performances in the implementation of the Five Year Plan, through the raising of the standard of living and through its consistent struggle for the maintenance of peace the working class helped the middle sectors of society to see for themselves the advantages of socialism. The parties of the democratic bloc worked out the ways to the transition from capitalism to socialism together with the craftsmen and undertakers of industry and trade.

In the course of the carrying through of the socialist transformation the relationship of the party and the working class with all sections of the population was increasingly consolidated.

The deep changes which took place from the anti-fascist–democratic transformation to the socialist revolution also changed the content of the alliance of the working class with the other parties, the mass organizations and non-party persons. The first big success of the democratic bloc policy was the elimination of the roots of German imperialism and the founding of the German Democratic Republic, the first German peace state.

The National Front of Democratic Germany was from the beginning the chief fighter for the strengthening of the GDR, for the conclusion of a peace treaty with Germany and for the establishment of

55

a united, peace-loving, democratic Germany. The policy of the government and the People's Chamber of the GDR is based on its program.

In the course of the struggle for the construction of the foundations of socialism in the GDR the content of the activity and the character of the National Front of Democratic Germany changed. It developed from an anti-fascist–democratic movement into a broad socialist popular movement, into the community of all patriots and democratically-minded citizens who, irrespective of their world outlook and creed, considered it an honour to do everything in their power to strengthen the GDR and the successful realization of the great socialist work of construction.

The development of the National Front of Democratic Germany testifies to the strength and ability of the working class to unite all sections of the people. The National Front is the model for all democratic, peace-loving people in West Germany. It is the force which is able to bring about the national rebirth of Germany in the struggle against German militarism and imperialism.

The transition to the socialist revolution introduced not only a deep-going reshaping of the social economic and state conditions but also of the ideology of the masses.

Naturally the development of socialist consciousness takes place most rapidly in the working class which is in the best position to understand socialist ideas because of its social and economic position and which is most closely connected with socialist construction, with material production. But this process does not take place in a simple way and without conflicts. There are, for example, contradictions and conflicts between personal and social interests, between special economic interests and socialist production interests, between the attitude to work originating from capitalism where work was a burden and a curse, and the new relation to work in socialism where work is a matter of honour and heroism and becomes the most vital need.

In the other sections, too, among working farmers, craftsmen, retailers, intellectuals and others, their way of thinking is changing profoundly. However, the development of socialist consciousness is slower in these strata and is connected with greater conflicts. With the small producers of commodities the ideology of the small owner who is primarily interested in augmenting his private property is effective. The bourgeois ideology, petty bourgeois habits of living, the centuries-old traditions and customs of individual small production have in part deep roots in them.

56

The party takes this situation into consideration and through its policy of alliance gradually and consciously leads these sections to the new life. It thereby develops forms and methods corresponding to our conditions which make it easier for these sections to take the step from I to We, to enter the road to the socialist transformation voluntarily and consciously.

With the formation of production cooperatives the individual working farmers, craftsmen and others begin to work and think in a socialist manner. They are changing from individual small producers into people working in a socialist way who increasingly come closer to the working class. This road is also used by private retailers through the conclusion of commission contracts with the state trading organization and by small and medium entrepreneurs through state participation in their enterprises.

The policy of the party is aimed at solving the contradictions between the working class and the other working strata of the population who are private owners of means of production as well as the private entrepreneurs in a peaceful manner, through a policy of socialist development which is in accord with the personal interests of these sections. The policy of the party is directed at overcoming contradictions by means of patient, comradely conviction with the direct participation of these sections themselves.

This is a very complicated way, and therefore it often happens that party and state officials approach these questions mechanically and do harm to the socialist construction through opportunistic behaviour or left-wing deviations.

As concerns the intelligentsia it is also developing into a new stratum which is closely connected with the working class and takes an active part in the construction of socialism. Its consciousness is changing by coming into ever closer contact with the problems and practice of the socialist revolution. Many scientists turn to socialism as a result of their own experiences as engineers and technicians or under the influence of the great successes of Soviet science and technology, others in recognition of the deeply humanist character of the socialist social system.

Thus the political-moral unity of the population of the German Democratic Republic is developing step by step along with the carrying through of the socialist revolution.

In the struggle for the solution of contradictions in the ideological, intellectual and cultural fields—the old conceptions are not yet eliminated and are constantly nourished by the enemy—a lively spiritual life is developing and socialist consciousness is increasingly winning in influence.

An important task was the development of the foreign policy of the GDR. A foreign policy corresponding to the interests of the population of the GDR and the national interests of the German people had to proceed from the fact that Germany must create firm friendly relations with the most progressive state in the world, the Soviet Union. The thoughts expressed by Karl Liebknecht and V. I. Lenin already at the end of the First World War, the ideas which were in part fixed in the Rapallo Treaty, all oriented around the idea that after the great turning point of the world as a result of the Great October Socialist Revolution Germany can occupy a worthy place in the circle of the peoples only if it renounces every imperialist policy and pursues a basically new foreign policy, a foreign policy of friendship with the Soviet Union and of peaceful relations with all peoples on the basis of equal rights and mutual respect for sovereignty. In developing the foreign policy of the GDR we also proceeded from the historical fact that the peoples of the Soviet Union had the main share in the liberation of the German people from fascist barbarism and that at the Potsdam Conference the Soviet Union was the only state which consistently supported the peaceful, anti-fascist and national interests of the German people. The firm, inviolable friendship of the population of the German Democratic Republic for the Soviet Union grew out of the USSR's role of liberator and out of the traditions of German-Soviet friendship as it had been cultivated by the vanguard of the German working class under the leadership of Ernst Thälmann, thanks to the purposeful activity of the SED, the National Front of Democratic Germany and the German-Soviet Friendship Society.

Of historic significance were the agreements between the governments of the Soviet Union and the GDR in 1955 which brought the German Democratic Republic the freedom of decision on all questions of home and foreign policy. Since then the German Democratic Republic has been the only German state which possesses full sovereignty. This cannot be said of the West German Federal Republic—as is shown by the content of the Paris Treaties. The Moscow agreements made it clear once and for all that the reunification of Germany is the affair of the Germans themselves and that it can only be agreed upon between the two German states. The reunification requires the will to muzzle German militarism and to create a peace-loving, democratic Germany.

The SED and the government of the German Democratic Republic were guided by those principles of foreign policy which were developed by Marx, Engels and Lenin and tested in practice by the Soviet Union. They proceeded from the fact that the national interests of our people do not require a "neutral" position between the two great world camps—as is propagated by the reactionary forces of the bourgeoisie—but firm relations with the camp of peace, democracy and socialism, especially with the Soviet Union. This means that the national interests of the German people require that the GDR should be an inseparable part of the socialist camp. On this basis mutual diplomatic relations with the Soviet Union and the other peoples' democracies were established immediately after the founding of the GDR and a number of important agreements and treaties were concluded with them which rely on the principles of proletarian internationalism. The agreements of our Republic with the People's Republic of Poland, especially on the demarcation of the Oder-Neisse Peace Frontier, as well as with the Czechoslovak Republic, the Hungarian People's Republic and others are of national significance. The close fraternal relations of our Republic with the Soviet Union and the peoples' democracies are not in contradiction to the interests of other peoples. Our government from the first declared its readiness to establish normal relations with all states, including capitalist states, on the basis of equal rights, mutual respect and non-interference.

The foreign policy of the German Democratic Republic has shown itself to be the only correct German foreign policy. Whereas the Adenauer regime has become increasingly isolated as a result of its revanchist and atomic armament policy our Republic has acquired great international prestige as a result of its consistent peace policy and it is making an important contribution to the maintenance of peace. It won its full sovereignty in this way. It has a responsible position on a basis of equality within the circle of the socialist family of peoples. When the western zones were incorporated into the aggressive NATO and, as a result of the open remilitarization, again became the main centre of war preparations in Europe, our Republic joined the Warsaw Treaty in May 1955 in the interest of the cause of peace and the nation without its sovereignty or the question of the reunification of Germany being thereby jeopardized. Its national and international position became still firmer and is unshakable. The conclusion of the Warsaw Treaty was the expression of the logical process of the growing mutual assistance and support of the socialist countries.

Our Republic bears a special responsibility towards Germany's western and northern neighbours. It must reveal to the peoples of these countries the dangers arising from West German militarism and win the masses of the peoples for the joint struggle against these dangers. Of great effect in this respect were the declaration of the president of our Republic, Comrade Wilhelm Pieck, that the German Democratic Republic will not tolerate another war against the French people from the German side and the initiative of our government to make the Baltic a sea of peace. The role of our Republic as a bulwark of peace in Europe is also increasingly recognized in the capitalist countries of Western and Northern Europe. The Geneva Foreign Ministers' Conference has clearly proved, along with the de facto recognition of the GDR by the participating western powers, that the German question can no longer be dealt with, to say nothing of being settled, without the participation of the German Democratic Republic.

The West German Militarist-Clerical Authoritative State

In the western zones of Germany developments have followed lines differing fundamentally from those in the GDR. With the active support of the imperialist occupation powers the restoration of the old, capitalist state apparatus and the restoration of the power of the German imperialists and militarists were completed after the formation of the western separatist state. Since the policy of German big capital under the mask of "national socialism" had failed and nazism was discredited with the masses of the people the state which had newly come into existence assumed the mantle of anti-Hitlerism and bourgeois parliamentarism. Ideologically a concoction of the old imperialist ideology and the ideas of nazism and political clericalism came into existence. At the session of the SED Central Committee in June 1951 the restoration of German imperialism was proved. It was stated that the restoration of German imperialism is expressed in the restoration of the power of the German monopolists and bankers and their solidarity with American and British monopoly capital, in the carrying out of a policy of revanchism, war agitation against the Soviet Union, against the GDR, against the People's Republic of Poland and other peoples' democracies. The restoration of German imperialism is further characterized by the struggle of the German monopolies for new positions on the world market, especially by ousting British big capital and through participation in the imperialist policy of the USA in Africa, the Near East and Asia. The remilitarization of West Germany, the domination of the machinery of state by the big capitalist monopolies, the interweaving of the monopolies with the state organs and the limitation of the democratic rights of the people are further characteristics of this development.

The past ten years of the policy and practice of the Adenauer regime show that the sham parliamentarism no longer suffices to give even scanty cover to the too open nakedness of the rule of monopolists and militarists. Examples like the facts that the Bonn constitution does not contain such an elementary democratic basic right of the people as the right to express one's will by means of a referendum, that in fact parliament has no right to recall the federal chancellor and the government, that the plebiscite against remilitarization is forbidden, that democratic newspapers were suppressed, etc., show that no one can speak of a parliamentary-democratic system in West Germany even in the first years of the West German state.

In the meantime the West German monopoly capitalist regime even dropped the initially existing formal democratic forms in connection with the joining of NATO and the atomic armament and increasingly assumes the form of a militarist-clerical dictatorship. The Bundestag in which in any case more than two-thirds of all seats belong to the representatives of monopoly capital and militarism is only a wretched facade. On the one hand a willing organ of the government, on the other, excluded from important decisions by the government, the West German parliament only represents the disregard of the will of its electors on the basic questions of the existence and future of the German nation.

Seen from the class point of view, the policy of the West German state is today determined by the same minority of militarist-revanchist forces of finance capital which in the last fifty years led Germany into the catastrophe of two world wars and at present intend to precipitate the West German population into a still greater catastrophe with atomic armament. The executive organ of this antinational policy of war and catastrophe is the West German government. Of the eighteen members of this cabinet of monopoly rulers and militarists nine are direct representatives of the trusts or independent employers, one is the representative of an association of big farmers and Junkers. Four ministers were active members of the nazi party or the SA, and six were officers of the nazi Wehrmacht during the Second World War.

The executive organs of the Bonn state, state apparatus, police, army, etc., are mainly in the hands of out-and-out militarists and former representatives of the Hitler regime. Bonn Economics Minister Erhard was in the period of fascism economic adviser to the Nuremberg nazi Gauleiter (district leader) Bürkel; Minister of the

Interior Schröder was a member of the NSDAP and SA man since 1933, today he is chief of the West German police. War Minister Strauss was formerly a specialist in the fascist Reich Ministry of Economic Affairs and national socialist educational officer of the fascist Wehrmacht. Refugee Minister Oberländer was SA Hauptsturmführer, Gauleiter of the NSDAP and since 1939 Reich leader of the "Federation of the German East". Already in 1952 85 per cent of the higher officials in the Foreign Office were former active members of the nazi party. Two-thirds of all judges and public prosecutors (9,000) active in the West German organs of justice are former members of the NSDAP. A large number of them worked in the fascist military courts and administered injustice in Hitler's blood-stained courts and special courts. All 104 generals and admirals of the Bundeswehr participated under Hitler in the drawing up and implementation of the plans for the attack on the peoples of Europe. Seventy-one generals were active in the fascist general staff, seven were sentenced as war criminals, etc. These facts disprove the lying allegations of an "anti-fascist" character of the Adenauer regime.

Already in 1951 there were in West Germany some 450 reactionary, revanchist soldier associations. Without including the many revanchist "associations of fellow countrymen" (Landsmannschaften) these organizations have meanwhile increased to some 1,200 "traditional associations", including 45 associations of the fascist SS, with almost 300,000 members. And finally the prohibition of the NSDAP was officially cancelled a year ago.

The fact that all these neo-fascist, militarist and revanchist organizations can work freely and are supported by the rulers and that the real and consistent democratic forces, the Communist Party of Germany, the National Front, the Free German Youth, the German-Soviet Friendship Society—altogether about 200 organizations and associations—are banned, however, and that their members are suppressed and persecuted every day shows very distinctly that neither democracy nor freedom exist in the western zones. Imperialism, militarism and atomic armament are incompatible with democracy and freedom.

The economic basis and in the final analysis the determining force of the rule of this militarist-clerical authoritative state in West Germany is the economic power and rule of monopoly capital and the financial oligarchy. Whereas in the GDR the workers and working people built up a true peace economy with the overcoming of the war damage in the course of economic reconstruction, the system of monopoly capitalist rule was restored in West Germany with the support of the imperialist occupation powers under the sign of "economic reconstruction". The workers toiled to remove the vestiges of the war, but the fruits of this labour were pocketed by the monopolies which were restored in the course of reconstruction and became stronger from year to year. To be sure, the great war losses and the economic help of the USA made it possible to preserve a boom for a relatively long period and improve the standard of living of certain parts of the population. But this so-called economic miracle was paid for by the workers and working people of West Germany at a very high price, the restoration of the power of imperialism, the maintenance of the capitalist system of exploitation, remilitarization and the Bonn policy of atomic armament.

The concentration of capital and the economic influence of the West German monopolies on the economy, state and policy are today greater than ever before in German history. In 1938, for example, there were 5,518 joint-stock companies in the whole of Germany with an original capital of 18.7 thousand million marks; today 2,379 joint-stock companies in West Germany have a capital of 27 thousand million marks. Of these 51 alone, i. e., only two per cent of all joint-stock companies, have 12.4 thousand million marks, i. e., 46 per cent of the total original capital of all joint-stock companies. Six mining trusts (Thyssen, Krupp, Mannesmann, Haniel, Klöckner and Dortmund-Hörder Hüttenunion) own 270 enterprises and dominate 70 per cent of the West German steel production.

The electrical engineering industry is controlled by the AEG and the Siemens trust, the chemical industry by the three successor companies of the IG-Farben trust. The Volkswagen Works as well as the Opel AG and the Daimler-Benz AG manufacture 70 per cent of all motor vehicles. In the foodstuffs industry 25 out of 180 enterprises dominate 80 per cent of the total production, of these one single trust controls 75 per cent of the entire production of margarine. In banking the Deutsche Bank (250 million marks original capital and 7.3 thousand million marks bank deposits), the Dresdner Bank (180 million marks original capital and 5.2 thousand million marks bank deposits) and the Commerzbank (150 million marks original capital and 4.4 thousand million marks bank deposits) with their some 700 branches, deposit cashiers and other subsidiaries exercise the decisive influence.

The ten years of development of the Federal Republic show quite clearly the results of the "economic miracle": tremendous profits and gains for the monopoly associations, intensified exploitation and oppression for the workers, whereby there was a temporary and partial raising of the standard of living for certain sections.

The average dividend of the West German joint-stock companies rose from 2.4 per cent of the capital stock in 1950 to 8.96 per cent in 1957, i. e., by some 350 per cent. Even Dr. Deist, economic expert of the SPD who had spoken for years of the "just participation in the social product" saw himself forced to declare in the Bundestag on 12 June 1959 that the Bonn economic policy serves solely the West German big shareholders and industrial concentration. Furthermore, Dr. Deist stated that more than 50 per cent of all West German workers have gross incomes of less than 400 marks. The "economic miracle" yielded the most instructive results in the Ruhr area. Although production was throttled by 3.6 million tons in the first half of 1959 the dump stocks increased from 13.1 million tons at the end of 1958 to 17.2 million tons in July 1959. In the first half of 1959 alone more than 16,000 workers had to leave the mines, as compared with some 19,000 in the last year. For those Ruhr miners remaining at work the "economic miracle" brought an increase in yields per man per shift of from 1,642 kilograms in 1958 to 1,891 kilograms in July 1959 and, in addition, more than four million hours not worked up to now, which equals a wage deficit of more than 100 million marks.

The facts clearly show that the policy of remilitarization and atomic armament camouflaged with the help of the "economic miracle" leads to a step-by-step sharpening of the internal contradictions in West Germany and thus prepares the ground for the development of a broad popular movement against the policy of atomic death conducted by Adenauer. The example of the German Democratic Republic where there is not and cannot be unemployment, short-time work and "overproduction", in which the national economy is constantly and soundly surging upward at a rapid speed, in which every worker himself sees how life improves from year to year without setbacks occurring, exerts an increasing influence on the development of West Germany under these conditions.

The existence and development of the German Democratic Republic, on the one hand, forced the imperialist circles of West Germany to make a few concessions regarding the improvement of the situation of the working people in West Germany; on the other hand, they made an essential contribution to the development of the class consciousness of the West German workers, strengthened the force of the masses of the people and thus gave an impetus and support to the popular movement against remilitarization and atomic armament.

Adherents of peace and friendship with the German Democratic Republic are therefore arbitrarily and illegally persecuted, citizens of the German Democratic Republic are arrested without grounds, the most elementary democratic rights and liberties are trampled underfoot in violation of the Bonn constitution and laws.

The goal of the ruling monopolist-militarist circles of the Bonn state is the dictatorship of West German finance capital over the whole of Germany and supremacy over the whole of Europe. This is expressed in the policy of the "integration of Europe", which is nothing but the old revived Hitler slogan of the "new order in Europe", and in the revanchist demands on Poland, Czechoslovakia and other countries which have been constantly sharpened since 1949. With the aid of the European Coal and Steel Community and the European Economic Community they seek to bring the capitalist countries of Western Europe under their influence. After the thus obtained hegemony of German imperialism in Western Europe the German Democratic Republic is to be annexed, as is shown by the "Outline" plan and further advances made to the east, to Czechoslovakia, Poland, the Balkans and the Soviet Union. At revanchist demonstrations which were especially numerous during the Geneva Conference these goals were shouted out to the world and could be heard everywhere. War Minister Strauss declared at the CSU Congress in Bavaria that a united Europe must also include Poland, Czechoslovakia, Rumania and Bulgaria.

After the German militarists had supported the counter-revolutionary putsch in Hungary in 1956 and intensified their undermining activity against the GDR, and after the plan of aggression of West German militarism and the NATO against the GDR had become known to us, the Central Committee of the SED, at its 30th session at the beginning of 1957, established the tasks in the struggle for the safeguarding of peace, for the construction of socialism in the GDR and the consolidation of the workers' and farmers' power and for the reunification of Germany by the formation of a confederation. The 30th session of the SED Central Committee gave a clear perspective to the population of the GDR, the working class of the whole of Germany and the peace-loving forces of West Germany. As to the reunification of Germany, the formation of an all-German council composed of representatives of the two German states on a parity basis was proposed at the 30th session. It was stated that such an all-German council would be an organ for the unification of East and West Germany on the basis of confederation, i. e., a union of states. The 30th session of the Central Committee devoted special attention to the internal strengthening of the party and state power and called for a struggle against revisionism and dogmatism.

In the meantime the proposal for the conclusion of a peace treaty and the formation of a confederation of the two German states has also met with a big response in West Germany and in all other countries. In West Germany, too, a growing number of people are coming to see that Adenauer's policy of revenge and atomic armament has led into a hopeless blind alley.

A deep antagonism has developed between the atomic armament and revanchist politicians and the will of the people in West Germany. The wishes of the peace-loving forces in West Germany correspond, even if they are not always aware of it, to the proposals of the German Democratic Republic for the relaxation of the situation in Germany through the transformation of West Berlin into a demilitarized Free City and through the conclusion of a peace treaty with the two German states which would put German militarism in its place and muzzle it.

The proposals of the government of the German Democratic Republic and the Soviet Union agree with views contained in the "Germany Plan" of the SPD, with the opinions of many members of the FDP (Free German Party) and also of some members of the CDU (Christian Democratic Union) in many points, especially as concerns the first steps. Regardless of the differences of opinion on questions of the second and third stages of development it is necessary in the interest of the safeguarding of peace and the relaxation of the situation to bring about cooperation for the immediate next steps. The more consistently the peace-loving forces oppose the disturbers of the peace and atomic politicians, the more successful will their struggle be, the greater and closer the prospects for peace and democracy.

Especially great is the responsibility of West German Social Democracy as the only legal workers' party in the Bonn state. Broad circles of the working class expect the SPD to make a real turn to an active, independent policy towards the Adenauer government.

In the interest of the future of the German people and the other European peoples, in the interest of peace in Europe and a real democracy in West Germany it is time that the SPD and DGB leaders also finally come to see that all opponents of the reactionary Adenauer policy must join together—the West German workers with their organizations, the intellectuals, the urban middle sectors and the progressive forces from the ranks of the West German bourgeoisie. Together with the workers, peasants and intellectuals of the

German Democratic Republic and the peace-loving forces of the entire world they have the strength to stop German militarism.

In view of developments in West Germany the strength and organization of the peace forces decisively depend on the strengthening of the German Democratic Republic and the tempo of the construction of socialism here. Alone the fact that in the GDR the foundations of German militarism have been removed and uprooted once and for all signifies a defeat of German imperialism and militarism.

The Road to the Victory of Socialism in the German Democratic Republic

Today one can say that the great ideas of socialism penetrate to the last corners of the world like the Soviet sputnik which is circling the globe calmly and surely, seen by all peoples. No power on earth is able to stop this movement, this law of development of our epoch. Indeed militarism in West Germany can temporarily throttle the will of the masses of the people opposing atomic armament with the help of its state power. But its limits are today considerably narrower than earlier. The political consciousness of the working class and broad circles of the people has grown. The contradictions in the individual capitalist states and between the imperialist powers have increased. These contradictions will further sharpen, especially in West Germany, because the German Democratic Republic continues the peaceful road of national development, the road of the people's power, because it has shown and successfully proceeded along the road of democracy and socialism.

When the bourgeoisie in the first phase of development, in the early period of capitalism, needed a certain measure of democracy to assert itself over the old, feudal relations it set up the slogan of democracy and freedom to assert its own class rule. But after the German bourgeoisie has reached the period of decline in its development and has to answer for two war catastrophes in Germany it favours the authoritative rule of the militarist-clerical state power over the people.

With the change in the relation of forces in the world, thanks to the steep rise of the Soviet Union and the socialist camp, an unheard-of upswing in the consciousness and activity of the masses of the people who are no longer ready to sacrifice themselves for imperialist interests can be recorded. The capitalist rule proves to be an outdated old social formation the ruling circles of which make vain efforts to turn back the wheel of history.

67

The basic contradiction between the interests of the imperialist rulers in West Germany and the vital interests of the German people which are represented by the German Democratic Republic comes to such a head because two German states, one with the capitalist and the other with the socialist social system exist in one country, because the frontier between the world socialist system and the imperialist sphere of influence goes right through the middle of Germany. The solution corresponding to historical development is the muzzling of German militarism and the renunciation by West Germany of an imperialist policy.

On the 10th anniversary of the founding of the German Democratic Republic every citizen can see what great forces of the people have become free and have unfolded after capitalist exploitation, the exploitation of man by man, has been abolished. In the German Democratic Republic, as in the other countries of the socialist camp, man consciously makes his own history.

Karl Marx, the greatest German scientist, wrote that the pre-history of human society ends with the capitalist formation of society and the proper, consciously shaped history of mankind begins. We can state that the working people of the German Democratic Republic have concluded the pre-history of the German nation with the elimination of the foundations of capitalist exploitation, with the transition to socialist production in the first German workers' and peasants' state. The German working people have also raised themselves to be masters of the means of production and thus to be conscious shapers of their history through the transition to the socialist social system.

Thus new, truly human relations have developed among the citizens of the German Democratic Republic. This process goes on. The development of the new, socialist human being, the way from I to We, to the socialist community, to the truly human society, that is the most significant result of socialist democracy. It is the law of historical development that socialism will triumph in the whole of Germany.

Fascist Dictatorship—the Last Resource of the Bourgeoisie

*From a speech to Berlin officials
of the Communist Party of Germany and mass organizations
on 15 December 1930*

The Brüning government has enacted the decisions of German finance capital through the Article-48 decrees, it has suspended the Reichstag and at the same time taken decisive measures to build up the fascist state system. The liquidation of the remains of bourgeois democracy, as at present by the implementation of the hunger and tribute laws by means of the Article-48 decrees shows that the "democratic means" of looting and oppressing the people have failed in view of the growing revolutionary upsurge. The fascist dictatorship is the bourgeoisie's last resource to stem the collapse of capitalist society and protect this exploiter society from the onslaught of the needy people.

The accelerated pace of the revolutionary upsurge in the last months, the strike of the Berlin metalworkers, the strike in Chemnitz, the creation of revolutionary defence corps in Hamburg, Leipzig and other cities, the powerful demonstrations of the unemployed in the Reich, the numerous token strikes against wage robbery and for improved working conditions in various enterprises all show that the working class is no longer willing to continue to live, starve and become impoverished as up to now. The bourgeoisie wants to quell this working-class counter-offensive as well as the growing radicalization of the petty bourgeois sections with fascist means.

The dictatorship of the Brüning government is based on the further sharpening of the world economic crisis and the political crisis in Germany. The present measures of trust capital and its semi-fascist Brüning government do not yet reflect the matured fascist system of domination. The Reich Association of German Industry itself declared that the 25 dictatorial laws and the methods of their implementation were only the beginning. Precisely for these reasons it is necessary to mobilize all working people in order to prevent the dictatorship from the very beginning attaining its full stature in the form of that bloody system of terror, famine and a war against the Soviet Union as in Poland, Yugoslavia and Italy. Fascism cannot give the working people employment and bread. As long as trust capital owns the factories, mines, banks and the land it will exploit the working people for its own profit as well as to collect the "Young" tribute.[1]) The road to fascism means hunger for millions of working people as well as increased armament to prepare a war of intervention against the Soviet Union.

The Institute of Business Research declares in its quarterly journal No. 3/1930 in referring to the development of the world economic crisis, which is undoubtedly decisive for the assessment of further developments in Germany:

"The international business recession (meaning the world economic crisis, W. U.) has reached such a magnitude and intensity as has never been observed before in the development of modern economy. The downward tendencies have further sharpened even in the last few months."

The present world economic crisis is not only characterized by a further stoppage of production and a tremendous increase of the army of the long-time unemployed but also by the fact that big capital maintains and increases its profits by an unprecedented exploitation of the workers and petty bourgeois sectors. The so-called stabilization of the Reich's finances by the reactionary Brüning government is nothing but a "shifting of income" by the state apparatus in favour of finance capital. This economic policy which means the road to famine for the working people was exposed by the Communist Party of Germany in the Reichstag when it denounced the following facts:

The unpropertied sections are robbed of more than 2,000 million marks by the dictatorial introduction of the head or Negro tax[2]), the bachelor's tax, the beverage tax, by a deterioration in health insurance, by cutting unemployment benefits and reducing the salaries of civil servants and office employees. By the new emergency decree and a

[1]) Young Plan: This plan named after the American monopolist and financier Owen Young was to "definitively" fix German reparations for decades and became effective on 1 September 1930. This plan aimed at the re-establishment of the German war potential. In reality it meant that the working people alone had to pay the burdens resulting from the military defeat and that the masses were brought under the yoke both of German and American monopoly capital. In 1931 the Young Plan was annulled by a moratorium of US President Hoover.

[2]) Negro tax:–the name for a so-called civil tax, a head tax, which was introduced by the Brüning government together with the emergency decree on 26 July 1930. The name of the tax goes back to the colonial practice of the imperialists who imposed a tax on the heads of that part of the natives whose income and consumption could not be checked. The Negro tax was a means to increase the exploitation of the working masses.

cut in the budget the unemployed are deprived of 475 million marks, the war-disabled servicemen of 104 million, the miners of 75 million marks by the stopping of payments to the miners' insurance system. In addition the invalids, the victims of the capitalist policy of exploitation, are deprived of 50 million marks, the expectant mothers of 15 million marks by a cut in family insurance payments, and hungry children of one million marks cut from expenditures for their school lunches. One hundred eighteen million marks are "saved" from housing and settlement development. As a result of the new decrees this amount already totals 838 million marks. In addition, there is a new tax on tobacco which amounts to 168 million marks.

The reactionary program furthermore leads to an unprecedented curbing of housing construction: The amounts for housing construction are reduced from 800 million to 400 million marks this year. Money for housing is eliminated entirely in the next five years and tenants' protection will be completely eliminated, entailing an unlimited increase in rents. All these measures mean an unheard-of restriction in housing construction so that after five years 1,700,000 families will still have no homes and 510,000 families will live in houses ready for demolition.

By this policy another 1,000 million marks are saved so that the unpropertied sectors are deprived of more than 4,000 million marks by the Brüning program. This is a level of exploitation as has never been reached before in the history of the German "Young" Republic. At the same time, however, huge sums are spent on armaments, on the armoured cruiser ABC-program and a further 750 million marks on a present for the propertied classes in the form of lower property taxes, in fact, 400 million marks from a cut in real taxes, 170 million marks from the reduction of industrial charges and the remaining part through cuts in the capital gains tax, the capital turnover tax, property taxes, etc.

Thus 750 million marks are cast into the hungry maw of big capital at a time when the poorest of the poor are deprived of the last slice of bread. No fewer than 700,000 unemployed have to live from hand to mouth on the most miserable starvation allocations of public relief.

Another 600,000 to 700,000 unemployed no longer receive any support at all. In the 1931 budget even the last million marks for children's school lunches have been cancelled.

The intensified armaments of the Reichswehr and the Schupo police in Germany, the strengthening of naval forces in the Baltic Sea (300 million marks are provided for the building of warships), the propaganda for "the right to arm", as it is spread especially with the help of the nazis, the negotiations of the Reichswehr commander in Paris, and the establishment of "border police" units from Königsberg to Silesia, all at the same time serve the integration of Germany into the anti-Soviet front. Never since 1914 has the danger of war been so acute as now, where, as a result of the world economic crisis, the antagonisms between the imperialist states and the basic contradiction between the country of socialist construction and the countries of capitalist collapse are driven to the extreme.

When I said that under the present conditions of the sharpening of the world economic crisis the bourgeoisie uses fascism as a last resort of capitalist society then I mean that this is not a special German phenomenon but is a typical phenomenon in all capitalist countries in the present third period. The fascist development began in those countries which were the weakest links of capitalism, Italy, Poland, the border states, in the Balkans, and Austria. Fascism is the direct dictatorship of finance capital under the cover of joint people's interests. The fascist dictatorship is exercised by a very strong centralization and militarization of the state power and by an extreme extension of the bourgeoisie's apparatus of oppression with the help of fascist organizations and the harnessing of other organizations in the service of the fascist dictatorship.

The fascist dictatorship is marked by different forms and methods of development according to the special conditions of the class struggle in the various countries. Fascism comes to power in different ways. Just as bourgeois-democratic rule has passed through different stages of development fascist rule does not suddenly emerge in its fully-developed form.

Brüning is abolishing the parliamentary form of government of the Weimar Republic. The government declares that it is going to implement the hunger laws "notwithstanding the combinations of parties" and the decisions of the Reichstag.

In its declaration the government is proclaiming its new course of "state policy" according to which only those parties and organizations have a right to exist which approve of capitalist society. What was introduced with the law on the protection of the Republic is now to be sharpened by changes in the constitution and right to vote in the interest of the "people's state". That is the justification for the suppression of all revolutionary organizations and particularly for the impudently announced prohibition of the Communist Party of Germany.

The dictatorial powers in the hands of the Reich president, the discussion of bills in the Reichsrat which is to become the future

First Chamber and the preparation of bills by the Reich Economic Council, that future professional corporate body of the fascist corporate state, as well as the fact that local self-government is abolished, all prove how far fascism has already penetrated the country.

The intensified preparation of the Schupo police and the Reichswehr as civil war troops against the working class and their cooperation with the Stahlhelm (steel helmet) organization and the newly-organized nazi storm troopers, with the border police and the Reichsbanner military organization show how the bourgeoisie is strengthening its Wehrmacht with fascist organizations in view of the workers' growing fighting strength.

The Brüning government, however, is already proclaiming fascist measures:

1. strengthening of the position of the Reich president,
2. changing the right to vote. In particular, the "unlimited participation of young people in political life" is to be ended,
3. further development of the Reichsrat into a First Chamber,
4. further extension of the Reich Economic Council into a professional corporate body, the so-called economic parliament, with the help of which the social democratic trade unions are to grow together with the fascist system,
5. change of local constitutions into fascist local constitutions, as already provided in a bill of the Prussian government (Greater Berlin Law). In this case the Brüning government need not make any changes in this bill,
6. developing and strengthening of fascism in the factories aiming at abolishing the inevitability of tariffs, i.e., wage contracts can be replaced by agreements between the employers and reformist shop committees. The factories shall have the greatest say in the conclusion of wage agreements,
7. open armament for a civil war, increased training of the police and the Reichswehr and their cooperation with the fascist murder organizations, with the SS and the Stahlhelm as tools in a civil war against the working class,
8. increased imperialist armament for the preparation of a war, stepped-up armaments propaganda and intensified anti-Soviet agitation.

Just as the period of bourgeois democracy from 1918 to 1930 was characterized by the most varied methods of rule depending on the development of class forces (from the 1918 social democratic government to the 1930 semi-fascist Brüning government), so will the fascist forms of rule and methods of oppression sharpen, according to the development of class forces, if the proletariat does not sweep them away.

Who are the rulers of the "Third Reich" which Herr Brüning has begun to establish? They are the ones who own the factories, the land and the banks, they are the Duisburgs, Klöckners, Siemens, Borsigs and company. They are the leaders of German trust capital and they determine the policy of the "Third Reich". The nazis and their organizations having ensnared broad masses of the petty bourgeoisie and parts of the workers by their radical phraseology can only lead the masses of the working people to the fascist state system in the interest of finance capital and on its orders, and can impose their bloody reign of terror on the vanguard of the working class only hand in hand with the fascist police and the Reichswehr.

Everything for the Anti-fascist United Front

15 February 1933

This is what is new, powerful, that the workers in the factories in Lübeck, Stassfurt, Dresden and many other places are carrying through the political protest strike against fascist terror and suppression. In Berlin and other places communist and Reichsbanner workers are forming joint self-defence units to protect themselves against fascist raids, for the protection of workers' dwellings, workers' premises, workers' property and workers' meetings.

What Is the United Front? What Is to Be Done at Once?

United front means joint struggle, united front means to follow the shining examples of Lübeck, Stassfurt and so on as models of joint actions of the workers everywhere. In strike actions and mass demonstrations in Dresden and Stassfurt, too, there were the old principled antagonisms between the communist and the social democratic policies. But it was possible to unite the masses of the workers for the joint struggle for the next anti-fascist demands of the workers. The working class does not need a united front philosophy but direct joint measures of struggle against the common enemy—against fascism. Membership cards or contrary instructions of organizational bodies must not prevent the working class from organizing the joint mass self-defence in view of the fascist raids on workers' dwellings and workers' premises in every enterprise, at every dole office, in every street and from protecting itself against the fascist terror through a well-organized communication and alarm system.

All existing obstacles must be overcome so that all workers meet in every enterprise, in every enterprise department, no matter what membership card they have in their pockets at staff and department meetings to deliberate on fighting measures against fascist terror and pay cuts, on strikes against terror measures of the enemy or the possible ban of the KPD (Communist Party of Germany), on the organization of a mass self-defence system of the enterprise and on the sending of representatives to the other enterprises to introduce the same fighting measures there.

The time is much too serious to allow the workers in the enterprises to wait until they receive instructions from organizational leadership. What is necessary now is the organization of struggle in every enterprise, and only when the struggle is waged in every enterprise against a pay cut of even one pfennig, against the cancellation of the wage tariffs, against dismissals as well as against the fascist terror and the bans on the press, meetings and demonstrations, will the wave of the anti-fascist mass struggle rise and the working class victoriously assert its demands.

What Are the Trade Unions Doing?

The working conditions and rights of the working class won in struggle are to be stolen through the Hugenberg-Hitler dictatorship. The fascist terror is to intimidate the workers so that the entrepreneurs can carry through the liquidation of the tariff agreements, pay cuts and mass dismissals more speedily. Wages based on performance and works tariffs, the elimination of tariff wages by means of pressure through obligatory labour service, elimination of the social insurance system and the worsening of the enterprise work order, cancellation of the rights of the shop-stewards to make them organs of the works community, these are the plans of the German National Party and the NSDAP (National Socialist German Workers' Party–nazi party).

But the trade union leaders are silent. The federal executive of the ADGB (General German Federation of Trade Unions) declares that the period of reaction must be endured and that the trade unions will not conduct a basic struggle against the Hitler-Hugenberg government but will only take a position on measures of the government from case to case. Is this not open capitulation to fascism?

The fascist measures against the social insurance system and the tariff agreements and those concerning obligatory labour service make it necessary for the trade union members themselves to decide what the trade union organizations should do in the struggle against fascism. The force of the trade unions must now be finally employed against fascism. Only when the trade union organizations exert their entire force in strikes against the fascist terror, in mass demonstrations, in the creation of the mass self-defence for the protection of the workers' property and for the defence of trade union buildings will they be able to avert the attacks on tariff wages, on the social insurance system and workers' rights. Leipart and Husemann, however, believe that they can conciliate Hitler and Hugenberg with a policy of "wait and see". Therefore, it is necessary to strengthen the revolutionary opposition in the trade unions so that the masses of their members exert the force of the trade union organizations in the anti-fascist struggle against the will of the Leiparts and Husemanns.

Who Is to Lead the Anti-fascist United Front?

The most active workers experienced in fighting who are elected by the workers themselves shall lead the anti-fascist united front. We communists are for proletarian democracy, we want the workers themselves to adopt the fighting measures in delegate conferences of the enterprise representatives of the individual areas and in meetings of unemployed workers and elect action committees to lead the struggle. The most active and experienced communist, social democratic and non-party workers should be elected to these action committees. Those convening the staff meetings and delegate conferences should of course invite representatives of the Communist and Social Democratic Parties and the trade union leaderships so that they can justify the proposals of their organization before the workers themselves.

Many social democratic workers want to make their cooperation in the fighting united front dependent on the negotiations of the top bodies. But will the fighting united front not come into existence much earlier if the workers themselves deliberate in their enterprises, in the dole offices or in delegate conferences and decide on joint anti-fascist fighting measures? Have not precisely these strikes brought the greatest success as, for example, against the Papen emergency decrees, when the workers did not wait for instructions from the trade union leaders but opposed the Papen wage cut in a joint strike as one man, shoulder by shoulder? This is what has to be done now, too.

Not only the fascist terror and the measures of the offensive of capital are directed against the fighting working class but also the disruptive theories of "wait and see" and "wait until they are done for" help Hitler and Hugenberg. It is the most dangerous illusion that the Hitler government will ruin itself because of the contradiction between its promises and its deeds. The belief in this illusion means renouncing struggle, means disarming the workers. The Hitler-Papen-Hugenberg government is not a government which can be overthrown as easily as the Brüning or the Schleicher government. The connection of state power with the mass organizations of the national socialists, the Steel Helmet and the German National Party, the cooperation of state power with these fighting organizations require the operation of the strongest forces of the proletariat, the broadest united front for the struggle against fascism. Only thus can the working class overcome fascism.

The interest of the entire working class demands that instead of general speeches on the "united front" it is concretely said what should be the fighting tasks of the united front.

The Communist Party has proposed to the working class:

1) strike against the fascist terror as was done in an exemplary way in Lübeck, Dresden, Stassfurt and elsewhere;

2) protection of the dwellings, property, meetings and the demonstrations of the workers through the creation of mass self-defence formations in every enterprise, at every dole office, in every working-class street;

3) leading the struggle through the action committees elected by the workers themselves; the most active and experienced communist, social democratic and non-party workers should be elected to these committees.

If the social democrats want to fight against fascism, why do they not make any concrete proposals? Why do the leaders issue no instructions to their organizations? The named proposals of our party correspond to the interests of the entire working class. The fact that strikes against the fascist terror were carried through in many enterprises, that the mass self-defence was formed with communist, Reichsbanner and non-party workers shows that our proposals for a united front correspond to the will of the masses of workers. We propose that shop meetings be carried through in all enterprises by the shop-stewards or in agreement between the communist and social democratic officials, staff meetings, where a position is taken on the tasks of the anti-fascist united front an action committee is elected and further appropriate measures adopted.

The seriousness of the situation, the tremendous fascist attack on the working class and the masses of the working people demand quick action. We therefore propose to the working class: Convene joint shop meetings at once and everywhere as well as department meetings, meetings of unemployed workers and meetings in the residential areas. Decide there yourselves the necessary measures of joint struggle, as they are presented above, elect action committees, combine the fighting activity of the shop staffs and organize delegate conferences in the individual areas to make joint decisions on the tasks of the anti-fascist united front and the elections of action committees. Invite representatives of the KPD, SPD and ADGB to the meetings and conferences so that they can justify their proposals and attitudes.

Trade unions members, decide the anti-fascist, trade union fighting tasks in trade union meetings in the enterprises as well as in meetings of the trade union organizations, trade union leadership bodies and in the meetings of the local executive bodies and demand from your leaders that they employ the organizational apparatus to implement the demand of the trade union members:

Raise the banner of the fighting united front!

Forward to victory through the fighting united front!

Only Unity against Hitler
Can Save the German People

1936

The Greatest National Interest of the People
Is the Maintenance of Peace

After Hitler has eliminated the arms restrictions within the country he is preparing the next step–the war measures for territorial conquests. Hitler combines the chauvinistic whipping up of the masses with the demagogic exploitation of the people's fear of war by repeatedly presenting himself as the "defender of peace". In fact, Hitler rejects all proposals for collective security and wants to conclude only bilateral treaties in order better to isolate the countries to be attacked.

Because Hitler cannot solve the economic problems of Germany fascism wants to save itself by wars of conquest, by the oppression and exploitation of other peoples. About the purpose of arms Hitler himself writes in *Mein Kampf:* "Armies for the maintenance of peace do not exist, but only for the victorious fighting of wars."

Hitler's policy of war for domination in Europe is at the same time meant to strengthen the power of the upper ten thousand in Germany. The army is also to be used for the holding down and chauvinistic poisoning of the people for the high honour of the profits of heavy industry and bank capital.

Do the armament and conquest interests of the Krupps and Thyssens, the Vöglers and Schachts, the trust lords and poison gas kings have anything to do with the national interest? No! Just as the interests of the Krupps and Stinnes, of the Junkers and generals, pushed forward to war against the will of the masses in the pre-war period, so it is today also. It is Germany's greatest misfortune that it is ruled by megalomaniacs Hitler, Göring, Goebbels and a small group of big capitalists. In order to deceive the masses, Hitler declared that he was prepared to sign a 25-year guarantee pact. He thereby wanted to achieve the neutrality of a few governments in order to isolate those to be attacked and to be able to wage war against the small states and the Soviet Union and France more successfully.

It corresponds to the greatest national interest of the German people to save Germany from the catastrophe of war which would lead to an even more terrible defeat than in 1918. How can a war of a few tens of millions of people against hundreds of millions of people of other nations end otherwise than in a catastrophe? Was Germany in 1914 not much stronger, militarily and financially, and did it not have more allies than now, when German fascism has allied itself with the most rotten and reactionary powers in Europe, like Poland, Italy and Hungary? No people wants to attack the German people; but no one can have confidence in the "peace declarations" of the fascist incendiaries. After Hitler himself declared that he wanted to transfer the methods of his domestic policy—the terrible suppression of the people—to his world policy, the German working people can only welcome it if the masses in the other countries make even greater efforts to fight against the scourge of Hitler fascism in fraternal solidarity with the German anti-fascists. Only he who fights against the main warmonger Hitler and for the support of the peace policy of the Soviet Union represents the real national interests of the German people.

The Union of Soviet Socialist Republics wants a firm and long peace for that corresponds to the socialist interests of the peoples of that country. The Soviet government desires the maintenance of peace in order to lead the people undisturbed to new heights of happiness, to the blossoming of their forces and abilities.

For the Unity of the Workers against Hitler Who Divides the People

Almost at the same time that fascism in Spain was beaten by the Popular Front in the elections Hitler was able to fool millions of German workers with chauvinistic phrases. Would not the struggle of the working people in Germany against the bloody rule of Hitler fascism have made greater progress if the organizations and personalities who want peace and freedom had formed a broad popular front? In Spain the parties and organizations which were opposed to the fascist regime agreed on a common program in which they demanded amnesty, the re-employment of workers and office employees dismissed for political reasons, higher wages, lower taxes on the peasants, lower land rents and the guarantee of agricultural credits, representation of the interests of the small business man, the implementation of a public works plan, the restoration of social legislation and support of the League of Nations. The gathering of all forces on the basis of these demands led to such a strengthening of

81

the fighting force of the workers, peasants, the middle class and the liberal bourgeoisie that this united force brought an end to the rule of the fascist gang leaders.

In Germany the fascist press daily pours scorn on the splintering into 47 parties which enabled Hitler to come to power. Hitler, the most cunning splitter of the working people, who sets the workers against the peasants, the middle class against the workers, the Catholics against the communists, young people against class-conscious workers, can pose as the representative of unity because it has not yet been possible to bring about a united front and popular front against Hitler in Germany. Never have the upper ten thousand, the rulers of the trusts and cartels, banks and stock exchanges, the Junkers and newly rich fascist party bosses had so much power over the 67 million German people as under Hitler. Fascism calls the terroristic subordination, the silencing and confusing of the German masses under the command of the upper ten thousand the "unity of the people". Is it not high time that the millions of people opposed to Hitler likewise unite for the struggle against barbaric Hitler fascism as the upper ten thousand is united against the millions? Let us create the popular front against Hitler, let us unite against the common enemy, and undreamed-of forces of countless heroes of the people's struggle will appear which will prepare an end to the rule of the fascist warmongers.

The German People Languish under the Reparations for the Upper Ten Thousand – The Rich Should Pay!

After 1918 the German people had to bear burdensome reparations. Big capital and governments shifted the reparations onto the working people by means of taxes on the masses and holding down wages. But even in the victorious countries big capital shifted the burdens of war onto the working people. The post-war profiteers did not earn less than the war profiteers. The Hitlers and Görings, the rulers of the war industry, the banks and the generals have the impudence to maintain that they were not to blame for the world war and therefore do not have any responsibility for the terrible defeat and for Versailles. Did not the arms capitalists, the coal and iron barons and the bank lords also press for the war of conquest, for the mineral deposits at Longwy and Briey as well as for the rich area of the Ukraine? Now, just as then, it is the upper ten thousand who are those really interested in war, who have the whole machinery of state power work to incite the peoples against each other.

The official statistics themselves admit that the huge profits of German industry in 1935 were twice as high as in 1934. Four hundred ninety million marks were ear-marked for dividends alone in 1935. That means that actual profits constituted several thousand million marks. The Vereinigten Stahlwerke (United Steelworks) shows an armaments profit of 150 million marks in its 1935 balance sheet. But the nazi bosses preach to the working people that they should eat less in the interest of building more cannons and tanks. The Vereinigten Stahlwerke paid out 19 million marks in dividends. If one takes into account the high profits still hidden in royalties, directors' salaries and the 130 million marks for "depreciation", it would be possible to raise the wages of 179,000 employees by 900 marks a year each, or 19 marks a week, without prejudicing production.

The workers justly demand higher wages. The raising of wages and the preventing of further price rises would bring full employment, whereas the witholding of a part of wages in the interest of building tanks and aircraft increases the distress of the workers and strengthens the power of armament capital. The workers correctly point to the aircraft and tanks and say: "There flies our butter," and "Outside our wages are rumbling by!"

We Want a Free, Strong and Happy Germany

Goebbels says that we are a people of have-nots. But look around you in Germany, at the highly-developed industry, at the rich stores of coal and other raw materials; think of the great achievements of the chemical industry.

The German worker is one of the most highly qualified workers in the world, the peasant industriously works his land and the middle class member could not manage his business more economically. Could not all workers in Germany have work if, in place of the senseless production of means of destruction, everything was produced that is necessary for the lives of the masses?

If, instead of the six thousand million marks of subsidies for the arms industry, the wages of the workers were improved, the mass taxes lowered and the price manipulations conducted by the cartel agreements were severely punished, then the factories would be working at full capacity to meet the needs of the masses.

A Germany in which the fascist war incendiaries do not sit in the government would have friendly relations with the other peoples and could exchange high-quality products of German industry for

83

6*

raw materials and foodstuffs from other countries. Why should the German people bleed to death on the battlefields when they can obtain everything they need through peaceful trade agreements?

The name of Germany will once more be respected in the world if a stop is put to the profanation of German culture in Germany by fascism. How should the other peoples have confidence in a Germany in which the great cultural values are destroyed, science and literature decay and in their place blind obedience and racial incitement triumph, and in which the development of the younger generation is put in chains? When great German writers and scientists like Heinrich Mann, Einstein and many others can once more freely work in their homeland, then Germany will once again be respected in the world.

If the German people put an end to the rule of the war incendiaries, liquidate the subsidized and corrupt economy of the "Third Reich" and create order in the German provinces (Länder), then the name of Germany will once again meet with respect and honour throughout the whole world, then the German people, as a really equal people, will be in a position to freely conclude treaties with the other peoples. It is therefore the highest obligation of honour of every German worker to do everything possible to bring about the popular front against Hitler and so that Germany will be freed from the fascist disgrace and so that the conditions for a really free, strong and happy Germany are created, in which free people live on free soil.

The Saving of Germany by the Popular Front

It is necessary to go new ways so that the workers and the working masses win the victory over Hitler. It is the highest obligation of honour of every individual to do everything to establish the unity of the working people and to bring all opponents of Hitler together.

The beginnings of the united front and popular front can be seen in the main industrial areas of Germany. Communists, social democrats, Catholics, trade unionists, and other anti-fascists are assisting each other in the struggle against terror, in representing trade union interests, in the distribution of agitation material and in the building of the organizations. This close friendship among anti-fascists, the great solidarity, this utilization of all opportunities to organize anti-fascist forces show the beginning of the creation of the popular front. At the same time a conference of representatives of the workers' organizations, of men of literature, art and science and representatives of the liberal bourgeoisie took place in Paris, a conference which accepted a joint declaration on the uniting of all anti-Hitler forces and on the struggle for freedom. That is a step forwards.

In the last few months the right-wing social democratic leaders have aggressively declared their opposition to such joint action of the anti-fascist forces. This vividly reminds one of the declarations against the united front of January 1933 which only benefited Hitler. Many social democratic leaders are speculating on cooperation with elements in the armed forces, place all their hopes on the League of Nations and believe that they can win petty bourgeois and bourgeois forces against Hitler with the propaganda of their earlier coalition policy. Here the view is also put that with increased efforts to build up the social democratic organization in Germany the forming of a united front is superfluous.

We hope that the imminently dangerous development of Hitler's war policy and the latest mass trials of social democrats in Germany will also cause those social democratic leaders who have recently been fighting with all means available against the forming of the united front and popular front to reflect on and correct their present standpoint. The present conception of some social democrats that one should march separately towards the common goal—the over-throwing of Hitler fascism—is also a bad recommendation. If in fighting against such an enemy as Hitler fascism, which controls a mighty power machinery under a unified command, every military column marches by itself it can only lead to the enemy smashing every column individually.

The KPD wants the united front at any price because only by the united front and popular front can Hitler be overthrown, can a democratic Germany be won and democratic freedom assured. We also believe that the reasons which caused the Prague Committee to reject the united front in November 1935 scarcely play a role any longer. It has turned out that most of the active social democrats in the country are for the united front and that an agreement between the two party leaderships corresponds to the wishes of the illegal fighters. The KPD has proved in the country that it seriously adheres to all united front obligations and works with the representatives of the social democratic groups in a comradely spirit. Practice in the country has taught how necessary it is that the communists and social democrats mutually assist each other, not only in guarding against Gestapo agents but also in establishing organizational links.

We want a new relationship between the SPD and the KPD and are therefore decisively opposed to the formation of "communist groups in the SPD," for that would only make the united front with the social democratic organizations and their party executive more difficult. Also coming to an understanding about the question of what comes after Hitler is certainly possible. After an understanding with leading social democratic officials has been possible at home and abroad on the common struggle against Hitler's war policies and for the maintenance of peace and a cooperation between communists, social democrats, Catholics, writers, scientists, artists and representatives of the liberal bourgeoisie ensues, cooperation between the Central Committee of the KPD and the Executive Committee of the SPD must also be possible. And the sooner the better since the KPD has committed itself to the consistent struggle for a democratic Germany.

We believe that in view of the increased terror against communists, social democrats, and Catholics, all honest anti-fascists are faced with the task, more seriously than ever since the Hitler memorandum of 7 March 1936, of doing everything to create the united front and popular front, and to save Germany from the fascist catastrophe of war and barbarism. The Central Committee of the KPD has therefore turned to the Executive Committee of the SPD as well as to all anti-Hitler organizations, groups and personalities, with the proposal for an agreement on joint action and for joint preparations for the forming of the popular front against Hitler.

The Prague Committee declared in a pronouncement in *Neuer Vorwärts* that it was prepared to work occasionally with the KPD if at the same time a truce were concluded. And in the *Sozialistische Aktion* of January 1936, the organ of the Executive Committee, we read:

"We must not underestimate the effect on morale of the united front... Where there is cooperation with other groups in conspiratorially thought out forms with trustworthy people and where it serves the purpose of making mutual assistance possible, exchanging information and experiences and contributing to the improvement of the methods of work and the clarification of the aims on both sides, then it is to be welcomed as one of the ways to be strived for in unifying illegal work."

Since the rapprochement and cooperation between communist and social democratic groups in the country are obviously making progress and a new relationship is being formed between the officials of the two organizations we are convinced that the leaderships of the two workers' parties will succeed in achieving joint action in individual cases and altogether to create a new relationship between the two parties. Since some of the demands of both organizations in the struggle for the maintenance of peace, against Hitler's policy of war, against the fascist terror and the mass trials as well as in the representation of the daily interests of the workers in the main are in complete harmony with each other, it must also be possible for the two party leaderships to come closer together by discussions from time to time and to agree on joint action with the signing of a truce.

For a Democratic Germany

In the manifesto of the Brussels party conference of the KPD, which contains proposals for the formation of the popular front, it was stressed that the central slogan of the anti-fascist struggle is the slogan of freedom and that it is necessary to draw together all anti-Hitler forces for the struggle for democratic freedoms. Just as we communists are doing everything in our power to induce the workers and working masses to achieve greater freedom of movement and form the united front and popular front for the struggle for democratic freedoms, so shall we do everything possible to secure the rights and freedoms of the working people after the overthrow of Hitler. We are prepared to fight with all anti-Hitler forces for a democratic Germany. The German people should themselves freely decide which regime they want.

Comrade Dimitrov, General Secretary of the Communist International, gave the fundamental directives for it in his great speech at the Seventh World Congress. He referred to Lenin's words:

"It would be a great error to believe that the struggle for democracy could divert the proletariat from the socialist revolution or even push this revolution into the background, to veil it and the like. On the contrary, as victorious socialism which does not realize complete democracy is impossible, so the proletariat which does not conduct a consistent, revolutionary struggle for democracy in every respect cannot prepare itself for the victory over the bourgeoisie."

The struggle for the democratic freedoms, for a democratic regime is necessary in Germany because there all bourgeois democratic rights and freedoms have been destroyed by fascism, and also because many demands of the bourgeois-democratic revolution have not yet been fulfilled, as, for instance, the elimination of the privileges of the Junkers, the property rights of the out-of-date princes and others.

The demands for action of the popular front of today are extremely closely bound up with the demands which are to be realized after the overthrow of Hitler. Today the workers begin by putting questions at meetings, with agreeing to passive resistance to bring about better working conditions and tomorrow they will force through the right to elections in the factory department and in the meeting. Today they agree to refuse to give the Hitler salute and soon they will be chasing the fascist party bosses away.

Thus the mass struggle for freedom from the smallest, daily petty demand will rise to a crescendo of the storm of the masses, to the overthrow of Hitler fascism. It would therefore be useless to discuss the design of the constitution instead of the tasks of action and the creating of an action program of the popular front, for that would only discredit the formation of the popular front.

The guiding principle of a democratic regime must be the protection of the basic interests of the workers. It is in this spirit that the victorious popular front will fight against the fascist reactionaries for the general, equal, secret right to vote for freely nominated candidates, for amnesty for imprisoned anti-fascists, for the closing of the concentration camps, for the annulling of the fascist legislation, for the cleansing of the state apparatus of enemies of the people, for the disarming of the fascists and reactionaries, for the freedom of coalition, assembly and of the press, for the ending of forced labour, for the right to organize trade unions and for the rights of the shop committees to represent the interests of the workers and office employees before the employer.

The victorious popular front will bring about the provision of work in the interests of the working people, the improvement of wages and working conditions through wage agreements with the aid of the trade unions, the restoration of social insurance, the lowering of taxes on the masses, the introduction of property taxes for high incomes and property, and the cancelling of tax debts and mortage debts. It will abolish forced labour and end the militarization of youth, and create the prerequisites for the opportunity for the German working youth to freely develop all their capabilities and to realize their ideals of freedom and socialism.

To realize the demands of the peasants for the ending of forced farming, the lowering of interest rates, changing of the lease agreements, the lowering of taxes and compulsory deliveries and to satisfy the peasants' need for land, all these belong to the main tasks of the popular front after the overthrow of Hitler. Similarly it is necessary to relieve the middle class of unpaid taxes and payments and to lower taxes. The popular front will implement the elimination of the corrupt and subsidized economy, the introduction of public reports and their inspection by bodies elected by the population itself as well as repayment of subsidies paid out to big industry and the Junkers. It will fight for the democratization of the army, for the elimination of reactionary officers and for the democratic rights of the soldiers. It will put an end to the persecution of religion as is daily practised in the "Third Reich" and protect the exercise of religious customs. With the victorious struggle of the popular front the bringing up of young people and the protection of the family in freedom will be guaranteed, the complete equality of women will be established, the freedom of art and science, the cultivating of a true people's art will be safeguarded and the great heritage of German culture will be made available to the masses of the people.

An alliance of friendship and close economic relations with the Soviet Union as well as with the other peoples will be created and all treaties which are contrary to the interests of the German people such as the German-Polish and the German-Japanese agreements will be annulled.

Germany will live properly and become a nation in freedom, honour and happiness only when the rule of the Hitlers and Krupps, Vöglers and Schachts has come to an end.

This is how the popular front will fight to restore the reputation and honour of Germany by overthrowing Hitler fascism and by safeguarding the freedom of the German people and international peace.

That is the way to a Germany of freedom and of peace.

New Tasks of the
Communist Party of Germany

June 1937

Both the internal and the international position of Germany testify to the growing difficulties of the fascist regime.

Whereas Hitler fascism is intensifying its war policy, driving the country towards the catastrophe of war the overwhelming majority of the German people do not want war, they want peace. They do not want to continue suffering under the unbearable burdens of armament. That is why this situation is marked by the most profound contradiction and constitutes the Achilles heel of the whole fascist dictatorship.

It is becoming increasingly clear that Hitler's policy is driving the German people towards war thus facing the nation with the question of the destiny of Germany. This policy can only end in defeat, plunging the German nation into the most dreadful disaster. That is why the struggle for peace, against the war economy, against the policy of conquest, against the intervention in Spain is a question which can and must unite all sections of the German people with the exception of the immediate beneficiaries of the war policy. Even today workers, office employees, peasants, craftsmen and small traders, intellectuals and even parts of the bourgeoisie are victims of and deceived by Hitler's war policy. They must all stand together in order to ward off the frightful disaster.

This decisive awareness has not yet penetrated throughout the entire Communist Party (KPD) or all other circles of German anti-fascists. The struggle for peace has not yet become the central issue with which all other tasks are linked, such as the struggle against the fascist instigation to national hatred, against armament burdens and war profiteers, for higher wages, against terror and coercion and in support of the demands of the peasants, the middle class, women, young people, scientists and artists.

Even today there are strong currents of opinion according to which no mass movement, no successful mass activity and mass policy by anti-fascists are possible under the present circumstances and that one can only wait passively until Hitler starts a war in Europe which would automatically lead to the overthrow of the Hitler regime. Such opinions are harmful because they keep the masses in a state of passivity under the cover of a radical mask, objectively facilitating Hitler's war policy.

This already became evident on the occasion of the fascist intervention in Spain. Whereas German anti-fascists were heroically defending democracy and world peace at the gates of Madrid, the struggle against Hitler's war of intervention was inadequately conducted inside Germany. Communists and anti-fascists in the country were not conducting a mass policy for the preservation of peace, for the withdrawal of fascist German troops and warships from Spain, for the cessation of arms deliveries which influenced all those sectors which did not have any interest in war. Broader mass movements are still lacking in Germany. This is a signal of great weakness and is a danger. Today, when Hitler has begun to drop his mask of "defence", when the masses are beginning to become aware of the way in which Hitler is driving Germany into the catastrophe of war, when the masses are groaning under the burdens of war, it is not enough to unmask the policy of war, it is necessary to conduct a direct struggle against economic distress and coercion which are the consequences of the war policy of ruling fascism. Anti-fascists must become aware that this struggle against the war policy, this delay of the war—also increasingly affected by international forces—is increasing the difficulties of the Hitler regime and providing an opportunity to overthrow it before its plans have been implemented, before the German people have been plunged into a terrible catastrophe.

If Hitler was able to come to power under the slogan against Versailles he can be overthrown under the slogan of peace, of the overthrow of the government of war, the creation of a democratic regime of peace, freedom and progress.

Hitler promised the masses that there would be sufficient food and raw materials and that wages could be increased once there was more "living space" available and once Germany ruled over colonies and other foreign territories.

The nazi propaganda for "more living space" and for "being masters in our own house" did not fail to produce an effect upon the masses. Fascism was able to take advantage of economic and social difficulties (shortage of food, low wages, lack of raw materials, high taxation and shortage of animal fodder in the villages) as a driving force for its policy of conquest. Fascism deluded broad masses with its social demagogy, its measures against individual small employers, against Jewish shareholders and against individual minor price speculators. Fascism has a particularly strong influence on women and the mass of young people who are forcibly united in the Hitler Youth. The still prevailing passivity among the masses and the feeling of helplessness are caused not only by the terror, by the pressure of the fascist apparatus and the influence of fascist propaganda, they are also the consequence of the previous social democratic policy of class collaboration, of the long years of rejection and suppression of the class struggle under the Weimar Republic, and of the rejection of united proletarian struggle and the anti-fascist popular front by the Social Democratic Party Executive Committee and social democratic trade union leaders.

The Communist Party is directing the main thrust of its struggle against the armament profiteers, against the upper ten thousand, against the millionaires, and is striving to influence the broadest masses in the direction of the class struggle. In this connection it is important to refer to the nazi promises to introduce a tax on millionaires, to confiscate war profits, etc. This does not mean any weakening of the struggle against the major enemy—Hitler—but it would help to unmask those who have an interest in war, to explain the big capitalist nature of the Hitler dictatorship to the masses in a comprehensible manner and to show them why the Krupps, Thyssens, Vöglers, Henckel-Donnersmarks, who have always made the biggest business from war, inflation, the Young Plan and armament are the old misfortune of Germany. In this way it will be possible to lead those parts of the masses which today still believe in Hitler to the struggle against the Hitler dictatorship.

There is no doubt that the overthrow of Hitler can be brought about only through the struggle of the broadest masses of the people. There is nothing Hitler fears more than the unity of the people for peace, for the vital interests of the masses. That is precisely the reason why he accuses us communists of being splitters of the people. In opposition to the "unity" desired by Hitler which is nothing but the subordination of the entire life of the people to the fascist war policy, the profit interests of the most reactionary circles of monopoly capital and the fascist bureaucracy, the task of all German anti-fascists should be to make every effort for the unification of the people, for the struggle for peace and against Hitler's war policy. Hitler can be overthrown only by the unification of the German popular masses in the struggle for peace, in defence of their vital interests, for law and justice in Germany.

The unity of the German people not only demands the unity of the working class and of all anti-fascist forces, but also the participation of broad sections of the national socialist masses without whom the overthrow of Hitler is not possible. Only the German Popular Front, which would at the same time guarantee that the unity of the anti-fascist forces should be preserved after the overthrow of Hitler to safeguard the newly acquired freedom, can be the basis of this unity.

Unity against Hitler, however, can only be achieved by agreement on the most immediate partial demands. The unification of the forces of the working class with those of the peasants, the middle class and democratic elements among the bourgeoisie, the unification of all these forces in the German Popular Front, can only be attained and led to victory if all anti-fascist forces have one common aim. This common aim is the democratic republic.

This goal unites the broadest masses in the present stage. In Germany fascism has liquidated all rights of the people and democratic institutions, it has thrown Germany back for centuries. Thus various tasks of the bourgeois-democratic revolution again stand on the agenda in Germany.

In the future democratic republic which represents a new and more advanced type of state, the people will have an overwhelming influence; the privileges of big capital will be destroyed and the roots of fascism will be extirpated. The working class, by upholding the slogan of the democratic republic assumes the role of the representative and vanguard for the unification of the people for the overthrow of the Hitler dictatorship.

In the recent period the feelings in favour of the popular front have grown in Germany. This is a result of the success of the French Popular Front and of the struggle of the Popular Front in Spain. But it is also a result of the appeals and propaganda of the preparatory committee for the establishment of a German Popular Front and the inspiring words of the great German writer Heinrich Mann. The masses have been roused.

In establishing a popular front in Germany the particular conditions of fascist terror, the destruction of the legal organizations of the workers, the peasants, the middle class and the democratic bourgeoisie must be taken into consideration. The chairman of the Communist Party of Germany, Comrade Wilhelm Pieck, indicated in his directives for the creation of a German Popular Front how the struggle, above all within the fascist mass organizations, must be organized with a broad popular front policy for peace, freedom and prosperity, directly linked up with the immediate interests of the masses. Just as the workers are united within the German Labour Front and other organizations—forcibly or voluntarily—the peasants are united within the organizations of the Reich Agricultural Board and the middle class, the doctors, scientists, writers, etc., are joined in the fascist mass organizations of their professions. There they are striving to represent their interests and these offer the most favourable ground for joint action.

If the popular front movement in Germany has so far included only a narrow circle of anti-fascist forces it is because it has only just started to take up a position in regard to the most urgent issues of concern to the broad masses. It is necessary to support partial demands of the masses in defence of their immediate interests and which they consider practicable. In this spirit it is necessary carefully to study, proceeding from the central question of the struggle against Hitler's war policy and for the maintenance of peace, the wages and food questions, the question of popular rights, of economic and finance policy, the situation of the peasants and the middle class, of women and young people, draw up legal demands for the various sections of the population and show to the masses the way by which they can struggle for the improvement of their situation, making use of all legal possibilities. It is not enough merely to reveal the anti-popular policy of Hitler fascism. It is also necessary to deploy direct mass initiative for the improvement of the conditions of the workers and to show them the way and aim by which the struggle of the Popular Front can solve the vital issues of the German people in the future German Democratic Republic.

The self-confidence of the working class and the popular masses, the belief in their own powerful strength must be reinforced; it must be proved to the entire people that the Popular Front, in fighting for the maintenance of peace and against Hitler's policy of war, is defending the real national interests of the German people and that it is the force which will lead the German people into a happy future.

From the illegally published pamphlet
Kriegsschauplatz Innerdeutschland
(Theatre of War Within Germany), published in 1938
under the camouflage title
Deutsche Scholle (German Soil)

The Alliance for Aggressive War

At the end of the fifth year of the Hitler dictatorship it is becoming increasingly clear that mankind is threatened by the danger of a new world war which is being prepared by the Berlin-Rome-Tokyo triangle. Since the middle of 1936 the war instigated by Hitler and Mussolini against the Spanish people and their democratically elected Popular Front government has been raging on Spanish soil. China is being devastated by the flames of battle and the Japanese military fascists are provokingly proclaiming their program of plunder and oppression against the Chinese people. The fascist dictators have not stopped at making menacing speeches, diplomatic surprise manoeuvres and rattling sabres. The Berlin-Rome war axis has united into a triple alliance with the rulers of Tokyo for the war of aggression already begun without official declarations of war in Abyssinia, Spain and China.

Hitler himself has stated plainly enough the purpose the fascist alliances are intended to serve. In *Mein Kampf* he wrote:

"An alliance which does not aim at war is devoid of sense and value. Alliances are only concluded for struggle."

It is characteristic of the method employed by the fascist powers that they are trying through rapid attacks and without declarations of war to break into other countries. For example, *Angriff*, the paper of Propaganda Minister Goebbels and the German Labour Front, wrote on this:

"The naive correctness of Herr von Bethmann Hollweg (German-Reich Chancellor at the outbreak of the war—W. U.) in August 1914 of studying with German diligence all the regulations of international law and then having an appropriate declaration of war handed over by the ambassador in Petersburg belongs to a time which has long since assumed the distant sound of baroque diplomacy. Wars have for long come about in a different way, without words, more reticently and with more cunning. The formation of the Manchukuo state and the events in Singkiang as well as the shooting incidents on the outskirts of Peking are classical examples of the new method of expanding domains of power."

This method of supporting an attack from without by organizing insurrections inside the attacked country is being employed by fascist governments in many countries.

This fascist method of war preparation is making clear even today to all peoples who the aggressor is. The aggressors are the despots of Berlin, Rome and Tokyo who have already violated peace and who are preparing a war of conquest against the democratic countries and the Soviet Union by their provocations. These warmongers are employing every conceivable method of intimidation with a view to splitting the front of governments interested in peace and finishing off one after another the countries threatened by fascist attacks. Hitler is applying the method by which he was able to defeat his political opponents in Germany as a result of their disunity, also in the arena of international politics.

The "World Mission" of Fascism

During the first years after the most reactionary forces of German monopoly capital had brought him to power Hitler declared to the German people that his aim consisted only in the "re-establishment of German honour and freedom and in breaking the fetters of Versailles", the "protection of the German frontiers and the maintenance of peace". In those declarations Hitler was still able to profit from the hatred of the masses of the people against Versailles. The policy of Weimar which had not resolutely settled accounts with the big capitalist and all German instigators of the war facilitated the use by Hitler of the demagogic catchword of "Struggle against Versailles" before and after his accession to power, just as the coalition policy favoured his lying instigation against "Marxism". If the German workers had placed those guilty of the war–the Krupps, Stinnes, Ludendorffs and others–before a people's court, had the German working-class movement followed the clear path of struggle against the Treaty of Versailles during the years of the Weimar Republic in the spirit of anti-imperialism and understanding among the peoples as consistently advocated by the Communist Party of Germany from 1919 to 1933, they would have deprived Hitler of the weapon of his demagogic struggle against Versailles. Instead the war criminals were entrusted with the commanding posts in the Reichswehr to conduct the struggle against the revolutionary proletariat.

Hitler proceeded step by step. In his speech of 17 May 1933 he stated for example that

"today there can be but one task: to safeguard the peace of the world. Germany is prepared to join every solemn non-aggression pact, for Germany is not thinking of an attack but of its security."

That was stated by Hitler at a time when he wanted to gain time for rearmament. Three years later, in March 1936, when German troops marched into the Rhineland in violation of the Locarno Treaty Hitler used the comparison in a speech which has since become well known, that Herr Müller wanted to be master in his own house. Hitler declared then that "the struggle for German equality could be considered as concluded" and he added that the first prerequisite for the earlier withdrawal of the "Third Reich" from European co-operation had thereby fallen away.

That statement also proved to be a conscious deceptive manoeuvre, for the Hitler government simultaneously began a violent campaign against the peace treaties between the Soviet Union, France and Czechoslovakia. The Franco-Soviet pact serves the safeguarding of peace and all states were invited to join. If Hitler had had no aggressive designs he would have had to declare the adherence of Germany to that pact. Yet Goebbels' propaganda twisted the truth about that pact and made it a "threat" to Germany. The Hitler government does not want to tolerate collective security agreements, but would like to leave the individual weaker countries without the assistance of stronger powers so as to be able to attack them more easily.

Contrary to Hitler's boasting that he tore up the Treaty of Versailles it is a fact that the Treaty of Versailles was already on its last legs when Hitler came to power. The debt and interest payments of the Young Plan had already been stopped by the Brüning government on 15 July 1931. The Saar poll was drawing near and would also have come off one hundred per cent for return to the Reich without the Hitler government.

Any other German government would also have succeeded in cancelling the last stipulations of the Treaty of Versailles peacefully without provocations against other peoples, without Germany's self-isolation and without transforming Germany into a barrack in which the entire people is drilled for war.

Some months before Hitler and Mussolini had started to give armed support to the insurgent generals in Spain Hitler declared in his speech of 7 March 1936:

"We raise no territorial demands in Europe. We know above all that the tensions which arise either out of false territorial provisions or from the disproportions between numbers of populations and their living space can not be solved by war in Europe."

How can this statement be compatible with Hitler's attack against the independence of Spain? Restoration of German honour? Spain was not among the signatories of the Versailles dictature. Protection of the German frontiers? Even a Goebbels could not claim that Spain was threatening the German frontiers. Thus the aggressive nature of Hitler's policy is becoming increasingly evident. The mask of defence is falling. The nazi leaders are substantiating their policy of conquest with increasing bluntness.

The armed intervention of Hitler and Mussolini is aiming at more than the conquest of Spanish natural resources; they are out to acquire a further strategic key position for the next world war in preparation by the Berlin-Rome-Tokyo triangle. A fascist Franco-Spain is to set up the third military front at the Pyrenees against the Popular Front in France and to cut off the communication routes of Britain and France in the Mediterranean. This war strategic interest was the principal motive inducing Hitler and Mussolini to plunge into the Spanish adventure under the banner of the "struggle against bolshevism".

Goebbels tried to camouflage the policy of conquest directed towards the establishment of military bases for the fascist war policy with his agitation against the Comintern. In his speech at the nazi party congress at Nuremberg he said:

"It can under no circumstances be tolerated that the Communist International should secure a new basis of operations in the west of Europe."

In fact it was Hitler and Mussolini who wanted to secure a basis of operations for themselves.

The national socialist leaders openly justified the "World Mission of Fascism" in Nuremberg, as it revealed itself in Abyssinia, Spain and China and in the organization of fascist insurrection in the democratic countries.

It is becoming increasingly clear to the peoples how right the German anti-fascists had been when they said right from the beginning that Hitler's slogans on "Equality", "Honour", "Freedom" and "Peace" were only to camouflage his war plans. Similarly the anti-communist slogan is now being used by Hitler, Mussolini and Japanese imperialism to cover up their imperialist program of conquest.

This slogan is by no means directed against the Soviet Union alone. Mussolini's speech at Palermo in which he proclaimed the struggle against bolshevism "or anything similar to it" shows that all blows are aimed against democracy, peace, the popular front and the freedom of all peoples. This is what Hitler and Mussolini call the "World Mission" of fascism. They are claiming for themselves the "right" to intervene in any way in the affairs of other countries. They are trying to "justify" the "right" of fascism to oppress, conquer and exploit foreign peoples.

The visit of the oppressor of the Italian people to Hitler underlined the sense of the 1937 Nuremberg party congress as a demonstration of the Berlin-Rome-Tokyo war axis. "Two peoples will hoist their knapsacks and rifles onto their shoulders and march into the future side by side"—thus Mussolini himself characterized the purpose of his pact with Hitler and the Mikado in an interview he granted to the pogrom hero Julius Streicher. Let us further recall his cynical confession on the Maifeld in Berlin (on which there was much discussion among the workers who had been ordered to the enforced rally):

"When words no longer suffice and when threatening circumstances require it one must reach for his weapons. That is what we did in Spain."

When Mussolini declared his withdrawal from the League of Nations the *Völkischer Beobachter* proclaimed that the "Berlin-Rome-Tokyo world-political triangle" was "today representing the will to life of three resolute peoples" and that peace will be guaranteed not by a world arbitration court but "by the popular force of the nations". This is the proclamation of naked arbitrariness, the tearing to shreds of all treaties, the rejection of all international arbitration courts. That is political gangsterism called fascist foreign policy. This policy combines a challenge to all forces of progress, to all acquisitions of freedom and human rights since the French Revolution of 1789 with the greed of Krupp and Thyssen, Hitler and Göring for the natural resources of other countries.

It is not the Soviet Union, whose peoples have great sympathy for the German people, which intends to attack Germany but Hitler and Mussolini who are preparing a war of aggression. It is not the Soviet Union which is to blame for the constant deterioration of economic and political relations between Germany and the Soviet Union but the brown dictatorship with its continuous campaign of defamation and warmongering against the Soviet Union. Germany could receive vast quantities of raw materials and food in peaceful exchange from the great country of socialism whose wealth is constantly growing if there were no brown dictatorship in Germany.

How strong and respected Germany would be if a free German nation were to conduct a genuine peace policy in alliance with the Soviet Union!

"We want to be masters in our own house!" Hitler screamed in his speeches during the election comedy in March 1936. Since then the destruction of Guernica by Junkers aircraft, the shelling of Almeria by German warships and the consignments of troops and war materials known to have been sent to the Spanish rebels have demonstrated with increasing clarity to the German people that Hitler wishes to be the master in other peoples' houses. The promises of the nazi leaders that Hitler's policy would lead to conquests of "new space" without war, thus becoming the "just reward" for the German workers are meeting with decreasing belief. Many workers and even certain bourgeois sections recognize that the conquest of foreign territories and the space of other countries means war—and probably (so they express with growing frequency) a new terrible defeat.

Germany's Destiny

The policy of the nazi regime, the aim of which is war, is cynically compared by Goebbels with a game of lottery. In his speech at Königsberg on 10 December 1937 he said:

"Politics is a game. And how have games always been won? By high stakes. Just as in a lottery. In a lottery those who buy the largest number of tickets have the best chances ... If we are asked whether the Four Year Plan was not also a plan of war, I reply: 'Yes indeed, it is!'"

But in every lottery millions lose and only a few win. In this case the loser is the German people. Conducting German policy like a lottery constitutes the most monstrous crime against the life of the German people and against the national existence of Germany. The "size of the stake" in the game of Hitler and Goebbels is the blood of our people, the life of millions of German men, women and children who would be torn to shreds by machine gun bullets, grenades and bombs in the approaching war. The "size of the stake" in the game of the fascist rulers is the destruction of our German towns, for despite all the insane armament of Hitler our country would be transformed into a battlefield of the modern war of extermination.

Let us keep to the words of Goebbels that the national socialist leaders know the size of the stake and that they are conducting their policy of imperialist aggressive war like a lottery—they are playing with the destiny of Germany.

The Hitler dictatorship will never attain what it is striving to achieve. If badly armed nations such as China and Spain are putting up a heroic and successful resistance against an aggressor equipped with modern arms, the militarily strong great powers will repulse all of Hitler's attacks with terrible superiority. The forces of resistance against the aggressive policy of the Berlin-Rome-Tokyo war axis are growing among the popular masses of all countries. Only irresponsible adventurers could try to convince the German people that the democratic governments will increasingly give way in the face of Hitler's provocations and the warmongering actions of Mussolini and the Japanese imperialists. A situation can very quickly come about in which the other great powers will have to protect themselves against Hitler's provocations and where the "highest stakes" are at issue unless it is possible to overthrow Hitler before then. With the "highest stakes" in a new terrible world war Germany, with its economically and financially weak, internally rotten allies Mussolini and the Japanese generals, hated by the peoples of their own countries, would inevitably be forced into defeat.

In this game for the life or death of the German people nazi spokesmen as a rule display a cheap optimism as to the outcome of a coming war: the strong German army would be able to defeat the enemy rapidly in a "blitz war". Discussions among various German generals on the other hand show that even some of them have begun to reflect about the lessons taught by Spain, no longer being convinced of the strength of the nazi system in the event of war. Lieutenant General von Metzsch significantly demanded that the possibility of defeat in a future war should be recognized in good time and that a corresponding education should be conducted among the popular masses so as to prevent being surprised by a new revolution. In the preface to his book *Der einzige Schutz gegen die Niederlage* (The Only Protection against Defeat) he wrote "... that we can only assert ourselves if we dared the ultimate, the most extreme and heroic even when there seems to be no prospect of success within the horizon of the individual ... For the question of whether there would be failure could be answered by us alone neither in nor before a war. Yet it does lie solely within our hands to determine how failures must be overcome so that they do not expand into a fatal defeat."

This preparation for the possibility of defeat is an admission that the Hitler war would not just be a cocksure "blitz war". The Hitler dictatorship has neither sufficient raw materials nor foodstuffs for a long war. "Substitutes" can stretch reserves and prolong starvation but they can not make victory possible. Whereas the other countries have large economic reserves, shortages have become a daily phenomenon in Germany even now and in the event of war Germany would have to reckon that its forces would run out.

Furthermore, Hitler, Mussolini and the Japanese militarists are internally weak because their power is based on the gagging of their own peoples and on the strangulation of all democratic freedoms. They fear that the idea of freedom might seize hold of their peoples, turning them into allies of the socialist Soviet Union and the democratic countries. The German workers and the entire German people are confronted with the great historic task of making every effort to prevent a Hitler war, in their own vital interests and in the interest of the whole of peace-loving mankind. Our entire struggle in Germany, the struggle of anti-fascists and of all progressive people is governed by the necessities of this human task. We have tried to show with examples how this struggle with its great significance is beginning in the daily life of our working people in hundreds of forms.

Prevention of war, defence of peace—could there be a morally more elevated or more imperative task for all those who love our people and who wish to guard our country against the horrors of war? Has there ever been any moment when the united front of the workers and the popular front for the struggle for peace have been of more urgent vital importance to our German people than today? May all opponents of Hitler become aware of their responsibility to German history and mankind! Our people would have to pay too high a price for any further war for anti-fascists to renounce constant struggle for peace and make concessions to the voices of those people who say that nothing can be done at the moment and who want to wait passively for the war. When anti-fascists discuss the question: "What shall we do if war breaks out?" after the bombing of Almeria, we reply:

The present joint resistance against armament burdens and "sacrifices", these forerunners of the misery of war a hunderd times worse, the present resistance to Hitler tyranny are also inseparably linked with vast tasks in the event that Hitler cannot be prevented from lighting the torch of war. If the popular movement against the war policy, "sacrifices" and for the rights of the people is developed with all forces, we shall not only increase the possibilities of preventing war but we shall also create broad prerequisites for more rapidly ending any war unleashed by Hitler, reducing the duration of the terrible period of war misery and overthrowing the war criminals.

The less done today the more easily can Hitler start a war and the more difficult will be the struggle against the fascist dictatorship during the war.

Thus there is no wall between the present tasks in the struggle to prevent war and the tasks during a war.

Hitler's policy does not serve the national interests of Germany or the well-being of the German popular masses. Hitler's policy is in truth endangering the entire national existence of Germany by his megalomaniacal ambitions for conquest which solely serve the interests of the Krupps, Thyssens, Flicks, Kirdorfs, Siemens and Blohms. Therefore there can today be no greater national task than the liberation of Germany from Hitler's tyranny and war policy. Those who strive to guard our people against the bloodshed and horror of a renewed war, fighting in alliance with the adherents of peace and freedom throughout the world are not "traitors to the country" but those who, like Hitler, play a game of lottery with the destiny of Germany in alliance with the world's warmongers are the ones who are betraying the nation.

Hitler speaks of his "thousand-year Reich" in order to create the impression that his rule is of unshakable firmness. His concluding speech at the Nuremberg party congress in 1937, however, indicated the fear of the unification of the workers and all his opponents. Today there are many streams and rivers of opposition in Germany. The desire for freedom is being expressed by the people in various ways. But all are unanimous in the call: "Down with Hitler! We want freedom again!" Today there is a whisper in our country: "We need a government of the people. The people must have power!" This can be achieved only through the creation of a German popular front.

The popular front embodies the idea of the unification of the popular masses for peace and freedom. The popular front embodies the struggle for justice, humanity and order. The popular front embodies the living continuation of those great ideals of freedom which are linked with the best names in German history. The popular front will ensure the new freedom after the overthrow of Hitler by eliminating the privileges of the big capitalists, nationalizing heavy industry and the banks, expropriating the big landowners and thus once and for all depriving fascism of the material basis for struggle against the people.

We communists are devoting our entire strength to the creation and strengthening of the German popular front for that is the way to the unity of our people for struggle against Hitler barbarism. Only the democratic people's republic can be the aim of the joint struggle uniting all opponents of Hitler, a republic which must not have the weaknesses of Weimar in the struggle against reaction. Every communist, every socialist will acknowledge this common aim as a great advance in the struggle for socialism.

We communists, faithful sons of the German working class, love our people and our country. We want to protect our country from the horrors of war. We love our German culture which in the past accomplished great things for mankind. We love our German language in which not only the poems of freedom of Schiller, Goethe, Büchner, Heine, Freiligrath and Herwegh were written but in which Marx and Engels wrote, the language in which Bebel and Liebknecht called upon the working class to fight for freedom. Because we love our people and our country we support every effort of the opponents of Hitler to unite.

Today there is a community of destiny that links Ernst Thälmann with Mierendorff, Chaplain Rossaint and Pastor Niemöller who are locked up in jail as hostages of the brown-shirted war provocateurs. Unity, unity and again unity, an end to all division among honest anti-fascists—that is the road by which the opponents of Hitler, today linked by a common destiny of suffering, must become the masters of tomorrow through their community of struggle for a new Germany of peace and freedom.

Hitler has raised the question of the destiny of Germany by his policy of war. The answer will be given by the German anti-fascists, by the German popular front movement:

Germany will live—therefore the Hitler dictatorship must fall!

Danzig and Hitler's War Plans

24 August 1939

The military preparations of German fascism to annex Danzig and destroy the independence of Poland are in full swing. The *Völkischer Beobachter* has the nerve to state that in its opinion the state territory of Poland is "too large". Nazi propaganda tries to cover up the fascist attack on the independence of Poland by screaming about the non-existent "Polish war threats", similarly to when they once maintained that Czechoslovakia was threatening Germany. Gruesome fairy-stories are spread about the citizens of Danzig being annoyed by Poland in order to detract from the fact of the terroristic rule of fascism over the population of Danzig.

Is it not obvious that with the exception of German fascism no one is threatening Danzig? Only since the German fascist war party has been using Danzig as a battering-ram against Poland has there been a Danzig question.

This attack is not only against Poland, but just as much against France and Great Britain. By strangling Poland Hitler believes he can secure himself a flank so that he can throw his main military forces against France and Great Britain.

Nazi propaganda tries to screen these tactics of German fascism of knocking out the European peoples separately, one after the other, by screaming about the "encirclement" of Germany.

Not so long ago German fascism tried to achieve the colonization of Poland by other tactics. It strove to increase its bases in this state with the assistance of reactionary circles in Poland and it proposed a treaty to the Polish government by which the country would have been degraded to an agricultural province of Berlin. The "military advisers" and the Gestapo agents were to follow in the footsteps of Hitler's economic agents.

As long as Hitler placed his hopes on Polish Foreign Minister Beck he did not think in terms of demanding the annexation of Danzig. It was not until this plan misfired, when Poland realized after the Czechoslovakian drama that its national independence was at stake–

that Hitler demanded Danzig and brusquely cancelled the ten-year treaty with Poland.

It is absolutely ridiculous for nazi propaganda to talk about Poland's "threat to Germany". Everyone knows that Hitler tore up the treaty between Germany and Poland, that Hitler sent German military personnel to Danzig, that the nazis wanted to cut off Poland's access to the sea, that the nazis create unrest and provoke clashes by organizing nationalistic incitement and that the nazis want to make Danzig into a war harbour and a battering-ram against Poland.

The Polish people have learned from the fate of Czechoslovakia about how fascism carries out its conquests by the organization of disintegration and putsches within the countries themselves, hand in hand with the military attack from abroad. The annexation of the whole of Czechoslovakia followed the military occupation of the Sudetenland. Warsaw is to follow Danzig; but Warsaw does not want to become a second Prague.

When Goebbels and Forster, the Danzig Gauleiter, today speak of the "right of self-determination" of the population of Danzig, millions of honest people point to the ten million Czechs and Slovaks, to the seven million Austrians, to Abyssinia and Albania and they think of the murder of women and children in Spain by the fascist Condor Legion. This Condor Legion today stands at the Polish border.

The fascist war party demagogically demands the right of self-determination for Danzig. Is it not the crudest demagogy when the fascist leaders use the phrase "right of self-determination" when it is just they who, in their own country take away the right of self-determination of the people, forbid all free expression and answer every free impulse with torture and prison?

The fascists speak of the "right of self-determination" for Danzig although they themselves have eliminated every right of the people of Danzig to self-determination. Self-determination without democratic liberties is not possible.

The fact that the representative of the German war party in Danzig appears but not one of the progressive deputies elected by the people of Danzig can speak is most characteristic. The most frightful terror regime was set up by the brown and black gangs of the nazis in the former Free City of Danzig. Because the fascists remained in the minority in the parliamentary elections they threw the parliamentary deputies of the workers into prison and thereby created a "majority" in the Volkstag. Many anti-nazis were sent to concentration camps in Germany or were subjected to forced labour. Only recently did it become known that representatives of the people of Danzig were hauled off to Berlin into the cellars of the Gestapo because they had led the struggle for the freedom of the people of Danzig.

The majority of the people of Danzig want the restoration of the legal state of affairs. This desire is also expressed in numerous leaflets distributed by anti-fascists in Danzig. They demand the withdrawal of the fascist units from the city, the restoration of democratic rights and the return of these Danzigers hauled off to Germany. All right-thinking people in Danzig want the restoration of the constitutional guarantees as laid down in the resolutions of the League of Nations. The people of Danzig are afraid of being "incorporated" into fascist Germany for this annexation is the annexation to a prison. The example of the Saar shows them that they have only terror, shortages of food and raw materials, devaluation and higher taxes to expect in Germany.

German fascism is not concerned about the "right of self-determination" of the people of Danzig or representing the interests of the German-speaking inhabitants but about the annexation of Danzig as a military base for the encirclement of Poland, as a deployment area in order to cut off Poland's access to the sea and to be able to squeeze it from the north and south.

This is also confirmed by the sabre rattling of Italian fascists. When the latter declare that they are prepared to go to war for 200,000 Danzigers while they chase 250,000 Tyroleans from their homes, it proves already that with Danzig it is not a national question of the German people which they are concerned with but an imperialist conspiracy against world peace.

These imperialist plans of conquest have nothing to do with the interests of the German people. Every such aggression brings the German people only new armaments burdens, intensifies the militarization of the country and restricts the living possibilities of the working people, until finally this fascist aggression comes up against the resistance of the threatened peoples and the German people must pay for these policies with monstrous sacrifices of property and blood. Every foot of soil that the fascist aggressors conquer, regardless of whether it once belonged to Germany or not, serves the interests of the fascist rulers and therefore harms the anti-fascist struggle for freedom.

In countering the race hatred and chauvinistic propaganda of fascism it is necessary to point out that in Danzig it is not a question of the national suppression of German-speaking sections of the population but of the suppression by German fascism of German-speaking and Polish inhabitants. This proves that the struggle for the maintenance of peace and for nations living together amicably poses the question of the fight against fascism.

German imperialism has always tried to stir up hatred for the Polish people among the German people. To some extent it has succeeded. Thus the active anti-fascists in Germany are now undertaking even greater efforts to make the masses understand the imperialist, anti-Polish slander and to strengthen solidarity with the just struggle of the Polish people for the defence of their national independence. Ernst Thälmann's call for solidarity with the French and Polish peoples must be made the guiding principle of the thoughts and actions of all progressive forces.

There is only one way for the fight for freedom for the German people and that is the fight against the fascist system ruling in Germany which is enslaving its own and other peoples.

Who Is Master in the German House?

From an illegal leaflet
which was also distributed among soldiers of the Hitler army,
published at the beginning of 1942

German men and women,

Hundreds of thousands of corpses of German soldiers cover the battlefields from the North Cape to the Black Sea. How many German women are in mourning, how many orphans weep for their fathers, how much suffering and misery have come over our homeland. Tomorrow it will be still worse. The unseeing eyes of those fallen at the front and killed by air-bombs stare at you questioningly.

Where is all this to lead, what, in fact, are the German people struggling for?

You have been told that you must fight and sacrifice for Germany because Germany is "a state of the people". Hitler, Goebbels and Ley often allege that in the Germany of today the people are the "master in the house", that the German people have to decide on everything.

But who are the German people? The German people are especially the workers and peasants, are those who create.

But do you govern the country? Do you make the laws? Do you decide on the fateful questions of Germany, on war and peace? Do you own all the riches of the country which were created by the work of your hands and the work of your fathers and grandfathers?

Just looking around a little in Germany and reflecting will make it clear to you who is really master in the German house.

Are there men from the people in the government, in the State Council, in the Reichstag? Not a single one. You will not find there a single genuine worker, not a single peasant from the soil. The entire state power is in the hands of persons who have nothing in common with the people. Take anyone of the present rulers of Germany, for example, Hermann Göring. He comes from the family of a big industrialist and had already absorbed an abhorrence of honest work with his mother's milk. In the war he was an air officer. After the war he made up his mind to live without work and care at the expense of his first wife, a rich Swedish baroness.

Or take another man, the noble Reich Foreign Minister von Ribbentrop. Before he was appointed Reich minister by Hitler he was already a capitalist, the son-in-law of Champagne Henkell, a rich wine merchant with a big export business.

And Hitler himself? He wrote in his book *Mein Kampf* that the very thought of regular work gave him a "yawning sickness" already from youth. As he himself admitted, he was busy as an informer of the Reichswehr against the workers after the First World War. He never really worked in his life.

Along with these and other nazi leaders, all of whom today are rich employers themselves, you can find in the leading state posts the old well-known rich capitalists and bankers from the Weimar period, the Krupps, Vöglers, Siemens and Klöckners.

The entire machinery of state dances to the tune of this handful of powerful men. They make the laws. They decide on your life and your death. They fix your wages and your bread ration. They jack up the taxes you have to pay. They decide whether the German worker is to toil for twelve or sixteen hours. It depends on them whether the German peasant can give his children half a litre of milk or an egg from what he himself has produced through hard work They send German soldiers to foreign countries where they bleed to death on the battlefields.

Only the rich rulers governing the German state and receiving millions from the war take an interest in this war. They are also the same who own the enterprises, the factories, the banks and the land, who own all of Germany's wealth. If, for example, you were to ask the question in Essen "To whom does this gigantic enterprise belong?" everybody will answer, "Don't you know? It belongs to Krupp!" Just as the entire works was owned by Krupp before he still owns it today. The only difference is that the wealth of the Krupp family grows dizzily from year to year, especially since Hitler has been in power.

You can wander through the whole of Germany. In all regions you will be told that this factory belongs to the Klöckner family and that one to Flick, Röchling or the like. They are the old capitalist sharks and tycoons.

But the old magnates and plutocrats were joined by new ones, the nazi leaders who have become rich. Herman Göring, for example, became one of the richest men in Germany during the Hitler rule. He has used his state and party posts as a springboard for his personal enrichment. Today he is the principal owner of the largest German metal trust, the "Hermann Göring Works". This enterprise was founded with the money of the German Reich, that means, the German tax-payers. The state makes available mines, monetary resources and loans. But this plant does not belong to the state, it is owned by a joint-stock company. Shareholders of this huge trust are Göring, Hitler, Ley and a few old capitalists. This is a hitherto unheard-of enrichment at state expense. But that is not all. The "Hermann Göring Works" has stolen dozens of factories and mines in all countries occupied by the German army. The German soldiers helped them to do it, that is why they fought and shed their blood. What good does it do you, German working people? Do you own any shares in the "Hermann Göring Works"? Do you perhaps receive a part of the millions made by those men?

Even official data give a clear answer to the question of who controls the German economy. According to official statements 500 of the 604 directors and leading employees of the 25 largest German companies held these posts already before Hitler seized power. The other 104 are nazi leaders who have risen to be shareholders and capitalists thanks to their positions of power. Among 114 chairmen of boards of directors and their deputies of the large German enterprises there are 101 who dominated the world of industry and finance already before 1933.

And what is the situation in the village? Who is the master there? Is perhaps the working peasant the master there? Not at all! According to official data 2,300,000, i.e., 60 per cent of all peasant families, have less than two hectares of land in Germany, from the yields of which they simply cannot live. This means that well over half of all German peasant families would not have enough bread to eat even if they could keep for themselves all that they produce. But they are not allowed to keep it for themselves. The peasants plough and sow, but the harvested crops are taken away by the nazi bosses of the Reich foodstuffs system.

Vast fields belong to the landowners. You can hike for days in East Prussia, Silesia, in North Bavaria, and when you ask "To whom do these fields and these forests belong?" you will be told "They belong to the Crown Prince!" or "They belong to the Duke of Coburg-Gotha!" or "All that belongs to Prince Hohenlohe-Oehringen!" And you will learn still more of the powerful men of the flat country, of the Count of Stolberg, the Count of Schaffgotsch, of Pless, of Putbus and whatever their names may be, these princes, counts and other noblemen who pretend to be the representatives of the German farmers but who never in their life held a plough in their hands or whetted a scythe. Hitler has not taken an inch of their land from these gentlemen. On the contrary, he has ruined 400,000 small peasants in the course of eight years but given back tens of thousands of hectares of land to the Hohenzollerns. He has presented the princes and counts with new vast landed property in occupied Poland.

Many officers and generals stem from the rural nobility and Junker families. If all these Junkers and big landowners were expropriated and their landed property distributed among the peasants who do not have enough land the German peasant could live better immediately on his own soil. But the German Junkers have no intention of giving up their large landed property to the poor German "fellow countryman". On the contrary. They drive the German soldiers to distant foreign countries to conquer more land for them there.

You can see from all this that the greatest disaster for Germany is that it is not the people who are master in their house, that it is not the people who have to decide in Germany but a handful of highly placed rich men. It is not enough for these men to squeeze profit out of the working German people. They want more and more, for the appetite comes from eating. They make war with your hands to subjugate and plunder foreign peoples. The blood of German soldiers is the purchase price they pay for mines, factories and mineral wealth in foreign countries. It does not matter to them that in doing so millions of German people perish, for they calculate that for every dead German they receive half a dozen other cheap workers.

Your sacrifices at the front and at home are senseless. You are fighting for a lost cause. Hitler can never subdue the mighty 200 million people of the Soviet Union defending a homeland which really belongs to them. And furthermore you are fighting against yourselves, for you are fighting for the cause of your worst enemies, for the cause of the men who keep the German people in misery and servitude. You cannot be interested in waging a war to help your plutocrats to obtain still greater power. Your interest is to put an end to the rule of the plutocrats in Germany and help the German people to their rights in their own house.

Take aim at the greedy and bloodthirsty German plutocrats! Overthrow Hitler and his clique!

Put an end to the criminal and hopeless war against the Soviet Union!

Take your destiny, the destiny of your families, the fate of Germany into your own hands!

Make yourselves masters in the German house!

All Weapons Against Hitler!

23 July 1944

The military crisis began at Stalingrad. Already at that time there was a lack of reserves, and Hitler had the encircled troops told: "The law orders you to die!" Now Hitler is giving this order to all soldiers on all fronts. This is his last military wisdom.

For under the blows which are falling on the Hitler regime from east, west and south the fronts have become yawning breaches which no Hitler can close again. The conquest of the world, the expedition to the Urals and to India, the theft of iron, oil, coal and wheat about which Hitler indulged in fancies before Stalingrad have become the nonsensical struggle for the prolongation of Hitler's respite on German soil. The existence of the nation is to be sacrificed to this private "war of defence" of the Hitler clique. This means the political crisis of the Hitler regime.

For five years Hitler sacrificed hundreds of thousands of men and sons of our people, month after month, for the rapacious interests of a small set of newly rich nazi bigwigs and big armament industrialists. Discontent is becoming ever louder among the people and in the Wehrmacht. Finally German generals picked up courage and declared: Enough!

Two fronts have formed in Germany, on the one side is the fighting front of patriotic men and women who want to save what can still be saved by the immediate ending of the war. On the other side is the bankrupt Hitler clique which wants to continue the war for its egoist interests until Germany is completely ruined.

The so-called Hitler government cannot be considered as the government of Germany, for its policy puts the future of the nation at stake. Another government must take the destiny of the nation in hand.

It must be done now. Either the patriotic, freedom-loving men and women of our people rise up to destroy the Hitler clique or they themselves will be destroyed by Hitler and his Gestapo. The appointment of Himmler as commander of the home army and the creation of an

113

inner-German air force against his own people show what crimes Hitler is capable of. Now force must be answered with force.

No one can say that Himmler's Gestapo and SS are still too powerful. This is not true. Hitler's apparatus of force is shaken by the defeats at the fronts. The brave national action of the people can render it harmless.

The Hitler clique is powerless if the workers, office employees, employees of the armament industry and the transport system at home stop production, paralyse traffic and thus make it impossible for Hitler to continue the war. To him who says that this endangers the existence of the population it may be replied that the excessive strain on the economy for a last absurd attempt to protract the war ruins the homeland and the front. But using every possible way to end the war saves hundreds of thousands of officers and soldiers at the front and the lives of hundreds of thousands of women and children at home.

The clique of generals subject to Hitler in the so-called supreme command of the Wehrmacht with its "national socialist leadership officers" is powerless if at the front generals, officers and soldiers stop fighting, make contact with the representatives of the National Committee and turn their weapons against the true enemy of the nation, against Hitler and his clique. It may be replied to him who says that this opens the front that the front has already been opened by the superior forces of the Red Army. Our German people have nothing to fear from the Red Army.

Himmler, the new commander of the home army is powerless if the men of the replacement battalions at home safeguard the struggle of the people with their arms and break the terror of the SS.

The strength of the people is tremendous when they struggle for a joint aim.

What Is the Commandment of the Hour?

The continuation of the war by the Hitler clique must be made impossible in every way.

In every way possible prevent Hitler from driving hundreds of thousands of the sons of our people into a senseless death shortly before his fall.

In every way possible prevent Hitler from dragging the war onto German territory and ruining Germany completely.

In every way possible prevent Hitler in his madness from destroying the last foundations for the reconstruction of Germany.

No German with a sense of responsibility may evade acting for these national tasks. Workers, office employees, employers, peasants and members of the middle classes, soldiers and generals—all are being ruined by Hitler. All must act jointly.

To hesitate now, to wait and see is fatal. He who by passive behaviour allows Hitler to drag the war onto German soil is himself guilty if he is killed in war action in the last hour, if his wife and his children are killed at home.

Hitler fears nothing more than the fighting community of the people. In his last need Hitler will try to stir up the working people against the generals and officers who oppose him. It would be inexcusable if an anti-fascist should stand apart passively out of distrust of the generals. We know that many men in the Wehrmacht and at home were on the wrong track earlier. But Hitler's mad deeds have opened the eyes of many of them, and today they are marching on a new way against Hitler for Germany together with all anti-fascists. Let us judge people by their present deeds against Hitler. The solidarity of all Hitler opponents is the supreme law of action. Hitler must be prevented by joint action from destroying the upright Germans who are courageously struggling for the cause of the people.

Hitler demands blind obedience in carrying out his orders. The German people reply: The traitor Hitler no longer has anything to command! Germany listens only to the instructions of those men who are struggling against Hitler in the midst of the people in unselfish action.

The rebellion of a group of generals against Hitler and the orders of generals on the eastern front to stop action show how deep the crisis of the Hitler regime has already become. Now the entire strength of the people must be displayed to overthrow Hitler as soon as possible and thus save people and homeland.

Hitler is the enemy of the nation! All weapons against Hitler!

The Program of the
Anti-fascist-Democratic Order

*From the speech at the First Conference of Officials
of the Communist Party of Germany of Greater Berlin
on 25 June 1945*

The German army which had set about conquering the world was finally smashed by the Red Army on the territory of Berlin. The Hitler clique left behind a heap of rubble. Who can still doubt today that the nazi leaders were the most unscrupulous enemies of the nation? Millions of Germans sacrificed themselves for the world conquest plans of nazism. The following words should stand above their graves: Fallen for the predatory interests of the German nazi leaders, armament industrialists and bankers!

We must state in deep sorrow that the big majority of the German people allowed itself to be misused as an instrument of the nazi leaders and armament industrialists. Hitler was able to carry through his war crime for six years because the ideological forces of opposition to the imperialist, militarist ideology were developed only insufficiently in the German people, because the poison of the predatory ideology and blind military obedience had deep roots in the people.

Why Was the Defeat of Germany Inevitable?

Many Germans today still regret that the war was lost. They seek the reasons in individual mistakes of the military leadership. But Germany was not defeated militarily because individual German generals made mistakes but because the road of imperialist conquest, the road of race hatred and war of extermination against other peoples had to lead to the catastrophe of Germany in any case. How could a war against the mighty Soviet Union, against the country with the most progressive democratic system, how could a war against all democratic peoples end otherwise than with catastrophe for Germany? A country like Hitler Germany which had written the hatred of other peoples and the extermination of other peoples on its banner had inevitably to call forth the alliance of all peoples against the common enemy.

The great friendship of the peoples existing in the Soviet Union and the alliance of the democratic states have been victorious over the medieval racial theory of nazism.

The heroism of the peoples defending their countries has defeated the German armies which wanted to assert the law of the jungle in Europe.

Soviet democracy and the democracy of the states allied against Hitler have proved stronger than the slave system of the Hitler state.

After the German people have themselves experienced through the victories of the Red Army that the entire Goebbels propaganda about the Soviet Union was lies and fraud it is high time that every German realizes what internal system gave the Soviet people such gigantic strength.

Germany's War Guilt and the Joint Responsibility of the German People

Hitler's defeat was inevitable. But the defeat of Hitler could have become a great historic victory of our German people if they had been able to utilize the military weakening of the Hitler regime and overthrow the nazi regime with their own force. It is the tragedy of the German people that it obeyed a gang of criminals. This is the most terrible thing! The perception of this guilt is the prerequisite for our people finally breaking with their reactionary past and entering resolutely upon a new road.

The joint responsibility of our people consists in the fact that they permitted those forces which were most rapacious and greedy for conquest in Germany, the nazi bureaucracy and the big armament industrialists, to take over the full state power.

The joint responsibility of our people consists in the fact that they permitted the hate propaganda against the French, Polish, Russian and English peoples and allowed the Hitler clique to break all treaties and even tear up the Soviet-German treaty.

The joint responsibility of our people consists in the fact that they allowed themselves to be deceived credulously, that the old Prussian spirit of submissiveness and blind obedience dominated great masses so that these masses again obeyed the orders of a gang of war criminals.

The joint responsibility consists in the fact that the majority of our people applauded the Hitler government during Hitler's temporary victories and imagined themselves to be superior to other peoples.

No one can say that the road to fascism was inevitable. It would not have been difficult after the First World War to break the power of German imperialism and, through a truly democratic system, destroy once and for all the rule of Prussian militarism, the armament industrialists and their accomplices. It is therefore aptly said in the appeal of the Communist Party of Germany:

"After all the suffering and misfortune, the shame and disgrace, after the darkest era of German history, today, at the end of the 'Third Reich', the social democratic worker must also admit that we were right in stating that the fascist pest was able to spread in Germany only because in 1918 the war criminals and those guilty of the war remained unpunished, because there was no struggle for real democracy, because the Weimar Republic granted reaction free play, because the anti-Soviet agitation of a few democratic leaders paved the way for Hitler and paralysed the strength of the people through the rejection of the anti-fascist united front."

In 1932 the united struggle of the workers and the entire working people could still have prevented the seizure of power by Hitlerism. It would be harmful to our own nation if we did not have the courage to recognize that the German working class and the working people failed historically. And this failure is the more terrible because it enabled German fascism since 1933 to organize the systematic destruction of the progressive forces in Germany and allowed nazism to carry through the systematic extermination of the opponents of the German fascist imperialism in gas cars and death ovens. Nobody can dispute today that Hitlerism made Germany a slave-keeping state and thus brought the deepest shame upon our country in the eyes of all peoples.

The bankrupt nazi regime historically doomed to failure raged like mad against all progressive forces of the working people. The nazi bosses and armament industrialists rightfully feared the progressive forces which were steeled in the heroic struggle against Hitler fascism and which are called upon by history to safeguard the future of Germany.

He who tries today to deny the war guilt of Hitler Germany acts against the interests of the nation, for the recognition of the war guilt is the prerequisite for the uprooting of nazism, for the destruction of the nazi war ideology, for the overcoming of the Prussian barracks spirit, for the determined struggle against the nazi racial ideology and every form of racial arrogance.

Only when our people feel deeply ashamed of the crimes of Hitlerism, only when they are deeply ashamed of having allowed these barbaric crimes, only then will they have the inner courage to enter upon a new, democratic and progressive road which alone can safeguard the future of the nation.

Let us see that our German people finally learn the historical lesson after having lost two world wars:

Not through a predatory war, not through race hatred but only through serious work and peaceful relations with the Soviet Union and the other peoples can the German people have a happy life.

The foundation for this is an anti-fascist democratic order in Germany itself.

The Consequences of the War of Conquest of German Imperialism

The fact that the forces of resistance against barbaric nazism in the German working class and in our people were too weak and nazism therefore had to be destroyed by the military forces of the Soviet Union and the allies has led to the occupation of Germany. We communists did everything we could do so that nazism would be destroyed by the forces of the German anti-fascists, with the forces of our own people. We were not successful. When today we have to record in Germany the beginning of a democratic development we owe this especially to the heroic Red Army. The fact that the German workers and working people could not with their own strength remove nazism, the enemy of the German nation, has had a number of serious consequences.

The first consequence is the military and economic disarmament of Germany. I need not deal in detail with military disarmament, for it is a matter of course that after two world wars the other peoples and even the German people themselves are interested in not giving the militarist and imperialist forces in Germany the opportunity to repeat their crimes a third time. The harder to be felt is the reparations for what was destroyed by the German troops in foreign countries. Only in connection with the compensation for the industrial plants destroyed by German troops in foreign countries did many Germans become aware of the magnitude of the crimes of the Hitler army.

Many German armament industrialists now appear in the toga of peace angels. They suddenly discover what beautiful durable consumer goods they could produce and want to make us forget that until yesterday they were manufacturing tanks and guns for the destruction of the towns and industries of other peoples. After Hitler Germany waged war for six years the other peoples have undoubtedly the right to receive at least reparations for what was destroyed from

German enterprises. We have no reason to feel sorry for Messrs. Krupp, Flick, Vögler, Hugenberg & Co., who are now to lose their trusts. These gentlemen must be be deprived of the material basis which earlier enabled them to finance nazism and lead Germany into the catastrophe of war. May our people prove to all peoples by their honest will to make reparations that never again will they go the road of imperialist conquest.

Another serious consequence of the criminal Hitler war is the separation of the territories east of the Oder and the Görlitzer Neisse. No people would have had the idea of demanding the separation of these territories if our German people themselves had had the strength to create a democratic system in these territories, break the power of the east Elbe Junkers and thus prevent these areas from again becoming the basis for military deployment. No German can dispute that in 1918 the working people would have had the opportunity to destroy for good the basis of Prussian militarism in the German eastern territories. Just as Poland was ready in 1848 to reach agreement on the frontiers with a democratic Germany it would also have been ready for it after 1918. But in Germany Stinnes and Hindenburg remained in power, men who continued the old Prussian policy of hatred against Poland and who conducted anti-Soviet agitation. German imperialism could again grow strong under the Weimar coalition governments. Ebert allowed the reactionary military formations to exist. Seeckt organized the cadre army with the old ideology. Stresemann supported the bloc formation against the Soviet Union in Locarno, and Brüning conducted the struggle against the anti-fascist front and let the nazis have their own way. Thus the Hitler party, the war party of the German armament industrialists, was able to seize power and lead Germany into the Second World War.

The war deployment against Poland and the Soviet Union took place out of the East Prussia-Upper Silesia pincers. Nazism, which set about conquering a world empire, not only managed to devastate the house of other peoples and destroy its own country but it gambled away the territories east of the Oder into the bargain. Goebbels once compared German policy to a lottery in which the highest stake brings high winnings. Hitler put the destiny of the entire nation at stake and in so doing lost parts of Germany.

It would be a fateful wrong way to try to repeat the way of Seeckt and Stresemann, as a few former German National Party and People's Party members want to do. This would be the way which could only lead to the complete extinction of Germany. Although it

120

is grievous we cannot blame the other peoples for now creating security for themselves after our people were not able to establish the necessary security in their own country against the forces of Prussian militarism and against the reactionary representatives of the "drive to the east". It is the course of historical development that at the end of a war between progressive and reactionary states the power of the democratic progressive states is strengthened and that of the reactionary states weakened.

Every patriotic German must courageously draw the historical lessons in this serious crisis of our fatherland and make efforts to bring about a new relationship with the other peoples, especially with the new, democratic Poland. The Prussian Junkers as well as the Pilsudski clique were interested in antagonisms between the two peoples and in stirring up hatred against the Soviet Union. After nazism is destroyed in Germany and the rule of the Prussian big landowners has come to an end, and after a new Poland has come into existence which for the first time in its history is carrying through the national unification on a democratic basis all the conditions for a new relationship between the German and the Polish peoples are given. We anti-fascists should always realize that the traditional hatred of the Poles which had been instigated by Prussian reaction for centuries was the forerunner of that race hatred and that predatory ideology which has covered our people with the deepest disgrace in the eyes of the entire world. It is therefore our first duty to put an end to all tendencies and moods of hatred against the Polish people in our own ranks. Then a truly friendly relationship between our German people and the Polish people will also grow in connection with the healing of the wounds of the war.

Some Germans assert that our people can not live within the framework of the present narrower frontiers. This is the old argument with which Hitler prepared the war. The perniciousness of the conception that the standard of living of the people depends on the number of square kilometres of territory was proved by this very war. Germany had increased its territory from 500,000 square kilometres to five million square kilometres through Hitler's war of conquest. But this was the very source of catastrophe for the country, and as a result of this campaign of conquest Hitler lost for ever the territories east of the Oder and Neisse rivers.

The fact that not the number of square kilometres is decisive for the standard of living of a people is shown by such countries as Switzerland, Sweden and others which lack many products which, however, they can always obtain through peaceful trade relations with other peoples. In contrast the people suffered the bitterest misery in huge Russia until 1917 although there was enough space. Only when the Soviet power, a really democratic system, was set up and the people had to decide, were distress and misery successfully overcome. This proves that not the number of square kilometres but the internal system and the relationship with the other peoples determine the standard of living of a people.

Let us learn from this that the standard of living of our people depends on the people never again permitting the forces of the people and the national property to be wasted for imperialist conquests and that they establish a democratic system in the country which makes peaceful coexistence with the other peoples possible. This means that the first task is to destroy nazism and Prussian militarism and not permit the reactionary militarists to be able to camouflage themselves in any way.

The Anti-fascist Democratic Republic as the Basic Political Orientation

Nazism has thrown the German people far behind. It has left ruins and rubble, intellectual confusion and moral corruption. It could only do that by continuing the tradition of Prussian militarism and the ideology of the master race of the Prussian Junkers and the big armament industrialists.

It would be self-deception to believe that Hitler would have been able to carry through his barbaric war policy only by means of the most cruel terror against his own people. He who recalls with what enthusiasm the majority of the German people cheered Hitler when the German armies stood before Moscow will not be able to deny that the imperialist and militarist ideology has deep roots in our people and that even those who were filled with anxiety about the future of Germany did not have the strength to swim against the stream. If the repetition of such crimes is to be prevented then we Germans ourselves must close the books on the past. Today every German can see the fateful consequences of the fact that our people were not even in a position to complete their bourgeois-democratic revolution in 1848. How fateful was the fact that the unification of the Reich in 1871 did not take place through the democratic will of the people but under the command of the Prussian Junkers. Even after the defeat in the First World War the German people were not able to see that the destruction of the rule of the big landowners and militarists was in the national interest.

For these reasons our basic orientation in the present situation is the completion of the bourgeois-democratic revolution which was begun in 1848. That means that the Junkers, princes and big land-owners are to be expropriated and Germany cleansed of the ideology of Prussian militarism. The active nazis who transformed Germany into a military prison and escalated the tradition of German milita-rism into the most barbaric campaign of extermination against other peoples must be severely sentenced by the German courts. The big industrialist war criminals, however, will be punished by the courts of the allied powers for their political, moral and material guilt for the war and for their crimes.

Why an Anti-fascist–Democratic System?

It is stated in the appeal of the Communist Party that the decisive interests of the German people prescribe
"the road of setting up an anti-fascist, democratic regime, a par-liamentary-democratic republic with all democratic rights and liber-ties for the people".
This road to the democratization of Germany is in the national interest and in the immediate vital interest of the working class, for such a democratic-parliamentary system gives the working class the opportunity to unite after long division and thus create the guarantee for the future unification of our people. A democratic system makes the complete destruction of nazism and the growth of progressive forces possible. It is the ground on which a solid bloc of anti-fascist–democratic parties can be formed.

A democratic system enables the anti-fascist forces to acquire the necessary experience in the administration of the towns, communities and the economy.

A democratic system makes it possible to develop all anti-fascist–democratic forces in all parts of the Reich and contributes to main-taining and safeguarding the national unity.

Many workers want to establish socialism at once. But how is this to take place in view of the ideological devastation which penetrates deeply into the ranks of the working class? How can this be possible after the working class was split for more than a decade and a large, united party of the working people is only just developing? How can this be possible without the working people uniting in their consistent struggle for democracy and acquiring the necessary experiences in their organizations as well as in their activity in economic life? If we German communists act as the most determined fighters for democ-

123

racy this does not happen for any momentary reasons of expediency but in the application of the deep theoretical perceptions which we have been taught by Marx, Engels, and Lenin.

We must enter upon that road in Germany which corresponds to the conditions of development in Germany, and this will not be exactly the same road as in other countries.

We also think that it is wrong to declare certain measures of the communal management of the economy as socialism as a few social democratic comrades do. This sounds very radical, it is true, but it would only discredit the socialist ideal. We have become acquainted with the demagogy of war socialism which was spread by a few social democratic leaders in the First World War. We recall the fairy tales about socialism which were once propagated by the social democratic Prussian government, and we do not want to forget with what demagogy about socialism the Hitler gang deceived the people. It is high time seriously to put an end to all manoeuvres, to all attempts to represent capitalist institutions as socialism, and to teach the working class and the working people scientific socialism as it was developed by Marx, Engels and Lenin.

Strenuous Work for the Construction of a Democratic System

Our people can emerge from the catastrophe of the Hitler war only if it works strenuously and puts forth all its strength for the construction of a democratic system. To this end it is necessary for the most progressive anti-fascist democratic forces organized in the anti-fascist parties to reach agreement on the great tasks to be fulfilled by our people and adopt a joint action program of construction. A step forward on this way is the agreement between representatives of the Central Committee of the Communist Party of Germany (KPD) and the Executive Committee of the Social Democratic Party of Germany (SPD).

This agreement is the expression of the serious will to create a new, confidential relationship between the Communist Party and the Social Democratic Party. Thus it is not only a question of good relations between the officials but also between the two organizations in the entire Reich from Frankfurt-on-Oder to the Ruhr and from Mecklenburg to Württemberg. Representatives of the Executive Committee of the SPD expressed the opinion that the merger of the Communist Party and the Social Democratic Party into a unified party of the working class should be brought about as soon as possible. We stated on this that we are convinced that the adopted agreement and the cooperation of the two organizations create the prerequisites for the merger. But the prerequisite for a unified party of the new type is not only the creation of a close community of action but also the scientific perception of the most progressive forces of the working class and the working people about socialism in the Soviet Union and on the world outlook of Marxism-Leninism.

We must not overlook the fact that the class consciousness of the workers was deeply shaken in the twelve-and-a-half years of fascist rule, that the workers had no possibility of continuing their theoretical education and that the further development of the scientific theory of Marxism-Leninism is for the greater part unknown to them. We therefore welcome the fact that joint deliberations on the clarification of ideological questions are foreseen in the agreement between the Executive Committee of the SPD and the Central Committee of the KPD. Nor may we overlook the fact that the creation of a unified party is not only the question of the workers but also a question of winning representatives of the progressive intellectuals and the antifascist peasants. They are to have their say, too.

Why a Bloc of Anti-fascist–Democratic Parties?

In addition to the united front of the workers we want the united front of all anti-fascist–democratic forces, the bloc of the antifascist–democratic parties. The prerequisites for the creation of such a bloc are given by the profound changes that have taken place in Germany. What are these changes?

Firstly, millions of people now see that the old imperialist way is directed against the interests of the nation. They are therefore willing to destroy nazism and militarism, these enemies of the nation, with their united forces.

Secondly, profound social changes have taken place as a result of Hitler's total war. Men and women from bourgeois circles have been thrown out of their customary ways of life.

Thirdly, people from all sections of the population who jointly suffered in the prisons and concentration camps have become friends and will now, too, continue to stick together and work together.

Fourthly, the old party leaderships of the Weimar coalition are bankrupt. The German National Party and the German People's Party were the main forces which brought about the restoration of German imperialism in the Weimar Republic. The German National Party members helped Hitler to power, and the armament industrialists, members of the German People's Party, helped them to do so. Brüning himself disbanded the Zentrum Party to give its members the opportunity, as he said, to cooperate under the new regime. In May 1933 the former social democratic leaders agreed to Hitler's foreign policy. And Herr Leipart–the chairman of the General German Trade Union Federation, committed the greatest offence in 1933 when he asked the workers to take part in the nazi rally on May Day under Hitler's bloody banners.

Fifthly, those people who fought against fascism and today stand at the head of the anti-fascist parties have achieved a new relationship to the Soviet Union and to the other democratic peoples. This is an important prerequisite for cooperation.

When we communists are for the bloc of anti-fascist parties we consistently continue that policy pursued by the great tribune of the people Georgi Dimitrov before the Leipzig Court and which he explained in detail in his later speeches and articles. Through his courageous appearance before the Leipzig Court Georgi Dimitrov contributed to the fact that since 1935 there has been cooperation between the various anti-fascist forces in Germany.

The Party of Construction, the Party of the People

The Communist Party is a truly national party, for it struggles for the elimination of the causes of the disaster of the nation. Our party is the party of the people, for it is the party of construction. Our program of action shows the people the way to a better future.

The Communist Party is the party of the people, for we say in the program of action what must be done to set the normal life of the population going again so that the people have bread and they are supplied with the commodities necessary for life. The Communist Party is the party of the unification of the working people. The action program of our party helps the working people to join on a common basis and create everywhere a strong bloc of the anti-fascist–democratic parties for the democratic renewal of Germany.

Our party is the party of peace, for since its founding it has struggled for peaceful coexistence and for friendship with other peoples and especially for friendship with the great Soviet people to whom we owe our deep gratitude. Our party is the party of the people, for it is the only party which is guided by a progressive scientific theory. Our party was able by reason of the theory of Marxism-Leninism to foresee the course of events and call our people in time to the struggle against the nazi war policy, and it is in a position to perceive the way of future development.

What We Want

31 December 1945

The year of catastrophe is over. What unspeakable suffering has been brought upon our German homeland by nazism. How many millions of men and sons of our people have been sacrificed by Hitler and his big industrial backers in their world conquest madness. With drums and trumpets they had shouted out into the world the beginning of a new age. The name-plate of the German state was newly painted, it is true, but the old forces continued to rule, only in a more barbaric and misanthropic way than before. Today every German asks himself : How was it possible that for twelve and a half years Germany was dominated by such people who replaced thinking with barbaric brutality, who stifled every free word and made the preaching of hatred the national morality?

Today the corrupters of Germany sit in the dock where our people see the ranters of the nazi government, the cannon king Krupp, Flick of the Central German Steel Trust and others with the deepest contempt and with burning indignation. But how many of the big war profiteers from the managements of the trusts and banks are still missing?

It is the first demand of our people to themselves and their demand to the allies that in the first months of the new year Germany should be purged of the war criminals, war profiteers and militarists. Just as the streets had to be cleared to be able to walk there must be a political cleansing to pave the way for the construction of the new, democratic Germany. We want the German workers, the peasantry and the intellectuals to become aware of their historic task.

Our second desire at the beginning of the new year is that the new democratic system will be built up in accordance with the will of the people. The basic conditions for the democratic construction are already created in the Soviet occupation zone of Germany. The militarist big landowners were made harmless by the land reform. In the economy the power of the monopolists has been broken in various parts of our country, and the large enterprises of the fascists and war profiteers are managed by provincial or municipal administrative bodies. This, too, is an important guarantee for the safeguarding of peace and the systematic reconstruction of the economy. Thus a number of material basic conditions have already been created.

The most important, however, the new intellectual will, the spiritual rebirth of our people makes but slow progress. Twelve and a half years of fascist power and mental confusion still weigh heavily on many of us. Every one may render account to himself at the beginning of the new year that only the breach with the reactionary past makes joyful work possible. Only the German who frees himself from the old submissive spirit and turns away from the mental dullness of the last twelve years can master the new work.

We want the new year to become the year of the rebirth of our people.

The rebirth of our people means responsibly learning, creating the new democratic system in which the welfare of the people is to be the supreme law of any action. The rebirth of our people means removing the rubble of the old in strenuous work, reconstructing the economy, doing more so that our people can again gradually live better.

The rebirth of our people means making the solidarity of the people the highest moral law. Only through mutual material and intellectual help can we overcome the most difficult period and ensure the growing up of the young generation.

The rebirth of our people means acquiring the spiritual treasures of the great thinkers of our people again. Nazism has done everything possible to cut off Lessing, Goethe, Schiller, Heine, Marx from our people. May our people now strengthen themselves on the works of our classical authors and learn to understand their deep democratic nature.

The rebirth of our people means helping the front soldiers who have returned from war captivity and the followers of nazism who for years engaged in destruction upon destruction on orders to take part in peaceful construction work.

The rebirth of our people means to fill our people with the spirit of peaceful relations with other peoples, especially with the spirit of friendship with the great Soviet people. It is time for our people to rise out of the despondency and direct their entire action and purpose at resolutely finding the way out of the catastrophe.

The future of Germany is ensured when the working people determine, when the sound forces within the people take a courageous part in the construction of democratic self-administration, in the construction of the economy, in the construction of the new democratic culture.

Learning to work in a democratic manner in the administration is the slogan of the new men. Learning to acquire the results of progressive science is the admonition for the new teachers and the many pupils who come out of the working people and will now attend the institutions of higher learning. Learning to work out and apply the new democratic law is the will of the new people's judges. Learning to manage the enterprises which are now under provincial or municipal administration according to the up-to-date methods of the science of industrial management is the task of the new works managers.

Only diligence, truth and humanity will enable us to overcome the catastrophe and regain the confidence of the other peoples. To unify the people in this spirit is the special task of the working class. It is the democratic force which was least connected with the old reactionary, militarist existence. Up to now the working class has never had decisive influence on the destiny of the state and economy in Germany. All the greater is the present responsibility of the working class. At the beginning of the new year, the year of construction, the year of the creation of the new democratic system it is our vow to do everything possible to forge the unity of the workers, the peasantry and the intelligentsia. The stronger the unity of action of the Communist and the Social Democratic Parties is forged and the sooner the common goal, the united working class party, is attained the better will the future of Germany be ensured.

We want the unity of Germany. It would be a minimization of this great task if one were to deal only with the questions of the zonal frontiers. The establishment of the unity of Germany is the democratic task of the German people themselves.

The unity of Germany means purging the administrative bodies and works managements of fascists and war profiteers in all parts of the country.

The unity of Germany means that new men, honest democrats must everywhere take over leadership in the provincial and communal administrative bodies.

The unity of Germany means the creation of the united front of the anti-fascist–democratic parties in all parts of our country.

The unity of Germany means carrying through the land reform in all parts of Germany. The unity of Germany means overcoming the barbaric nazi ideology and the cultivation of progressive science and democratic culture in town and village.

The Communist Party will exert all its strength to solve these tasks in the new year. Only the democratic rule of the people can save Germany and bring about a better future of our people.

The Union of the Working-class Parties —
a National Task

Interview with a representative of Radio Berlin
on 11 January 1946

Question : Can you give me a few details about how the decision to unite the working class came into being at the joint conference of the Social Democratic Party of Germany and the Communist Party of Germany on 20 and 21 December?

Answer : As you certainly know, the joint conference lasted for two days. Representatives of the two parties from the districts reported on the ever closer cooperation in confidence of officials of the two working-class parties. Especially since the beginning of November last year many joint membership meetings of social democrats and communists have taken place in the enterprises and in the local groups. In most towns joint demonstrations took place in November at which the lessons of 1918 were discussed. These reports from the lower party organizations have convinced all participants in the conference that the second phase of unity has already begun. The joint decision was accordingly formulated. The decisions which have become known to us from Bremen, Wiesbaden, Munich and other cities of the western zones show that the will to the unification of the working class is growing there, too.

Question: Was there a special reason which induced the two party leaderships to carry through this joint conference in December?

Answer : Yes, there was. The real reason was the fact that the fascist and reactionary forces are active and are carrying through their malicious activity under various camouflages. The decision of the joint conference states that the enemy of peace and freedom, namely, fascist reaction, has not yet been destroyed.

The experiences after the First World War are recalled when the militarists and reactionary forces first assumed a democratic camouflage to wait for the suitable moment for the attack on democratic achievements. This great danger exists today, too. And for this reason the officials of the two workers' parties were of the opinion at the joint conference that the unification of the working class is necessary in order to create a strong centre of strength which is in a position, together with the other anti-fascist–democratic parties, to destroy fascist reaction for good.

Question : It is obvious from the press that a group of social democratic leaders in the west does not agree with the decisions of the December conference on the establishment of the unity of the working class.

Answer : I am of the opinion and I believe that I express the conception of the workers in the west, too, when I say that it would be better if these social democratic leaders were to use their forces in the struggle against the fascist reactionaries instead of fighting against unity. Before all workers in West Germany I want to ask the clear question of which way are you to go? There are two ways; one is the way of the unity of the working class, the union of the two working-class parties, because only this can create that centre of strength which safeguards peace and democratic development. After the repeated failures of the old forces since the founding of the Reich now the working class as a united force must take over the leading role in the democratic development.

Question : And what is the other way?

Answer : The other way which a group of social democratic leaders in the west want to go is the old way which in the Weimar Republic led to the step-by-step liquidation of the democratic achievements. It will again lead to the formation by these social democrats of a coalition with bourgeois parties and the bourgeois parties will take the social democrats in tow. We consider this way fatal from the national aspect, too, for such a policy allows the old reactionary forces to play one part of the people off against the other and hold their old positions. I ask all working people, would it not be better for the German working class to unite and carry through a uniform German policy?

Question : Do you not see a connection between the decision of the joint conference of December and the will in our people to unify Germany?

Answer : To ask the question in this way does not seem to me to suffice. The decision to establish the unity of the working class means more, it directly serves the safeguarding of the unity of Germany. We communists are a united party for the whole of Germany led by a central committee. We can therefore not understand it when a group of social democratic leaders in the west demands that the parties separate according to zones. This means to play directly into the hands of those forces which want the division of Germany. I say frankly that we also want the unity of the working class because that is the decisive guarantee for a unity of Germany. And therefore the union of the two working-class parties is a question of interest to the entire German people. Everyone who opposes the establishment of the unity of the German working class acts, consciously or not, against the safeguarding of peace and democracy and thus against the unity of Germany.

Question : You think, then, that the establishment of the unity of the working class is the most important task of a national German policy?

Answer : By all means. It is no coincidence that the joint unity committee of the four anti-fascist–democratic parties–the Communist Party, the Social Democratic Party, the Liberal Democratic Party and the Christian Democratic Union–recently expressly declared itself to be for the union of all democratic forces. At the end of this joint declaration which was signed by Wilhelm Pieck, Otto Grotewohl, Wilhelm Külz and Jakob Kaiser it is stated :

"The more strongly this will gains ground within the united working class and among the entire people, the more secure will the foundations which are to bear a new, democratic and peaceful Germany be."

I am deeply convinced that in all parts of Germany the working people yearn for this unity and will therefore welcome the decision of the two working-class parties to unite.

The Policy of the Communist Party of Germany from 1935 to the Unity Congress in 1946

From the report at the
Fifteenth Congress of the Communist Party of Germany
on 19 and 20 April 1946

The political report of the Central Committee of our party covers the period from the 1935 Brussels conference up to the end of 1945. We report on the Communist Party's policy in the period of Germany's greatest disgrace, the period of the most barbarous war policy pursued by the German fascist rulers. The report also includes the second half of 1945, the period following the defeat of Hitler fascism by the allied armies. What has been done in this period to get our country out of the catastrophe and to save Germany?

Our party made the greatest sacrifices in the struggle against fascist German imperialism. It did not give up the struggle against Hitler's war policy for a single hour and it acted during the Hitler period in a way faithful to its historic task. It is fully justified to say today that the history of our party is a history of struggle against the imperialist rulers in Germany, against the domination of the armament plutocrats, the bankers and big landowners. During the First World War Karl Liebknecht demanded "War against the imperialist war! Down with the government!" and from the beginning of the Hitler rule onwards leaflets of the illegal Communist Party organizations said "Hitler is driving Germany into a war! If you are for peace, then struggle for the overthrow of Hitler!"

When Hitler in 1935 set the Reich course for war, enacted the national service act and proclaimed his fight for "more space" it became obvious that a war was imminent.

Our party considered it necessary in this serious situation to re-examine its policy pursued up to then in order to help the party and the working class to draw the lessons from the past and to pursue a correct policy in the struggle against the Hitler system. The party left no doubt in its self-criticism at the Brussels conference that it had not drawn the political conclusions from the changed situation in 1932 early enough. The general change in the situation demanded that all forces be concentrated and united to defend the last remnants of democracy and to destroy all fascist elements. It was also not

133

recognized in time that the situation in the Social Democratic Party had changed. The social democratic representatives had been removed from their posts in the government and administrative services. Thus Social Democracy was placed in a new situation which made it easier to win the social democratic organizations for the creation of a firm united front.

Only on the basis of the Brussels conference decisions was a change in the united front policy made. These decisions stated that the struggle for a democratic republic was the strategic aim of struggle for which all anti-Hitler forces should be united in a broad front. Big sectarian obstacles were present in our party against the implementation of this policy and only by struggling against these sectarian tendencies did the party reach a turning-point in its line and thereby create the prerequisites for a broad front of the anti-fascist–democratic struggle against fascism and reaction. By this turn our party was strengthened politically and morally and more closely united with the broad masses of our people's progressive forces.

Our party declared at the Brussels meeting in October 1935:

"The whole country has been changed into a real war camp by the preparations for a war for the imperialist aims of German monopoly capital. The Nuremberg party congress of the National Socialist German Workers' Party (NSDAP–nazi party) was characterized by a general mobilization for war during its preparation and the course of the congress. The speeches made there aimed at the preparation of war, and a stepped-up chauvinist instigation of the people. The imperialist objective of this war policy was underlined by the threats against Lithuania and the shameless instigation against the Soviet Union. The war, however, will lead Germany into a new defeat and the German people will fall into even greater misery and servitude."

The Communist Party confronted the war policy of the Hitler government with its peace policy as outlined in the Brussels decisions:

"Germany must live in peace and cooperation with other peoples, and above all needs to reach understanding with the Soviet Union. Hitler's policy makes enemies of the German people everywhere. The racism of Rosenberg and Goebbels is understood all over the world as an expression of the hunger for power of German imperialism which wants to dominate the globe."

In the knowledge that the fascist tyranny can only be abolished by the broadest popular action the Communist Party proposed that all opponents of Hitler establish a united front and people's front. In the decisions of the Brussels conference an agreement on a united front is proposed to the Social Democratic Party as an organization and at the same time it is proposed that all anti-fascist and democratic forces unite in a people's front to struggle for peace, freedom and bread, and for the overthrow of fascist rule. When certain opponents of unity maintain today that the communists struggled for the unity of the anti-fascist and democratic forces only after Hitler fascism had collapsed, the actual struggle of the party organization and the decisions of the party prove that our party did everything possible during the Hitler rule to establish a broad anti-fascist–democratic front. The decision of the Brussels conference reads:

"In the conviction that the cause of the proletariat requires the creation of a united political mass party of the German working class the Communist Party is endeavouring to win all class-conscious workers for it. The practical prerequisite for the implementation of this aim consists in the establishment of united action. The bitter experiences of the German working class arising out of its defeat and the coming to power of fascism have called forth its will to reunite in a united mass political party."

We said in our decisions already then that the most urgent need of the hour was to establish united action, but that the historic task requires the reunification of the working class in a united mass political party. This shall be a reminder to all those who have forgotten or want to forget that the Communist Party worked for the reunification of the two working-class parties already during the Hitler period.

The solidarity of the anti-fascist forces developed under the unheard-of difficult conditions of the fascist terror. The unity of action between individual groups of communists and social democrats and of communists and Catholics grew from below. In 1936–37 groups of communists and Catholics struggled against fascist suppression and enlightened the people about Hitler's war policy.

At that time unity of action came about in many German towns. In Württemberg social democratic and communist officials agreed upon mutual aid for the support of the victims of the fascist terror. In Lower Saxony such an agreement was also reached in which former Reichsbanner comrades also participated. In Baden the joint help for imprisoned persons and the joint resistance against wage robbery was agreed upon through the organization of the opposition in the Labour Front. In Berlin deliberations took place between the SPD district executive and the communists. Joint defence measures were agreed upon against the fascist terror, against informers and provocateurs as well as joint support for the victims of the fascist terror without consideration of party membership and world outlook.

In the Zeitz area a united front agreement for joint help for the victims of fascism and for joint struggle against provocateurs was made.

In Dortmund the district executives of the KPD and SPD issued a joint appeal against the intensified exploitation in the enterprises.

On the occasion of the shop stewards' elections in Stuttgart a joint leaflet was distributed in which the workers were asked to strike the entrepreneurs' lackeys and Hitler agents off the lists.

In February 1937 a social democratic delegation from Berlin submitted a program with ten demands of the Berlin social democrats to the foreign office of the SPD. The provincial leadership of the Communist Party in Berlin had approved this program. It was stated at the end of this social democratic platform:

"There exists a deep longing for unity in the proletariat. The best way to give shape to this striving for unity is the Popular Front."

It was further stated in the document that it is necessary to do everything possible to conduct the struggle against the fascist war economy and for the democratic rights of the people. This agreement was reached with Comrade Brass who at that time was still a member of the Social Democratic Party with the approval of the earlier Chairman Künstler of Berlin Social Democracy.

This development of cooperation between individual communist and social democratic groups, the cooperation of groups of young people who were former members of the social democratic or communist youth movements was repeatedly suppressed by the fascist terror. Thousands of our best were thrown into the prisons and concentration camps and perished there.

German fascism attacked the Spanish people. Thousands of non-party people, communist and social democratic workers answered the appeal to join the international brigades in Spain. Communist, social democratic and other anti-fascist working people who had been driven out of Germany went to the front.

But from Germany itself, from the Ruhr and from Central Germany, anti-fascist fighters went to Spain to struggle against the fascist war of intervention there. Honour and glory to the countless anti-fascist fighters who gave their lives in the struggle against German fascism on Spanish soil.

Following the aggression in Spain German imperialism attacked Austria and Czechoslovakia. It became obvious that it was Hitler's military strategy first to conquer a deployment area which gave him a favourable jumping-off place for the implementation of his further war objectives.

At that time officials from the various districts of Germany and comrades who were living abroad met at the Bern party conference of the KPD in January 1939 to deliberate on the imminent danger of war. The decision of the Bern conference stated that developments since the conquest of Austria and the annexation of the Sudeten area justifies the statement that the slogans of the Hitler regime like "Greater Germany" and "right of self-determination of the German people" were only slogans for the carrying out of the plans of conquest against other peoples and for an imperialist "redivision" of the world by fascism. The decision further reads:

"The Hitler regime is creating a situation in the East and West so that the German people can be plunged into the catastrophe of war overnight, a war against the powerful front of all peoples threatened and attacked by Hitler and the war axis."

It was possible to see already in January 1939 that Hitler was completely isolating Germany and was doing everything in his power to drive Germany into the greatest catastrophe of its history.

In this serious situation our party proposed that all social democrats, Catholics, democrats and all other Germans conscious of their responsibility unite to struggle together for the preservation of peace and for the freedom of the German people with the aim of forming a people's government and a new democratic republic. The decisions of that time essentially stated on the spirit of this democratic republic what was developed in the action program of our party of June 1945. This proposal for joint action was welcomed by a part of the social democratic leaders. We agreed with such leaders as Dr. Breitscheid on a joint propaganda against Hitler's war policy.

The German anti-fascist forces, however, were unable to succeed in their struggle against the chauvinist instigation, the temporary foreign policy successes of Hitler and against the fascist terror. Nevertheless the activities of the resistance movement and the joint propaganda of anti-fascists belonging to various parties are of great historical significance.

The sacrifices made in this struggle were not in vain. By the resistance, by the joint propaganda against the fascist war policy part of the workers retained and strengthened their anti-fascist thinking and wherever possible an attempt was made to throw a spanner into the fascist war machinery.

Hitler fascism was unfortunately able to attack Poland without any resistance from the German working class. It was by no means a question of Danzig, but was a question of the deployment against the Soviet Union.

Hitler then marched into France to expand his European war and economic basis and to win Britain for a military alliance against the Soviet Union.

The Communist Party of Germany at that time explained to the German people that Hitler Germany was the imperialist aggressor and that therefore the German people had to do everything possible to prevent any further expansion of the war and to struggle for an immediate end to the war. When the British press attacked our party in connection with our attitude towards the German-Soviet treaty then these attacks are obviously based on a distortion of the facts. Our position was to do everything possible to limit the war, to come to an immediate peace and thus to wage a successful struggle for the overthrow of the Hitler government. The Communist Party declared in an appeal to the German people at that time:

"The Communist Party of Germany warns the German people against any illusions that the Hitler regime will pursue such a policy (i.e., a peace policy–W. U.) which would only be in the interest of the German people... The whole German people must guarantee that the non-aggression pact between the Soviet Union and Germany is observed. Only if the German people take the destiny of the German nation into their hands will peace be ensured."

This means that we warned the German people and the German working class: Only if you yourselves decide on the destiny of the country, only if you successfully struggle against the Hitler rule, only then can peace be safeguarded.

Our statement clearly shows that we struggled for an immediate end to the war. We would have wished that it had been possible to prevent Hitler's aggression against Czechoslovakia right from the beginning by a united front of all anti-fascist and democratic organizations in Germany and the world and by agreements on mutual security between the four big powers, the United States, the Soviet Union, Britain and France. Unfortunately Mr. Runciman had too much influence on policy in Central Europe at that time. Instead of helping to safeguard peace he tried to direct Hitler's aggression into other channels.

When Hitler attacked Norway the communists distributed a leaflet in Berlin which read: "We consider it a great shame that the Norwegian people are now violated, subjugated and starved by the German rulers."

When German imperialism launched its aggressive war against

Yugoslavia and Greece the communists told the German people that the German rulers took this step in contradiction to the national interests of our people and that only the working people themselves in struggle against Hitler's rule can save the country and the people.

Hitler's temporary foreign policy successes made it easier for him to spread the imperialist ideology, the ideology of race hatred and world conquest deep within our people. The consequence was that the anti-fascist propaganda of the active anti-fascist and democratic forces was not very effective in the country itself. In addition, it was only possible in a number of towns to create a united front between small groups of communists, social democrats and other anti-fascists. Fascist German imperialism was able, as a result of this situation in Germany and as a result of the failure of the German working class, to commit its war crime, the war against the Soviet Union. This was the biggest crime against its own nation. The attack on the Soviet Union, Hitler's total war against the country in which no monopolists and bankers, no big landowners and no old tsarist officials ruled the country any longer, the war against the country in which the people made the decisions, was the most reactionary and barbaric war ever to be waged. Hitler believed that he could overwhelm the country of socialism with his concentrated technical war forces in a blitz war. Pillaging, looting and murdering, Hitler's troops pushed into the Ukraine and White Russia until they were crushed by the Red Army and the working people at Leningrad, Moscow and Stalingrad. As was to be foreseen the German army was defeated.

When the German troops had reached the Dnieper German opponents of Hitler declared that it would be possible to induce many German officers and soldiers to separate from Hitler if we first were to confine ourselves to the demand that the German troops should withdraw to the old borders of the Reich. We wanted to do everything in our power to prevent the continuation of the mad bloodshedding and Germany itself from finally becoming the theatre of war. But it became clear that there were not enough men in the German army and in the German officer circles who were able to revolt against Hitler and stop the war. It turned out that many German soldiers and officers drew conclusions only when they had become prisoners of war. We, however, pay great respect to those officers who after having been taken prisoners of war laid down their Hitler decorations and did everything in their power to induce the German troops to cease fighting. They were able to save the lives of hundreds of thousands of soldiers who voluntarily became prisoners of war.

Hitler was able to plunge Germany into the deepest national catastrophe. In sharp self-criticism we must state that German imperialism was able for decades to split the working class and to deepen the division. Thus the resistance of the German people against the imperialist war policy was weakened and paralysed. Those officials of the labour movement who in 1918, 1923, 1932 and 1933 prevented the working class from fulfilling its most fundamental tasks in its struggle because of alleged unnecessary sacrifices, will not be able to deny today that their policy at that time contributed to the most frightful sacrifices of the German working class and the worst sacrifices of blood of the German people. The road on which the German people embarked led to the greatest catastrophe possible.

Germany was ruined by the crimes of Hitler. One year ago the Red Army dealt the last, decisive blow to the Hitler army in Berlin. Hitler's headquarters were destroyed by Soviet troops and Hitler himself perished.

Following the collapse of Hitler a new situation arose which was fundamentally different from that after the First World War. Then Wilhelm II and his military clique were removed from power. But the generals and monopolists remained and Prussian bureaucracy continued as if nothing had happened.

In the Second World War the German imperialist rulers continued the war until the German army was completely wiped out on German soil. This means that the entire state machinery, industry and agriculture had supported Hitler's war policy to the end. The top industrial leaders were fully conscious that the war was lost, but they hoped right up to the last hour that they could provoke differences among the allies in order to save the foundation of German imperialism. They recalled their successes after the First World War when they had been able to maintain the foundations of German imperialism under the slogan of the struggle against the Soviet Union.

It was a matter of course that the German reactionary forces tried to pursue a similar policy after 8 May 1945 and they had obviously not without reason reckoned with the sympathy of such conservatives as Lord Vansittart. At the beginning the war profiteers sabotaged the restarting of the economy, but at the same time they called their old organizations into being again under new names. They were clever enough to mobilize the press under the slogan of struggling against "centralism", meaning the reconstruction of free trade unions, while under the cover of this propaganda they renamed the Metallurgical Federation the Engineering Federation and dozens of other associations which had served the fascist war economy. The second echelon of German imperialists was brought into the leadership. In a number of German regions, above all in the Bavaria "order cells" reaction began its struggle under the slogan of federalism. In the western regions of Germany it is the next tactical aim of the reactionaries to tie the social democrats more firmly to the Christian Democratic Union or the Zentrum Party in order thus to prevent the unity of the working class. Schumacher is obviously following the instructions of western reactionaries in that he has rejected united action with the Communist Party. It is clear that the present line that is taken in some regions of Germany is the same which was taken after 1919 and which allowed German imperialism and militarism to salvage their foundations.

The fundamental question in present-day Germany is the elimination of the material bases of German imperialism and militarism and the struggle against imperialist and militarist ideologies. The reactionary and imperialist forces, the monopolists, bankers and big landowners must not again be allowed to exploit democracy in the struggle against a democratic system and to re-establish their reactionary organizations.

The national misfortune of our people consists precisely in the fact that the reactionary forces got the upper hand over the progressive forces at all decisive turning-points of German history. It is the fundamental national task at present to remove all those from power who pursue this reactionary, predatory policy hostile to the people. They are the rulers of the trusts and banks and other war profiteers, the big landowners and the fascist bureaucracy.

The German people must know that if the reactionary forces continue to influence the state and economy, then this will entail periodical crises and constant conflicts with other peoples. But if peaceful work and the reconstruction of Germany are finally safeguarded then the people must take the destiny of the country in their own hands.

It is our great historic task to help our country to overcome the catastrophe left behind by fascism. Therefore it was the first step of our Central Committee following the defeat of Hitler to propose that all anti-fascist–democratic forces form a united front against fascism and reaction, for the safeguarding of peace, and for the democratic reconstruction of Germany.

The prerequisite for a real preservation of peace is based on the recognition of the causes of war and of the roots of nazi ideology. Some people now make it too easy in that they describe the accused in the Nuremberg trials as those solely responsible. They want to have it forgotten that Hitler would never have been able to continue the war until the end of April if he had not been supported by the German state machinery, by the German army, by the German economic bodies as well as by the fascist system of terror. The program of the Communist Party of 11 June 1945 therefore says that in addition to Hitler, Göring, Keitel and Jodl, the imperialist order-givers of the nazi party, the rulers of the big banks and trusts, the Krupps, Röchlings, Poensgens and Siemens are guilty of and fully responsible for the war. The nazi ideology is also not only the product of Hitler's war mania but a consistent continuation of the ideology of the Prussian Junkers and German monopolists as well as their war and colonial associations.

The old "Führer principle" of the leader of the German Coal Syndicate, Kirdorf, of the Krupps, the Oldenburg-Januschaus, the Donnersmarcks and their ilk was declared by fascism to be the highest principle of state.

The responsibility of the economic and state administrative officials and of the army officers therefore demands that the old Hitler state and economic apparatus be crushed. Therefore it was not a question in the Soviet occupation zone of who was to be dismissed from the apparatus, but an end was put to the past and it was determined who of the former officials could be employed in the new democratic administration. The Soviet Military Administration ordered the closure of banks, finally ending Hitler's financial bankruptcy. Order No. 124 on the confiscation of the enterprises of the war profiteers and active nazis made it possible to confiscate their enterprises and to place them under the management of democratic self-administrative bodies provided they were not to be put under the control of the occupation authorities.

Fundamentally new was the fact that the anti-fascist and democratic forces were given every possibility in the Soviet occupation zone on the basis of the Potsdam decisions of the allies to purge the economy and administrative services. In addition, the reactionary forces were not given any legal right to organize themselves again. After twelve and a half years of fascist subjugation and after the deep depression which gripped many people after May 1945 it was gradually possible to stimulate the initiative of the popular forces. Those men and women who stood the test in restoring traffic, organizing the supply of foodstuffs, organizing repairs of buildings and starting production in factories again especially well were called into leading functions in the bodies of self-administration. If at present one year after the end of the Hitler war transport is to some extent in operation again and the largest part of industry is working again then we have to thank those working men and women, engineers and office employees who set about the job on their own initiative.

Now, one year after the fall of Hitler rule we can report that the democratic agrarian reform has been concluded. It has been carried through by the people themselves in the truest sense of the word.

The agrarian reform is a great historic victory of the democratic forces in Germany, for it helps to safeguard peace, consolidate democracy and improve the nutrition of our people.

In industry developments were slower due to the aftermath of the war. In the Soviet occupation zone the works managements have been cleared of fascists and war profiteers and the trusts and syndicates liquidated through measures of the occupation authorities as well as through the initiative taken by the shop committees and trade union officials.

What is basically new in this? What is new is that the enterprises of the war profiteers have been confiscated, that the enterprises of the war profiteers and nazis which are not claimed by the occupation authorities will be placed in the hands of the organs of democratic self-administration in the near future. If those enterprises had remained in the hands of the former war profiteers, these forces would have another opportunity to continue their old policy of crises and war. Therefore, in the interests of peace and for the proper use of those enterprises for reconstruction, it is necessary for them to be put in the hands of the Länder or provincial administrations, that is, that they become enterprises of a state character. They are to be run by directors to be appointed by the provincial administration. The directors will be assisted by administrative committees.

It would be wrong to speak of state capitalism in this connection as Bavarian social democratic Prime Minister Dr. Hoegner did. It is wrong because there are no representatives of big capital in the Land and provincial administrative bodies. The democratic organs of self-administration are directed by real anti-fascist democratic forces which guarantee that the enterprises which are owned by the provincial administration really work in the interest of the people. It is correct, therefore, to speak of a democratic economic system.

The reactionary forces doing mischief in various parts of Germany represent the main danger to the unity of Germany. It would be much easier to convince the other peoples of the necessity of maintaining German unity if democratic forces had taken over throughout the whole of Germany and if the danger of fascism and reaction

143

had been overcome. Today in the west of Germany the armament profiteers are again proving to be the deadly enemies of the nation. For it is they who support and finance the separatist organizations. We call upon all German people to do everything in their power to fight against those reactionary separatist elements and to make their propaganda activity impossible. This is a vital interest of our people, for Germany cannot live without the Ruhr area and the Rhineland. Nor would France benefit from cutting off the Ruhr because this would merely create a permanent political trouble-spot.

We understand the concern of the French people about the Ruhr again becoming a deployment area of imperialist armed forces. We are of the opinion, however, that the Ruhr can be turned into a base of peace within Germany. Therefore we request the occupation forces to allow the democratic forces of the German people to purge the enterprise managements of fascists and war profiteers, to democratically reorganize the chambers of industry and commerce, and to prohibit employers' organizations, those traditional carriers of Germany's imperialist policy of conquest. The employers have sufficient opportunity to look after their interests in the chambers of industry and commerce. When the former fascist engineering economic group is now organizing over entire occupation zones, that is a strong centralized organization headed by representatives of German imperialism. To tolerate the activities of such organizations will yield no good.

No less is the danger of federalism. The division of Germany into Länder and provinces with independent economies can only serve the purpose of maintaining fascist and reactionary positions in several parts of Germany.

We are struggling against federalism because it also hampers economic reconstruction. One part of Germany is dependent on the other. Even with the formal existence of zonal borders the economic unity of Germany can be implemented in accordance with the Potsdam decisions. We therefore request the Allied Control Council to allow central administrations to be established to make possible normal traffic and economic exchange between the zones.

Most dangerous to our German people is the attempt by certain reactionaries, backed by the social democrat Schumacher, to split Germany into two parts.

Today it is obvious that the fascist and reactionary forces in Germany are the backbone of separatism and the idea of splitting Germany. It is therefore the national task of our people to struggle against reaction. There is only one way to bar the road to reaction once and for all—that is the unity of the anti-fascist and democratic forces, the united front of the anti-fascist–democratic parties!

At today's 15th party congress, one year after the allies smashed Hitler fascism, we can state that a great deal of our program of action proclaimed on 11 June 1945 has already been implemented. There are certain circles which are dissatisfied about the strong influence of the communists, we can proudly say to them today:

Our party has grown because it has worked for the implementation of the present-day demands of the working people, demands which serve the real national interests of our people and the reconstruction of our country.

Our party has grown because we did not confine ourselves to propaganda but actively supported the people and helped them overcome the worst misery by means of popular aid.

Our influence has grown because we fought most decisively, together with the social democratic comrades, for the agrarian reform and thereby for the greatest historical progress and the safeguarding of food for our people.

Our influence has grown because we are working on the reconstruction of Germany on the basis of a democratic program and because we are the most decisive fighters for the unity of Germany.

What we have achieved together with the Social Democratic Party, the Liberal Democratic Party, and the Christian Democratic Union in this one year is but a little step forward. Only the formation of the Socialist Unity Party, the party of millions of working people, gives the anti-fascist, democratic forces an organization which is able to consolidate the unity of the working class and the united front of the anti-fascist–democratic forces and with these tremendous forces implement the great plan of the democratic reconstruction of Germany. Our supreme law remains: Everything by the people! Everything for the people! Everything for our new German fatherland!

The Meaning of the People's Congress

Radio interview on 3 December 1947

Question: Does the convocation of the People's Congress for unity and a just peace mean the beginning of a great popular movement?

Answer: After the Allied Control Council had refused to receive representatives of the German democratic forces and, on the other hand, Germany was divided by the institution of a bizonal administration for the British and American occupation zones it is high time that the will of our people for unity and a just peace is clearly expressed.

A delegation of German democratic representatives is to be elected at the People's Congress to put forward the attitude of the German people at the deliberations on the peace treaty in London.

This the first purpose of the People's Congress.

Question: Who are the representatives of the unity movement?

Answer: The representatives of the unity movement are all peace-loving and democratically-minded women, men and young people in the whole of Germany. The Socialist Unity Party of Germany has taken the initiative because it is the strongest party in Germany, because in it members of all sections of the people are organized and because its organizational network spreads over the whole of Germany through the teamwork of the Socialist Unity Party of Germany (SED) and the Communist Party of Germany (KPD). Declarations of approval from all parts of Germany show that the People's Congress is the affair of all circles of our people, especially the democratic forces which are organized in the democratic parties, trade unions, youth associations, women's and farmers' organizations.

Question: Are other circles also admitted, apart from the former anti-fascists?

Answer: It is left to the democratic right of determination of the enterprise employees and the members of the mass organizations to decide freely at their own discretion whom they will send as delegates. As far as a survey is available, there are also women, men and young people among the delegates who were formerly nominal

146

members of nazi organizations. Such working people, members of the technical intelligentsia, also scientists and artists who in recent years have honestly worked on the reconstruction can of course be delegated, for they are citizens of the state enjoying equal rights.

Question: Is there not a danger of nationalism?

Answer: The struggle for the right of self-determination of the German people, for unity and for a new democratic system does not involve any nationalist danger. The nature of German nationalism consisted in the struggle for the imperialist conquest of other countries, for the enslavement of other peoples and shows itself today in the attitude of certain circles against reparations. The present democratic popular movement for a just peace, however, wants to safeguard the national future of Germany through peaceful work, the creation of a progressive, democratic system in a united Germany and through peaceful relations with other peoples.

Question: What do you think is necessary to bring about the unity of Germany?

Answer: Above all the peace-loving and progressive forces of the German people must unite, contribute to the formation of an all-German government through joint proposals and support the carrying through of a referendum for the unity of Germany with the rights of the all-German government and the provinces fixed in the Weimar Constitution. The People's Congress will be a step forward in the solution of this task.

Thus it is no longer enough today to declare oneself in favour of the unity of Germany. He who is serious about this unity must be against the creation of the bi-zonal council and against the preparation of a West German separatist government as well as against the attempt of American-British imperialism to dominate the Ruhr district and make it its armament basis in Europe.

Why National Front of Democratic Germany?

From the report to the party workers' conference
of the Greater Berlin Socialist Unity Party of Germany
on 17 May 1949

When the representatives of the USA and Britain divided and split Germany after the London Conference the German People's Council declared a national state of emergency and called for national self-help. We can say that the elections in which the questions of peace and the unity of Germany were put to the vote and the Third German People's Congress was elected ended with a victory of the peace-loving forces. The warmongers in the USA and in Britain, the warmongers in Frankfurt-on-Main and in Bonn have suffered a defeat.

When the First German People's Congress met at the time of the London Conference many Germans looked to London fatalistically and maintained that everything depends on the negotiations of the big powers. At that time we declared that the decisive thing is the unfolding of the forces of the German people, that it is necessary to join all forces which favour the unity of Germany and jointly wage the struggle against division and for the unity of Germany. The elections for the Third German People's Congress have shown that the forces wanting peace and the unity of Germany have grown and that they have achieved a tremendous success in secret ballot in the Soviet occupation zone and in Berlin.

The result of the referendum on 15 and 16 May in the Soviet occupation zone and in Berlin is as follows: 13,533,071 were entitled to vote; 12,887,234 voted, that is a poll of 95.2 per cent; 12,024,221 votes were valid, 7,943,949 or 66.1 per cent voted "Yes". The number of "No" votes was 33.9 per cent. Nobody can say that it was not a correct electoral contest with free voting.

The result of the election shows firstly that the People's Congress is indeed the representative of the German people and that the majority of the population stands behind the German People's Council.

The result of the election shows secondly that the majority of our people is against the western occupation statute and against the forty-year occupation period, that it wants a peace treaty and the rapid establishment of the unity of Germany and the withdrawal of the occupation troops.

When a few days ago the western divisionist press was still declaring before the referendum: Why is a referendum not held in the Soviet occupation zone? we now ask: Why is a referendum not held in the western zones? We are for a free referendum; we favour the final holding of a free referendum in the western sectors of Berlin and in West Germany on whether the population wants a peace treaty or a colonial occupation statute.

We want a referendum on whether the German people have the freedom to shape their internal system themselves.

We want a referendum on whether the German people are to have the freedom to determine their future destiny themselves and finally bring about the unity of Germany.

We want a referendum on whether the German people are for the rapid conclusion of a peace treaty and the subsequent withdrawal of the occupation troops or whether, as certain forces in West Germany maintain, the population in West Germany most ardently desires that the American and British colonial troops stay in West Germany as long as possible. We are for the freedom of the referendum on this question.

The result of the election shows thirdly that the elections gave the German People's Congress the legitimate right to demand that representatives of the German people be heard at the Paris Foreign Ministers' Conference.

But the election has shown something else, namely, that the peace-loving forces and the supporters of unity must not indulge in self-satisfaction. After all some 30 per cent of the electors voted "No". Thus the enemy has done an organized systematic work in the democratic sector of Berlin as well as in the Soviet occupation zone. We must in no way underrate the activity of the enemy.

We conclude that we have made a big step forward but that the chief work is still ahead of us.

The danger of the final division of Germany can be averted only if all patriotic forces unite in a great national front. There is undoubtedly a large part among the 30 per cent who voted "No" which can and must be won. There are undoubtedly people among the 30 per cent who are not against the unity of Germany but who allowed themselves to be influenced by certain arguments of hostile propaganda. We must convince these people that our people can only live in peace if the unity of Germany is established and if through a peace treaty and the withdrawal of the occupation troops it is assured that West Germany does not become a military basis for the aggressive forces in the USA and thus a constant threat to peace. We want the unity of Germany to be restored, its independence to be guaranteed and its economy strengthened through a peace treaty.

The objective conditions are given for a broader National Front extending from the working class to the employers in West Germany and also in the Soviet occupation zone. This is no new perception. We already had the beginnings of such a development earlier, also after the First World War. I recall the discussions in connection with the conference of Genoa in 1922 at the conclusion of the Rapallo Treaty. At that time Germany was isolated and not only the progressive parts of the working class but also bourgeois economists were interested in a treaty between Germany and the Soviet Union to develop trade relations with this rich country and thus abolish the dependence on the western allies. At that time, too, it was not only the most progressive representatives of the working class but also representatives of bourgeois parties who demanded the establishment of peaceful and normal economic relations with the Soviet Union. These circles recognized that a deep antagonism existed between the egoistic interests of the rulers in the USA and in Britain and the economic interests of the German people. At that time Germany could have set out on the way of peaceful upward development if the forces of German monopoly capital had not used their power to undermine the treaty of Rapallo and get themselves in the tow of a bloc policy with Britain and France.

After the defeat of Hitler Germany in 1945 certain circles in West Germany already had the illusion that this time it will be different; they believed in the "unselfish help from the USA". In the meantime they have had much experience, have become disillusioned and are beginning to think. This is expressed by the fact that they declare themselves in favour of the restoration of the national independence of Germany on the basis of a peace treaty. The representatives of the Bonn Parliamentary Council and the Frankfurt Economic Council have rejected direct negotiations and deliberations with the People's Council on the establishment of the unity of Germany, it is true, but they could not prevent talks on the joint struggle for the unity of Germany from beginning in fact. Talks are being held between representatives of the People's Council and circles of the West German intelligentsia as well as circles of businessmen in Hamburg and circles of young people in West Germany. It is being shown that the indignation at the occupation policy and the colonial measures taken by the aggressive forces of American imperialism in West Germany is growing and that in West Germany, too, a broader national movement to save Germany is developing.

It would be wrong, therefore, to formulate the question so: Are all these supporters of the unity of Germany convinced democrats and are they people who are unreservedly for an independent Germany? That cannot yet be said today but it is the task of the democratic forces to convince all these peace-loving people.

German Young People
in the Struggle for Peace

*From the speech at the Congress of Young Peace Fighters
in Berlin on 27 May 1950*

Our German fatherland has been in a national emergency since the western occupation powers divided Germany and since they departed from the Potsdam Agreement, What is new in the situation in West Germany today is that the American imperialists are turning this part of our fatherland into a military base, i.e., they intend to expose the whole of Germany to destruction. This would be the worst thing not only for the workers but also for the West German employers, no matter how much they are prejudiced against our democratic system: it would be the greatest evil for all Germans.

Precisely the results of the London Conference have shown that the American imperialists do not intend to give the German people a free hand in their economic activities. They do not even give the German businessmen the possibility of selling their goods on the world market. Whether it is the Marshall Plan, the Atlantic War Pact or a so-called European Union the integration of West Germany into these associations under US command means nothing but the misuse of West Germany for the interests of the rulers of the trusts and banks of the USA.

How is it possible to achieve the unity of a peace-loving and free Germany? Who can doubt that our people deeply long for a lasting peace? Everyone sees the ruins every day; millions are mourning for their relatives who were devoured by the Hitler war. Seventy-eight per cent of the population came out in favour of the preservation of peace in a poll recently organized in West Germany.

But it is not enough to be for the preservation of peace. It is necessary to fight for the maintenance of peace. If the American rulers are promising, just as Hitler did, that a strong Germany would emerge from a war, then this is to be regarded as the most cruel deception. Every German can easily check that a war starting from the West German military base would signify the complete devastation of Germany whereby only the American armaments industrialists would be the laughing third man. That is why the vital interests of every German demand that the American war plans be thwarted by the struggle for peace and for the objectives of the National Front of Democratic Germany. The next step is the unification of all patriotic forces in the National Front of Democratic Germany.

I ask: Is not every German, whether worker or peasant, intellectual or business-man, likewise interested in re-establishing the national sovereignty of Germany on a peaceful basis? The next thing is therefore the cooperation of all patriotic forces in the capital of Germany, in the West and in the East of our German fatherland.

German-Soviet friendship is a vital question for the nation seen from the point of view of the German people's national interests. The catastrophe of Germany and the Versailles dictatorship could have been avoided already at the end of the First World War if the working people had accepted Lenin's peace offer and had made the continuation of the war on two fronts impossible. If the German people had entered into an alliance with Soviet Russia at that time the road would have been free for a peaceful and democratic development and today our young people would be just as happy as young people of the Soviet Union are.

One of the most urgent demands we put forward is the demand that the German people shall finally be given a peace treaty. Instead of granting the German people a peace treaty and thus fulfilling the provisions of the Potsdam Agreement the gentlemen in London and Washington had the idea of proposing voting regulations for Germany.

We are for all-German elections which will serve the unity of Germany and the freedom of the people. The gentlemen in Washington and London seem to have forgotten that they solemnly signed the Potsdam Agreement in which measures for bringing about the unity of Germany are laid down.

They speak of "freedom". But how can one speak of freedom in Germany as long as the American occupation officers put their feet on the table of the German people. It may be an American way of life to put one's feet on the table. This is an internal affair of the people of the United States of America, but in Germany we have other concepts and other habits, and we do not like American tycoons to put their feet on our table. If they write so much about "freedom" in the warmongers' press, we frankly say to the entire people:

The first commandment of freedom is freedom of peace propaganda in the whole of Germany.

The second commandment of freedom is the demand that, if one signs treaties, like the Potsdam Agreement on the demilitarization and democratization of the whole of Germany, i.e., also of West Germany, this democratization must be carried out in West Germany, too.

The third commandment of freedom is that the American, British and French occupation authorities shall give the German people the freedom to decide on their democratic and peaceful order in their own house.

The best the Americans, the British and the French can do in order to allow a peaceful development in Germany is to go back to their own countries, to the USA, Great Britain and France, as soon as possible.

What is important and new in Germany's situation is that we in the German Democratic Republic are demonstrating to the West German people through our living labour how Germany can be reconstructed, more beautiful and magnificent than it has ever been. In the German Democratic Republic the working people are showing how a state can be built up peacefully and properly in the interests of the entire people.

The Peace Treaty with Germany and the National Right of Self-determination of the German People

From the speech to the Scientific Conference
of Professors, Lecturers and Assistants
in the Basic Social Science Course at the Humboldt University
in Berlin on 3 May 1952

The Historic Significance of the Note of the Government of the USSR on the Peace Treaty with Germany

On 10 March 1952 the government of the Union of Soviet Socialist Republics presented to the diplomatic representatives of Great Britain, France and the USA a note on the subject of the preparation of a peace treaty with Germany.

The historic significance of the Soviet government's note is that it points out the way to the peaceful solution of the German question. The Soviet government proposes the preparation in the very near future of a draft peace treaty and its submission for examination to an appropriate international conference attended by all interested states. Such a peace treaty, according to the proposal of the Soviet government, is to be worked out with the direct participation of Germany. To facilitate the preparing of a draft peace treaty the Soviet government has presented to the governments of the USA, Great Britain and France the draft of a peace treaty with Germany. This draft meets the national interests of the German people. The proposals of the Soviet government are in complete accord with the aspirations and demands of the German people and, therefore, were enthusiastically welcomed by all peace-loving people in the German Democratic Republic and in West Germany.

The note of the Soviet government contains the conclusions from the lessons of German history, particularly from the experiences of the Hitler war. German history teaches that an imperialist Germany ruins Germany itself by its agressive policies, by oppressing its own people and by launching aggression against other peoples. Germany can never become strong by conquering foreign territories and enslaving foreign peoples. Such a road has twice led into catastrophe for Germany. Only a Germany governed by the people and not by the egoistic interests of cliques of finance capital, only a democratic Germany capable of establishing friendly relations with its neighbours and, above all, allied in firm friendship with the Soviet Union, will be a member with equal rights in the community of peace-loving nations.

In the Potsdam decisions it is clearly said that the allies are willing to give the German people the opportunity to rebuild their life on a democratic and peaceful foundation. Such a peaceful solution of the German question through a peace treaty with Germany will render possible the final settlement of all problems that have arisen out of the Second World War.

The Right of National Self-determination

The German people fought for centuries to establish a united German state. The German people—as any other people—have a right to self-determination and to existence as an autonomous state.

The vast majority of the people in West Germany resents most profoundly the national suppression of the German people by the western occupation powers. The national suppression becomes manifest in the prolongation of the occupation. Seven years have elapsed since the end of the war and the number of troops stationed in West Germany is steadily increasing. The national suppression is reflected in the outrageous terms of the General Treaty. With this General Treaty the Adenauer government gives its consent to the unlimited occupation of West Germany.

The General Treaty is the most blatant violation of the national interests of the German people, for it is to ensure the continuance of the division of Germany for an unlimited period.

National suppression finds its crassest expression in the creation of a military-strategic deployment zone in West Germany which is to be used, above all, in a fratricidal war of Germans against Germans.

The idea of cosmopolitanism is being propounded to repress the sound patriotic feelings of the German people. The German is to be made to believe that it is no use fighting for the future of Germany, that the national interests, as it is said in *Der Tagesspiegel* of 26 March 1952, "must be sacrificed to boost the chances of success of the western world outlook", that means, of the aims of conquest of the American armament millionaires.

Also in *Der Tagesspiegel*, a paper subservient to the US, Adenauer warns on 6 April 1952 against the "relapse into untimely, unfruitful nationalism". American Governor McCloy said quite bluntly:

"What I demand of the Germans is to abandon national pride and national honour."

By contrast to the policy of the Adenauer government the German people demand the full national right of self-determination. The program of the National Front of Democratic Germany rightly emphasises that the peaceful coexistence of the peoples is only possible on the basis of respect for every people's national right of self-determination. This calls for a resolute struggle for democracy in the different countries.

All peoples which have suffered from Hitler's aggression are interested in the conclusion of a peace treaty with Germany.

Within the framework of imperialist US policy West Germany is also to be the main economic and military position of the US with regard to other capitalist states of Europe. There can be no doubt that the re-establishment of militarism in West Germany constitutes a threat to the French, the Belgian and the Dutch people. The transformation of West Germany into a military base of the US means encouragement to American armament capital to pursue its aggressive aims with increased determination. In this way the British people and the peoples of the Scandinavian countries are also included in the war preparations of the United States of America.

The peoples of the European states therefore have a profound interest in the peaceful solution of the German question and the re-establishment of the unity of Germany.

The Re-establishment of German Militarism and Imperialism— A Serious Threat to the German People

The note of the Soviet government states:

"The necessity of speeding up the conclusion of a peace treaty with Germany is dictated by the fact that the danger of a restoration of German militarism which unleashed two world wars is not abolished and because the corresponding provisions of the Potsdam Conference are still not implemented. A peace treaty with Germany is to guarantee that a revival of German militarism and a German aggression are impossible."

In the decisions of Potsdam it is stipulated that German militarism and nazism be exterminated. This includes the disbandment of all military and para-military organizations, the prohibition of all fascist activity, the political transformation on a democratic basis, the arrest and punishment of the war criminals, the conviction of active fascists and the purging of the education system of all fascist and militarist doctrines. Furthermore, these decisions demand that the industrial tycoons and bankers be deprived of power and the German Junkers—a class which for centuries was the supporter and mainstay of German militarism—be expropriated.

It has been the object of the American, British and French occupation policy to prevent the destruction of German militarism. The American imperialists needed the re-establishment of German militarism to implement their aggressive war plans.

What does the resurgence of German militarism mean? It means:

the formation of a mercenary army which, according to the General Treaty and the supplementary Troops Treaty, is to fight where it is ordered by the rulers of the US, Britain and France, which means, both in Korea and Vietnam or in South America. The command over this mercenary army is to be assumed by the old fascist generals who were pardoned by the American rulers for the purpose;

the resurgence of revanchist policies and the preparation of war to conquer the territories of the People's Republic of Poland and of democratic Czechoslovakia;

an unbridled campaign of instigation against the socialist Soviet Union and against the peoples' democracies for the ideological preparation of a new war;

the re-establishment of the power of the German armament monopolies and banks;

the implementation of the Schuman Plan, the plan of the mining industry to provide the equipment for the army of aggression;

the establishment of military bases in West Germany;

the consolidation of the power and dictatorship of the armament capital in the state and economy of West Germany, and the lowering of the working people's living standards through price increases on consumer goods and higher tax pressure, the preparations for an imperialist war thus being made at the expense of the working people;

the abolition of democratic rights and the suppression of the free expression of the will of the German people;

the formation of German divisions is to help to establish a military dictatorship in West Germany.

Us imperialism pursues the aim of making West German militarism its main pillar in Western Europe and converting West Germany into the chief war base in Europe. This striving reveals itself in the fact that the industrial and financial magnates, Hitler's old war economy leaders, have been reinstated in their old positions of power. The trusts were not broken up, but there was new concentration, particularly of coal and steel companies, and also in the chemical industry.

Under the cover of "decartelization" there was a renewed concentration of the armament trusts. All those people who share responsibility for Germany's great catastrophe, the Krupps, Pferdmenges, Dinkelbachs, Reuchs, Zangens and Abs, are again exerting their ominous influence in West Germany.

Adenauer demands the incorporation of West Germany in the so-called United Europe and the formation of a mercenary army as a prerequisite for the reunification of Germany. *Der Tagesspiegel* of 16 March, the paper subservient to the US, divulges how this is to be done. The reunification of Germany is to be effected as "part of the great problem of freeing the world from Sovietism". It should be mentioned here that in Bonn "an advisory research council on questions of German reunification" has been established which has to prepare everything for "X Day", that is the day when the war and, consequently, fratricidal war is to be provoked according to the plans of the US and German militarists.

The American imperialists and West German militarists have proclaimed their aggressive program so openly that no peace-loving German will be able to say he does not know what the General Treaty and the resurgence of militarism in West Germany mean.

It is up to the German people to decide. The draft peace treaty of the government of the Soviet Union shows that a peaceful solution of the German question is possible. Every German should be aware that the signing of the general war treaty in Bonn will have fateful consequences for the German people. The general war treaty is to prevent the conclusion of a peace treaty with Germany and thus deprive the German people of the prospect of peaceful reunification. Therefore, it is said in the Appeal of the Central Committee of the Socialist Unity Party of Germany to the nation that all Germans face the far-reaching decision:

"Either the conclusion of a peace treaty with Germany by the four great powers—this means peace."

"Or Adenauer's general treaty of war—this means establishing a military dictatorship in West Germany and aggravating the danger of war."

This grave situation necessitates an immediate understanding of all Germans on the holding of free elections in the whole of Germany.

The Present Situation
and the Struggle for the New Germany

From the report to the
Fourth Congress of the Socialist Unity Party of Germany
from 30 March to 6 April 1954 in Berlin

The Fourth Congress of the Socialist Unity Party of Germany (SED) takes place at a time when the peace-loving peoples led by the Soviet Union are making great efforts to bring about a relaxation of international tensions. In Germany the struggle between the peace-loving and militaristic forces is being waged for the alternatives, a peace treaty for the united and democratic Germany linked with an early withdrawal of the occupation troops—or Bonn and Paris war treaties providing for a fifty-year foreign occupation of West Germany. The German people are at the crossroads. Do they want to embark upon the road of peace, the democratic unity of Germany and of peaceful coexistence with the European peoples or upon the road of aggressive German militarism under the leadership of the USA which would result in the continuation of the division of Germany and which would lead to war?

In the period since the Third Congress of the Socialist Unity Party of Germany our party, the government of the German Democratic Republic and the National Front of Democratic Germany have waged a tireless struggle for a united, peace-loving, democratic and independent Germany. The German Democratic Republic, the first peace-loving and democratic state in Germany, has acquired great respect. The German Democratic Republic has shown itself to be a reliable bastion of peace, a source of power for the development of a national people's movement in West Germany for a united, peace-loving and democratic Germany.

The Socialist Unity Party of Germany is being guided in its policy by the great idea of the safeguarding of peace and the peaceful solution of the German question.

We must not allow the German people to be dragged into the Anglo-American military bloc for the preparation of a new war. The plans of this Anglo-American military bloc form the main obstacle to the reunification of Germany on a peaceful and democratic basis.

That is why we are concentrating all forces on developing a people's struggle against the resurgence of German militarism.

The Road to a Peace Treaty for the United, Democratic, Peace-loving and Independent Germany

The main questions of the German people which have not yet been solved nine years after the end of the war are the reunification of Germany on a democratic basis, the conclusion of a peace treaty with Germany and the withdrawal of the occupation troops. After the defeat of Hitler fascism in the Second World War there were favourable conditions prevailing in Germany completely to deprive the old imperialist forces which had led Germany from disaster to disaster of their power. It was a matter of drawing the historical conclusions and of embarking upon a new road, a road of peace and democracy. Immediately after 8 May 1945 the foundations for an anti-fascist– democratic system were created in East Germany with the help of the Soviet occupation authorities, and later, as an answer to the division of Germany by the western powers, the German Democratic Republic, the first peace-loving and democratic state in Germany, was founded.

The western occupation powers prevented those who were mainly to blame for the two world wars from being deprived of their power in the western zones of Germany; they saved the big landlords, bankers and armaments tycoons from the people's wrath and turned West Germany with their help into a satellite state of the USA on which treaties had been imposed providing for a fifty-year foreign occupation and the conversion of West Germany into a military base.

As is well known the western powers already during the war spoke openly of carving up Germany. Thus, the then US President Truman submitted to the Potsdam Conference a proposal in 1945 which read:

"The President believes that the partition of Germany into separate sovereign states will be beneficial to future peace and security."

Mr. Morgenthau, an adviser to American President Roosevelt, declared:

"It will be easier to deal with two Germanys than with one ... for, according to the peculiar international arithmetic, two halves do not make a whole. They amount to considerably less."

This conception failed because of the Soviet Union's resistance which always worked for and continues to work for an indivisible

161

Germany, and it was agreed at the Potsdam Conference to treat Germany as an economic entity.

American and British newspapers report with cynical frankness that a united Germany would be too dangerous a competitor and that they had not waged the war in order to be faced with such a competitor again. That is a typical point of view of imperialists who proceed from the safeguarding of their monopoly profits. But the imperialists' plans are far more fateful both for the German people and for Germany's neighbours because they want to make West Germany the shock troops against the democratic forces of Europe, the gendarme of Europe obeying the orders of the American imperialists.

The great task of the German working class and the peace movement is to save the whole of Germany from the consequences of such a policy. Out of pure class interests the German big bourgeoisie sold the interests of the nation in return for dollars. The striving for monopoly profits, the exploitation and oppression of the workers of one's own people are of greater value to it than the interests of the nation, the independence and the sovereignty of one's own country. The working class, on the other hand, is not linked up with the foreign oppressors. It has the power to shake off the double yoke by organizing the people's struggle. That is also why the German working class holds aloft the banner of national independence around which all patriots are rallying.

The parties of the anti-fascist–democratic bloc and the government of the German Democratic Republic have done everything possible since the Third Congress of the Socialist Unity Party of Germany to bring about the reunification of Germany on a democratic and peaceful basis. In September 1951 the People's Chamber and the government of the German Democratic Republic took the initiative and demanded an all-German discussion between representatives from East and West Germany who should negotiate on the holding of free elections and the conclusion of a peace treaty with Germany. At the United Nations General Assembly held in Paris in December 1951 the government delegation of the German Democratic Republic presented the view that the holding of all-German elections and the peaceful reunification of Germany were the internal and basic affair of the German people themselves. The fact that the representatives of the government of the German Democratic Republic and of the Bonn government appeared before the United Nations was not only a recognition of the existence of the two governments but also expressed the perception that the reunification of Germany is not possible without an understanding between the representatives of the two states. On 13 February 1952 the government of the German Democratic Republic addressed a letter to the four big powers requesting that the conclusion of a peace treaty with Germany be speeded up. Only the Soviet government answered this letter and submitted to public opinion the draft of the "Fundamental Principles for a Peace Treaty with Germany" on 10 March 1952.

The year 1952 brought at the same time a sharpening of the war course pursued by Adenauer in West Germany. On 26 May 1952 Adenauer signed the General War Treaty in Bonn and, one day later, the treaty on the so-called European Army in Paris. This was the occasion for the party and government to intensify the struggle for the reunification of Germany. The result of this struggle was that a delegation elected by the People's Chamber went to Bonn in September 1952 to discuss the possibilities for beginning all-German deliberations. The rulers in Bonn, however, rejected any understanding among the Germans, for, on the basis of the General Treaty they signed, they have turned over to the western powers exclusively the decision on all vital questions of Germany.

The fundamental principles of the continuous policy of our party and government on Germany's reunification have been repeatedly submitted to the German public and again summarized in the significant Government Declaration of 25 November 1953 and in the Memorandum of the Government of the German Democratic Republic of 30 January 1954.

It was pointed out in these documents that the reunification of Germany is possible immediately if the West German parliament renounces the European Defence Community, the revival of German militarism and if the representatives of East and West Germany come to an understanding on the formation of a provisional all-German government the most important task of which is to prepare and hold general, free, secret and democratic elections throughout Germany.

It is obvious that all these proposals are an important contribution to relaxing international tensions.

On the Results of the Berlin Conference of the Four Foreign Ministers

There is no doubt that the Berlin Conference was a success for the peace movement. The Conference showed that fundamental issues can be settled and possibilities for understanding initiated through negotiations. The Soviet government, proceeding from the point of view that at present any issue in international relations can be peacefully solved, submitted to the representatives of the three western powers significant and constructive proposals on the relaxation of international tensions, on the peaceful solution of the German question and on the establishment of peaceful relations between the European states through an all-European agreement on collective security.

The proposals of the Soviet government on the conclusion of a peace treaty with a united, democratic and peace-loving German state, on the withdrawal of the occupation troops from Germany, on measures promoting the economic and cultural relations between the two parts of Germany, on the formation of a provisional all-German government and on the holding of free, democratic elections throughout Germany as well as on the establishment of a system of collective security in Europe are fully in accord with the proposals put forward in the Memorandum of the Government of the German Democratic Republic that had been submitted to the Foreign Ministers' Conference.

The western powers answered the constructive proposals of the Soviet Union with a stubborn "No". In their efforts to prevent the restoration of the unity of Germany, and to turn West Germany into a US protectorate they even went so far as to reject the participation of representatives of the two parts of Germany in the negotiations on the German question.

The Berlin Conference of the four foreign ministers resulted in a clarification of the German question but in no agreement. The representatives of the USA and Great Britain were only concerned about their military pacts; they insisted on the remilitarization of West Germany, on the maintenance of the foreign occupation troops and refused to take a stand on the conclusion of a peace treaty with Germany. It is not difficult to understand that the Soviet Union can, under no circumstances, put up with the resurgence of German militarism. The Soviet foreign minister therefore declared on 5 March:

"The solution of the German question depends upon one main problem: Will German militarism be re-established or not?"

The Bonn Government in a Blind Alley

The West German government parties answered the proposals on a peace treaty and on the withdrawal of the occupation troops put forward by the Soviet government with the demand that the foreign occupation troops be left in Germany and that the EDC be implemented, that military pact of a few West European states under US command. Adenauer even went so far as to propose that the USA rattle the atomic bomb at the Berlin Conference in order to force the Soviet Union to make concessions to the warmongers.

Adenauer's peace assurances collapsed at the Berlin Conference of the Four Foreign Ministers. The leaders of the Bonn government parties had made the West German population believe before the elections that it would be possible through rearmament, the re-establishment of German militarism and through the EDC to enforce "peacefully" the aims of the West German warmongers towards the German Democratic Republic, the Czechoslovak Republic, the People's Republic of Poland and the Soviet Union. The Berlin Foreign Ministers' Conference made clear to the West German population that the policy of West German militarism will result in war if the working class and the peace-loving people do not put an end to the activities of the Bonn militarists in time.

If the Adenauer government now hopes for concessions from the Soviet Union to German imperialism at future international conferences these are empty speculations.

There can only be concessions in the interest of the maintenance of peace, there will never be concessions for the benefit of West German warmongers.

The Adenauer government is confronted with the question of either altering its policy, declaring its readiness to enter into negotiations with the government of the German Democratic Republic or being unmasked as a government that has embarked upon the road of war.

The road to the unity of Germany can easily be found if the goal to be achieved is a peace-loving and democratic Germany. A unity of Germany under American command, under the rule of West German trust lords and militarists, however, is not possible.

What is new is that it has been made clear that the reunification of Germany depends primarily upon the Germans themselves, that reunification will only be possible through an understanding between the representatives of the two parts of Germany, that reunification will be possible only after the EDC Treaty and the Bonn General Treaty have been abolished.

The German Democratic Republic has done everything and is doing everything on its part to pave the way for the reunification of Germany.

On the Sovereignty of the German Democratic Republic

As a result of the negotiations with the government of the German Democratic Republic the Soviet government has given the German Democratic Republic the right, in the interest of safeguarding peace and guaranteeing the national reunification of Germany on a democratic basis, to decide on its internal and external affairs–including the question of relations with West Germany–as it thinks fit. Thereupon, the government of the German Democratic Republic declared that it will observe the obligations arising from the Potsdam Agreement for the German Democratic Republic on the development of Germany as a democratic and peace-loving state as well as the obligations connected with the temporary stay of Soviet troops on the territory of the German Democratic Republic.

The most recent declaration by the Soviet government was possible because the working people in the German Democratic Republic established a democratic state system serving the safeguarding of peace. The Soviet Union and the people's democracies rely on the fact that a firm foundation for a policy of peace and friendship among peoples has been created in the German Democratic Republic.

For a Peace Pact between All European States

The proposal the Soviet government put forward at the Berlin Conference to conclude an all-European treaty on collective security between all thirty-two European states instead of the military pact entered into by six states of Western Europe met with a wide response in all European countries. Instead of a military pact, a peace pact! Instead of setting up fronts right through Germany–peaceful coexistence of the European peoples on the basis of the peoples' right of self-determination! Instead of the armaments race–agreements on the reduction of armament for the benefit of the peoples' prosperity!

The proposal of the Soviet Union on an all-European treaty on collective security between all European states means that all European states may become parties to this treaty irrespective of their social system. The all-European treaty will also be of great benefit to the cause of the reunification of Germany. Germany would be neutralized as a sovereign state having equal rights and thus escape the danger of being dragged into military conflicts.

The government of the German Democratic Republic has declared its readiness to participate in an all-European treaty on collective security up to the reunification of Germany, since such a collective system embracing all European states is appropriate to safeguard peace in Europe and to provide favourable prerequisites for a peaceful solution of the German question. The Soviet proposal means a direct easing of the situation for Germany, for example through the withdrawal of the occupation troops. As long as the unity of Germany has not been restored the two parts of Germany may accede to the treaty. If one of the parties is attacked by armed force the other parties to the treaty are to come to its help with every means at their disposal, including the use of armed forces in order to restore peace. Thus an all-European treaty on collective security will prevent the setting-up of military blocs directed against each other. This great idea of the peaceful coexistence of the European peoples has met the approval of the broadest circles in all countries of Europe. How well could the European peoples live without foreign occupation, without economic interference by the United States, without inroads by some trust lords of the Coal and Steel Community, without military pacts.

If the opponents of peace in Europe maintain that the proposal of the Soviet government means a Sovietization of Europe there is no evidence of that. Mr. Dulles demands the maintenance of American monopoly capitalist rule over Western Europe, the Soviet Union, however, did not demand the introduction of the Soviet system but suggested that every people in Europe, in the spirit of the national right of self-determination, shall decide on its internal system itself. A peace-loving and democratic Germany would occupy a significant position among the European peoples and among the peoples of the world because of the great achievements of its science, its technology and culture. Why shall the peoples of Europe not have the right to protect their peaceful coexistence by such a treaty on all-European security when the American states in America also enter into certain firm agreements? In any case the proposal of the Soviet government holds out a great perspective to the European peoples if they eliminate the American bases in their own country and the economic interference by the USA and if the peace-loving forces take the rudder in their hand.

The question is asked: how can such an all-European peace pact on collective security come into being?

The most important contribution the German Democratic Republic can make for the conclusion of an all-European peace pact is the struggle against the revival of German militarism which is one of the main obstacles on the road to understanding among the European peoples.

The German Democratic Republic will also do everything to develop peaceful relations with the capitalist countries of Western Europe. Through the expansion of economic and cultural relations, through mutual visits of scientists, artists and sportsmen mutual understanding shall be developed and a closer cooperation with the peace-loving forces of other peoples brought about. The most important thing is to strengthen the friendly relations with the Soviet Union and to promote relations with the peace-loving forces in France.

The German Democratic Republic will do everything possible to promote relations between the trade union organizations, cultural organizations and other mass organizations of the European countries.

The German Democratic Republic favours cooperation and the organization of discussions of the peace-loving forces of all European states in the struggle against the resurgence of German militarism, against the imperialist ideology of race hatred, against the propaganda of the "New Order in Europe" taken over from Hitler and against the anti-Soviet instigation.

The German Democratic Republic is convinced that the respect for the national independence of the European states is the basic condition for the conclusion of a treaty serving close peaceful and friendly cooperation.

The Foreign Policy of the German Democratic Republic

The foreign policy of the German state proceeding from the interests of the nation can only be a policy of peace. However, the policy of revenge-seeking and war alliances followed by the German imperialists will result in isolation from the peace-loving peoples and is doomed to failure. It must be opposed in order to save the German people from new disasters. Only the democratic forces of the German people can establish a united German state on a peaceful and democratic road. This Germany will work for good-neighbourly relations with all adjoining states. To achieve this goal, it is necessary:

1. to strengthen the friendship with the Soviet Union, the bulwark of peace, democracy and socialism, continuously and indefatigably; to develop the friendly relations with the great People's Republic of China and the other peoples' democracies;

2. to maintain friendly relations with all other states on the basis of mutual respect for the national interests and equality of rights, and especially to promote trade for mutual benefit;

3. to establish with the peace-loving forces in the neighbouring states of Germany, especially with France, a joint struggle against the common enemy of the European peoples, against the US forces of intervention, against their military bases and against militarism in West Germany;

4. to make every effort to contribute to the preparation of an all-European treaty on collective security in order to replace the dismemberment of Europe by the EDC with the peaceful coexistence of all peoples and states of Europe;

5. to support all peoples who are waging a just national liberation struggle and who have become the victim of an aggression.

The peaceful solution of the German question is a part of the great task of reducing international tensions.

The Warsaw Conference and the New Tasks in Germany

*From the report at the 24th session
of the Central Committee of the Socialist Unity Party of Germany
on 1 and 2 June 1955*

What Are the Results of the Warsaw Conference?

The deliberations and decisions of the Warsaw Conference serve the safeguarding of peace and collective security of the states of Europe. The cooperation and mutual assistance laid down in the Warsaw Treaty serve the strengthening of friendly relations between the member states, their security and economic upsurge. The speeches at the Warsaw Conference were imbued with the great ideas of proletarian internationalism.

At the Warsaw Conference the necessary joint defence measures for safeguarding the peaceful work of our peoples were agreed upon and it was decided to set up a joint military command of the member states. This was necessitated by the coming into force of the Paris war treaties and the incorporation of West Germany into the Atlantic pact constituting an open threat to the peace-loving peoples of Europe. The readiness of the military forces under the joint command is to protect the peoples of the Soviet Union, Poland, Czechoslovakia, the German Democratic Republic, Hungary, Rumania, Bulgaria and Albania from surprise attacks by imperialist adventurers.

The firm will to an easing of tension and understanding between the peoples is expressed by the fact that it is explicitly stated in the agreements of the Warsaw Conference that the reunification of Germany is desirable and that after the conclusion of a treaty on the collective security of all European states the Warsaw treaty will be superfluous and will be invalidated. The states participating in the Warsaw Conference agreed to the proposal by the government of the German Democratic Republic according to which the government of the German Democratic Republic has the right to negotiate independently on the reunification of Germany as a peace-loving and democratic state.

West German politicians now ask what securities a reunified Germany not aligned to any military pact has. If the two parts of Germany had no military links and were members of a treaty of security for all European states, a threat or danger to Germany would be out of the question. The best security is to ensure in an agreement the right of national self-determination and the guarantee of the borders which were laid down in the agreements of Yalta and Potsdam. Such a settlement is possible even now without Germany being reunified. Such a settlement would give a new impetus to reunification and would enable the nationally conscious forces in Germany to clarify with the four powers and the European states the terms of a peace treaty to be concluded on the reunification of Germany which must guarantee the full sovereignty of Germany.

Such a treaty should in its entire contents correspond with the United Nations Charter. Against the argument of certain West German politicians it must be said that such a Germany would not be defenceless, for first it would have its own police forces or a militia and, if it requests it, it would receive the full military support of the signatory states of the treaty on collective European security in the case of a threat.

According to the decisions of the People's Chamber—the highest representative body of the people in the German Democratic Republic—we are ready at any time to take part in negotiations with representatives of West Germany serving a relaxation of tension in Germany and the reunification of Germany. We are also ready to take part in all negotiations with other states.

We expect that, if a conference of the four powers is held, representatives from the two parts of Germany will be given the opportunity to explain their stand on the reunification of Germany and a German contribution to the safeguarding of peace. The Adenauer government has declared that it renounces the opportunity to express its point of view at a four-power conference since it is of the opinion that the representatives of the United States of America and Great Britain would do this. This undignified attitude is an effect of the Paris Treaties and only shows that the Bonn government is the government of a protectorate.

The National Foreign Policy of the Government of the German Democratic Republic

Since West Germany has been turned into a protectorate of the USA it is the national duty of the German Democratic Republic, its People's Chamber and its government to pursue a foreign policy which is always in the interest of the entire nation and which is a model for the foreign policy of a united peace-loving and democratic Germany.

The foreign policy of the German Democratic Republic proceeds from the necessity that the whole of the German people must live in peace and good neighbourly relations with all the peoples of Europe. All its foreign policy steps are aimed at creating a relationship of confidence between the German people and their neighbours. It is a fact that all peace-loving peoples distrust the Bonn state. Even the governments of those countries which are linked to West Germany in a pact system do not conceal their lack of confidence in the Bonn chancellor. This is understandable for the restoration of German militarism is the most unsuitable way conceivable of creating good neighbourly relations. The participation in the Warsaw Conference of a delegation of the German Democratic Republic and its attitude, on the other hand, have shown anew that there is a German state today with which normal and peaceful relations can be maintained.

We were set the task of developing such relations by the Fourth Party Congress. The report of the Central Committee said that it was necessary to maintain friendly relations with all states on the basis of mutual respect for national interests and on an equal footing. It also said that it is particularly necessary to promote trade with mutual benefit. The German Democratic Republic in the Warsaw Treaty has once again bound itself to such a constructive foreign policy directed at the peaceful solution of all questions. The Warsaw Treaty strengthens the German Democratic Republic's influence and reputation in the world and gives us new possibilities to pursue such a policy. We must take advantage of them.

The growth of our friendly relations with Finland, especially in the economic and cultural fields, shows that these serve the interests of our two peoples and help them to greater mutual understanding. But we think that the possibilities for the expansion of the economic and cultural relations are by no means yet fully utilized and that a further normalization of political relations could only have a positive effect for both peoples.

In the recent period we succeeded in solving a few questions of traffic with Sweden and Denmark of interest to our two countries. It will also be possible to settle other important questions of trade, cultural and inter-state relations satisfactorily if the principle of equality of rights is guaranteed and there is no giving in to the pressure of foreign powers.

The relations between the peoples of the Baltic states have old traditions. If all Baltic states reach agreement on joint efforts to make the Baltic a sea of peace and friendly cooperation a great service would be rendered to peace throughout Europe.

The government of the German Democratic Republic is convinced that the normalization of relations between the German Democratic Republic and Austria, too, corresponds not only to the mutual economic and cultural interests of our two peoples but also meets the need of the two peoples for independence, security and peace.

The National Betrayal of the German Big Bourgeoisie and Its Adenauer Government

Because of its class interests, which are associated with the interests of American, British and French big capital, the imperialist West German bourgeoisie is neither willing nor able to safeguard the national interest of the German people. This is borne out among other things by the fact that Adenauer has transferred to the United States of America and Great Britain the right to negotiate questions of reunification. The class combination of the interests of the German big bourgeoisie and the interests of US and British finance capital are a sign of the fear of the growth of the democratic forces in Germany.

Adenauer by his talking about love of peace and the necessity of general disarmament is trying to veil the Paris agreements on the creation of the West German army under the command of fascist officers and the incorporation of West Germany into the Atlantic war pact. However, the stationing of atomic guns in West Germany and the armament, the arming of fascist officers and Adenauer's revanchist propaganda campaign against the Oder-Neisse frontier do not suggest that the Bonn government favours disarmament. The Adenauer government talks of peace because people in West Germany also advocate a relaxation of international tension and understanding between the peoples and governments. Precisely because Adenauer is in the process of restoring fascist military power positions in West Germany he speaks of peace and disarmament. At the same time he announces that the West German army is to be built at a slow rate only. However, the speedy introduction of the first military law on the call-up of volunteers proves the contrary. Adenauer and his Hitler generals are planning to build up the West German army in the shortest possible time. But Adenauer's plans are one thing and the will of West German young people, the working class and the peasants in West Germany is something else again. It will be shown that the resistance of the West German people will continue to seriously upset Adenauer's plans. In connection with the

call-up of volunteers, that is, of officers of the Hitler Wehrmacht Adenauer has given instructions that the will for peace and understanding
of the West German people is to be opposed by kindling chauvinism.

After talks with Mr. Conant, the US representative, Adenauer
called for the revision of the Oder-Neisse frontier at a rally at
Mainz. Every realistically thinking German realizes that the Oder-
Neisse frontier, which has been laid down by agreements of the
powers at Yalta and Potsdam, can never be altered. Those who in
connection with the talks on German reunification call for the revision of the Oder-Neisse frontier are only seeking a pretext for preventing reunification. Other representatives of the West German
CDU in addition have claimed the northern part of Czechoslovakia,
the Sudeten area. Under the slogan of "From the Maas to the
Memel" they try to kindle chauvinism and destroy every possibility
of an understanding on the reunification of Germany. The leadership
of the CDU parliamentary group in Bonn holds the view that a US-
Soviet agreement on the German question must be prevented by all
means. After the conclusion of the Austria treaty State Secretary
Hallstein expressly stated that the Adenauer government could agree
to reunification only on the condition that the reunified Germany
will be given the opportunity to join the western alliance system, i.e.,
the system of alliances between the imperialist forces of the big
bourgeoisie of the USA, Great Britain and West Germany. That is
why Adenauer is opposed to any talks on a peace treaty with Germany. He does not want the German people to see where the path
leads.

The Struggle Against the Revival of Militarism in West Germany

The new situation is presenting the working class, working peasants and all peace forces in West Germany new tasks. Since the
Paris Treaties are now valid the struggle against the Paris Treaties
must be combined with the complete exposure of remilitarization and
other war preparations as they are being carried out in West Germany, and they must be resisted. It is the task of all peace fighters
systematically and patiently to convince people in West Germany
and to explain the peace policy of the Soviet Union and the World
Peace Council as well as the policy of the reunification of Germany
as pursued by the government of the German Democratic Republic
and the National Front of Democratic Germany. A resolute struggle
must be waged against war-mongering. After the imperialist West
German bourgeoisie has embarked on the road of preparing a new

war everything must be done to weaken the power of the capitalist monopolies and militarists in West Germany. Following the ratification of the Paris Treaties certain sections of the public were in a mood of hopelessness and unclarity as to what should happen next. The proposals of the Soviet government on disarmament, the Warsaw Pact and the Austrian Treaty gave new strength to the opponents of the Paris Treaties and remilitarization in West Germany, and gave them a clear perspective.

Following the Moscow discussions on the Austrian Treaty activity against the Bonn policy of remilitarization and of further deepening the division of Germany grew among the working class, especially among the young workers, the working peasants and sections of the petty bourgeoisie. The hope of the Adenauer government that the ratification of the Paris Treaties would impress the majority of the working class and the other working people in such a way that they would relax their struggle against remilitarization has proved wrong. The working people, especially members of the trade unions, quite correctly recognized that the new situation requires grave measures of the working class in the struggle against the brazen activities of the fascist military.

Adenauer's volunteers' law and the meetings of soldiers of various SS divisions strikingly illuminate the new situation. Every peace-loving citizen in West Germany asks himself the question: Who are these 150,000 volunteers? These 150,000 "volunteers" are the newly dressed SS officers, the active nazis who were prepared by Hitler especially in his order castles for entry in the German Wehrmacht and who made quick progress in the officer's career. These "volunteers" are the vanguard of fascist reaction in West Germany. At their head are such Hitler generals as Speidel, Manteuffel, Heusinger, the generals of the SS divisions, Gestapo men such as the commander of the first mountain division, Müller, generals who fought for the Hitler regime up to the last hour like General Wenk and others who are fully responsible for the destruction of our German homeland.

After the Paris Treaties have become valid in Germany there is no doubt that one must create such conditions as make possible an understanding of the four powers on the peaceful solution of the German question. We recall that the prerequisites for an understanding at the Geneva conference on an armistice in Vietnam were created through the strength of democratic forces in Vietnam themselves. The same is true of Austria. There, too, the conditions for an understanding were created after the influence of the bridge-head politicians had been repulsed. In divided Germany it is the most important task to isolate the separatists and divisionist politicians who want to erect a barrier between the two German states. It is thus necessary to bring about a rapprochement between the two parts of Germany, with the influence of the militarists in West Germany being repulsed.

We propose that all peace-loving and democratic forces in the whole of Germany unite and develop a strong people's movement on the following basis:

1. Understanding among the powers on disarmament, the prohibition of atomic bombs and other means of mass extermination.

2. The stopping of all war propaganda and race hatred in the press, literature, radio and in the schools.

3. The normalization of the situation in Berlin by the closing of all sabotage and espionage centres in West Berlin. The banning of the fascist Bärendivision and of activities of soldiers' organizations of the Hitler Wehrmacht in West Berlin.

4. The promotion of the reunification of Germany as a democratic state by demanding the withdrawal of the occupation troops, the removal of all military bases and the preparation of a peace treaty for a non-aligned Germany whose territory is guaranteed by a treaty on collective security.

5. The normalization of economic relations between West Germany and the German Democratic Republic.

6. The removal of all fascist war criminals, especially all SS people, from the state and police apparatus in West Germany.

7. Cooperation and exchange of delegations between factory workers, trade unions, women's and youth organizations of West Germany and the German Democratic Republic.

8. Cooperation of all youth organizations for the step-by-step implementation of the basic rights of the younger generation as adopted by the All-German Youth Congress. The restoration of the right of the Free German Youth to function in West Germany.

9. Cooperation between the sports federations and clubs to promote all-German sports.

10. Cooperation between institutions in the fields of science and culture, between the associations of scientists, artists, and other cultural workers to foster the German humanistic cultural heritage and the development of German culture.

Strengthening of the German Democratic Republic as a Bastion
of Peace and Democracy

The importance of the German Democratic Republic has grown as a result of the development of political events in Germany and of the international situation. After West Germany has become a protectorate of the United States the German Democratic Republic faces still more than before the task of acting as the protector of the national interests of the German people and further developing democracy in internal policy so that the majority of the working class, the working peasants and intellectuals in West Germany endorse this policy. The Fourth Congress of the Socialist Unity Party of Germany proclaimed in its resolution the rebirth of Germany as a peace-loving democratic state so it is now a question of leading to the victory of progressive ideas in all fields, in relations with other states, in the economy, in agriculture and in the development of social life and culture, thereby unfolding that great force which has an influence on West Germany. It is now a question of making the German Democratic Republic a basis for the struggle for a united, democratic and peace-loving Germany by developing German science, German pedogogics, literature and art and by fostering the humanistic traditions of German culture.

The Warsaw treaty has created new favourable conditions for the struggle for the reunification of Germany because by this treaty the German Democratic Republic is strengthened, its defence is guaranteed and the GDR is given a free hand to agree on reunification with West Germany.

Now that the big bourgeoisie in West Germany and its complaisant parliamentary majority have trampled upon the national interests of Germany it is the task of the German Democratic Republic to raise still higher the banner of the national interests of the German people and always to represent all the national interests in the struggle for the reunification with West Germany as well as for bringing about collective security in Europe and the conclusion of a peace treaty with Germany.

Our Policy Embodies the Future of Germany

Speech before the People's Chamber
on the Treaty on the Relations between the GDR and the USSR
on 26 September 1955

The Socialist Unity Party of Germany declares its full approval of the report of Prime Minister Otto Grotewohl on the negotiations between the government delegation of the German Democratic Republic and the government of the USSR. The Moscow negotiations have brought the German Democratic Republic the freedom of decision on all questions of home and foreign policy. The relations between the USSR and the German Democratic Republic are "penetrated by the spirit of mutual confidence and solidarity" as was stated by the chairman of the Council of Ministers of the USSR during the negotiations. The German Democratic Republic has strong and reliable friends.

The conclusion of this treaty of historic significance is the result of the consistent and purposeful policy of the construction of our workers' and peasants' power and the struggle for the safeguarding of peace. The conclusion of the treaty is the expression of the confidence of the peoples of the Soviet Union in the working class and in all patriotic forces in the German Democratic Republic which have taken the cause of peace, democracy and socialism in Germany firmly in their hands. Achieving this success was possible only thanks to the sacrificial work of ordinary people, the workers, farmers, intellectuals and the other working people in the German Democratic Republic who have removed the consequences of the Hitler war with great effort and entered upon the road of progress.

The GDR–the Legitimate German State

West German bourgeois and social democratic newspapers write that the conclusion of the treaty on relations between the German Democratic Republic and the USSR has led to an essential shifting of the relation of forces in favour of the German Democratic Republic. The German Democratic Republic has become a piece on the chess-board of European policy which cannot be taken so easily. They are quite right. The situation in Germany has developed in such a way that the German Democratic Republic is the legitimate German state, the state whose policy embodies the future of Germany. Why is this so?

Firstly, the German Democratic Republic is the only German state which has full sovereignty, which cannot be said of the West German Federal Republic in view of the conclusion of the Paris Treaties.

Secondly, only in the German Democratic Republic was the solid basis for the development of Germany into a peace-loving, democratic state created by depriving fascism and militarism and their chief supports, the monopolists, bankers and big landowners of power. The joint decisions of the allies on the destruction of German militarism, the carrying through of the land reform and the breaking up of the monopolies were realized in the German Democratic Republic.

Thirdly, the German Democratic Republic is the progressive part of Germany in which the working class in alliance with the working farmers, intellectuals and other working sections exercises state power. This fully corresponds to the conditions of social development in Germany.

Fourthly, the German Democratic Republic sets an example for peaceful and friendly relations with other peoples for the whole of Germany. The relations of the German Democratic Republic with the Soviet Union, with the People's Republic of China and with many other states are based on the full equality of rights, mutual respect for sovereignty and non-interference in internal affairs.

When a few American politicians say that the treaty does not contain anything new it is obviously meant to serve the purpose of deceiving the population in West Germany. Who can contest the recognition of the German Democratic Republic as a state by all progressive states in the world? The consistent policy of the struggle against German militarism, for the abolition of the power of the imperialist forces in Germany, of the monopolists, bankers and Junkers who have brought unheard of sufferings to the peoples, has strengthened the international authority of the German Democratic Republic. And it will continue to grow.

Today already the peace-loving peoples see a bulwark of peace in the German Democratic Republic and the peace-loving people in all countries welcome the fact that the German Democratic Republic has barred the way to German militarism. They are convinced that the working people of the German Democratic Republic will never allow NATO's military deployment area to be extended up to the Oder.

The Moscow negotiations again expressed very clearly the fact that the unity of Germany is possible only when understanding is reached on the annulment of the Paris Treaties and the disbandment of the military groupings in Europe.

This means that the power of militarism must be broken in West Germany. The consolidation of the workers' and peasants' power of the German Democratic Republic and the consistent continuation of its policy is therefore of the greatest national significance precisely because the reunification of Germany is possible only on a peaceful and democratic basis and can be reached only through negotiations.

A few West German newspapers write that "the German Democratic Republic approaches West Germany". This is undoubtedly correct. In these words it is expressed that also in West Germany ever broader circles are coming to see that a reunification of Germany is only possible through the establisment of normal relations between the West German federal government and the government of the German Democratic Republic.

Up to now there were many people who doubted that the peace-loving and progressive forces will be in a position to shape the new, united Germany. The "propaganda of strength" had influenced them as well as some citizens of the GDR. The Geneva Conference of the four heads of government already made the bankruptcy of the "policy of strength" obvious. Meanwhile Herr Adenauer has gone to Moscow with the Paris Treaties in his briefcase to have it certified again with special emphasis that the "policy of strength" is bankrupt.

Two German government delegations have been in Moscow within ten days. One government delegation came as a friend to friends. This government delegation included all parties belonging to the National Front of Democratic Germany. It included representatives of the working class, the working farmers, intellectuals and the middle classes, that means it was a delegation which really spoke in the name of the People's Chamber of the German Democratic Republic, in the name of the population of the GDR.

The government delegation of the West German Federal Republic consisted of Herr Adenauer, his foreign minister and a few officials of his ministry. This West German government delegation represented the interests of the big capitalist forces of West Germany and the North Atlantic pact.

May the entire German population itself make its comparisons with what different basic declarations the two German government delegations appeared in Moscow. The social democrats reproach Herr Adenauer with having gone to Moscow without a conception on the reunification of Germany. But where is Herr Adenauer to get such a conception when he already had the Paris Treaties in his luggage and demanded that the whole of Germany become a member of the North Atlantic Treaty Organization which would mean shifting the military basis of the imperialist powers to the Oder. This is also recognized by West German newspapers. The *Rheinisch-Westfälische Zeitung,* for example, expresses the fear that the Bonn government's policy is oriented on a perpetuation of the division of Germany and writes:

"This becomes the more probable since in the Federal Republic powerful circles close to the federal chancellor prefer a 'New Occident' with its frontier on the Elbe in which they believe they will be able to realize their reactionary, feudalist, monarchic and Catholic-authoritative dreams to a reunification with the Protestant part of the German people of the Soviet Zone which have a strong socialist, even if not Bolshevist attitude—people who were not able to realize their natural longing for an authoritarian regime and an 'imperial doctrine'—even though no longer German—in the 'Third Reich' and now hope to make up for what they missed in their own way." I think that the West German newspaper of the heavy industry must know about these things.

When West German politicians called it the task of the Bonn government delegation in Moscow to induce the Soviet government to speak its mind openly it can be stated that the Soviet government fully complied with this request. It was clearly declared to Herr Adenauer that the Paris Treaties are incompatible with the reunification of Germany and that the Bonn government cannot expect the Soviet Union to support NATO plans which are obviously directed against the Soviet Union.

A Treaty of Historic Significance

The government delegation of the German Democratic Republic went to Moscow as a friend to friends. It set forth there the all-German interests in the truest sense of the word. Accordingly, the concluded treaty states:

"Convinced that the joining of the efforts of the German Democratic Republic and the Soviet Union for cooperation in the maintenance and consolidation of peace and security in Europe and the reunification of Germany as a peace-loving and democratic state and the conclusion of a peace treaty with Germany corresponds to the interests of the German people and the Soviet people as well as with the interests of the other peoples of Europe . . ."

Everyone can see for himself that the government delegation of the German Democratic Republic went to Moscow with constructive proposals which were in full accord with the interests of the peoples of the Soviet Union and the conception of the government of the USSR. Article 2 of the treaty states expressly that the two governments will consult on all important international questions

"which concern the interests of the two states and take all measures within their power with the aim of not permitting a violation of peace."

And Article 5 speaks of the joint efforts for the conclusion of a peace treaty and the restoration of the unity of Germany on a peaceful and democratic basis.

The Soviet government has told the entire German people that above all the Germans themselves must settle the German question. It is true that at international conferences favourable conditions can be created for the peaceful settlement of the German question through the conclusion of a treaty on the collective security of all European states, but the two German states must first of all take part in them, too, until reunification. It is necessary, therefore, for them to come closer to one another and for their governments to carry through joint consultations.

The negotiations between the government delegations of the GDR and the USSR were the expression of the firm friendship which has developed between our two states. This friendship corresponds with the national vital interests of the entire German people. It serves the happiness of the German people when they are connected in firm friendship with the USSR which is the biggest and at the same time most progressive European state. The fact that the representatives of such states as the People's Republic of China, the European people's democracies, India, Burma, Egypt, Yugoslavia, Finland, Sweden, Iran and others took part in the receptions in Moscow which took place on the occasion of the presence of the government delegation of the GDR shows that the German Democratic Republic enjoys especially great esteem in those states which have liberated themselves from imperialist oppression or which are on the way to achieving their national independence.

The National Policy of the GDR and the Role of the Working Class

Thus what is new in the situation is the existence of two German states. The German Democratic Republic is that state which has full sovereignty whereas West Germany is bound by the Germany Treaty and the Paris Treaties. The restoration of the unity of a peace-loving, democraticGermany is obviously only possible through the overcoming of the Paris Treaties by the conclusion of a treaty of all European states on collective security and through a rapprochement of the two German states and the cooperation of the two governments.

The treaty which legally confirms the freedom of the German Democratic Republic to decide on its internal and external affairs bears witness to the entire German people that the workers' and peasants' government of the GDR firmly bears the banner of peace, democracy and national reunification in its hands. The Moscow Treaty is the expression of a truly national policy of the government of the German Democratic Republic. The treaty expressly states that the bringing about of a "peaceful settlement for the whole of Germany" is the main goal of the parties to the treaty.

The new situation in Germany and the stubborn clinging of the Bonn government to the Paris Treaties show that in the present period of history the representation of the national interests and the struggle for the reunification of a peace-loving, democratic Germany necessitate the joining of all democratic forces in the National Front of Democratic Germany. The National Front embraces workers and farmers, intellectuals, craftsmen and tradesmen, people with different world outlooks and different pasts. The National Front whose main force is the working class must now be developed into a still stronger force. The German working class bears an especially great responsibility. It suffers most under the dictatorship of the militarist trust rulers, bankers and big landowners in West Germany and is the most consistent force in the struggle for the safeguarding of peace and for depriving the militarists of power. Therefore, the creation of the union of action of the working class in the whole of Germany, the cooperation of the working-class parties, the trade unions and mass organizations are of the greatest significance. The working class is not only the most consistent force in the struggle for the safeguarding of peace, it is also the strongest force because it bears the banner of progress, because it has set up the workers' and peasants' power in the German Democratic Republic and is linked in firm friendship with the working class of the states of the new world of socialism.

Change of Bonn's Government Policy – Prerequisite for Reunification

Since the Bonn Bundestag ratified the Paris war treaties, the Bonn government parties have been speaking a great deal about the reunification of Germany. They do not mean reunification but the integration of the territory of the German Democratic Republic as far as the Oder in the North Atlantic Treaty Organization. Thus they conceal their policy of the remilitarization of the whole of Germany and the exploitation and the subjection of the entire German people by West German finance capital behind the words "unity of Germany". It is high time to unmask the Bonn government politicians who speak on the unity of Germany in a deceptive manner. The time has come to recall that the ruling class of Germany has twice driven the united Germany into the catastrophe of war. When the militarist forces now raise the demand for the reunification of Germany to advance their military basis to the east the peace-loving population may answer them unmistakably that there must not and will not be such a "unity" of Germany. A "reunification" under the command of German militarism would lead to war and the ruin of Germany.

All that is said by western politicians on the reunification of Germany is empty talk as long as the western powers and with them Adenauer cling to the policy of NATO and the restoration of German militarism. The reunification of Germany is only possible through the creation of a democratic, peace-loving state. This requires the overcoming of the North Atlantic military grouping which is hostile to peace and directed against the interests of the German people through the establishment of a comprehensive system of collective security including all European states.

This is confirmed by the *Rheinisch-Westfälische Zeitung* which writes under the title "Fiasco after the Germany Song":

West Germany will "remain occupied if a change of opinion does not take place here, we shall pay and pay, we shall pine away as a satellite and set a young generation on the false powder barrel which tomorrow already can tear the entire European body into pieces if Dr. Adenauer sticks to his conviction that this part of Germany with the western bloc could face and defy the eastern bloc".

And it is further stated that "anyone who has taken the oath on the western International is no longer able to make a contribution to the bringing about of an independent Reich unity".

We see that there are forces in West Germany which assess things realistically. The time has come for the population of West Germany to throw its own vote and its force into the political scene and see that the Bonn government abandons its NATO policy and declares its readiness to cooperate with the government of the German Democratic Republic in the interest of the establishment of collective security in Europe and the reunification of Germany.

Herr Adenauer has declared in Bonn that the Bonn government is the spokesman for the whole of Germany. This allegation stands in contrast to the real facts. The Bonn government has forfeited any right to speak for the whole of Germany through its policy of division which began with the formation of the bi-zone and found its high point in the ratification of the Paris Treaties. It represents only the interests of the West German big capitalist circles. If it intended to speak for Germany the Bonn government would not have expressly put the right of negotiations on all-German questions into the hands of the western powers in the Paris Treaties. If the Bonn government wanted to speak for Germany it would not have bound itself one-sidedly to the imperialist western powers through the Paris Treaties since it knew very well that a peaceful settlement of the German question is only possible through the understanding of all four big powers and the German people themselves.

Herr Adenauer was so friendly as to threaten other states, saying that the taking up of diplomatic relations with the GDR must be considered as an unfriendly act in Bonn. The normalization of relations between other states and the GDR does not at all depend on Herr Adenauer. The taking up of diplomatic relations corresponds with the interests of these countries as well as with those of the GDR. The arrogant appearance of western representatives was already replied to by the press chief of the government of the Yugoslav Federative People's Republic at the press conference of the Yugoslav Foreign Ministry when he said that the Yugoslav government will not allow itself to be advised by anybody but will make its own decision.

It appears ridiculous that Adenauer utters threats in the style of the German imperialist foreign policy whereas the world's largest states such as the Soviet Union and the People's Republic of China have long since maintained normal friendly relations with the German Democratic Republic.

This stubborn policy as it is expressed in Adenauer's speech may show the West German population how necessary it is for the working class and the working people to make their peaceful and democratic views respected.

May the taking up of diplomatic, economic and cultural relations between the West German Federal Republic and the Soviet Union not remain a governmental act only but lead to firm friendship between the West German population and the peoples of the Soviet Union through the active participation of the people. This will also be an important contribution to the relaxation of the situation in Europe.

The Prerequisites for the Peaceful
Reunification of Germany

*Answer to a question put in the 15th session
of the People's Chamber of the German Democratic Republic
on 29 and 30 August 1956*

Question of People's Chamber member Heinrich Homan: I should like to ask Herr Walter Ulbricht, first deputy chairman of the Council of Ministers, the following question: How does the government of the German Democratic Republic assess the question of reunification after the Adenauer government has demonstrated by integrating West Germany into NATO, by introducing conscription, banning the Communist Party of Germany and taking other anti-democratic measures that it is opposed to the peaceful reunification of Germany?

Answer: Along with all peace-loving people we regret that the present Bonn government constantly places new obstacles in the way of German reunification. The rejection of the proposals of the German Democratic Republic to renounce conscription in the whole of Germany, not to allow the stationing of atomic weapons in Germany and to reduce foreign troops shows that the Bonn government is not only against a policy of relaxation but also against the peaceful re-unification of Germany. The prohibition of the Communist Party of Germany is specifically directed against the reunification of Germany, for with this ban the Bonn government shows that it is against a democratic Germany and is striving to suppress the progressive, democratic forces in the whole of Germany.

The statement of Herr Adenauer and Hitler General Heusinger on the preparation of a war have already been dealt with in the government declaration delivered by Foreign Minister Dr. Bolz. These aggressive goals of the ruling circles in West Germany show why the Adenauer government rejects negotiations with the German Democratic Republic.

West Germany is now advertising some kind of memorandum on the reunification of Germany directed to the four powers. To camouflage their militarist and anti-democratic policy, the leading Bonn government circles resort to cheap tricks. We recall that the Adenauer government declared when joining the North Atlantic pact that this step served reunification. The contrary has proved to be true.

The Adenauer government should not indulge in illusory hopes. This time it will not be able to mislead the people.

It is necessary to tell the people the whole truth. The truth is that according to the plans of the ruling West German monopolists, bankers and big landowners the Bonn government has erected not only a barrier through the middle of Germany, but this barrier is made higher by such fascist measures as the prohibition of the Communist Party of Germany. The whole truth is that one can bring about reunification only if the barrier built by the West German militarists is removed. This can only be done with the forces of the united working class and all friends of peace. Since the majority of the German people are of the opinion that Germany should become a peaceful, democratic, and progressive country the key to reunification is in the hands of the workers, peasants, intellectuals, the middle classes, the progressive bourgeoisie and above all German young people. Only they can create the internal prerequisites for peaceful reunification in the struggle against German militarism. This great national task can be solved if the workers' organizations in West Germany and in the German Democratic Republic cooperate fraternally and if all peace-loving forces in West Germany together with the German Democratic Republic defend and promote the cause of peace and democracy. It would be absurd to speak about all-German elections at all as long as the West German armament millionaires, the Hitler generals, and other warmongering forces have the opportunity to use their economic and state power to influence the elections. He who wants a peace-loving and democratic Germany should help to create conditions in West Germany which make possible the peaceful reunification of Germany.

The national interests of our people and fatherland, the cause of peace and reunification demand:

1. The limitation of armed forces in the two parts of Germany. It should be agreed that the replenishment of the armed forces should be made only on the basis of volunteers. When reunited, Germany should belong to a zone of limited armament. A German army, let us say, could number some 200,000 men.

2. Removal of all Hitler generals and other revanchists from the state machinery and the army. The armament monopolies, whose owners are the main supporters of the policy of revenge and fascism, should be nationalized.

3. The step-by-step withdrawal of foreign troops from Germany.

4. The lifting of the ban on the Communist Party of Germany. A ban on all militarist organizations and associations.

5. Cooperation between the government of the German Democratic Republic and the government of the German Federal Republic in the interest of the rapprochement of the two German states. Negotiations between representatives of the People's Chamber of the GDR and the Bonn Bundestag and between representatives of the two governments on questions of the reunification of Germany.

Since the Adenauer government, as a result of its dependence on the armament monopolies and militarist forces, is not prepared and not able to embark on the peaceful road towards reunification which corresponds to the national and social interests of the German people, real conditions for reunification will probably exist only when the West German people draw the conclusions from the bankruptcy of the policy pursued by the West German government party, the CDU, force the Adenauer government to resign and form a government which is prepared to solve the national tasks in a peaceful way together with the People's Chamber and the government of the German Democratic Republic.

As a result of the bankruptcy of the political line of the Bonn government a certain part of the West German press is trying to make Adenauer alone responsible for the disastrous policy of the Bonn government. We consider it our duty to tell the German people that the real rulers of the Federal Republic, i. e., the armament monopolies, the Adenauer party, the CDU, and other forces which have set themselves the aim of re-establishing German militarism and fascism are responsible for the political course directed against the national interests of Germany pursued by the West German government led by Adenauer. May the West German people themselves draw the necessary conclusions from this.

We will make every effort to see that the great ideas of peace, freedom, democracy and socialism spread from the German Democratic Republic to West Germany. The government of the German Democratic Republic welcomes the decision of the National Front of Democratic Germany on the development of socialist democracy in the GDR.

We will do everything possible to demonstrate in the German Democratic Republic the superiority of the progressive democratic order and of socialist construction. The strengthening of the GDR and its friendly ties with the Soviet Union, the states of the socialist camp and with all peace-loving countries will encourage the West German people in their struggle to safeguard peace and for the victory of the forces of progress. This road will lead to the reunification of Germany into a peace-loving democratic state.

of the Policy of the Socialist Unity Party of Germany

*From the report to the 30th session of the
Central Committee of the Socialist Unity Party of Germany
from 30 January to 1 February 1957*

*On German Imperialism and the Responsibility of the German
Working Class for the Destiny of Germany*

To develop a realistic policy one must start from an evaluation
of the class forces. Both parts of Germany are highly industrialized
states. The numerically largest class, upon whose attitude the entire
development depends, is the working class. At present the struggle
in Germany is being waged between two main political forces and
two social systems. In the German Democratic Republic the working
class led by the SED has the political power and exercises it in
alliance with the working farmers and other strata of the working
population. The German Democratic Republic is based on the bloc
parties and mass organizations united in the National Front of Democratic Germany. The workers' and peasants' rule in the German
Democratic Republic is also the basis for the struggle of the working
class and all peace-loving forces in West Germany. Every economic
or cultural success in the GDR means support for the struggle of the
working class and the working people in West Germany. Through
the establishment of a people's democratic power in the German
Democratic Republic the prerequisites were created for the fraternal
alliance with the Soviet Union, the People's Republic of China and
other states of the socialist camp, as well as for cooperation with
peace forces throughout the world.

The construction of socialism in the German Democratic Republic
and the strengthening of the workers' and peasants' state is a necessary prerequisite for the struggle for the reunification of Germany on
a peaceful and democratic basis.

The construction of socialism in the German Democratic Republic
is being carried out under the complicated conditions of an open
border with West Germany. But this is not simply an open border
between the two German states. It is at the same time an open
border between the two social systems. The German Democratic
Republic and West Germany are engaged in an open economic com-

petition. West Germany has an advantage in this competition in its industrial development, because Germany's most important traditional industrial areas are located in the West of our country. Reactionary West German circles use this fact for their propaganda and subversive activities against socialist construction in the German Democratic Republic. Thus they want to discredit the idea of socialism among the German population. That is why we must face the task of strengthening the German Democratic Republic in every way, increasing political vigilance and conducting the struggle against the rule of German imperialism.

But the very fact of successful socialist construction in the German Democratic Republic means that a decisive blow has been dealt to German imperialism. The foundations of German imperialism have been uprooted in the German Democratic Republic for ever. Our struggle for the construction of socialism in the German Democratic Republic is shaking the keystone of West German monopoly capital and dealing blow upon blow to it. The existence of the German Democratic Republic of course must make its mark on developments in West Germany. There is no reason to doubt that in time the German working class and all progressive forces of the nation will understand the advantages of the socialist system and irrevocably side with the German Democratic Republic against West German imperialism. The struggle for the construction of socialism in the German Democratic Republic is therefore the basis and main prerequisite for the struggle for the reunification of Germany on a peaceful and democratic basis. The attitude towards the German Democratic Republic is the test of every honest socialist, of every real German patriot and of every supporter of the reunification of Germany.

In West Germany political and economic power is in the hands of monopoly capital. Some 300 bankers and monopolists in West Germany exercise the dictatorship of finance capital. What is new in West Germany is the active appearance of German imperialism.

In his work *Imperialism: the Highest Stage of Capitalism* Lenin showed that imperialism is to be assessed as a further development and direct continuation of the basic properties of capitalism. Lenin scientifically proved the five characteristics of imperialism.

The monopolist development of capitalism has been strengthened in West Germany since the introduction of the West German currency. At present, West German heavy industry is controlled by six trusts. The chemical industry is controlled by the successors of the IG-Farben trust. The electrical engineering industry is controlled by the Siemens and AEG trusts. West Germany's large banks–the Deutsche Bank, Dresdner Bank and Commerzbank–have again become a decisive power of finance capital. German imperialism of today is characterized by its attempts to bring the highly developed industrial countries of Western Europe under its dictatorship and its efforts to make capital investments and win influence in those countries where, in the process of the liberation from colonialism, British and French imperialism have more or less lost influence.

A characteristic of German imperialism of today is its dependence on American finance capital. After the defeat of Germany in the Second World War the American and British occupation authorities helped German monopoly capital to restore its former positions of power under the condition that West Germany be prepared to support the plans of US imperialism and take part in aggressive military blocs.

What is new is that a part of the plans of US finance capital for economic expansion in Europe, the Middle East and Asia are carried out by German finance capital. Cooperation between American and West German trusts is developing in the form of the participation of West German big enterprises in projects in Asia, the Near East, South America, Africa and other countries.

Trusts of the two states exchange technical information whereby the American trusts place special value on utilizing the basic research in West Germany. It is characteristic that branch offices of American trusts have been shifted to Düsseldorf from other capitalist states of Western Europe. On the other hand, West German trusts have established business bases in the USA.

Under the leadership of the United States the German imperialists are eager to bring a part of the heritage of the British and French colonial rulers in the Near and Middle East and in Africa under their influence. We recall in this connection that during the aggression against Egypt committed by the two NATO states Britain and France together with Israel, West Germany sided with the imperialist aggressors. West Germany supports the policy of the American semi-colony Israel against the Arab states. Lately, the Bonn government has not only supported the Eisenhower-Dulles doctrine directed against Egypt and other Arab states, but also rejected a request by Yemen for economic assistance, stating that its relations with the NATO states do not permit such assistance.

German imperialism is fighting for its leading role in Western Europe, taking advantage of its superior industrial power. Through West Germany's affiliation to the North Atlantic pact and the creation of a West German NATO army to be equipped with atomic arms with US assistance, the political weight of German imperialism has grown in the past year. The activities of German finance capital aimed at establishing a Common Market of Western European capitalist nations show the methods with which the German monopolies are leading the struggle for supremacy over the capitalist countries of Western Europe. In this way German imperialism is aiming at rapidly strengthening its own positions and ruthlessly pressing its own interests.

It is aided in this by the policy of the French government with the socialist Mollet at the head. The Western European Union which was created to hamper the independent initiative of German imperialism now stands under the leadership of German imperialism. Thus a new situation has come into existence for France, Belgium, Holland and Denmark. The national interest of these states and their populations demands rapprochement with and cooperation on certain questions with the peoples' democracies in Europe, especially with the German Democratic Republic.

West Germany as NATO's main base in Europe has become a dangerous hotbed of war. The activity of German imperialism is finding its military expression in winning leading positions in NATO with the approval of the Defence Department and the general staff of the United States.

It is only in a limited sense that one can speak of West German sovereignty, for the policy of the representatives of monopoly capital in West Germany is conducted within the framework of US policy. The aim of West German ruling circles is the dictatorship of West German finance capital over the whole of Germany and supremacy in Europe. This aggressive imperialist policy is the deeper reason for the rejection of all realistic attempts for a rapprochement of the two German states and for bringing about the reunification of Germany as a peace-loving democratic state.

It is a lesson of history that the external activities of imperialism are closely connected with an extension of the internal positions of power of monopoly capital, as well as with the increased exploitation of the workers and the restriction of democratic rights.

Remilitarization is at the same time a weapon of the West German monopolies against the working class, the working farmers and other strata of the working population. It serves as a means of still more heavily burdening the masses of the people and restricting the democratic rights of workers in enterprises and of the working population. The banning of the Communist Party of Germany, the banning of the communist press and the suppression of numerous mass organizations of the working people are designed to break the resistance of the working people to remilitarization.

In view of the strengthening of the workers' and peasants' power in the German Democratic Republic on the one hand, and in view of the existence of German imperialism in the Federal Republic on the other hand, the destiny of Germany is dependent on the activity or passivity of the German working class and on the influence of the National Front of Democratic Germany. Under the leadership of the monopolists and bankers West Germany has embarked upon a road leading to the deepening of the division of Germany and to West Germany's isolation from the peoples of Europe.

Only with united forces can the working class curb its powerful enemy, West German monopoly capital and its state power.

For the SED, unity of action of the German working class is not a tactical question which—today in the foreground—may be set aside again tomorrow. It is the general line of the party, on the realization of which depends the solution of national and class demands of the German working people as well as the future of the German nation in general. Joint action of the German working class is the only real force which can offer resistance to militarism and the reactionary policy of German finance capital.

Problems of German Reunification

The national desire of our people for reunification is barred by the NATO policy and by the rule of capitalist monopolies in West Germany. Reunification shall lead to happiness for our people and to a peaceful and democratic Germany. Reunification is, however, not realistic if it means an extension of the power of West German monopoly capital and militarism over the whole of Germany.

A decisive particularity of the division of Germany consists in the fact that it is closely connected with the class struggle between the working class and the imperialist bourgeoisie. Whereas in the past, let us say in the period of feudalism or the early stage of capitalism, a divided Germany had remained within the framework of a single social system, the division has now taken place under the conditions of the struggle between two antagonistic social systems.

The smashing of the state and military machine of German imperialism in the Second World War deprived it of its main instrument of class rule. The consistent implementation of the Potsdam principles on the democratization of Germany would have led inevi-

193

tably to the development of revolutionary activities of the working masses, primarily, of course, of the German working class, as well as to a transformation of the country's social and political system on a new, democratic basis. Proof of this is the development in the eastern part of Germany where, as a result of the Potsdam decisions, the first democratic state of workers and peasants in German history was created, a state in which socialism is now being constructed. German monopoly capital, which no longer had the forces and resources to maintain its position in Eastern Germany, established itself with the support of American imperialism in the western part of the country, pursuing a policy of splitting Germany with the intention of prolonging its existence.

The ruling circles in Bonn fear a democratic way of German reunification in the interests of peace and of the German working people, because that would mean the end of German imperialism. That is why militarism is being re-established in West Germany as a force with the help of which the West German rulers want to solve the problems of reunification. Their idea of reunification is the swallowing up of the German Democratic Republic by West Germany. The consequence of this would be the elimination of all achievements which the working class and the working people of the German Democratic Republic have attained.

These plans, however, are inevitably doomed to failure because the workers and farmers of the German Democratic Republic, once liberated from the slavery of the monopolies and landlords, will not allow themselves to be enslaved again. The German Democratic Republic is being backed on the one hand by the united force of the socialist camp, on the other hand by the solidarity of the workers and the exploited in the capitalist countries, as well as by the sympathies of all progressive people and friends of peace the world over.

Under present conditions, reunification can be achieved only through the successful struggle of peace-loving democratic forces against the reactionary militarist forces and against German monopoly capital. The defeat of the Adenauer party in the Bundestag elections can lead to a step forward. It is necessary to repeat that reunification cannot be brought about through negotiations between the four powers, but that it is an affair of the German people. Only through the struggle of the working class and all peace-loving forces in Germany against militarism and the power of the monopolies can the reunification of Germany be achieved.

If the stability of the German Democratic Republic and its fraternal alliance with the socialist states are supported by the increased struggle of the working class and the forces of peace in West Germany against militarism, then it will be possible to bring about a reorientation in West Germany which will facilitate a rapprochement of the two states. If through a defeat of the Adenauer CDU and by strengthening the will to action of the working class a new situation is created in West Germany then it is possible to come to an agreement between the two German governments on a solemn renunciation of the mutual use of force. Representatives of both German states could form a standing commission to deliberate on the measures to be taken to bring about inner-German relaxation of tension and cooperation. Members of such a standing commission could be elected either by both parliaments or in general, free, direct and secret elections along the lines of the valid election regulations in both states.

Create Realistic Conditions for Reunification

After a whole mountain of obstacles against reunification has been piled up through decisions of the Bonn Bundestag and NATO, it is first necessary to remove these obstacles, that is, to create realistic prerequisites for reunification. This includes the withdrawal of the West German Federal Republic from NATO and other military groupings. It would be practicable if a plebiscite on this question were held in West Germany as a next step towards preparing reunification.

In order to make the future united Germany a peace-loving and democratic Germany, it is necessary to abolish conscription in West Germany, to limit the armed forces in both German states and to remove leading nazi officials from positions in West Germany's state and economy. In addition, a collective European security system should be established with both German states participating, and a zone of reduced armament created.

The German Democratic Republic has not made it a condition for reunification that socialist transformations should take place in West Germany. We support the efforts of those circles of the West German population which are for the neutralization of Germany. We point out, however, that the neutralization of Germany can be guaranteed only if the imperialist and militarist forces in Germany, the supporters of a policy of revenge and war, are eliminated.

The preparation of the peaceful and democratic reunification of Germany demands that the working class in alliance with the middle class and strata of the national bourgeoisie itself create the foundation on which to establish the new building of a united, peace-loving and democratic Germany.

All-German Council and Confederation

If such conditions are created which make possible a peaceful solution of the German question, one could also succeed in forming an all-German council, composed on a parity basis of representatives of both German states. Members of the council should be elected in both parts of Germany on the basis of valid election laws. Such an all-German council would be an organ for the unification of East and West Germany on the basis of a confederation, that is to say of a federation of states to be composed of the two German states, the German Democratic Republic and the West German Federal Republic. The all-German council would exercise the functions of a government of the German confederation and prepare measures such as the creation of a uniform administration in Germany, in particular for creating a customs and currency union, a coordinating commission for questions of nationalized industry, for the creation of a unitary bank of issue, a uniform currency, a united transport and communication system, etc. In negotiations on the basis of equality, the all-German council would further work out measures for carrying out free, all-German elections to the national assembly.

These proposals bear a truly democratic character because, during the subsequent general, free, all-German elections, the interference by foreign troops, the financing of political parties by monopoly capital, the purchase of deputies and control of the press and radio by big capitalist monopolies are excluded. Free, all-German elections are thus the result of the process of reunification. They become possible at a time when the free and independent exercise of the rights of the people is being guaranteed with respect to the economy, politics and international law—that means, when all foreign troops have been withdrawn from German territory and all foreign military bases have been liquidated.

The national assembly emerging from these all-German elections bears the high responsibility of drafting the constitution and forming from its ranks a government which serves peace, democracy and progress and which has no room for an imperialist policy.

In this way conditions would be created by the working class and all peace-loving democratic forces, enabling the new Germany to live in friendship with all peoples and take a worthy place among the peoples.

Reply to Konrad Adenauer

9 June 1957

On 24 May the Bonn government sent the government of the USSR a memorandum on the German question. The brief content of this long memorandum is that the Adenauer government proposes to the government of the USSR no more and no less than to allow the German Democratic Republic to be annexed by imperialist West Germany. The government of the USSR is to permit the rule of the German militarists to be expanded over the whole of Germany, thus changing the relation of forces in Germany and Europe in favour of German imperialism. The Adenauer government would be ready under this condition to have closer relations with the USSR.

It would be incorrect to call the memorandum a "reunification note" as is done by the western press, for it does not contain a single constructive idea of its authors which could contribute to paving the way for the reunification of Germany. Ten months of work of the Bonn jurists and not a single idea was born.

The Adenauer government does not want to admit that the reunification of Germany is primarily a question of the German people. Moreover, the German Democratic Republic is a sovereign state on whose future nobody but its people can decide.

The Perspective of Germany

The basic question of the safeguarding of peace and the reunification of Germany is what kind of a united Germany is to be created, a peace-loving and democratic Germany which does not belong to any military bloc or a militarist Germany in which the dictatorship of the trusts, big banks and big landowners and other militarist forces rules and which belongs to a bloc of imperialist powers?

The question on the perspective of Germany must be considered from the aspect of the national interests of our people and the lessons of the two world wars.

The memorandum of the Adenauer government supports Germany's right of self-determination in words. This cannot gloss over the fact that through the restoration of the power of the big monopolies and of militarism and through the integration of West Germany in the North Atlantic Treaty Organization West Germany became a state dependent on the USA.

In the Paris Treaties the Bonn government expressly declared itself for a united Germany "integrated in the European community" (Article 7 of the Germany Treaty), thus renouncing important principles of the national right of self-determination. In addition Adenauer consented to the reservation of the right of the three western powers on questions of the reunification of Germany, thus trying to deprive the German people of their right of self-determination.

Despite repeated warnings from the government of the German Democratic Republic Adenauer, in choosing between the Paris Treaties and the unity of Germany, clearly decided against reunification and for the integration of West Germany in the aggressive NATO military pact system. Adenauer himself confirmed this in a talk with the then French High Commissioner François-Poncet in which he stated:

"Please do not forget that I am the only German chancellor who gives preference to the unity of Europe over the unity of his own fatherland."

The integration of West Germany in the NATO pursues the direct aim of making the reunification of Germany impossible, for the NATO pact is not limited in time.

According to the will of the Bonn government Germany is to become the main NATO war basis, and the GDR is to be retransformed into a domain of exploitation of the Junkers and the trust managers of the Rhine and Ruhr. The facts confirm that the German Democratic Republic, in which the principles of the Potsdam Agreement were implemented and where the basic conditions for a peaceful and democratic settlement of the German question have been created, is the legitimate German state whereas the West German Federal Republic is a state dependent on the USA, a state of injustice whose government makes the country of West Germany available to the USA as its chief military basis in Europe.

In view of the restoration of the rule of militarism in West Germany there is only one way to the perspective of a peace-loving, democratic Germany—the relaxation of tension, the creation of a zone of diminished armament in Europe, the development of the people's struggle against militarism in West Germany, negotiations between the government of the two German states.

The Bonn government asks in its memorandum what policy corresponds to the traditions of the fatherland. There are various traditions in Germany. There is the tradition of the great German humanists, the classical masters of German art and literature, the tradition of the great struggles of the German working class against capitalist exploitation and imperialist war and, on the other hand, the tradition of the dictatorship of the bourgeoisie, the traditions of disregarding the vital national interests of the people. Such traditions are the sale of Germans to foreign powers, reactionary Prussianism, the rapacity of the trust managers and bankers since the beginning of the 20th century, the terror of the bourgeoisie against the working class from the law against socialists to the Hitler dictatorship. These reactionary traditions reached their deepest point in the division of Germany by the German trust and bank managers and in the dependence of the Adenauer government on the USA. A final stop must be put to these traditions of national treachery, of sabre-rattling, the master race theory of the monopolists, Junkers and Hitler generals so that the good traditions of the German people can also freely develop in West Germany.

The patriotic traditions of the struggle for national unity, for the rights and liberties of the people, for peace and socialism are preserved and continued by the German working class and its party. The program of the German working class for reunification is based on the experiences and lessons of German history. It is in accord with the longing and intention of the best Germans who struggled for the democratic unity of our country and the power of the people during the reformation and the Peasants' War, in the liberation war against the Napoleonic foreign rule and in the revolution of 1848, in the struggle against Bismarck's sabre rule and the arbitrary regime of Wilhelm II and in the heroic resistance against Hitler fascism. It relies on those ideas of peace, friendship among the peoples, democracy and humanism which were defended by Thomas Müntzer, Lessing, Herder, Goethe and Schiller, Fichte and Feuerbach, Marx and Engels, Bebel and Wilhelm Liebknecht, Rosa Luxemburg and Karl Liebknecht, by Ernst Thälmann and all the uncounted heroes of the struggle against militarism and imperialism.

The Adenauer government whose deeds include the splitting of Germany and the militarization of West Germany, the aggressive NATO policy and the preparation of atomic war has forfeited any right to appear in the name of the fatherland. True patriotic sentiment demands the struggle against the anti-national policy of German finance capital. Today it is a patriotic duty to struggle with all strength and passion against German imperialism and militarism. It requires checking the aggressive and revenge-seeking forces in West Germany which pursue the atomic armament of the West German army and the preparation of atomic war. It requires the strengthening of the German Democratic Republic as the basis of the struggle for the peaceful, democratic reunification of Germany. The interests of the people and the good traditions of the fatherland can only be preserved through the realization of the program of the German working class and the National Front of Democratic Germany for the reunification.

The aggressive, revenge-seeking forces of German monopoly capital maintain their rule in West Germany with the help of deception and suppression. They try to assume a parliamentary and social disguise and falsify such noble ideas as "freedom" and "democracy". In reality the domination of the state and economy in West Germany by a handful of multimillionaires and militarists is the greatest social injustice and the worst violation of freedom and democracy. Only when the working people have power in their hands in the whole of Germany are a truly social system and true freedom of the people and democracy possible.

The rule of the militarists and monopolist war criminals leads to the destruction of the German spirit. Science and research are made serviceable to the interests of the big monopolies and transformed from the seeking for knowledge into a dirty business. Art becomes the scene of action of disgusting, decadent efforts. Public education and science are neglected in favour of militarization. Philistines like Foreign Minister von Brentano dare to slander the great performances of a dramatist like Bertolt Brecht. This Bonn regime does not have a single constructive idea. It embodies those forces which history has condemned to defeat.

The rebirth of Germany is now on the agenda. The new is born in the struggle against militarism and reaction in West Germany, the peace-loving, democratic forces will grow and the conditions created for the reunification of our German fatherland. Germany can only be reunified as a peace-loving, democratic state. To promote this process of unification the strengthening of the German Democratic Republic is the first prerequisite, for it is the basis of the struggle of all peace-loving, democratic forces of Germany.

The German Democratic Republic
Is for Peaceful Coexistence in the Baltic Sea Area

From the speech at the
District Sports Festival of Youth in Rostock on 7 July 1957

Rostock citizens have asked me what are the possibilities for winning all Baltic Sea countries for the cause of peace. Without doubt all Baltic Sea states are interested in maintaining peace. Relations between the Baltic Sea countries with different social systems are therefore necessary, relations which are based on mutual respect for their sovereignty, the national independence of all Baltic Sea countries, and non-interference in their internal affairs. The Baltic Sea does not separate these states, but connects them.

That is why the GDR advocates close relations with all Baltic Sea states. Progress has already been made, for example, the development of our trade relations with the Republic of Finland, the increasing exchange of delegations, many sports competitions, the visits of Finnish parliamentarians to the Leipzig Fair, the development of our cultural relations and the visit of Finnish ministers to our Republic. Shipping is also developing satisfactorily and the GDR is prepared to further expand tourist traffic, cultural exchange, air traffic and postal communications.

The Swedish policy of neutrality and non-alignment as outlined by Swedish Prime Minister Erlander on the occasion of Indian Prime Minister Nehru's visit to Sweden can only be welcomed by us. The GDR has shown its will for good neighbourly cooperation. The upswing in trade and traffic provided the possibility of establishing a general agency of the German Railways in Stockholm and a representation of our foreign trade organs. In the interest of Sweden itself Swedish transit traffic over GDR routes is developing, Swedish charter aircraft land in Berlin-Schönefeld. The GDR is very accommodating in issuing visas. Cultural exchange is growing and we are ready to welcome delegations of Swedish parliamentarians, politicians and journalists on our territory.

The GDR wants to have good relations with Denmark. We all regret very much that trade relations have not developed more rapidly. Good relations with the GDR are in Denmark's national interest. Precisely Denmark, like no other Baltic Sea country, is threatened by the same German militarists who occupied Denmark in 1940.

With the policy of strength the German militarists are methodically striving to turn the Baltic Sea into a deployment area against every peaceful state. It would be a disadvantage to all Baltic Sea states if the German militarists ever reach their goals. The head of the navy department in the Federal Defence Ministry in Bonn, Vice-Admiral Ruge, declared openly in Pensacola, Florida that it was important that the Danish position "at the entrances to the Baltic Sea be covered in every way. It is the strategic position No. 1 (!) in Europe. If it remains in the hands of the West it could be used in case of a conflict as an arm of the sea which reaches far into the Eastern land mass!" He called the Baltic Sea a "runway" for major mass transports.

Nobody outside of German imperialism conjures up terrible dangers for the Baltic Sea countries. The atomic strategy of NATO hits most severely countries like Denmark which must reckon with a decisive counter-blow. The military plans of the German imperialists and of NATO coldly and diabolically oppose the vital interests of the Baltic Sea peoples.

The peace-loving states cannot remain indifferent in the face of these machinations. The Soviet Union has clearly formulated its peace policy. Its aim is to maintain the Baltic as a sea of peace. The governments of the German Democratic Republic and the People's Republic of Poland have reaffirmed their desire for the peaceful coexistence of all Baltic Sea states in a joint declaration of 20 June 1957:

"The governments of the German Democratic Republic and the People's Republic of Poland unanimously agreed that in the interest of the peaceful development of the European peoples the Baltic must be a sea of peace. The two governments will therefore make efforts to come to an understanding with their neighbouring countries on the Baltic and take steps to achieve this aim."

Highly important, therefore, are all steps aimed at bringing about the true coexistence of all Baltic Sea peoples and of creating a system of collective European security—because the peaceful coexistence of all Baltic Sea peoples would strengthen peace in the whole of Europe. The GDR, which is resolutely fighting the aggressive plans of German imperialism, is thus rendering an important contribution to the security of all Baltic Sea states. The Baltic Sea countries are considered by German imperialism as deployment areas and suppliers of raw materials. German imperialism wants to bring the Baltic Sea peoples under the yoke of its misanthropic plans. The GDR favours relations on the basis of mutual advantage, mutual respect for the sovereignty of all Baltic Sea states. It is in the interest of the Baltic Sea states to strengthen relations with the GDR. The GDR is prepared to take steps in this direction.

The Struggle for Peace, the Victory of Socialism, for the National Rebirth of Germany as a Peace-loving, Democratic State

From the report to the Fifth Congress
of the Socialist Unity Party of Germany from 10 to 16 July 1958

10 July 1958

The Fifth Congress is focused on the national task of showing the working class and all peace-loving people in Germany ways and means of maintaining peace. In order to safeguard peace and protect it from all attacks it is most important to consolidate our workers' and peasants' state and to go unswervingly ahead on our march to socialism.

The question: peaceful coexistence or war? has become the basic problem of world policy. Two roads are visible; one road leads into a peaceful future without war, the other into the holocaust of a nuclear war. Nobody can avoid a decision on this. The Soviet Union, the states of the socialist camp and other peaceloving peoples have embarked upon the road of peace. They demand not only disarmament, they are also giving an example. The Soviet Union and other socialist countries have frequently reduced the strength of their troops. The German Democratic Republic, too, has reduced the originally planned strength of the National People's Army to 90,000 men. The Soviet Union not only demands the cessation of nuclear testing, but has already stopped it, whereas the United States continues to poison the atmosphere with radioactivity in new series of tests.

The centre of world reaction is American imperialism. The aggressive imperialist circles of the United States are striving for world domination. They are attempting to avoid an economic crisis by pushing ahead with the armaments race and foiling international disarmament in every way possible. With the assistance of NATO and other war pacts they ensure themselves the command over the military forces of other countries, thus preparing aggression against the socialist camp. German imperialism is the closest ally of American imperialism. West Germany is today the centre of the danger to peace in Europe.

Again and again West German CDU politicians name the GDR, Czechoslovakia, Poland and the Soviet Union as enemies in a future war. German imperialism tries to penetrate the peoples' democracies politically and economically as well as through ideological subversive activities. German imperialism plays a leading role in sabotaging the relaxation of tension and in developing nuclear weapons and missiles in West European NATO states. It is clear that this aggressive policy is incompatible with the idea of peaceful coexistence. The consequence of these predatory demands is war, and German militarism—as part of the US-controlled NATO—is preparing for this war.

The victory of socialism cannot be prevented through war. On the contrary, a third world war would inevitably mean an end to the capitalist system. But the terrible devastations of the war would bring immeasurable sufferings to the people, it would hamper socialist construction and mean a temporary set-back. Socialism is strong enough to convince the peoples through its successes and to win the victory in peaceful competition. Socialism does not need, nor does it want war. Socialism is the most humane order that ever existed. Marxism-Leninism is the most human of all existing teachings. Therefore, the basic political task in our present situation can only be the struggle to safeguard peace and against atomic death.

Principles of a German Peace Treaty

Thus the German people are deeply interested in having the principles of a peace treaty with Germany finally discussed. We recall in this connection that already in 1952 the Soviet Union as well as the People's Chamber and the government of the German Democratic Republic had established the principles for a peace treaty. A peace treaty with Germany shall truly serve the safeguarding of peace, but this is only possible if the draft of the peace treaty contributes towards promoting the reunification of Germany into a peace-loving, democratic German state. The drawing up of such a draft of a peace treaty is directly linked with the proposals for the creation of an atomic-weapon-free zone in Europe, a zone of reduced armament, the step-by-step withdrawal of foreign troops from Germany and the elimination of foreign military bases in both German states and the other European countries. It is therefore necessary to do away with the wall which has been built up through the remilitarization of West Germany and the integration of West Germany in NATO, to remove it with the assistance of the draft of a peace treaty in order to make possible the reunification of Germany. What must be the foundations of a peace treaty to be worked out under such conditions?

1. Germany becomes a peace-loving, democratic and independent state by means of the establishment of a confederation of the two German states.

2. Germany becomes a sovereign state, not affiliated to any military bloc or economic associations such as the European Coal and Steel Community. This means West Germany's withdrawal from NATO and the GDR's withdrawal from the Warsaw pact.

3. In a reunited Germany, the German people and all German citizens irrespective of race, sex and religion are guaranteed human rights and basic freedoms. Democratic political parties and organizations have the right to engage in activity freely and the right of free decision on their own affairs. They enjoy freedom of the press and of publications. It is not sufficient, however, to fix these human rights and basic liberties legally. They must be created in reality whereby the supremacy of militarist and fascist forces is eliminated. That is to say, in a peace-loving, democratic Germany no organizations will be tolerated which are hostile to the cause of peace and democracy.

4. Germany is guaranteed the full development of its peaceful economy and unhindered access to world markets.

5. The territory of Germany is defined by the frontiers fixed in the decisions of the Potsdam Conference of the four great powers. On this basis only can friendly relations with the People's Republic of Poland be guaranteed. All revanchist efforts currently to be seen in West Germany must be resolutely rejected because they are directed against the maintenance of peace in Europe.

6. Germany will be permitted to have its own national armed forces for defence purposes, consisting of land, air and naval forces. Preparations for fixing the military armed forces are arranged through agreement between the two German states on the number, equipment and location of garrisons of the military armed forces.

Also in West Germany, the proposal for a discussion of the principles of a peace treaty with Germany at a conference of representatives of the great powers has met with approval. A public discussion between the peace-loving democratic forces in both parts of Germany on this vital national question can only be beneficial.

The Safeguarding of Peace Has Become the Main Content of the German Question

The Soviet Union's peace policy is finding special support from the German people, because in Germany the world problem of maintaining peace appears in a particularly acute form. The policies of peace and war sharply confront each other in the form of the two German states. The maintenance of peace has become the main content of the German question.

Since the Adenauer government signed the Paris Treaties and made West Germany a member of NATO, since the majority of the Bundestag agreed on the nuclear armament of the West German army West Germany has become a hotbed of an atomic war in Europe. But not only that. The atomic armament of West Germany would prevent a rapprochement of the two German states as well as the reunification of Germany. How could one think of a confederation of the two German states if West Germany confronts the GDR as its mortal enemy and threatens cities of our Republic such as Leipzig, Dresden and Magdeburg with atomic rockets? Atomic armament would bury for a long time not only any hope of reunification, but also of any normal relations between the two German states.

In evaluating the relation of forces and judging the prospects for the maintenance of peace, one has to take into consideration, however, that today the radius of action of German imperialism is limited thanks to the existence of the German Democratic Republic. The territories used by Hitler as a deployment area for his armies against the East are today firmly in the hands of the GDR and the peace camp. Manpower and material employed by Hitler for German imperialism's plans of conquest are today ready to bar the way to the German militarists. The very existence of the GDR means that one arm of German imperialism has been cut off. The "other Germany", which during Hitler's days fought illegally or from exile for peace, is today a state on German soil which also offers a firm backing to peace fighters in West Germany.

When in autumn 1956 the danger of war came to a head, when the imperialists attacked Egypt, staged a counter-revolutionary thrust against Hungary and sought to put pressure on the GDR, the working class of the German Democratic Republic firmly sided with its workers' and peasants' power, so that all provocations failed and the militarists were given no pretext for intervening and unleashing a war. Even the conservative London *Times* later confirmed that the firmness of our party and our state saved peace in those days.

Experience teaches us that the more unshakable our workers' and peasants' power in the GDR is, the firmer is peace in Europe. Experience teaches further that any lack of vigilance, any giving in to attempts of the class enemy to soften our position means playing with the fire of war.

The safeguarding of peace and the national rebirth of Germany as a peace-loving democratic state thus demand the further internal consolidation and the further strengthening of the international position of our Republic. First and foremost we will further consolidate and expand our fraternal relations with the Soviet Union and other states of the socialist camp. In addition, we want to have normal relations with all countries which are ready to establish such relations on the basis of equality, respect for sovereignty and non-interference. The German Democratic Republic's foreign policy, guided by the principles of socialist internationalism and by the desire to safeguard peace with all peoples as well as to strengthen the world socialist system, is the only national German foreign policy which, in contrast to Bonn's imperialist policy of war, serves the interests of all Germans.

In the draft resolution of the Party Congress, the peace program of our party is presented, a program which corresponds to the wishes of the German people and the interests of the nation. Of special importance for us Germans is the proposal which in the first line concerns our security—the creation of an atomic and hydrogen weapon and rocket-free zone in Central Europe.

The atomic armament of West Germany would place a means of mass extermination into the hands of militarists and fascists who under Hitler developed industrial mass extermination and who today again occupy leading positions in Bonn, a means of mass extermination which, however, would be much more effective than the gases of IG-Farben. This would mean an immense intensification of the danger of an atomic war.

The creation of an atomic-weapon-free zone, on the other hand, would not only ban all atomic weapons from Germany, Poland and Czechoslovakia, it would also include an obligation by the atomic powers not to employ atomic arms in case of war against the territory of this zone. The Soviet Union has declared its readiness to give such a guarantee.

That is to say, a zone of extraordinary danger would become a zone of relative security, quite apart from the fact that an atomic-weapon-free zone would be a step towards the complete liquidation of nuclear weapons. From a national point of view it is almost criminal to reject such guarantees for the security of the German people, as the Bonn government is doing. The struggle against the atomic armament of the German militarists and for an atomic-weapon-free zone is therefore in the centre of the struggle for peace in West Germany.

The head of the opposition in the British parliament, Hugh Gaitskell, published an essay in which he states that the policy of determent is not effective and that the temptation to use the atomic bomb exists in view of the fact that a growing number of countries possess atomic bombs. In this connection he speaks of the special case of West Germany. He says that it would be necessary to remove such zones "which could be the starting point for small armed conflicts which then develop into bigger wars". In view of such a situation Hugh Gaitskell recommends making the proposals for the creation of an atomic-weapon-free zone the basis of international negotiations. Although in this connection Hugh Gaitskell develops viewpoints which differ from ours his proposal to consider the plan of the creation of an atomic-weapon-free zone as the basis for such negotiations at a summit conference is nevertheless worth dealing with. His view corresponds to the conception of many nuclear research scientists and broad bourgeois circles in West Germany. I want to state explicitly that we consider the discussion of the question of the creation of an atomic-weapon-free zone in Europe a main question of the summit conference, for this corresponds with the will of the peoples.

When the West German CDU politicians try to camouflage their murderous plots against peace and the population of the GDR by hypocritically talking of "human contacts", we tell them quite frankly: We are for contacts of any kind which serve the maintenance of peace, but not for contacts aimed at undermining the GDR, the centre of peace in Germany. We are above all for contacts between the peace movement of the GDR and the committees against nuclear death and the peace movement in West Germany.

We agree with the West German friends of peace who say that the prevention of atomic armament in West Germany constitutes a decisive step towards normal relations between the two German states. We greet the friends of peace in West Germany who are courageously struggling against atomic armament despite persecution by the Adenauer state and clerical instigation.

The temporary injunction by the so-called Federal Constitutional Court banning a plebiscite against nuclear death is rightly being characterized by the West German population as an undemocratic measure directed against the vital interests of the nation, which has no legal force. One can increasingly hear among the West German population that we must not wait until it is too late. Or they say: if the provincial government does not prepare the plebiscite we must carry it out ourselves. The West German population does not want the transformation of its home country into a rocket base and a deployment area of the United States. The population does not want American policy to be conducted in West Germany and the NATO general staff to be superior to parliament.

Peace-loving people throughout Germany are rightly alarmed and demand steps for the safeguarding of peace and the relaxation of tension. We submit the following proposals to the German public:

1. The people's movement against nuclear death and for an atomic-weapon-free zone is to be expanded on a still broader scale.

2. The government of the German Democratic Republic declares its readiness to meet for discussions with representatives of the West German Bundestag or the West German federal government with the aim of not erecting missile bases in Germany, not equipping German troops with nuclear weapons and refraining from test-flights with atomic bombs over German territory. The GDR representatives will thereby propose that the two German states work for a non-aggression pact between the Warsaw Treaty states and the NATO states as well as the step-by-step withdrawal of foreign troops.

3. Representatives of the Central Committee of the SED and representatives of the Party Executive of the SPD get into contact with each other to pave the way for a relaxation of tension and for understanding on certain questions. It could be the purpose of these discussions to consult each other on measures against atomic armament and for the creation of an atomic-weapon-free zone as well as to promote the unification of all peace-loving democratic forces.

The Way to the Safeguarding of Peace and the Raising of the Material and Cultural Living Conditions of the People

*From the report to the fourth session
of the Central Committee of the Socialist Unity Party of Germany
from 15 to 17 January 1959*

Through Peace Treaty to the National Rebirth of Germany

The government of the USSR has submitted to the states which participated in the war against Germany, as well as to the German Democratic Republic and the German Federal Republic, the draft of a German peace treaty, and has proposed the convocation of a peace conference to be held in Warsaw or Prague within two months. As this peace treaty concerns not only the vital interests of the German people but also world peace, no state will be able to avoid defining its attitude to this treaty. It is necessary, plain and realistic to define one's attitude towards it. After the government of the USSR and the government of the German Democratic Republic have proposed the preparation of a German peace treaty several times the Soviet government has now presented to the states named the precisely drawn up and paragraphed draft of a peace treaty with Germany.

Nobody will deny that it is a completely abnormal, nationally scarcely longer endurable situation that a country like Germany still has no peace treaty fourteen years after the Hitler war. This is bound to complicate both the internal relations between the two German states and international relations as well. It is therefore in accord with the national interests of the German people to propose, as the Soviet government does, finally to close the books on the war fourteen years after the end of the Second World War and to create such conditions which would guarantee that Germany will not become for a third time a spring-board for war provocations or the initiator of a war. A final closing of the books on the last and a barrier against a new war—that is the great significance of the peace treaty.

Article 22 of the draft states that the allied and associated powers shall respect the right of the German people to re-establish the unity of Germany, and shall be ready to grant the two German states any assistance to reach this goal through rapprochement and understanding between the German Democratic Republic and the Federal

Republic of Germany. It also says that these powers—in accordance with the national aspirations of the German people and, also, in accordance with the interests of security in Europe and throughout the world—shall regard the peace treaty as an important contribution to the reunification of Germany.

Every German citizen will understand that, after Germany has been split by western finance capital and militarism has been re-established in the western part of Germany and a drive for atomic armament is even being made, the re-establishment of the unity of Germany is possible only step by step, i.e., in several stages. The proposal for a peace treaty creates the most important prerequisite for the reunification of the two German states. The peace treaty is a national bond for holding together the divided Germany.

It is of very great significance that Article 23 contains an obligation for the two German states to bring about the reunification of Germany only by peaceful means. By signing the peace treaty the two German states undertake never to resort to the use of force or the threat of force to bring about the reunification of Germany, and to settle all disputes that might arise in their relations by peaceful means.

With regard to Berlin, the present capital of the German Democratic Republic and future capital of all Germany, it is stipulated that pending the establishment of the unity of Germany West Berlin shall be accorded the status of a demilitarized Free City.

The provisions of the proposed peace treaty with Germany signify the establishment and safeguarding of Germany's full sovereignty. The German people will finally be given the opportunity to arrange their internal affairs in national freedom, free from military pressure, free from the commitment to military blocs.

According to Article 14 of the peace treaty Germany pledges to build up a democratic order. All persons subject to German sovereignty irrespective of race, sex, language, religion, nationality, shall enjoy all human rights and fundamental liberties including personal freedom, freedom of speech, freedom of press and publication, religious worship, political opinion, the right to join associations and public assembly.

Under Article 17 Germany assumes the obligation to eliminate nazism. The restoration, existence and activities of the NSDAP (nazi party) and its organizations including political, military and para-military organizations, as well as the establishment and activities of other similar parties and organizations shall not be permitted, and any new attempt is to be prohibited.

The provisions of this draft peace treaty have long become reality in the GDR. The People's Chamber and the government of the German Democratic Republic, relying on the anti-fascist and democratic forces of the people, have put into effect the principles of the anti-Hitler coalition and the Potsdam Agreement in the GDR, for these principles are in keeping with the national interests of the German people.

The eradication of German militarism and imperialism created a sound foundation for a consistent policy of peace by the GDR. At the same time, the GDR government has set an example of peaceful and friendly relations for the whole of Germany.

The draft peace treaty makes no reference to the social system existing in Germany for that is the affair of the Germans alone. The peace treaty thus does not affect in any way the existence and development of the socialist social system in the GDR. But it also does not affect the existence of capitalist society in West Germany. It is equally acceptable both to socialists and capitalists. Thus, the peace treaty contains only such provisions as refer to the sovereignty of Germany as a peace-loving, democratic state, and to its relations with other peoples. The question as to who, in view of the existence of two German states, is to sign a peace treaty is also answered. It is proposed that pending reunification the term Germany shall be interpreted as the two existing German states—the German Democratic Republic and the German Federal Republic—and all rights and obligations of Germany contained in the treaty shall refer to both German states to the same extent. The conclusion of a peace treaty would, of course, be considerably accelerated by the formation of a confederation of the two German states. In this case two representatives of the German confederation as well as representatives of the German Democratic Republic and of the German Federal Republic would sign the treaty. The draft peace treaty of the USSR confirms that the re-establishment of the sovereignty of Germany through the conclusion of a peace treaty and the creation of peaceful, democratic conditions also in West Germany are the prerequisites for the reunification of Germany.

The people of the German Democratic Republic and all peace-loving forces in Germany are grateful to the Union of Soviet Socialist Republics for this great initiative serving the cause of peace and promoting the settlement of the German people's vital national question. The position of the Soviet government corresponds to the Marxist-Leninist principles of respect for other peoples' sovereignty and equality. The draft peace treaty is in harmony with the longing of the German people for peace, understanding and the unity of Germany.

The conclusion of a peace treaty is the shortest and speediest way to safeguard peace, a way by which the German people can bring about the unity of Germany through their own strength and on their own responsibility. The draft peace treaty contains all the principles of a program for the peaceful solution of the German question. It creates the prerequisites for the national rebirth of Germany as a peace-loving, democratic state. The future of Germany emerges from the fog. The bells of peace will resound throughout Germany and Europe.

Within the framework of the great program for the peaceful solution of the German question the Fifth Party Congress proposed that the people of Berlin make joint efforts so that Berlin shall become a city of peace. The congress noted that the front-line city policy of the West Berlin Senate, the stationing of armed forces of the three western powers and maintenance of the occupation regime in the western part of the city have given rise to an abnormal situation presenting a danger to peace.

The West Berlin authorities have been called upon to revoke all measures constituting an interference in the internal affairs of the GDR. We proposed the establishment of normal economic relations between the government of the GDR, the Municipal Council of Greater Berlin and the West Berlin Senate. For this purpose, we proposed that negotiations be held on a basis of equal rights and declared ourselves also ready to settle such questions as the initiating of unrestricted city traffic, the entry of West Berlin citizens into the GDR, etc. We declared the readiness of the GDR and the Municipal Council of Greater Berlin to make arrangements for the provisioning of West Berlin with fresh vegetables and fresh milk from the GDR. We declared ourselves ready to purchase industrial products from West Berlin, which would have been beneficial to West Berlin, too, as it would provide workers with an assured job. We are ready to reach understanding on the status of West Berlin as a Free City, and we, on our part, shall of course respect that status.

We are ready to ensure West Berlin's communications both to the East and to the West, and to guarantee, on the basis of an appropriate agreement, unrestricted use of the railway lines, roads and waterways of the German Democratic Republic. We are also ready, on the basis of an agreement, to grant the Free City of West Berlin the opportunity to establish air connections with other countries.

The German Democratic Republic has hitherto made several

proposals to re-establish and develop economic relations between the GDR and West Berlin. The policy pursued by the West Berlin authorities and the Adenauer government had now led to a situation in which West Berlin is being not only politically isolated, but also increasingly economically isolated from the German Democratic Republic in the centre of which it is situated. This, of course, is by no means a normal situation and will eventually entail serious consequences for West Berlin.

West Berlin's one-sided western orientation makes that part of the city dependent upon changes in the economic situation from the effects of which the German Federal Republic and the entire capitalist world are suffering today.

The policy of economic isolation from the GDR pursued by West Berlin and West German circles sometimes takes the most curious forms. It is a fact that, by this policy, West Berlin is deprived of the opportunity to procure the most essential commodities from its immediate vicinity, the GDR, beginning with milk, vegetables and other products and ending with gravel for building purposes. All these goods have to be brought from far away, which, of course, adds to their prices. I think that every rationally thinking Berliner will understand that such a situation cannot be called normal.

In the case of the conversion of West Berlin into a Free City the German Democratic Republic will do everything in its power to create the necessary conditions for a normal economic development of West Berlin.

We are ready to contribute towards providing West Berlin enterprises with the necessary orders. Moreover, I think that our enterprises, in cooperation with West Berlin enterprises, could carry out orders for other countries, as is being done already in a number of cases. We could, furthermore, make available to West Berlin workers a substantial number of jobs in our industries.

The Bonn Government Against the National Rights of the German People

The replies of the USA, Great Britain and France are completely negative. The note of the Bonn federal government must be characterized as worthless. It is worthless because it does not contain one single proposal serving to lessen tensions in Germany and to solve the German question peacefully, but only reflects the views of a small coterie including Adenauer, his Ribbentrop diplomats and Hitler generals. This statement is devoid of any real sense of reality and of the relation of forces in Europe and the world. The reply of the Bonn government reveals the anti-national character of the policies of German imperialism. The characteristic feature of those policies is their complete disregard for the national interests of the German people. The anti-national character becomes manifest in the following:

The Bonn government opposes the abolition of the occupation statute and occupation practice of the western powers in West Berlin.

The Bonn government refuses to define its attitude to the activities of the centres of espionage and subversion in West Berlin, that is to say, it wants the activities of the foreign and West German centres of provocation to continue.

The bonn government has transferred inalienable national rights of the German people—as far as the West Germans are concerned—to the states of the North Atlantic war pact.

The Bonn government declares that, by virtue of the Paris Agreement with the three western powers of 23 October 1954, it has delegated to those powers only the rights affecting Germany as a whole, including the reunification of Germany and the conclusion of a peace treaty.

The Bonn government's renunciation of the sovereign right to take the initiative in reunifying Germany means yielding the right of decision on the national questions of the German people to the western powers which are not in the least interested in the reunification of Germany. The Bonn government thus wants to conceal from the German people its own decisive responsibility for the splitting of Germany and the exacerbation of the division of Germany by the policy of atomic armament. The Paris Treaties have no validity, either for the people of West Germany or for other peoples, because the Bonn government concluded them without asking the West German population. The Bonn government even forbade a referendum in West Germany on the question: General Treaty and European Defence Community Treaty or peace treaty and withdrawal of occupation troops. Could anyone act more anti-democratically and anti-nationally?

Why Do Bonn and the Western Powers Have No Constructive Proposals?

People in West Germany, Great Britain, France and other countries have justifiably asked how is it to be explained that the replies of the western powers and the reply of the Bonn government which claimst to be a German government, contain not a single proposal for the peaceful solution of the German question? The explanation is that these notes are directed against a peaceful solution of the German question. As long as the Bonn government pursues aggressive imperialist aims it will not be able to make constructive proposals for a peaceful settlement of the West Berlin problem or for the peaceful reunification of Germany. It is not by chance that the Bonn government has long been treating the question of German reunification not as a German question any more, but has left it to the NATO authorities. It was noted especially by the German people that at the show staged by the West German Bundestag on 1 October 1958 in West Berlin, not a word was said about the road to the reunification of Germany, that, moreover, that word was not even mentioned. Adenauer once declared: "... my idea of developments is as follows: When the West is stronger than Soviet Russia then the day will have come for negotiations with Soviet Russia."

It follows from this statement that Adenauer intends to employ a policy of strength to blackmail the Soviet Union and the GDR. Adhering to such a policy the Bonn government first carried out remilitarization and rejected any proposal for rapprochement and understanding between the two German states, as well as for reunification. That policy has run into a blind alley, however, as a result of a change in the relation of forces in the world and the tremendous upsurge of science and the economy in the Soviet Union making possible the launching of intercontinental and interplanetary rockets. This is the talk of the town in Bonn. That is why Herr Adenauer is trying now—as was formerly done by Hitler—to extend NATO's sphere of influence to the East by combining subversive activities in the peoples' democracies with political and military pressure. The Bonn government proposed that the USA, Great Britain, France and the Soviet Union call a conference and set up a commission to deal with the German question. It does not say, however, what its proposals are for such a commission. Why does the Bonn government keep silent about its plans to the German people? What kind of plans are these that will not bear the light of publicity? I should like to inform the people of West Germany about the secret plan "Outline" (i.e., an outline of the basic features of common policy) which was agreed upon between the western powers and Bonn.

After the GDR, at the Fifth Party Congress, set forth a program for solving the national question of the German people and the Soviet Union presented the draft of a peace treaty with Germany the time has now come for the public to be informed about Bonn's

and the western powers' plan so that the German people can form
their own judgment.

"Outline"–Crusade Instead of Peace Treaty

Since spring 1957 when it was assumed by the Bonn government
that there would be a summit conference, consultations were held
by a four-power work-team for drafting directives for German
reunification. At the same time, deliberations on these directives
were conducted in the NATO council for European security. What
now is the content of the "Outline of a Plan for German Reunification and Agreements on European Security"? The plan proceeds
from the idea that an agreement on security in Europe will be concluded in which the parties undertake "to renounce the use of force
in any form that is incompatible with the aims". This means little
since the West German government is not envisaged as a signatory
to such an agreement. So the gentlemen want to make the peace-
loving people in Germany believe that a general declaration on the
safeguarding of peace alone will turn the West German militarists
into peaceful lambs. In the disguise of champions of reunification
they want to advance up to the Oder river to issue there security
declarations as they understand them. Moreover, the NATO troops
are to remain in Germany during this period.

Three months after such principal statements on security, elections
for an all-German national assembly are to be held in Germany with
the mode of election being worked out by the four great powers. On
13 January 1959 Herr Adenauer remarked on this that atomic armament was quite consistent with free elections. So Herr Adenauer
chooses to call elections under the pressure of atomic weapons and
under the pressure of NATO militarists "free elections".

This "Outline" stands the German question on its head. It
proceeds from a completely false assessment of the situation in Germany and in the world. The basic tenets of this plan for reunification issue from a platonic declaration on security obligations, but do
not envisage any measures to make security prevail as a prerequisite
for reunification, as they are provided for in the Soviet draft peace
treaty with Germany.

The ruling circles of the western powers should finally take notice
of the fact that the reunification of Germany is the affair of the German people alone, and that it can never be tolerated that a reunification of Germany will be effected under pressure from the imperialist
western powers, with the aim of incorporating the whole of Germany

into NATO. There never can be and never will be such a thing! The mere fact that this "Outline" was first dealt with in the NATO working committee shows where it is to lead.

So the plan proper starts with a proposal for so-called all-German elections. But the Bonn government itself took all-German elections off the agenda when it began to introduce compulsory military service in NATO and atomic armament. As long as there is remilitarization in West Germany, as long as atomic armament is continued and West Germany remains occupied by foreign troops it is impossible to speak of free elections. The plan spells out the western powers' and Bonn's intentions to hold all-German elections under the pressure of the atomic bomb and the pressure of foreign occupation. That means that the three imperialist western powers and Bonn are to have the right to bring the necessary political, military and clerical pressure to bear during the elections, as is in accord with the spirit of the Paris Agreement. The proposal to hold all-German elections under conditions of militarist domination, of atomic armament, and under the pressure of the bayonets of foreign imperialist troops means nothing but organizing civil war. Under the pressure of atomic weapons and foreign troops in West Germany as well as its own notorious methods, the Bonn government hopes to be able to forge ahead up to the Oder river. The joker in the "Outline" is that Germany may take part in a European security arrangement only after an aggression against the GDR.

If one examines the whole, the section on security obligations serves only the purpose of obligating the states of the Warsaw Treaty to keep still and calmly watch how the realm of NATO is extended, as a first step, up to the Oder river. Thus it is not security in Europe which is to be created, but only security to ensure the success of the first stage of the crusade to the East. When the German NATO forces have advanced up to the Oder German imperialism and NATO will need a certain time to be able to carry out their undermining activities against Poland and Czechoslovakia. They will then, following Hitler's method, make solemn statements that they are willing to settle all questions only with peaceful means, until they are adequately prepared for the next stage of aggression.

This "Outline of a Plan" makes it clear why Herr Adenauer rejected free all-German elections in 1952. He feared the free decision of the German people. Therefore, he wanted to complete remilitarization and atomic armament first, hoping that this would effect such a change in the relation of forces in Europe as to make his crusade to the East successful. But Herr Adenauer was grossly mistaken. Such a thing can and will never happen. That is why this "Outline" is not even worth the paper it was written on.

Some Questions to the Governments of the Western Powers

Now the question crops up: Why do the representatives of the western powers take such pains to work out such an unserious document with officials of the Bonn government? That policy is designed to sway certain unstable sections of the world public favouring an understanding between the two German states. It appears that some representatives of the western powers had the intention to present a comedy at a summit conference.

How would it be if the leading political circles of the western powers threw this unrealistic plan in the waste-paper basket and began to create peaceful conditions in Germany and Europe so as to provide the basic conditions for the reunification of Germany? With the western powers themselves admitting the necessity of a peace treaty with Germany it is only natural to call a peace conference at long last. As the Soviet Union's draft peace treaty is strictly in keeping with the agreed-upon principles of the anti-Hitler coalition, consultations could be started now. If, in the opinion of the western powers, a provisional all-German agency may initiate preliminary negotiations on a peace treaty, why could this not also be done by the council of a confederation composed of representatives of the two German states? If—in the words of their own plan—the setting up of a zone for restricting armed forces and armaments is to be started later on, including, of course, the control of restrictions, why should it not be started already today? Why is it that the western powers only want consultations by German experts on the draft of an election law which is to be laid down by the great powers? Why can one not begin by inviting German representatives to consultations on questions of safeguarding peace and preparing a peace treaty? If the western powers are really of the opinion that European security must be linked with German reunification, it would, in fact, be the most obvious thing to reach an agreement between NATO and the Warsaw Treaty states on the renunciation of the use of force as is envisaged in the Soviet draft peace treaty for the two German states.

If the western powers declare themselves to be ready for security obligations it would really be the most obvious thing to arrive at agreement on the withdrawal of foreign troops in stages. This would result in an immediate relaxation of the situation.

Proposal on the Formation and Activity of a Confederation to Bring about the Reunification of Germany

The draft peace treaty answers the question of who may sign such a treaty on behalf of Germany. It is proposed that if a German confederation is established the peace treaty shall be signed for Germany by representatives of the confederation and representatives of the two German states. It would of course be better if, at the time of the conclusion of a peace treaty, a confederation already existed, that is to say, if such a decisive rapprochement had been reached between the two German states.

Already in autumn 1957 we proposed that negotiations be started so that the confederation could be formed as from 1 January 1958. If negotiations had been held then a confederation with a certain amount of experience would exist today which could take part in preparing a peace treaty. The Bonn government rejected the proposals at that time. It adopted the following tactics: If we propose creating a zone of restricted armaments it says, first reunification of Germany; if we propose reuniting Germany it will reject negotiations maintaining that this question is one of international policy, which is to mean that this question is subject to the competence of NATO.

The draft peace treaty gives a fresh impetus to the efforts of the peace-loving, democratic forces in Germany seeking to reach reunification by the formation of a confederation of the two German states.

I recall that an extensive discussion on our proposal for a confederation, for a federation of the two German states, developed after the 30th session of the Central Committee of the Socialist Unity Party of Germany. After negotiations between Bonn government Minister Dr. Schäffer and representatives of the GDR we made proposals for the formation of a confederation which in every respect are acceptable to a West German bourgeois-democratic government. We have left no doubt that confederation and reunification cannot be linked up with demands to the effect that the social system of the GDR be extended to the Federal Republic, or that of the Federal Republic to the GDR. The idea of a confederation was then expounded in detail in interviews with the West German, British and American press.

Thus the point now is not a discussion about the two social systems, but the safeguarding of peace and the reunification of Germany. To arrive at reunification the main obstacle must be recognized and abolished. The Fifth Party Congress said about this:

"As long as atomic cannons are trained on the German Democratic Republic from West Germany and plans of annexation and revision of the frontiers of the peoples' democracies are being juggled with, the necessary climate for rapprochement and understanding will be lacking."[1])

We are of the opinion that the necessary climate for rapprochement and understanding can be created through a broad discussion on a peace treaty with Germany. The time has come for the peace-loving, democratic forces in Germany to take the business of the safeguarding of peace and the unification of the two German states into their own hands. We therefore propose that the National Council of the National Front of Democratic Germany initiate consultations with representatives of the democratic parties, the trade unions and other organizations in West Germany on the formation of a confederation for the purpose of reunifying Germany.

Tasks, Organization and Aims of the Confederation

We should like to give a clear-cut answer to, and put up for discussion, the question of the conditions under which the formation of a confederation between the German states could be agreed upon, a question which is repeatedly asked by workers, SPD members of the Bundestag, trade union leaders and members of the West German bourgeoisie.

The formation of a confederation is connected with the fulfilment of the basic demands of the peace treaty. The conclusion of a peace treaty would create the necessary prerequisite for the rapprochement of the two German states and for a close cooperation between them. The ultimate aim of the confederation is the reunification of Germany as a peace-loving, democratic state. The confederation will only be of a transitory nature.

Such basic demands of a peace treaty the fulfilment of which would at the same time constitute a stable foundation for a German confederation might, perhaps, include:

the comprehensive democratization of social and political life in Germany;

the renunciation by both German states of the production, acquisition or the testing of nuclear weapons;

the withdrawal of all foreign troops from the territory of Germany

[1]) Protokoll der Verhandlungen des V. Parteitages der Sozialistischen Einheitspartei Deutschlands (Minutes of the Deliberations of the Fifth Congress of the Socialist Unity Party of Germany), Dietz Verlag, Berlin, 1959, p. 187.

and the elimination of foreign military bases on German soil within the time-limits stipulated in the peace treaty;

the withdrawal of the Federal Republic and the GDR from NATO and from the organization of the Warsaw Treaty, respectively, and renunciation of participation in military alliances.

The organization and activities of the future German confederation could, in our view, be the following:

As the supreme body of the confederation a 100-strong all-German council will be formed composed of equal numbers of members of parliament named by the parliaments of the two German states. The all-German council of the confederation is to include representatives of all democratic parties and mass organizations, such as trade unions, which are represented in the parliaments of the two German states or which have political significance.

The all-German council of the confederation elects an executive body, the presidium of the council.

During the initial period of its activity, the tasks of the all-German council will obviously include such questions as the signing of the peace treaty in the name of the confederation and the maintaining of contacts with other parties to the peace treaty on all questions concerning the fulfilment of the individual articles of the treaty. Subsequently, the scope of the functions of the all-German council might eventually be supplemented by such questions as the conclusion of agreements with foreign states on securing foreign trade conditions for the German confederation, on sea navigation, on access to world markets, on accession to international organizations and conventions including the UN auxiliary organizations.

The all-German council of the confederation will undertake to regulate relations between the German Democratic Republic and the German Federal Republic. This will, in particular, affect such questions as the abolition of military conscription in the Federal Republic, the fixing of the numerical strength of the armed forces, the regulation of inter-German trade, mutual clearing payments, currency transactions, transportation, goods traffic, questions of labour law, social insurance, culture and statistics. The council will form commissions and committees to prepare the various questions.

The all-German council of the confederation will not have the right to issue instructions to the parliaments and governments of the two German states. It will only make recommendations. The two contracting parties shall retain their sovereignty and equality of rights within the confederation.

The confederation shall only be of a provisional nature. It shall cease to exist as soon as the provisions of the peace treaty have been implemented, the reunification of Germany effected and all-German elections for a national assembly held.

The preparation of such elections will also form part of the duties of the German confederation. For this purpose a special body may be set up under the council of the confederation to deal with the questions of drawing up the constitution for the future united German state.

The government of the German Democratic Republic intends to present in due time a detailed plan for establishing a German confederation on the basis of the above principles. We think that a major discussion should be conducted on these proposals in all political parties and organizations, for the formation of a German confederation under present conditions is the only realistic way to re-establish the unity of our country.

What can the peoples of the anti-imperialist and capitalist states do to facilitate the peaceful solution of the German question?

It follows from the existence of two German states that a peaceful solution of the German question could be considerably promoted if all states maintained normal diplomatic, economic and cultural relations with both German states. The Bonn government indulges in a policy of intrigue against the GDR in foreign countries because it does not want a peaceful solution of the German question. But the peoples of both the newly independent anti-imperialist states and of the capitalist countries do not feel any inclination to let themselves be drawn into adventures by the West German militarists. The Soviet Union's proposal for the conclusion of a peace treaty shows what great importance it would have if as many states as possible spoke out in favour of this draft and decided now to establish normal relations with the peaceful German state, the GDR. The unilateral diplomatic relations of the states of the West with the Bonn government constitute an encouragement of the aggressive militarist forces in West Germany.

All states desiring understanding and a peaceful solution of the German question could express their desire by establishing diplomatic relations with the German Democratic Republic. He who wants peace and is willing to do something for it cannot but establish normal relations with the first peace state in Germany, the German Democratic Republic.

Open Letter to Konrad Adenauer

23 January 1960

To the Chairman of the CDU/CSU,

Herr Dr. Konrad Adenauer

Bonn

The signs of change in world policy from cold war to peaceful coexistence, and the necessity that particularly we Germans make a contribution to relaxing international tension, prompt me to write to you.

I must say–quite frankly–that I have no illusions as to your past policy and the aims of your government. Ever since leading political forces in West Germany, under your leadership, introduced a separate currency, set up the west zone state and began to arm, the clouds of a national catastrophe have been gathering over Germany.

As early as 1950 we proposed to you the formation of an all-German council and the preparation of a peace treaty in the belief that this was the only way to reunification. Unfortunately, already then, you rejected joint preparations for free, democratic, all-German elections because you thought that, with arms and a policy of military pressure, you could force the annexation of the German Democratic Republic.

You answered our proposal for a peaceful solution of the German question with a coup d'état and took it upon yourself to sign the Paris Treaties and link West Germany with NATO and so rend Germany asunder.

In past years and particularly last year the CDU/CSU leadership sacrificed every chance of reunifying Germany, as well as any possibility of relaxing international tension, for what I must call the very short-sighted policy of armament and revenge. You have rejected everything which could have served the cause of peace. It will not have escaped your attention that West Germany is becoming more and more isolated as a result.

225

Naturally, I am not writing to you because I am concerned about the isolation of your government. You certainly don't expect that of me anyway. But I am bound to approach you because you and your party still exercise power in West Germany. I am taking this step because there is nothing I will not try—not a single thing—to divert you and your party members from a path detrimental to the national interests of the German people and European peace.

The speech which your Minister Strauss made to NATO induced me to write this letter. This speech agreed with the political introduction to your report on your government's activities in 1959. Our people have hardly recovered from the catastrophe of the Hitler war when the West German federal government again begins to lead the West German state back on to the same path. Basically your government has given the West German army the very same tasks which once faced the Hitler Wehrmacht. Is it so difficult to calculate that the policy of the ruling military circles which has already failed in two world wars can, in the present period, only end in a dreadful catastrophe?

It would obviously be useless to attempt to convince each other on political aims. But I would like to suppose that it is not entirely impossible to reach a certain measure of agreement, at least on a few fundamental questions which concern all Germans.

I am thinking here, for example, of the life and future existence of the German nation which is endangered by your policy. For example, the question of a nuclear war on German soil which all Germans with normal powers of reasoning should be interested in preventing, irrespective of their world outlook or party membership. I still resist the belief that you consciously consider the possibility of a nuclear war on German soil to be part of your policy as many of your closest associates apparently do, which would lead among other things to the physical extermination of large sections of the West German population, as Hitler once considered all eventualities including as you know, the elimination of the German nation.

I believe that everything possible must be done to prevent Germany from being the point of departure for a third world war.

You will answer that you do not want war. That is quite possible. Former political rulers have said the same. Even Hitler believed that he could step by step impose German military and fascist rule upon other countries without war.

It is a contradiction to speak of peace and to speed up atomic armament in West Germany. The German people's experiences teach that armament, aimed at revenge, can only lead to ever larger conflicts and war. But this time it is not a question of a war that could be compared with previous wars.

West German armament and the inevitable war provocation from West Germany which result from the policy of revenge would act as a boomerang and the unavoidable counterblow would descend upon West Germany as though it were a magnet. This would mean the annihilation of the majority of the German people.

At the NATO ministerial meeting on 16 December 1959 the remarks that your Minister of War Strauss made on this point seem to confirm the worst apprehensions. In connection with demands that the West German NATO army should be armed with atomic weapons and that nuclear weapons should be stored in West Germany, Herr Strauss declared in Paris:

"Despite the high population density in the Federal Republic we are prepared to carry the burden attached to this and to bear the responsibility to our own people for the risks involved!"

And on Herr Strauss' orders, the general staff of the West German army is already working out plans for the evacuation of millions of West German citizens. This is, indeed, insanity, Herr Adenauer, but indicative of the methods.

Do you really agree with this, Herr Adenauer?

Are you really prepared to take the risk on behalf of the German people, for instance, of the physical annihilation of large sections of the West German population in a nuclear war on German territory?

Have you, like your minister of war, made allowance for this in your political plans?

I would like to have a plain answer to this question and I take it for granted that all Germans in East and West are entitled to demand from you this clear answer.

But please do not try to make us believe the stale nonsense that West Germany needs atomic armament because it is threatened, and intends to prevent atomic war with the help of atomic bombs. Nobody is threatening West Germany. No ordinary person in the whole world believes that the Soviet Union or the German Democratic Republic is threatening West Germany. If you believe it yourself, why not support such far-reaching proposals for general and complete disarmament as were put forward by Prime Minister N. S. Khrushchov at the United Nations General Assembly? By participating in preparations for a peace treaty with Germany, you could have proposed international guarantees ensuring a peaceful future for Germany. Instead of this you are the only prime minister in Europe demanding territorial changes and revenge.

Neither the Soviet Union, the German Democratic Republic nor other peoples' democracies have made any sort of demand in respect of the territory or the political regime in West Germany. Nobody has demanded that capitalism in West Germany be abolished by action from outside. It is the West German population's own internal affair to determine their economic system and form of government.

But because the CDU/CSU, under your leadership, demands revenge and fights for the revision of the decisions of the Potsdam Agreement, West Germany has become a trouble-maker in Europe and the world. The demands for revenge, the talk about "liberating eastern countries" and the simultaneous speed-up in the arms drive, are reminiscent of methods used by ruling circles in Germany from 1933 to 1939.

Herr Dr. Adenauer, you have repeatedly declared that you are in favour of disarmament. I take you at your word.

It is known to you that the Soviet government through Prime Minister Khrushchov made a reasoned proposal to the United Nations General Assembly on general and complete disarmament. In line with this proposal, the Soviet Union unilaterally set an example and reduced its military forces by one-third.

At a moment when leading statesmen are concerned with the question of general and complete disarmament, and are seriously taking steps to disarmament and to dissolving foreign military bases, has not the time come for Germany, in particular, to show its own initiative in this question?

Would it not be a blessing for the German people if both states agreed on complete disarmament?

What would be the outcome? The German people would live in peace. Their ingenuity would enable them to accomplish outstanding peaceful work resulting in true well-being. If a break with the past could be made in this manner, peaceful relations could develop between the German people and all other peoples and states. Our two German states, situated in the centre of Western Europe, would, under conditions of disarmament and the conclusion of a peace treaty, be in a better position to reach unification quickly.

How would it be if both German states were to agree to a plebiscite on general and complete disarmament and the conclusion of a peace treaty based on the United Nations Charter?

We deeply regret, Herr Adenauer, that you use so much energy arming, while declaring that you are in favour of disarmament.

Why do you speed up the arms drive and unsettle negotiations between the great powers preparing the Summit Conference?

Why are you not prepared to renounce atomic armament in West Germany?

Why do you abuse the people's democratic right to reject atomic armament through a plebiscite?

Why do you reject the arms stop?

Why are you not prepared to conclude an agreement between the two German states on the strength, equipment and location of military forces?

You refer to your Christian beliefs. Does it not correspond to Christian teachings to renounce force, and to testify to this by signing an agreement between both German states renouncing the use of force?

We judge very seriously the fact that there are no signs of willingness on your part to cooperate in a German contribution to the maintenance of peace and the improvement of international relations in Europe.

If, as you say, you want peace, it is madness to train West German troops for an aggressive war against the East and to store nuclear weapons on West German territory. But if you really are opposed to nuclear war on German territory, please prove this by your deeds and take steps to see that atomic and hydrogen weapons of all descriptions are banned from German territory. Here, pious words are of no avail. Deeds alone count.

During the last ten years you have waged a cold war aimed at undermining the GDR and, by a surprise attack, you intend to cause a civil war in Germany to supply you with your motive for a military advance to the East. You cannot deny that you have not succeeded in accomplishing this cold war aim. And it cannot be accomplished. The people of the German Democratic Republic are proud of their work of the last ten years and remain steadfast to their achievement, the first workers' and peasants' state in Germany.

The historic struggle between reactionary and progressive forces in Germany resulted in the existence of two German states.

One state embodies the traditions of German militarism and revenge policy.

The other state embodies the best humanist traditions of the German people and the realization of the aims of the German working-class movement founded under the leadership of Marx, Engels, Bebel and Liebknecht.

The forces of German finance capital determine the policy of the leadership of your party, the CDU/CSU. The Socialist Unity Party is the party of the working class which in alliance with the working

229

farmers, the intelligentsia, the small tradesman and businessmen, has succeeded in unifying all peace-loving and progressive forces in the National Front of Democratic Germany.

I do not intend to argue with you which is the legitimate German state, that is to say, the state which represents the true national interests of the German people.

The legitimate German state can only be that which fights in the spirit of the anti-Hitler coalition against the rebirth of German militarism and fascism and facilitates the reunification of our German fatherland by negotiating a peace treaty.

I quite understand your desire for the non-existence of the GDR. The fact that the GDR exists is the great obstacle in the way of the old German imperialist policy of aggression and conquest which you and your political friends would like to continue.

But you, too, should realize that there is obviously no sense in denying the existence of facts which everyone can see and the existence of which can be verified by all. I cannot believe you are so foolish as to assert that a rock on which you have just knocked your nose, does not exist. The fact that the rock exists does not depend upon your recognition. Your government spends hundreds of millions of marks on financing gangs of spies and criminals who organize crime in the GDR, which obviously does not burden your Christian conscience.

All your statements that you are unable to negotiate with the GDR because you cannot support the "impossible two-state theory" is empty talk. This is not a question of some theory but of the fact that the Hitler war and the fight for the liquidation of militarism and fascism in Germany resulted in two German states.

When you refuse to negotiate with the GDR, you do this in order to keep your hands free for military aggression, and that means for war. We know your war minister's plans to speed up atomic armament for a blitzkrieg against the GDR.

You know as well as I do that manoeuvres in West Germany in 1959 took place with this idea in mind. The leaderships of the West German political parties are aware of this military conception even though for fear of you they speak of it only in small circles. These war plans are behind your cross-fire against preparations for a Summit Conference.

You can hardly expect us to believe you when, in such a situation, you talk about peace and your actions prove the contrary.

Misuse of the word peace has caused the German people untold suffering in the past, but they have gained ample experience. No doubt you still remember that the more the Hitler regime talked about peace, the more feverishly it armed and consequently the day drew nearer when it was ready to attack other countries. When Hitler believed himself to be at the peak of his success, he disclosed his formula. I am convinced that you know it. The Hitler formula was more or less like this:

First speak only of peace to distract attention from the arms drive; suppress opposition or break its resistance so that it can no longer operate; promote a feeling of revenge, propagate the aims of conquest one at a time, connected with assurances that these aims should only be attained by peaceful means; finally, when fully armed, begin psychological preparations for the use of force and war.

Do you not think, Herr Dr. Adenauer, that your government shows a remarkable lack of embarrassment at having adopted this formula?

To begin with, you, too, talked only of peace and even coined the phrase of the hand that might wither rather then ever touch a weapon again.

Then—accompanied by tirades on peace—you began a feverish arms drive, whereby at first you rejected with disgust any thought of equipping the West German NATO army with atomic weapons.

The policy of atomic armament followed, and with it the ban on the Communist Party and a ban on and persecution of many democratic organizations.

Hand in hand with this you promoted the feeling of revenge and propagated aims of conquest, at the same time giving assurances that this could only be achieved by peaceful means. Who can be expected to believe that?

The more your arms program nears completion—you are aiming at being ready by the end of 1961 or in 1962—the more your regime in West Germany under your personal participation increases its internal political terror against all supporters of peace and opponents of atomic war, while psychologically preparing the West German population for a switch-over to the open use of force, that is, to the systematically prepared war of revenge.

It naturally follows that your policy of revenge is connected with the development of facist ideology, race-hatred and anti-Semitism. I know that you reject the swastika. Former Hitler officers reject it, too, because they suffered defeat under this symbol.

Naturally you are in favour of a different symbol which is not so discredited. That is, however, not decisive.

It is unavoidable that many people in West Germany, who do not clearly understand the intricacies of your tactics, are encouraged by your policy of revenge and come out into the open and show the true face of German militarism and its race hatred.

If we take into account that this policy of yours is being carried out, in the main, by people who practised the same policy under Hitler, then you need not be surprised that not only GDR citizens, but many other peoples and their governments watch your steps with the greatest distrust, and take the necessary precautions to nip in the bud any new German imperialist aggression or—as far as governments closely connected with you are concerned—take steps to see that they are not dragged into a suicidal adventure.

You have a habit, Herr Dr. Adenauer, of decisively rejecting any comparison of your policy with the policy of the Hitler regime. You emphasize that you yourself were not a follower of Hitler and that you even came into certain conflicts with the nazi regime. I will not dispute that. But the fact that you were not a public supporter of Hitler does not prevent you, as far as one can see, from continuing Hitler's policy of revenge and conquest using slightly altered methods, allowing for the completely changed international situation.

Neo-fascism and anti-Semitism are running wild on the fertile soil of your military-clerical regime. Almost all sections of your state apparatus, including the police, the judiciary and also the schools, colleges, literary life, etc., are affected by this fascist restoration.

It is really no merit to your present government that it does not openly favour anti-Semitism. Germany is discredited by anti-Semitism to such an extent that only narrow-minded fascists would back this horse today. But the swastikas on the synagogues, the desecrated cemeteries and desecrated monuments to the victims of the Hitler regime prove all too clearly how abundantly these weeds flourish in your allegedly so free and democratic rose garden.

Are you actually completely aware of what you are doing? You are, after all, a rose gardener? Aren't you astonished that the plants you so carefully tended sprout brown blossoms with steel helmets, and vultures often enough adorned with swastikas?

Let me put it quite frankly. The aggressive imperialist and militarist plans which you, your government and your general staff pursue are a threat to the future of the German people as a nation.

It is absolutely incomprehensible to me how you can hope for the success of such an aggressive policy. The German ruling class has already plunged our people into two catastrophic wars. Is it not obvious that Germany will never progress through force and war?

I have already said that your plans are well known to us and that not only the GDR, but also our allies, are taking the necessary defensive measures. Apparently you were not prepared to listen to warnings from the Soviet Union and the government of the German Democratic Republic and wrongly interpreted our drive for peace. I therefore publicly inform you that

if the West German federal government does not end atomic armament in the near future and introduce a general arms stop, the government of the German Democratic Republic will be compelled to take necessary defence measures and will apply to its allies for rocket weapons to be put at its disposal. Your atomic war preparations and revenge policy literally drive us into a position where we are forced to take defensive measures.

According to the speech made by Minister of War Strauss to NATO and preparations of your general staff, you are speculating with the idea that, as a result of international negotiations, our allies will be prevented from taking immediate action to come to the aid of the GDR, in accordance with their obligations in the event of a military provocation by the Bonn government.

If, therefore, other arguments cannot convince you, it is to be hoped that the presence of modern rockets on GDR soil will help you to recognize once and for all that your plans of revenge are doomed to failure.

Nobody reasonably capable to some extent of assessing the relation of forces in the world can doubt that within a few minutes of a military attack on the German Democratic Republic, Bonn and other military centres in West Germany will have ceased to exist.

What do you actually hope to gain from your aggressive policy? Are you absolutely determined to speed up radically the end of capitalist rule in West Germany?

We certainly have no reason to prolong the rule of monopoly capitalism in West Germany or to regret its decline.

We are not fighting for peace in order to extend this rule. But we are against war. We want to protect the German people from the fate of an atomic war on German soil.

Thus we discuss even with you, although we have no illusions about your plans. Thus we attempt to persuade you to change your course. And if humanist reasons have no effect upon you, we hope at least that you are still capable of assessing the true relation of forces.

Let me give you some advice: throw your plans for a war of conquest in the East into the waste-paper basket.

Think seriously for once about the atomic inferno awaiting the West German population, your children and your grandchildren, if your policy is applied.

Do not play with atomic war, cancel the atomic armament of the West German NATO Army.

Give the people of West Germany the right to decide for themselves on atomic armament and a peace treaty.

You yourself once said that people should not live in fear. How can West German citizens not live in fear under the Damocles sword of atomic armament?

The German people can only live free from fear if atomic armament is cancelled in West Germany and the militarists and revanchists brought to a halt.

Listen to reason at last and stop being a trouble-maker during preparations for the Summit Conference and other possible international conferences to ease tension and promote understanding. If representatives of the USA realize that the continuation of a policy directed at war is equivalent to national suicide and that it is necessary to direct policy into the channels of peaceful competition between countries with different social systems, then you and your political friends should also recognize this. Are you so afraid of the prospect of peaceful competition between the two German states that you prefer to drag our people into a catastrophe?

You maintain that we are introducing communism into West Germany through our peace proposals. You have distributed posters throughout West Germany to impress this upon the population. Obviously you thus wish to divert attention from your own aggressive plans.

People here were greatly astonished that at a time when the German people were hoping for relaxation, you misused your Christmas message to disturb festivities by spreading slander, hatred and threats of aggression. If, although you know better, you bear false witness against the GDR and speak of misery, poverty, the suppression of religious service and slavery in the GDR, only to justify your stupid demands for "liberation", this shows that you have set the course for war.

Let me be quite frank on this point. I neither believe you are so badly informed that your misrepresentations of the GDR are explained by lack of knowledge, nor do I consider you so inexperienced that you are not aware to what terrible end such a policy leads. In the final analysis, you are not a greenhorn in politics. We can therefore only come to the conclusion that by slandering the GDR and other socialist countries you are consciously sowing hatred in order to prepare the population of West Germany for civil war in Germany and a war of revenge.

I would like to give you a sober, matter-of-fact answer to your tirades of hate: You are living in the past, following the footsteps of reactionary forces of the old Germany. You are dreaming of the Carlovingian Empire, of the German knights who crusaded in the East and of the clerical rule of the middle ages. You are integrating these dead ideas of the past with plans for a West European economic and arms community.

We find it difficult to understand why you and your Minister of War Strauss oppose a German nation-state. You are obviously allowing yourself to be guided by the interests of the 25 trust groups in West Germany which, under the protection of supranational agreements, are out to exploit foreign territories. Of what use to the German people are these links to finance groups in western countries? What has West Germany's participation in NATO brought the German people other than deepening the rift between the two parts of Germany?

Put Germany first for once. Only here in Germany can the roots of the future peace-loving, democratic Germany be found and not in Paris with NATO.

Listen to the voice of the West German population which greatly desires a peaceful solution of the German question. Your "little Europe" policy and the abandonment of the idea of German reunification is against the national sentiments of our people.

What use to the German people would Bonn's domination of Western Europe be? It is an idea built on sand anyway. The peaceful solution of the German question is the greatest national task facing the German people.

Think of Germany and help to utilize the great opportunity offered to the German people by the Summit Conference and the international conference which will probably follow.

Talks at the Geneva Conference and between Prime Minister Khrushchov and President Eisenhower on the question of disarmament, a peace treaty with Germany and the peaceful solution of the West Berlin question prove that steady progress can be made by a policy of mutual understanding and negotiations. The Soviet Union's proposal to create the basis for the German people themselves to achieve a peaceful and democratic reunification through a peace treaty is in the national interest of our people and makes possible a peaceful future for our nation.

In his speech in New Delhi President Eisenhower said that war is made by people who are influenced by the past, the dead past, by men who believe that the problems of mankind can be solved by force. Political leaders in West Germany must free themselves from the dead past. They must, as President Eisenhower said, forget the past and face the future together.

The reason why other nations look upon your government as a trouble-maker is that your "policy of strength" which only contemplates a solution by using force, is in contradiction to the real relation of forces in the world. Leave the evil traditions of revenge policy and race hatred to the past, turn your attention to the best traditions of our people, the traditions of humanism and friendship among the peoples. Help to put an end to the disastrous circle of crisis–arms-boom–war–post-war boom–rearmament–war, which still grips West Germany today.

Our national question is to overcome the contradiction between our people's peace interests and the aggressive plans of certain ruling circles in West Germany. The way to a solution is a policy of relaxation, of rapprochement and understanding between the two German states and their participation in the preparation for a peace treaty.

The aim of the Socialist Unity Party and the National Front is to prove to the whole of the German people with a policy of peace, democracy and progress, that the whole German people can live in peace, prosperity and happiness in a united Germany as long as West German ruling circles are halted in their policy of militarism, revenge and the restoration of fascism.

Last year, true to these principles, the GDR persevered in making a German contribution to peace. We were, and still are, above all, working for the conclusion of a peace treaty with Germany which would finally, after 15 years, close the books on the Second World War and thus eliminate dangerous inflammable material which could cause a new catastrophe. We demand that agencies and spy centres in West Berlin be cleared out and that this potential hot-bed of war be changed into a peaceful, Free City whose inhabitants themselves select their form of government. This aim will be achieved sooner or later in the interest of the security and liberty of the West Berliners and of peace in Europe.

Although you have rejected all our proposals we have always been ready for cooperation between the two German states. We even invited you to visit the German Democratic Republic on the assumption that our Prime Minister Otto Grotewohl could return that visit to West Germany. You rejected all these proposals.

You maintain that we are interfering in the internal affairs of West Germany and intend to impose socialist democracy upon it. We have no such intentions. We are one section of our peace-loving people and

seek only a peaceful future for Germany which is only possible in a

Germany without militarism and fascism. As long as West Germany continues to build up atomic armament and prepares for a war of revenge, we are of course obliged to carry out our peace propaganda in West Germany in order to prevent war.

In connection with a treaty on the renunciation of the use of force and the formation of an all-German commission we are prepared to conclude a mutual non-intervention agreement. This would lead to improved relations between the two German states.

I assume that you fully understand that in view of the high standard of missile technology, the question is of war or peace. You know very well that Minister of War Strauss' speech and West German revenge policy leave you no chance to deny responsibility for military provocations in the same way that you deny that the Bonn government has anything to do with anti-Semitic outrages and swastika daubing.

Take heed of the new situation and remember our people who can only exist in peace. Think of our fatherland which can only be reunited as a peaceful state.

We shall continue to do all we can to promote relaxation in Germany, to fight against any military and revenge policy and put the case for a peace treaty with Germany to the great powers to clear the way for the reunification of our German fatherland in peace and freedom.

Think over thoroughly whether it is not in your interest, too, for representatives of both German states to meet on a parity basis as soon as possible in an all-German commission to consider such questions as how to safeguard peace in Germany, how to draw up a peace treaty and how to overcome the division of Germany step by step.

In the hope that you will give serious thought to this letter and that it encourages frank, matter-of-fact discussion on "peace or war" and the reunification of our German fatherland into a peace-loving democratic, progressive state,

I remain,

Walter Ulbricht
First Secretary of the Central Committee
of the Socialist Unity Party of Germany,
First Vice-Chairman
of the Council of Ministers of the GDR

The People's Plan for Germany

Open letter of the Central Committee of the Socialist Unity Party of Germany
to West German Workers of 17 April 1960

Dear West German Workers,

Just like you, the social democratic, Christian and non-party workers of West Germany, we, too, are worried about the maintenance of peace, relations between the two German states and the future of the German nation. We appeal to you, because without understanding between the working people, understanding between the governments hardly seems possible. It is absolutely necessary that we approach each other and reach agreement on questions decisive for the life and future of our people. Time presses. The date of the Summit Conference is drawing near. We should hurry so that the German people do not once more miss the chance of peace. What we do not do today, we will have to do tomorrow, in more difficult and perhaps more dangerous circumstances.

You know that it took the kaiser's empire about fifteen years to prepare the First World War and to lead the German people into catastrophe. Fifteen years after the First World War the night of fascism closed in upon Germany and with it, as everybody knows today, the Second World War which plunged the German people into an even greater catastrophe, today fifteen years have passed since the end of the Second World War, and we see the same old forces active in West Germany, feverishly preparing a new war which in the era of atomic weapons threatens the physical existence of the German nation.

You know the facts. The atomic armament of the West German army is going ahead without regard to your wishes and your democratic right of decision. You may not agree with this, but that scarcely moves the rulers of West Germany. Missile bases are being erected next to your homes and places of work, threatening magnets which, in an emergency, will concentrate death and destruction on you. You may be against the activities of the militarists. But already the old Hitler generals are drilling your sons for a civil war against the GDR's working people, and to be sacrificed in a hopeless revanchist war against the socialist countries, just as your fathers and brothers were senselessly sacrificed in the First and Second World Wars.

You know all this. You know about the manoeuvre "Winter Shield" and the staff exercise "Side Step" which were rehearsals for a blitzkrieg against the German Democratic Republic. You know the drafts for the emergency laws and the emergency service law which are to give the ruling circles in Bonn the possibility of preparing war more quickly and, to this end, controlling the working class more closely. You know the plans to establish military bases in Spain and in other countries. Like us you are shocked and dismayed at the evacuation plans according to which 14 million West German men, women, children and old people are to be driven on the road to death on X Day. Even your own papers write that there is already in West Germany an atmosphere "as though it will break out tomorrow." Remember that it is a year since the Social Democratic Party of Germany published its Plan for Germany which began with the warning: "The German people face a terrible danger." Since then the danger has grown.

Adenauer and Strauss, Globke and Oberländer, Speidel and Heusinger, Blank and Schröder, 1,100 Hitler hanging judges and the SS and Gestapo leaders in the police force have no use for democracy and freedom in their plans—the democracy and freedom so much talked of, and so abused in the Federal Republic. Democracy and freedom, as well as social rights and health services, including health insurance, are being reduced step by step.

The democratic right of self-determination is also denied you by the ruling circles. What kind of self-determination is there when an atomic war is being systematically prepared against the wishes of the people? The West German revenge politicians understand the right of self-determination as their "right" to prepare and unleash war. The right of self-determination was understood in the same way under the kaiser and under Hitler. No German should forget that Hitler attacked Austria, Czechoslovakia and Poland under the pretence of self-determination.

By the right of self-determination, the German people understand first and foremost the democratic right to prevent war and preparations for war in all circumstances. All responsible Germans, the German workers and their organizations in both German states must fight together for this elementary right of self-determination for our nation.

Let us fight together then! All German people should decide in a plebiscite whether or not they agree with our proposal that both German states should renounce atomic armament. All German people should also decide whether they agree or not with our proposal for complete disarmament in both German states.

A person's attitude toward this proposal shows whether he is really for self-determination of the German people or is only misusing the term "self-determination" for fraudulent ends in the interests of NATO policy.

Let national peaceful interests and national reason have their say!

We have spoken of our common anxiety concerning relations between the two German states. Why are relations between the two German states so decisive for the fate of the nation? Let us consider the matter quite soberly.

At present there are only three alternatives for the German people.

First alternative: The Road of War

One German state tries to conquer the other by force. This would mean a terrible civil war, a war in which German workers fight against German workers, German farmers against German farmers, German citizens against German citizens and which would unleash an atomic world war about the result of which there can be no doubt. This is the policy at present pursued by the Bonn government, which plans a civil war and war of revenge under the slogan of "liberation" if its attempted blackmail with atomic weapons is unsuccessful.

We must state quite frankly that no attempts at blackmail and threats of a war of revenge can impress the GDR and the socialist camp. The relation of forces throughout the world today is obviously such that it is completely out of the question for the West German militarists to take over power in the whole of Germany. Blitzkrieg would be blitz-suicide. 1960 is not 1933.

Those who believe that the West German government is so powerful today are mistaken. They should remember the words of Bertolt Brecht: "The great do not remain great, nor do the small remain small. The night has twelve hours, then comes the day." It is well known that the world has changed and is changing ever more rapidly in favour of socialism.

Herr Adenauer knows, of course, that atomic war means the total destruction of West Germany. This is why the Bonn government is seeking military bases and facilities for retreat and refuge for the West German government in Spain and other places outside West Germany.

This first alternative is unacceptable to you, to us, to the German people.

Second alternative: Deepening the Division of Germany

Strong outside influence and the resistance of the Germans themselves prevent a war. Thus peace would be saved, but without understanding between the two German states there would still be no rapprochement nor the beginnings of reunification. Twenty or thirty years could thus be lost for reunification. This is the aim of Adenauer's policy. If its aggressive military plans do not succeed, the present Bonn government will in all circumstances try to prevent the reunification of Germany. The aim of these gentlemen is that if they cannot rule over Germany then Germany must remain divided. Basically this is the old reactionary conception of the Carolingian Reich at the cost of the unity of the German nation. Neither this everlasting division of Germany nor a German civil war and a war of revenge must be allowed to become a fact. We cannot be satisfied with this alternative. The road to understanding between the two German states must be found under all circumstances.

Third alternative: Understanding and Peace

The workers in East and West come to an understanding and through their joint struggle bring about an understanding between the two German states. Through the conclusion of a peace treaty with the two German states, the remains of the Second World War will finally be liquidated. The third world war will be prevented. West German militarism will be eliminated. An understanding between the German workers in East and West and between the two German states will be implemented on the basis of a national compromise, acceptable not only to the workers in West Germany and the German Democratic Republic but also to other classes and sections of the population including the West German bourgeoisie. This is the one and only possible Plan for Germany for every reasonable and responsible German. This is the People's Plan for Germany.

Such a national compromise is the foundation for peaceful reunification of the German nation. Why is this so? The citizens of the German Democratic Republic have long ago and finally decided their governmental and social system and do not tolerate any interference from the West German Federal Republic. The citizens of West Germany should use their own judgment in deciding on the governmental and social system in West Germany without any interference from the GDR. Both German states will then come to an understanding about the future. This is true self-determination. This is also the basic idea of confederation, of a German federation, in which the two German states are linked with each other on a basis of parity. This is the only remaining way to the peaceful reunification of Germany. No one in Germany except the incorrigible militarists and revenge-seekers would lose anything by it. But every individual and the nation as a whole would benefit by it. We would all win peace and the right of self-determination, overcome the division of Germany and strengthen international esteem for Germany. We workers would benefit, the farmers, the craftsmen and small businessmen and the intellectuals would benefit and even big businessmen would not do so badly; atomic weapons have no respect for shares. The removal of the enormous armament burden in West Germany and the rapidly growing possibilities of the huge socialist world market would guarantee German industry full employment for a long time, thereby guaranteeing the workers their jobs and protecting them from the inevitable fluctuations on the capitalist world market.

Some people speak about a "freezing" of the military status as a result of which everything else would follow automatically. They simply mean, however, that the two German states would each leave its system of alliance and they obviously do not want any change in the rule of the militarists and revanchists and their armament plans. The "military status" that the German people need must consist of the abolition of atomic and rocket bases and over and above this, general and complete disarmament. This would indeed be a big step forward. There is only one good "military status" for Germany: that is general and complete disarmament.

The implementation of the People's Plan for Germany can be decisively encouraged through the forthcoming Summit Conference. If we agree on this point, West German colleagues, then we must reach an understanding on our common standpoint at the Summit Conference. We have a great common interest in the success of the forthcoming Summit Conference. We should therefore do everything in our power to contribute towards this success instead of obstructing the conference as the Bonn government is doing. We should not allow ourselves to wait passively.

The Great Responsibility of the Social Democratic Party of Germany

Some years ago some people in West Germany had hoped that it would be possible to conquer the GDR by subversion and through military pressure exerted by the Adenauer government. In this connection some social democrats hoped to be admitted into a coalition led by Adenauer's Christian Democratic Union. This was always unrealistic. But political speculators seldom trouble themselves with realities. The Ostbüro was ordered to work against the GDR and anti-communist propaganda was made the central question of policy. Who profited by the Ostbüro's activities? Does a single West German worker profit from sabotage in a nationally-owned enterprise of the GDR or in an agricultural production cooperative? Or do any of you perhaps need espionage reports from the GDR or falsified documents designed to obstruct the GDR's economic development? You certainly do not. These are activities which only serve Adenauer's policies. In the GDR we are able to cope with the provocateurs and saboteurs of the Ostbüro whose cooperation with the official West German espionage service is by no means accidental. This is not the point.

But this policy is directed against you, the West German workers, and your interests.

The GDR was to have been attacked as long ago as 1957. This can be confirmed by those SPD officials who—on various boards of trustees and "research councils"—have been working out senseless programs for the re-establishment of capitalist rule in the GDR. But these policies had and have no chance of success. They did not lead to anything and they cannot lead to anything in the future either, except a petrification of German division. We hope that the Social Democratic Party executive does not want to be an accessory to this.

We ask you, social democratic workers: if the German policy of Adenauer and Strauss has already led into a blind alley is it absolutely necessary for the SPD to follow them? Surely it is a question of abolishing the power of these reactionary militarists in West Germany, which is only possible in cooperation with the GDR, and not of maintaining their power by undermining the GDR. Why does the SPD leadership want to tie itself to the West German imperialists' policy? This policy has no prospects.

It lies in your own interest, in the interest of all German workers, in the interest of Germany's peaceful future, to see to it that a decisive change takes place in your party's policies on the questions of peace, the German problem and relations with the German Democratic Republic; to see to it that the road of understanding between the German workers and between the two German states is smoothed and taken. Without such an understanding you will never be able to remove militarism. It is still not too late. It is not yet too late finally to take a determined stand against a militarism that is overgrowing

16*

democracy and against the mad revanchist policy. Surely this is the least that could be expected from a party like the SPD.

Please understand us correctly. In this connection we criticize the policy pursued by some of your leaders, not because it is not a socialist policy—although we regret this very much. We criticize the fact that some of your party leaders are injuring the peaceful and democratic interests of the West German workers and citizens and the national interests of the German people by abandoning their own Plan for Germany. Party leaders will not be pardoned if they allow an adventurer like Strauss to push them around. Quite frankly, we do not want the SPD to get lost in a morass under pressure from the militarists and to the benefit of the Adenauer government. But this danger threatens. Erler, Mommer and Wehner are already adopting a more than doubtful attitude. They have abandoned their own conception of reunification for the benefit of Adenauer and Strauss. They decline a policy of conciliation between the two German states. They are not taking serious action against a militarism that is overgrowing democracy. They lack all courage before Adenauer's throne. How much longer, dear social democratic friends, are you going to look on? Who else can change things but you? Napoleon said on one occasion that even an army of lions cannot conquer if it is led by lambs. This can also be applied to a party.

What are we to do in this situation in Germany? This is the question we ask you, workers from West Germany. Are you, too, of the opinion—as shown by some questions West German citizens put to us—that we have no choice but to resign ourselves to the fact that an understanding in Germany has become impossible; that at the very worst, our country will become the scene of civil war and atomic world war; and that at the best, a war might be prevented but that the division of Germany can no longer be overcome? Should we resign ourselves to such a prospect for our German people? We are not prepared to resign and we are convinced that you, the West German workers, are not prepared to do so, either. There is already a movement against the threatening developments in West Germany. Workers stage token strikes and demonstrations against the deterioration of social services. The people of towns and villages protest against atomic rocket bases and the militarist government's measures of oppression, such as, for instance, the "emergency law". There are also strikes for higher wages and the right of co-determination in industry.

The West German working class is indeed a great force! The 6.2 million trade union members with their resistance to militarism and the threat of atomic death are a force to be reckoned with. At congresses held by the West German Trade Union Federation–the DGB–, at innumerable trade union meetings and conferences, trade unionists time and time again warned against the development of the militarist state, of atomic armament and of all armament policy. However, pursuing the same policy as Erler, Mommer and Wehner, the right-wing DGB leaders are giving more and more room to Adenauer's endeavours to coordinate the trade union leadership with his fatal policy. This has already had disastrous effects on the West German workers, as is proved, for instance, by the attack on health insurance, the decisions made against the engineering workers' union (IG Metall) and the continuous price increases. Those trade union members and workers who offer determined trade union resistance to militarism and armament burdens and who demand that a persistent struggle be put up for peace and rapprochement between the two German states, are right. Just think: the thousands of millions now being wasted on armament and preparations for an attack on the GDR could be utilized for social and cultural purposes and for the benefit of the working masses if a policy of peace and understanding between two German states, based primarily on the unity of action of the working class, were to be pursued in West Germany.

The situation is developing so dangerously that no worker can afford to sit back with arms folded, waiting for what may come. If the militarists in Bonn, Adenauer, Strauss, Oberländer, Schröder and their incorrigible Hitler generals once manage to kindle the fires of war, who will be the first to pay? The workers and their families, the whole of the working people. This was the case in the First and Second World War, and if things go according to the wishes of the gentlemen in Bonn it will be the same in a third world war.

What can be done in this situation? That is the question you will ask us. And indeed, this question is asked by many West German workers who have lately approached us, the Central Committee of the Socialist Unity Party of Germany. They see the danger but they see no way out. We have shown them the way out, the way which leads to peace for our German people and at the same time to understanding and the overcoming of the division of Germany. And this is the way we must walk jointly, in both German states, through understanding between the workers, the workers' parties and organizations–social democratic as well as Christian. This is what we must fight for. We are certain that the day must and will come when the SED, the SPD, the KPD, the trade unions and the Christian workers' organizations will come to an understanding concerning the future of Germany. There will be negotiations between executive members of the SED,

the SPD, the KPD, the trade unions and other democratic mass organizations as well as official negotiations. But there are many obstacles as yet. There are obscurities and prejudices, differences of
opinion and artificially stirred up conflicts.

German Workers in East and West Are Brothers

Some people say that there is no common interest between the
workers in East and West nor between the workers' parties and the
trade unions in both parts of Germany. This would please the enemies
of the working class but it is not so. You are German workers and
we are German workers. We are brothers and sisters of the great
family of German working people. We have a long common history
of class struggle, misery, the struggle for peace, freedom, human rights
and democracy. It can not be otherwise than that we remain brothers
and complete our joint struggle and together lead the German people
into a peaceful, happy and prosperous future. Apart from the working
class, which as a result of historical development is called upon to
undertake the leadership of the nation, there is no other force in
Germany capable of uniting all peace-loving democratic forces of the
various classes and strata. If we do not do this jointly then Germany
faces a dark future.

The Five Common Interests of the Whole of Germany

Unity of action of the working class is vital for our people. Do
you feel the same? Here then is our first great common interest. Are
there any differences of opinion about the road we have to take? Yes,
there are. For this very reason we must consult each other and reach
agreement.

With regard to peace, which is your concern as much as ours, we
the workers of the two German states, are dependent upon each other.
The working class of the German Democratic Republic, in alliance
with the farmers and other working people, has uprooted German
militarism. It will never return. Neither we, the GDR workers, nor
you, the West German workers, can alone guarantee peace throughout
Germany. The failure of one of us endangers peace for the other, too.
We workers simply must not fail. We depend upon each other and
are therefore forced to unite and act jointly. This is our second great
common interest. In maintaining peace we serve the interests of the
widest sections of the farmers, lower middle class, intelligentsia,
bourgeoisie, including even some capitalists.

As workers we cannot resign ourselves to our class and our Germany being divided for all eternity. Since we hate civil and revanchist war and must guarantee peace, an understanding between the two German states is for us a national duty. And this is our third great common interest.

Like us you are determined to fight for the greatest degree of prosperity and social security for the working class and all working people. It is easier for us because our state is a socialist workers' and farmers' state. It is more difficult for you because West Germany is a capitalist state. The wish for a better life and unlimited social and cultural progress for all workers and working people is common to us all. This is our fourth great common interest.

West German workers are just as interested in friendly relations with all peoples as GDR workers. This friendship between the peoples is our fifth great common interest.

As compared to the great common interests concerning the saving of the nation, the securing of peace and friendship between the peoples, the reunification of Germany and the social security and prosperity of the people, all other questions must—we feel—remain in the background. We must always be on our guard that the enemies of the working class have no chance to erect artificial barriers between us. The enemies of the working class are all for quarrels between the workers under the slogan of "divide and rule". How is it with the alleged conflicts between us? Let us say frankly: We are of the opinion that there are no conflicts between workers in West Germany and workers in the GDR which could prevent us from cooperating.

The West German Workers and the GDR

Some workers say: "We cannot see how things are finally going to turn out in the GDR. We would rather wait and for the time being maintain capitalism in West Germany. We have no illusions about the monopolists but at least we know for certain now what we have got and what we have not got. If we should go along with you we would also have to take over socialism." We can only answer: Many of you are today still sceptical or have different opinions than us concerning socialism. All right! We do not intend to force socialism upon West Germany. We know that it is a good thing. Socialism is incomparably better than capitalism and far superior to it. This superiority will be proved increasingly from year to year in Germany, too. But nobody wants to force our social system upon you. Everybody here is happy to be rid of capitalism. Nobody here any longer wants capitalist exploitation. We working people have taken a decision and we know that we have taken the right one. You will have to decide for yourselves on your social system. We are certain that you will sooner or later take the right decision.

Some social democratic, Christian and non-party West German workers say: "But we have another conception of democracy than you." To this we can only answer: We judge democracy according to who are the political and economic rulers and what they offer the masses of the people. We do not think much of a democracy such as yours where seven thousand millionaires own the factories, mines and estates, forcing you to work under their conditions and for their profits and who control the state, economy, judicial apparatus, the army and the domestic and foreign policy thanks to their ownership. In our socialist democracy the factories, mines and the land belong to the people and the representatives of the working people form the government, run the state machinery, economy, police, army, judicial apparatus, the entire domestic and foreign policy in their interests. Come to us and you will see for yourselves.

But we do not wish to force our socialist democracy upon you. As things are at present it would be a step forward if you would see to it that the military-clerical system in West Germany was changed and at least a bourgeois-democratic system established that would renounce war and adhere to the rules of bourgeois-parliamentary democracy. But choose your own democratic system. We keep the socialist democracy which we have found to be best. Our proposals are based on the fact that there are today in Germany two separate German states with different political systems and that neither must force upon the other its political system and threaten it with violence, blackmail or war. Close examination will show that there are no contradictions in this which could prevent us from cooperating.

Some Christian workers from West Germany ask: "What is your attitude, comrades of the SED, towards religion? You are atheists and I would prefer to keep my belief." To this we can only answer: First, not all the workers in the GDR are atheists. Catholic and Protestant workers and other working people also whole-heartedly participate in the building of socialism. Here everybody has the right of religious freedom. Stick to your belief, brother, if you want to. We do not want to force our ideology upon you. Do not believe the malevolent fairy stories about alleged persecution of Christians in the GDR which are spread particularly by atomic-war-supporting bishops whose clerical intolerance is well known. In their heart they are only

too sorry that they can no longer–as in earlier times–have un-
believers and those of a different faith burned at the stake. It is their
aim to prevent you from seeing that we are your brothers and from
struggling with us for the maintenance of peace and the peaceful
democratic reunification of our country. Atomic war makes no distinction between creeds and ideologies. Therefore we all, and particularly
we workers, who must jointly safeguard peace for our people, must
make no such distinction.

The Great National Compromise

There are in West Germany serious and well-meaning people who
say: But we cannot get together with the two political systems. How
then is reunification supposed to be possible? The problem does not
lie in the existence of two political systems in Germany but in the
fact that the present West German state is a militarist aggressive
state, whereas the GDR is a socialist peaceful state which is basically
opposed to any aggressive intentions and actions. Naturally the question of the existence of two political systems in Germany is a problem
which is not easy to solve.

But if we do not want to abandon reunification or wage war against
each other there is no other possibility than to secure–by means of
a German confederation–the maximum rapprochement of the two
German states and their peaceful cooperation in overcoming the division, despite the difference in our social systems. Within the framework of this peaceful cooperation between the two German states,
the two social systems will compete with each other and show which
is capable of accomplishing most for the German people.

Peaceful competition will bring many pleasant and useful things
not only for the workers in the two German states but also for all
other sections of our people.

We assure you that in the interests of the whole German people
and their peaceful reunification we will do everything in our power
to prove, through the development of socialism in the German Democratic Republic, that the whole German people can live in peace,
prosperity and happiness and occupy a respected place in the life of
the peoples if they reject a revanchist policy and militarism, if they
devote the great creative power of the German working class and
all other strata of the nation only to the work of peace and prosperity.
The victory of socialism in the German Democratic Republic will
also make easier the great national compromise for which we are
striving.

The road of peaceful democratic development is complicated for you in West Germany. We know that besides the working class, there are many forces among the intelligentsia, farmers, other members of the lower middle class and bourgeoisie, and even including employers in West Germany, who have in the past years already proved that they advocate peace and understanding. Not a few have fought for peace and made sacrifices. Let us remember the West German scientists' struggle against atomic armament and the struggle of many farmers against the seizing of their land for military purposes. Many are traditionally bound in their way of thinking, but even they feel that things cannot go on like this any longer. They are opposed to the inflexible policy of Adenauer and his militarists and are prepared to cooperate in the establishment of a peaceful, democratic Germany. But they are also afraid of the future. They have doubts as to whether their daily life and social position would be endangered if the policy of the Bonn government were changed. They are disappointed by Adenauer's breach of trust when, after having promised not to tolerate any experiments, he plunged West Germany into the adventurous and extremely dangerous "experiment" of revanchist policy and atomic war preparations.

The working class must set a good example for the intelligentsia, farmers, middle class and bourgeoisie and show them the way to safeguard peace and the peaceful reunification of Germany. Only the working class can do this. We can and will honestly cooperate with all these strata. The working class will then also consider their interests, that is to say, agree to a great national compromise. The national compromise could be accomplished in the spirit of this Plan for Germany.

The People's Plan for Germany means no civil war and war, no threats, blackmail and violence!

The People's Plan for Germany means understanding among the Germans! Understanding means understanding between the German workers and their organizations, understanding between the farmers, the intelligentsia and all peace-loving Germans.

The People's Plan for Germany means negotiations between the two German states aiming at peaceful understanding, agreement between the two German states on the renunciation of the use of force, understanding on the establishment of an all-German commission on the basis of parity.

The People's Plan for Germany means understanding on the next step towards safeguarding peace through the renunciation by the two German states of atomic armament and the establishment of missile

y

250

bases, understanding on disarmament and the strength of the military forces, understanding on the joint struggle for general and complete disarmament, understanding on our German proposals for the conclusion of a peace treaty, understanding on rapprochement between the two parts of Germany through economic and cultural cooperation.

The aim of the People's Plan for Germany is the reunification of Germany as one peace-loving, democratic state by means of a German confederation.

Dear Social Democratic, Christian and non-party workers, let us rally around the People's Plan for Germany. Discuss the Plan at your meetings. Let us hope that discussions on the Plan will lead to understanding between the workers and all peace-loving forces. Come to us. Even if some of your leaders do not agree they are not in a position to prevent it. We shall talk with each other. We shall discuss with each other. We will fight jointly for our common aim. If the German workers do this then the cause of peace and peaceful reunification will triumph throughout Germany.

The People's Plan for Germany is the plan to save the German nation.

Central Committee of the
Socialist Unity Party of Germany
First Secretary
Walter Ulbricht

Speech to the Diplomatic Corps

26 September 1960

Your Excellency, Gentlemen,

Thank you for your congratulations on my election as chairman of the Council of State of the German Democratic Republic. I especially thank you for your readiness for further good and friendly cooperation in the interest of peace in Europe and in the whole world as well as for the maintenance and further development of good and friendly relations between our governments and peoples.

At the same time I may assure you in the name of all members of the Council of State of the GDR that, in the spirit of our late President Wilhelm Pieck, we shall do everything possible to support your responsible work for the strengthening and consolidation of the political, economic and cultural relations of your countries with the German Democratic Republic, in the service of friendship among the peoples, in the service of international understanding and cooperation.

We, the citizens of the German Democratic Republic, have definitively broken with the bad traditions of German history. As a consequence the German Democratic Republic as the first German workers' and peasants' state in which the working people exercise political power has made the safeguarding of peace and disarmament its primary objective. Our coat of arms is the symbol of peaceful work.

The lessons of German history, especially of the two world wars, have been drawn in the German Democratic Republic and it is the German Democratic Republic which has again brought honour to the German name which had been disgraced by the militarists, colonial rulers, fascists and revenge-seekers. It is the German Democratic Republic which has endeavoured to create an honest relation of mutual confidence, respect for the interests of others and friendship with all peoples, both large and small. That is true—as was said—of our relation with all countries including those whose governments for one or another illogical reason today still promote or support those forces in West Germany which embody and continue the evil and ruinous traditions of our German history, namely, the German militarists and revenge-seeking politicians in Bonn. The German Democratic Republic, through its foreign policy of peace and friendship among the peoples has again brought the German name to a position of esteem in the world.

It cannot be otherwise than that the two so basically different traditions of German history should also be conspicuous in the foreign policy of the two German states. The foreign policy of the German Democratic Republic is rooted in the traditions of true humanism, the love of mankind and friendship among the peoples, regularly cultivated and further developed by the working class, all truly patriotic Germans and the most outstanding heroes of the spirit of our history, in the tradition of respect for mankind and for the culture and achievement of every other people. Many peoples have already made a large contribution to human culture. We consider that every people makes its contribution to human culture. As we have drawn the lessons of the two world wars we see our first task to be to help to ban war from the life of the German people and all peoples.

The foreign policy of the West German Federal Republic, on the contrary, is determined by the traditions of the German militarists and revenge-seekers, the reactionary "master race", the oppressors and exploiters of foreign peoples.

The test of the character and the policy of the two German states is their position on the question which is today arousing the whole of humanity, the question of disarmament and peaceful coexistence between states with different social systems. Who promotes and continues the evil traditions of Germany, the traditions of militarism and imperialism—as does the Bonn government—opposes disarmament. It is therefore understandable that the ruling circles of the West German Federal Republic do everything possible to prevent disarmament in opposition to the will of the majority of the people. The government in Bonn does everything possible to thwart any lessening of the dangerous international tension because it could not otherwise continue to carry out its policy of revenge.

Our proposal to the session of the General Assembly of the United Nations for the stage-by-stage carrying out of complete and general disarmament in the two German states in three steps by 1964 is the expression of our consistent policy of peace. If the militaristic rule in West Germany is eliminated by means of disarmament and democratic development there, then the destruction of all weapons in Germany can be undertaken as we propose for the third step of disarmament. That would make possible the military neutrality of both disarmed German states. The German people would thereby once and for all be saved from war. It would stop the world from once again being plunged into the inferno of a war started from Germany.

To preserve peace in Germany it is above all necessary to eliminate the vestiges of the Second World War so that Germany cannot again—as is occurring today in West Germany—be used for the preparation of a new war. The fact that up to now there is still no peace treaty with Germany in which the principles of a lasting peace are set forth along the lines of the principles of the anti-Hitler coalition and the United Nations Charter is used by the militarists in West Germany for their preparations for revenge.

The elimination of the vestiges of the Second World War and disarmament are prerequisites for the peaceful solution of the German question. Therefore the proposal on the "Principles for a Treaty on General and Complete Disarmament" laid before the General Assembly of the United Nations by the Soviet government, has a vital significance for our German people. We especially welcome the fact that the proposals of the Soviet government include the complete prohibition of nuclear weapons as well as the ending of their production and testing, including the destruction of all stocks of these weapons. The adoption of these proposals by the United Nations General Assembly would free mankind of the menacing danger of atomic war and our German people, especially, would breathe more easily.

We are of the opinion that precisely we Germans have reason not to wait until the whole world has disarmed. The German people must make a special contribution. We have already initiated it in our proposals to the United Nations General Assembly. Basing ourselves on the humanistic traditions of the German people, we are of the opinion that the German people have every reason to go ahead on the question of disarmament and to make a good beginning here on the blood-soaked soil of Europe which would bring peace and security not only to the German people but to all the peoples of Europe. The disarmament of both German states and the final conclusion of a peace treaty would serve the cause of the peaceful coexistence of the peoples and at the same time would remove the greatest obstacle which today still stands in the way of the rapprochement and agreement of the two German states and their ultimate reunification. We Germans have a still further reason for going ahead with disarmament. As German militarism in West Germany has again raised its head and is pursuing dangerous revenge-seeking aims, it would be precisely the German people upon whom frightful afflictions and ruin would be imposed in the event of a war. A special German contribution to disarmament such as we have proposed would free the German people from this terrible danger.

We are firmly convinced that the complete and general disarmament of both German states would also have an exceptionally favourable effect on the relations of the GDR as with those of the West German Federal Republic with other states and peoples. Then no one would need fear any attack from a German state.

We are of the view that the German people should never again seek greatness and everlasting glory on the battlefield, but that their greatness and their glory can be found solely on the field of science and culture and economic and social achievement. We see in this, in noble, peaceful competition with the other nations, jointly to bring progress to the whole of mankind, the greatest and finest purpose the achievement of which deserves every effort.

The two basically different traditions in the history of Germany are also apparent in the attitude of the two German states towards the anti-colonial liberation movement and towards the nation-states of Latin America and the new nation-states of Asia and Africa. Most of these nation-states have but recently thrown off the yoke of an inhuman colonial oppression. They are now in a difficult struggle for the complete liberation from political and economic dependence and exploitation, for the liberation from economic backwardness, from hunger and want and from all the sad heritage of the rule of imperialism. To support them is a humanistic obligation and the commandment of international solidarity.

In contrast the ruling circles of West Germany are led by the tradition of imperialist colonial policy, to be sure, with the employment of new methods. This is characterized by the slaughter of the Hereros, by the shameful participation of German troops in the putting down of the so-called Boxer rebellion in China and by the colonial oppression of African and Asian peoples. The result of this inhuman tradition of German militarism is that today in West Germany there are once again special "colonial schools" where now, of course, somewhat refined methods of colonial exploitation and oppression are taught. The result of this tradition is that today in West Germany imperial generals who commanded the bloody annihilation of African peoples are commemorated. The attitude of the Bonn militarists to the new nation-states and their peoples struggling for their freedom is shown by the fact that the exponents of West German finance capital are today attempting to characterize these as "delinquent" peoples who urgently need the paternal rod of correction; that means, of course, the rod of the "white men" of Washington, Bonn and vicinity. The white race, it is further indicated, must take over the role of an authoritative educator to these "delinquent peoples" so that they will learn how "to grow gradually into civilization". The West German militarists and imperialists—in the closest cooperation with United States monopoly capital—would thus like to turn back the wheel of history and to put the peoples of Africa, Asia and Latin America in struggle for their freedom into chains and to force the new nation-states under the sign of neo-colonialism once again into imperialist domination. Those are the worst traditions of the German colonial rulers and militarists who are again influencing policy and exercising ever more control in West Germany.

The German Democratic Republic is following another tradition of the German people in relation to the countries and peoples who languished under colonial oppression and are carrying out their struggle for national liberation, namely, the tradition of the German working class and the German humanists who always despised and opposed the colonial oppression and exploitation and always championed the sacred right of the colonially-oppressed peoples to freedom, human dignity and a happy life in an independent nation-state for every people.

On the basis of this good, humanistic German tradition the German Democratic Republic, within the limits of its ability, everywhere and on every occasion supports the new nation-states and the peoples in struggle for freedom and rights. "Africa for the Africans"—that is the foundation of our African policy. The GDR supports the new nation-states and their peoples fighting for their freedom in their difficult struggle for political and economic liberation and also helps them in increasing the necessary knowledge and in the more rapid training of skills for the development of their own economy and administration.

The German Democratic Republic fully agrees with the view of the Soviet government that the time has come for the complete and definitive elimination of the colonial regime in every form. The German Democratic Republic greets the peoples of Africa who are courageously carrying out the struggle for their political and economic liberation from centuries-long exploitation and servitude. We have a feeling of solidarity with the peoples of Africa, Asia and Latin America who are courageously fighting for their liberation. We greet the people of the young nation-states of Africa in which the people are forging their new life. May the organizations of the United Nations fulfil their historic tasks and support the peoples who are struggling for their national independence and their liberation from the exploitation of foreign monopolies.

The German Democratic Republic supports the demands of President Kwame Nkrumah of the Republic of Ghana for the immediate liquidation of all foreign military bases on African soil and for the support of the legitimate government of the Congo headed by Prime Minister Lumumba. The nation-states of Africa are right when they request a permanent seat in the UN Security Council in view of the growing significance of the African continent. The government and population of the GDR are, with all their hearts, at the side of the Cuban people who have freed themselves from the shackles of United States neo-colonialism, on the side of the peoples of Africa fighting for their freedom, as with all peoples who have stood out against the oppressor and the exploiter, for freedom and rights.

The German Democratic Republic, the first German peace state, has existed for eleven years. Looking back we can confirm that our entire policy has been and still is oriented on peace and the peaceful living together of the peoples. In these eleven years the German Democratic Republic has proved its vital force and stability and in the economic sphere has long equalled and surpassed many large countries of the capitalist West. It is good and useful that in these years commercial relations of mutual benefit have been established between the GDR and nearly all states on earth.

But today commercial relations alone are no longer enough. We think the time has come, universally to normalize relations with all countries, for it is becoming absolutely necessary. It is now absolutely necessary to establish truly normal interstate relations, that is, to take up normal political and diplomatic relations along with the commercial and cultural relations where they do not yet exist.

In view of the complexity of the German question, I understand that in the first years of the existence of the two German states it may not have been easy for many foreign statesmen and politicians to have a clear picture of the character and the policies of the two German states. But today everything is clear. The past eleven years have brought to the light of day what the two German states represent and what policy they follow and that they embody two completely different traditions of the German people. No one can any longer overlook that. No one can overlook the fact that today the majority of the citizens of West Germany are speaking in favour of a policy of peace and of complete and general disarmament, just as are the citizens of the German Democratic Republic and their government. No one can overlook the fact that the GDR has thereby become the legitimate representative of the peaceful interests of the large majority of the German nation.

257

Thus there stand opposed to each other the peace-loving German Democratic Republic and the forces of peace in West Germany on the one side, and the revenge-seekers and militarists with their federal government in West Germany on the other side. Under these circumstances the one-sided diplomatic relations of some states with the West German Federal Republic—whether intended or not—are a support for militarism and revanchism in West Germany. Such states thereby repudiate the very principle of neutrality which they have often called upon, in their attitude to the two German states. The West German militarists not infrequently base themselves on that position of some states which violates the principle of neutrality in their revenge-seeking policy which is so dangerous for peace in Europe. The hesitation of the governments of some countries on the question of the full normalization of relations with the German Democratic Republic is improperly interpreted by the West German militarists as a support for their claims for conquest. The government of the West German Federal Republic attacks with blackmailing threats to break off relations and impose economic disadvantages in order to prevent the governments of such countries from carrying out their own policy. But it is really the question of peace, its maintenance and lasting preservation which is involved here. Therefore the basic principle of neutrality imperatively demands complete consistency precisely today.

The interest of peace in Europe thus requires that precisely those states which are not allied to one of the great power blocs now implement the policy of neutrality with respect to Germany whereby they place their relations with the two German states on an equal basis without discrimination between the one or the other, that is, that they maintain the same normal relations with each of them.

The governments concerned should understand me correctly. We have no so-called "Hallstein doctrine" in reverse. We do not demand that any country relax or break its normal relations with the West German Federal Republic. It is also not primarily a question of recognizing the GDR but the question of the safeguarding of peace and of peaceful coexistence. The German Democratic Republic exists and is developing in any case, may some states sooner or later come to normalize their relations. But in the interest of peace, equal, normal relations with both German states are a no-longer-postponable necessity. One-sided relations with the West German state of militarists and revenge-seekers increase the danger of war in Europe because they—whether desired or not—advance the revenge-seeking endeavours of the West German state and at the same time make more difficult the solution of the national question of the German people by means of a rapprochement of the two German states, by means of their ultimate reunification.

The assumption that the split would be widened through recognition of the German Democratic Republic is thus completely unfounded. The split can only be overcome by the muzzling of German militarism, the conclusion of a peace treaty, the transformation of West Berlin into a demilitarized, Free City and negotiations between the two German states on the basis of equality. If all foreign states which are interested in the maintenance of peace would concern themselves with normal relations on a basis of equality with both German states it would be advantageous for the reunification of Germany.

The peaceful solution of the German question is only possible on the basis of peaceful coexistence, especially through respect for the principle of non-interference in the internal affairs of another state.

The establishment of normal relations with the German Democratic Republic is especially important for the states which have liberated themselves from foreign rule. The timely consolidation of such relations is especially important in the interest of the new nation-states for they contribute to the strengthening of the peace camp and to the taking from the imperialist forces right from the start the inclination to engage in such interventions and attacks as were undertaken against Egypt and against the Republic of the Congo.

It also seems to me to be time for some western countries which are allied with the West German Federal Republic in an aggressive military alliance to examine their relations with the German Democratic Republic. May the western powers, too, recall the experience of history that German militarism above all struggles for the domination of Western Europe and attempts to draw its western allies into adventures. There is no advantage to western states if some of them carry out a policy of pin-pricks and discrimination against citizens of the German Democratic Republic under the influence of the Bonn government. The constant attempts to subject citizens of the German Democratic Republic to discriminatory treatment on various occasions are vestiges of the Second World War and methods of the cold war which should disappear, preferably today rather than tomorrow.

We say quite frankly that we do not want to use this very healthy principle of reciprocity to reply in kind to these negative appearances. We also do not want unfriendly to say nothing of hostile feelings towards the USA, Great Britain, France or other countries to arise on the part of citizens of the German Democratic Republic as a consequence of this discriminatory treatment which has been continued for years. We have been most successful in bringing up the young people of the

German Democratic Republic in the spirit of international friendship, international cooperation and peaceful coexistence with countries with other social systems. We have today become a peaceful people, German people who love peace above everything. That is a fact of the highest significance for the peace of mankind. But if because of the extremely absurd and short-sighted policy of discrimination which is in violation of the United Nations Charter our citizens are further subjected to regular and ingenious difficulties and if the exercise of their rights is further encroached upon, these actions can only lead to the most harmful consequences. The governments of the states addressed here should consider that in the long run their interests and the interests of their peoples can only be harmed if they continue the policy of discrimination against citizens of the GDR. We are always ready to settle existing or newly-arisen questions in dispute in normal negotiations conducted on a basis of equality.

Your Excellency, Gentlemen, I have taken this opportunity to define our attitude on some basic questions of the foreign policy of the German Democratic Republic. You have assured me of your readiness for further friendly cooperation which has proved itself in the past. I am convinced that our cooperative work and our joint struggle for peace and friendship among the peoples will contribute to the overcoming of all obstacles which stand in the way of humanity's peaceful and happy future.

From the Programmatic Statement to the
People's Chamber of the German Democratic Republic
on 4 October 1960

Honourable Members of the People's Chamber,

The German Democratic Republic is the first German peace-loving state. Each of us, the whole of the German people—with the exception of a small group of mad militarists and revenge-seeking politicians in West Germany—is longing for peace, needs peace as the air to breathe or his daily bread. We love our people and we love humanity and we are constantly working to secure a happy life in peace and prosperity. But militarist adventurers are once again threatening peace and the lives of our people.

Today the protection of peace is the main content of the German question. That is why it is the most urgent desire of the German Democratic Republic to do everything which serves total disarmament in Germany so that in West Germany, too, the forces of peace will prevail and the national rebirth of Germany as a peace-loving and democratic state will become a reality.

It puts us Germans to shame. It took the German empire some fifteen years to prepare the First World War and to plunge our German people into a grave catastrophe. Fifteen years after the First World War those bitter experiences had already been forgotten and the night of fascism closed upon Germany, and with it—as everyone knows today—the Second World War which plunged the German people into an even worse catastrophe. And now again fifteen years have elapsed since the end of the Second World War. And again in one part of Germany we perceive the same old forces feverishly attempting to prepare a new war which is already lost before it has started and which, in the face of atomic weapons, is threatening the physical existence of our nation.

The West German militarists want to revise the irrevocable results of the Second World War and they have the illusion—this time relying on the American imperialists, and as their satellite—that they will ultimately succeed in putting their old plans of imperialist conquest into practice. What a foolish notion! Even the First World War was bound to be lost because German imperialism did not have a chance to acquire world domination. The Second World War was also bound to be lost because after the socialist Soviet Union had come into existence, the struggle of the peoples, oppressed and exploited by imperialism, for their freedom was the beginning of the end of imperialist domination over other countries and the time for an imperialist redivision of the world had long since been ended. Today there exists the big socialist part of the world whose influence in every respect is growing from day to day and which has a superiority in the field of the latest weapons. The strength of the socialist camp is the guarantee that any aggressor who should dare to attack a socialist country would be destroyed within a short time.

GDR–Representative of the Peace-loving German Nation

The historical lessons of the wars and crises in Germany during the first half of our century consist in the knowledge that Germany in that new period of world history, in the period of the struggle for freedom of all peoples which began at the time of the Great October Socialist Revolution, will never be able to move forward by employing an imperialist policy. Our German people will be able to occupy a respected place in the community of nations only if they concentrate all their efforts on developing the creative talents of the people for the advance of science, technology and culture and if they engage with honour in peaceful competition with other nations.

Based on that historical knowledge of Germany's position during the new epoch of the history of mankind the decision was made, after the surrender of the Hitler army and the bankruptcy of the German bourgeoisie, to take the cause of peace and reconstruction and democratic progress into the hands of the working class, the peasants and progressive intellectuals. The coalition of anti-fascist democratic forces faithfully fulfilled the agreements concluded between the states of the anti-Hitler coalition in 1945 which demanded the ultimate liquidation of nazism and militarism.

If, during these weeks in the Fifteenth Session of the UN General Assembly, the delegates of the peace-loving peoples and above all of the Soviet Union, had to call for a halt to the actions of the West German militarists, it only shows to what extent the ruling military circles in West Germany have again discredited the German name, and that they are again endangering peace.

The population of the German Democratic Republic may be proud that our first workers' and peasants' state succeeded in drawing the lesson of history, in achieving the greatest revolution in German history, in eliminating the roots of German militarism and abolishing the exploitation of man by man and in overcoming the disease of race hatred against other peoples. And this far-reaching revolution was carried out by peaceful means. It was founded upon the unity of the working class and its alliance with the peasantry, the intelligentsia and other sections of working people. This revolution required a great deal of work of explanation and persuasion but not one shot of ammunition. Thus, the German Democratic Republic today is a stable state which represents the peace-loving interests of the entire German nation throughout the world and which is gladly prepared to make the special contribution towards reaching disarmament which is essential for both German states.

Here, in the GDR, the social changes which have been absolutely necessary in order to free the development of the forces of production from all the chains of the capitalist system and to bring the creative capacities of the people to full flower have been brought about. In the age of automation, space navigation, the utilization of atomic energy in all spheres of production, the insoluble contradiction between the social character of production and the capitalist form of the private appropriation of the products by a small group of finance capitalists becomes increasingly evident. Especially in West Germany this concentration of capital and the exploitation of the masses of workers has been practiced to the utmost. In this situation German finance capital is tightening its domination by seeking to secure its rule with the aid of militarism and by employing fascist methods and emergency laws. It is typical of the character of the Bonn government's emergency legislation that the Adenauer party itself explained in the Bonn Bundestag that the population is "always an unreliable factor". It could not have been expressed more cynically. So, the emergency laws exclusively serve the suppression and brutal oppression of the people should they demand democratic rights and express their opposition to the policy of war. But it is precisely atomic armament and the establishment of positions of power by militarism within the country which are sharpening the economic and political contradictions in West Germany. The people of West Germany are already looking for a way out. The German Democratic Republic, firmly advancing along the path of democracy and social progress, is showing that way out.

After the German militarists, sponsored and supported by the most reactionary forces of American monopoly capital, closely chained the West German state to the United States and consolidated their own power in West Germany, and after having reached a certain stage of armament, they are expressing their rapacity and desires for conquests with a fantastic outspokenness. Federal Chancellor Adenauer raves about the conquest of East Prussia, his deputy Erhard speaks of Upper Silesia and another member of the government, Herr Seebohm, is already busying himself with carving up the Czechoslovak Socialist Republic on paper.

The West German Hitler generals who prepared, carried out and lost the Hitler war and who are responsible for the death and maiming of millions of German soldiers, unceremoniously submit memoranda to the public prescribing to the West German state what policy to pursue in home and foreign affairs. Even during the time of the Weimar Republic the German militarists were able to feel themselves masters of the state, thanks to the incomprehensible abstinence of the Social Democratic Party and the bourgeois democratic parties.

But what they did during those days is nothing compared with their present claims as set forth in the infamous memorandum of the Bonn Hitler generals. They are demanding, as a matter of course, atomic and missile weapons for aggressive purposes, the complete militarization of life, a total readiness for war on the part of the entire population, and the employment of other western states, such as France, Great Britain, Spain and others for West German military purposes. It is typical of the German situation that at a time when general and complete disarmament are on the world's agenda and the German Democratic Republic is proposing a program for disarmament in the two German states and military neutrality, the Bonn government is planning its highest military budget to finance increased atomic armament.

Only the German Peace State Can Be the Legitimate German State

I ask you, honourable members of the People's Chamber, I ask all citizens of the German Democratic Republic and I ask all citizens of the West German state:

Is what the West German militarists are doing legitimate? Can a state and a regime which are leading their population to ruin be legitimate? Is it not rather the test for any German state and its regime that they do everything to strengthen peace and to secure a future in peace, prosperity and happiness to the German people? If we take all that into account we must say that only the German Democratic Republic is the legitimate German state. The West German federal government has forfeited its right to be looked upon as the legitimate representative of German interests before the German people and the peoples of Europe and the world.

Not even the payment of a few debts of the Hitler regime will ever be able to justify to the German people and their history or to other peoples, the continuation of the abominable Hitler policy of revenge and conquest with but slightly-changed methods.

The Bonn government asserts that it came into power by general secret ballot and that consequently the people themselves have decided this policy with their votes.

That is not true. The formation of the West German state was decided on at the conference of the western powers held in London in 1948 on the initiative of the United States. The Bonn government was installed by the American occupation power. The people of West Germany have never been allowed to decide whether its government should pursue a policy of war or a policy of peace. They were denied the most elementary right of any people to make their own decision on the question of war and peace, on atomic armament, on conscription, on the right to prepare and unleash an atomic war. Completely deprived of their most primitive right of self-determination, the West German people are now to be made a tool without a will for the West German militarists' plans. People who only mention peace are hunted like the worst criminals in the West German state of injustice. Hundreds and thousands of West German patriots have been sentenced and imprisoned for the sole reason that they dared publicly to demand peace and agreement.

Questions to the German Nation

I ask you, honourable members of the People's Chamber, citizens of the GDR and West Germany: How can a German state such as the West German Federal Republic be legitimate if it sabotages the implementation of the Potsdam Agreement which was designed to prevent a resurrection of German militarism and to secure a peaceful and democratic development in Germany? How can such a German state be legitimate if it persecutes peace and has as its main object not the interests and requirements of the German people but the interests of the US imperialists and NATO?

No, a state such as the West German Federal Republic is a state of injustice. After all that has happened to the German people during two world wars and two difficult post-war periods we can only recognize as legitimate that German state which represents the German people's desire for peace, which has become the firm homeland of peace and whose main objects are the interests of the German nation. The German Democratic Republic is the legitimate German state. The time will come in West Germany, too, when the forces of peace will determine events and when West Germany can be called a peaceful state. Then the reunification of Germany will soon be possible.

But only such a German state can be legitimate which does everything in its power to promote agreement between the two German states and which does not widen the gap between them but tries instead gradually to bridge it. But what is taking place in West Germany in 1960? Quite obviously, the Bonn government has abandoned any form of peaceful reunification. It is preparing for war and in the event war does not break out–the division of Germany for an indefinite period. And that is taking place quite systematically in all spheres. Not even the towns and municipalities in the East and West of Germany are to be allowed mutually to discuss their problems. According to the intentions of the Bonn militarists, Dresden and Stuttgart, for example, are to be sworn enemies. Cultural exchange is to be prevented. Is it not a disgrace that the world-famous Berliner Ensemble, which has with such outstanding success advocated humanist German culture in London, Paris, Moscow and other cities of the world, has been exposed to disgusting attacks from the ruling party of the Bonn chancellor on the occasion of its tour of West Germany? But it must be stated for the sake of the West German population that neither the director of the theatre nor the West German theatre-goers were in any way impressed by the official attempts to paralyze cultural contacts. In spite of these machinations the outstanding artists of the German Democratic Republic found an enthusiastic audience in West Germany and an applause which could not have been better. But the Bonn government is continuing its attempts radically to suppress all cultural relations and any exchange in the field of culture between the two German states.

Publicists and philosophers were mobilized to prove that a reunification of Germany in peace, democracy and freedom was neither essential nor desired. The West German big business organs write pages and pages on that theme. It is quite openly stated that only military conquest and the complete subjection of the GDR to the Bonn regime would be accepted. And in case that should not be possible, course should be set for an indefinite separation.

I ask you, honourable members of the People's Chamber, all citizens of the GDR and West Germany: Can a West German state be legitimate which consciously and systematically widens and deepens the gap which splits the German nation by carrying out atomic armament, which disapproves of reunification in peace and freedom, which has determined either to let the German people be decimated by an atomic war or to continue the division of Germany for an indefinite period? No, never!

We believe that only that German state which constantly and consistently fights for agreement between the two German states and their citizens, for a step-by-step rapprochement and the ultimate overcoming of the division can claim to be the legitimate German state. In view of the existence of two social systems in Germany the only way to achieve reunification is the conclusion of a peace treaty with both German states and the establishment of a confederation. Confederation signifies, in fact, nothing else than to agree to a rapprochement so as to advance step by step along the path of peaceful reunification.

As you know, that is just what the German Democratic Republic is doing. Although the Bonn government stands for anti-national interests, the GDR government has time and again stretched out its hands to come to an agreement. It has again and again submitted proposals for the safeguarding of peace and for overcoming the division. It has only recently proposed general disarmament in Germany to the General Assembly of the United Nations so as to remove any obstacles which at present hinder a rapprochement of the two German states, their cooperation within the framework of a confederation and their ultimate reunification. Thus the attitude towards the question of reunification also proves that the German Democratic Republic is the only legitimate German state.

The legitimacy of a German state also includes its ability to take the lessons of history to heart.

The German Democratic Republic has drawn those lessons and has carried out the Potsdam Agreement.

In the German Democratic Republic the consequences were drawn from the lessons of history. The forces which plunged the German people into the misery of two world wars have been eliminated. They have been removed from all influential positions. By placing the enterprises of the big trusts and monopolies into the hands of the people and the big estates into the hands of the peasants we have taken good care once and for all that those circles will never be able to raise their heads again.

There are good and bad traditions in the German people. The bad traditions which caused the two world wars in the course of half a century of the history of German wars of conquest, have caused the German name to be shamed and befouled. We had to start with a very bitter inheritance.

Those bad traditions are again fostered in West Germany. Can a state, I ask, where those responsible for the murder of millions of innocent people hold responsible positions again, even including government posts, can such a state be looked upon as a legitimate German state? I say no. Only that German state which clears the German name of the disgrace of contempt for human dignity and which promotes the good and humanist traditions among the German people can claim to be the legitimate German state. Such a state is the German Democratic Republic.

Those who doubt the legitimacy of the GDR also doubt the legitimacy of the peoples' struggle against the murderous regime of Hitler fascism the policy of which is being continued by the West German state of injustice. For the ideals pursued in the peoples' struggle against the murderous Hitler regime also show that the German Democratic Republic is the only legitimate German state.

The policy of the German Democratic Republic is in accordance with the international treaties, especially the Potsdam agreements and with other agreements concluded by the anti-Hitler coalition. I need no longer dwell on this subject. But that also shows that the West German Federal Republic is the state of injustice. And from the point of view of international law, as well, the German Democratic Republic is the only legitimate German state.

These facts lead to the following conclusions: The principal contradiction in Germany between the interests of the people of the German Democratic Republic and all peace-loving people in West Germany, on the one hand, and the forces of militarism and revanchism in West Germany, on the other, can only be overcome by putting German militarism into a strait-jacket, by disarmament and the conclusion of a peace treaty with the two German states which would pave the way towards overcoming the division of our nation.

The Safeguarding of Peace–the Major National Task

The historic task of the German Democratic Republic consists in banning war once and for all from the life of the German people in a joint effort with the forces of peace in West Germany. This is a task of national and European, and even of world significance. Once this task is fulfilled there will be no more wars in Europe, and at least one potential source of world war would be eliminated. No state in Europe other than West Germany raises territorial claims against other countries. Only in West Germany are the same militarist forces still in power, those forces which prepared and conducted the Second World War and who are once again voicing revenge-seeking claims. Their adventurous policy is being promoted by the present government of the United States. If the governments of the United States, Great Britain and France would finally stop supporting West German militarists and revenge seekers in their war preparations, if these governments would at last be willing to cooperate in the elimination of the vestiges of the Second World War and in the conclusion of a peace treaty with the two German states, peace could be assured in Germany and in Europe.

So you see, honourable members of the People's Chamber, that we have a very special situation here in Germany.

This situation is marked by the fact that the two main forces active in the world today, the socialist states, headed by the Soviet Union, and the imperialist states, led by the USA, are immediately and simultaneously effective in Germany. All our internal conflicts encounter the interests of these two main world forces. Our specific situation leads us to take a vital interest in the safeguarding of the peaceful coexistence of states with different social systems and in the bringing about of general and complete disarmament throughout the world. The logical consequence of things as they are is that any potential conflict between the two great powers—regardless of whether it was originally concerned with Germany or not—would be fought out immediately upon German soil as long as American troops are stationed in West Germany and as long as West Germany belongs to NATO. That is precisely the reason why it is utter madness to equip the West German state with atomic weapons and to assign to it a role that may be compared to that of a death brigade.

The atomic armament of West Germany and the establishment of an offensive force in NATO uniform is senseless in every respect. In view of the fact that no one intends to attack West Germany, least of all the socialist countries which are accused by Bonn of having such intentions, West Germany has no need to prepare a defence against any attack. If Bonn really pursued no aggressive designs it would have to agree to general and complete disarmament for it would offer the safest guarantee against all attacks. Yet Bonn will have nothing to do with it.

The atomic armament of West Germany is also useless as a means of political blackmail. No one will be blackmailed by West German threats of war. It has finally become historically notorious how German militarists are to be restrained.

What should be done in the first place in the face of these facts? We believe that we should above all take serious steps to safeguard peace in Germany. It is necessary that we should at least once take the lead in ensuring peace, that we should effect general and complete disarmament in the two German states. All of you, honourable members of the People's Chamber, know our proposal to the General Assembly of the United Nations envisaging general and complete disarmament in the two German states in three stages—beginning in 1960–61 and ending in 1963–64—and the neutrality of both German states guaranteed by the great powers. We set forth this disarmament proposal in great detail. I may refer in this connection to the many publications on the matter and to my statement on the Memorandum of the Council of Ministers of the German Democratic Republic.

Ruling circles in West Germany have rejected the proposal for a German contribution to world peace. The majority of the West German population, however, welcomes the proposals for disarmament and for the military neutralization of Germany. It recognizes our proposals as being decisive measures to ensure peace and at the same time as a means of solving the national problem. West German militarists and revenge-seeking politicians do not care for our proposal. Even the thought of disarmament makes them nervous because they are pursuing plans of aggression.

What Is to Be Done?

What is to be done, many will ask, so that the great discussions at the Fifteenth UN General Assembly will be followed up in Germany by the first step to relaxation?

I should like to give the following reply: the foremost necessity is an open dicussion among the people, among members of parliament, officials of parties and mass organizations in both German states. The subject matter of this frank discussion should be the renunciation by both German states of the use of force, all forms of war propaganda, territorial claims and revenge propaganda, full freedom of action for the peace movement in West Germany, i. e., the renunciation of the emergency legislation in West Germany which serves the purpose of war preparation.

The fundamental task in connection with the safeguarding of peace is the negotiation of a peace treaty. The representatives of the

West German state have recently asserted that a peace treaty was unnecessary, since the western powers had ended the war with the Paris treaties. In other words they maintain that the Paris treaties replace a peace treaty.

That is a very peculiar explanation with which we cannot agree. The Paris treaties served the purpose of separating West Germany from the German state unit and transforming it into the central military base of the aggressive American system of alliances in Europe. The Paris treaties were intended to clear the road for West German rearmament, for the establishment of the reign of German militarism and neo-nazism. The Paris treaties were and are in no way comparable to the Potsdam Agreement and the aims of the anti-Hitler coalition. The principal aim of the anti-Hitler coalition, also laid down in the Potsdam Agreement and in full agreement with the interests of the German people was, in fact, to ensure for all time that peace should never again be threatened from German soil. Any peace treaty deserving to be called by that name must also have this content today. For this very reason Bonn and its American sponsors are trying to evade the conclusion of a peace treaty.

Many individuals in Bonn claim to be in favour of a peace treaty on principle, but only a peace treaty concluded with a united Germany. This statement will not bear close scrutiny. It is generally known that Bonn has for years been systematically obstructing every possibility for an agreement between the two German states and their cooperation to safeguard peace and overcome the division of Germany. In truth the Bonn government does not want a peace treaty; it wants neither peace for the German people nor for Europe because it has built its entire existence on the policy of war preparation.

I should like to take this opportunity to emphasize that we shall make every effort to see that the peace treaty remains on the agenda until this problem has been solved in the interest of peace and the future of the German nation.

People's Democratic State and Council of State

Our policy has a scientific foundation. It is one of its principles always to start from a realistic assessment of the international relation of forces and the development of the situation in Germany, to recognize the New and progressive in good time and to think over, discuss and decide in due time on the problems which newly arise in the development of socialism and society. The most important things are truthfulness and clarity. All progress in the German Democratic Republic presupposes the unfolding of the creative forces of the people. For this reason it is the task of the Council of State as of all state organs of the German Democratic Republic to maintain close contacts with the people, to learn from the experiences of the workers, peasants, intellectuals and other working people, to evaluate the most progressive experiences of the Soviet Union and the peoples' democracies and to shape further developments with a view to the future.

There is no contradiction between our people's democratic state and its policy, and the interests of the citizens. Therefore every one can become a conscious member of society. He does not seek the satisfaction of his interests at the cost of others, but together with the others, through joint collaboration for the benefit of all and for his own benefit. It is a truly humanist task to cooperate in the construction of such a society in which the capitalist law of dog eat dog, the fight of each against all, is abolished, in which every individual occupies a respected place and feels responsible for the whole, a society in which people not only live side by side but together, who work together and who form a real community.

The frank and open discussions of the deputies of the People's Chamber and the local representatives, the members of the state apparatus from the government down to the mayors, the officials of the parties and mass organizations and economic and cultural officials with the citizens of the German Democratic Republic about the basic questions of our policy and its implementation in the enterprises, towns and communities has already become a practice accepted as a matter of course. The cooperation of the citizens of the German Democratic Republic in the drafting and implementation of the resolutions adopted by the party of the working class, the People's Chamber and the government as well as the National Front takes place in the most varied ways. They have an effect on the sessions of the Central Committee of the SED, the People's Chamber and the parties and organizations united in the National Front of Democratic Germany as well as in the discussions of the production teams. This constitutes our tremendous superiority over the imperialist regime which the mass of the citizens declares to be incapable of having a say in political life, let alone in conducting the affairs of state.

It is therefore the decisive, fundamental right of the citizens of our Republic to cooperate in the conscious shaping of the entire economic, cultural and above all the political life of our Republic. This makes most evident the deep-going transformation which took place in the position of the working people compared to former conditions of rule in Germany. The working people have become the masters of the country and they exercise this rule ever more consciously and better, by implementing ever more actively their rights, for example, to participate in the work of the peoples' representative bodies, to control and help implement the work of the state organs. The working people exercise their rule ever more consciously and better by exerting an active influence on the production and working conditions in the enterprises and agricultural production cooperatives and above all by discussions on production, the innovators' movement, the socialist teams and work groups. In the residential areas and schools they have a share in the many activities in committees and other spheres of life which they help to shape.

The right to work which, for the first time in German history, was transformed by our Republic from a mere declaration on paper into an ensured social reality, is already today becoming a matter of responsible behaviour by people towards society in the socialist teams and work groups, is consciously becoming a matter of personal responsibility of every individual towards society. The fulfilment and over-fulfilment of the plans are increasingly becoming a matter of personal honour, and work becomes a genuine requirement of life.

Thus a new discipline is coming into existence in our society—the voluntary, conscious discipline of a community of free and equal persons who rationally employ their strength for the more speedy attainment of a jointly set objective, without unproductive and egoistic opposition. The stronger and more quickly this discipline develops, the more consciously we work, the more productive will be our work in all fields, which makes possible the step-by-step reduction of hours of work.

I believe that all deputies of the People's Chamber and the entire people agree with me when I say:

Everything we are proud of, which we have achieved, the workers of our Republic have created with their hands and their brains. It has cost hard work, much effort, heroism and also large sacrifices. The German Democratic Republic, in the position it occupies today in the world, internally consolidated and stable, with a strong economy, is the work of our workers and office employees, our farmers, our scientists and artists and members of the middle classes.

Millions of people from all sections of the population, including also hundreds of thousands of housewives and old-age pensioners, created extensive values in voluntary work within the National Construction Program, which contributes to making the life of all better and richer. All these workers deserve esteem, respect and thanks. Communal spirit has become the decisive factor in the relations between the people. The principle of bourgeois individualism is being increasingly overcome by the humanist principle of the socialist community which is based on the mutuality of interests of all working people. Individual, personal interests are best satisfied by giving priority to the social interests, the mutual interests of all.

The decisive sphere, in which the new man is developing, is work under socialist relations of production. The character of work has experienced a fundamental change under the conditions of the workers' and peasants' power as they exist in the German Democratic Republic. Many have already realized that the struggle for the welfare of the whole of society and thus the contribution which every individual makes by his work for the benefit of the socialist society is at the same time the decisive prerequisite for the well-being of every individual citizen of our Republic. The perception of the agreement of their personal interests with the social interests has, with millions of workers, already caused a deep-going change of their attitude to society, to work and to the socialist state. A deep-going process of transformation has also been accomplished with craftsmen, tradesmen, owners of enterprises and other businessmen. Many of them have shifted over to community work and in the process of joint work the seeds of a new consciousness also developed in them.

It is truly worth working for the perspectives which socialism is able to give to man. The time will come when wars will only be a matter of recollection. That will be the time when mankind has finally achieved true humanism through its rise to the heights of socialism, when Maxim Gorky's words: To be a human being, how proud that sounds—will receive a deep meaning.

The people of the German Democratic Republic are shaping their new life in this sense.

The victory of socialism is certain!

From the Statement to the
People's Chamber of the German Democratic Republic
on 6 July 1961

Honourable Members of the People's Chamber, Dear Friends,

Two important documents are submitted to the People's Chamber for adoption, the German Peace Plan which is to be our contribution to the safeguarding of peace in Germany and Europe as well as to the settlement of other national questions of the German people, and an appeal to all Germans in East and West.

It is a question of the long due peace treaty with the two German states and the peaceful and reasonable settlement of the West Berlin question. The German Peace Plan contains the proposal that a German peace commission be formed from representatives of the parliaments and governments of the two German states to draft German proposals for a peace treaty and for the conclusion of a good will agreement serving the purpose of immediately improving relations between the two German states.

Our proposals for a peace treaty are based on the principles of the United Nations Charter. A peace treaty is to prevent a war from ever again beginning in Germany.

The peace treaty is to guarantee the German people peace for ever and full equality of rights in the family of nations. The West Berlin question is also to be settled on the basis of the peace treaty by giving West Berlin the status of a neutral Free City until the re-unification of Germany. Our proposals to guarantee security in Europe and for the rapprochement of the two German states and their peaceful reunification correspond to the peaceful interests of our entire people. We are convinced that the peace treaty also paves the way for the reunification of the two German states which in the present situation is only possible through the formation of a con-federation.

This, our Peace Plan, these, our proposals serve peace alone, peace for our German people, peace for the neighbouring peoples in Europe, peace for all peoples of the world. No people is to be in-jured, nobody's honour and dignity are to be impugned, no one is

275

expected to do anything impossible. All are to benefit from it. This is the heart of our Peace Plan with which today we turn to the German people and the peoples of the world.

It is indeed high time to prevent the flames of a third world war from flaring up out of the vestiges of the Second World War. There is to be no shooting, but negotiations must be held! I want to say that especially to all those among our West German fellow countrymen who allowed themselves to be frightened by the shouts and war threats of the West German militarists and extremists. There will be negotiations! Everything will proceed peacefully. Nothing else has been proposed. We shall never use unpeaceful means unless we are attacked.

Is it right, many of you will perhaps ask, that once again we address ourselves so insistently to the government of the West German Federal Republic? I know that many citizens of the German Democratic Republic are thoroughly tired of repeatedly seeing how our offers for peace and understanding are answered by ruling circles in Bonn with threats and insults.

We fully understand the impatience and indignation of the citizens of the German Democratic Republic, but here peace and the future of the German nation are at stake, and we therefore must not spare any efforts. We must not omit any attempt and never abandon hope, despite everything, to reach agreement on a peace treaty between the German Democratic Republic and the West German Federal Republic in order thus to muzzle West German militarism and pave the way for a rapprochement of the two German states, for their cooperation within the framework of a German confederation. And I do not yet want to give up the hope today that some day responsible personalities in Bonn will in fact find the courage to make a contribution to the safeguarding of peace in Germany and Europe.

There are clear-sighted people in West Germany, too, who openly express the view that history would find no justification and even no mitigating circumstances for a policy which wants to obliterate the consequences of the war begun by Hitler with new force. It is impossible for the Bonn government over and over again to thwart the conclusion of a peace treaty on the grounds that a peace treaty can only be concluded with a previously united Germany, for the very coming into existence of this united Germany was and is indeed made impossible by West Germany's membership in NATO, through the policy of the West German government and its allies.

People in West Germany with a sense of responsibility say that a war would with certainty seal the final downfall of the Federal

Republic. Thus the West German ruling circles should leave the flags, the torches, drums and trumpets in the properties room. These things are at the best suitable for making West Germany suspicious also to its western allies. No one should have any illusions in West Germany: de Gaulle has long since recognized the Oder-Neisse frontier, and neither an Englishman nor an American or Frenchman would take the smallest risk of a war to change the frontiers which have existed for sixteen years. A policy of illusions which has often plunged the Germans into national disaster is more untenable today than ever. Those people who did not oppose it in due time because they "were not interested in politics" have had to pay for it over and over again. This could only bring a bad awakening. There is also widespread indignation that a few people in Bonn rattle the atomic bomb as if West Germany were the Sahara desert, the Nevada desert or Bikini atoll.

Any further delay in the conclusion of a peace treaty and the transformation of West Berlin into a demilitarized Free City is a growing danger to the German people, the peoples of the Soviet Union, the Polish people, the Czechoslovak people and to all other European peoples, and also to the population of the United States of America.

The peace treaty would prepare a militarily neutral Germany which could devote all its forces to peaceful work and the securing and raising of the prosperity of all its inhabitants. Such a peace treaty would at the same time be a link for the two German states. I think that the entire German people should be interested in such a peace treaty with the two German states, apart, perhaps, from a small minority of incorrigible and unconvincible revenge warriors and specialists in lost wars who are especially esteemed as advisers in West Germany—in contrast to the customs of other countries.

It is perhaps quite interesting to recall today that there was a time in which a Herr Adenauer expressed the following conception in public—I quote:

"We agree that we are to be completely disarmed, that our purely war industry is destroyed, that we are put under a long control in both directions, and I want to go even farther, I believe that the majority of the German people would agree that we . . . should be neutralized by international law."

This was stated by Herr Adenauer on 29 December 1946.

But only a few years later Herr Adenauer feared the democratic forces in the German people and was therefore against a peace treaty. In 1949 Dr. Adenauer declared in Hamburg:

277

"Germany needs to be occupied for fifty years because the German people cannot govern themselves."

This expression showed the deep fear of the CDU leadership of the democratic forces in the German people. Later Dr. Adenauer indeed took part in working out the Germany Treaties envisaging foreign occupation for fifty years, and signed them.

It is demagogy when in connection with the demand for the conclusion of a peace treaty with the two German states a few people in Bonn speak of an intended dictated peace. A draft peace treaty has been submitted as the basis of negotiations, and the two German states are called upon to develop conceptions themselves which they will present at the peace conference. The Soviet Union even went so far as to propose in its memorandum to the late President Kennedy that the four powers might obligate themselves from the outset to accept what the two German states agree upon jointly. When had a defeated country ever had the opportunity after a crushing defeat and unconditional capitulation to exert such a great influence on the content of a peace treaty?

Naturally the peace would also fix the frontier juridically. As is known, we did not fix it. The victor powers drew this frontier. Hitler and the German militarists and imperialists who twice in half a century wanted to annex the whole of Europe and practised the physical extermination of entire peoples have these frontiers on their conscience.

Many of these people sit in Bonn today and this time intend to ruin the German people for good with their criminal policy of revenge. They must be stopped. No one can change the frontiers which have existed for fifteen years! In view of the alarm caused by the revanchist policy in West Germany and in view of the consequences which a continuation of this revanchist policy can entail I want to say that it would be a blessing for the German people if the frontiers were fixed in a peace treaty as soon as possible. This would cut the ground from under the policy of revenge.

According to the only draft which has thus far been submitted a peace treaty would stipulate that Germany is not allowed to join military alliances which are directed against one of the powers of the anti-Hitler coalition. Germany would be militarily neutral, to put it quite clearly. Would it really be so terrible to be militarily neutral and live in peace, without war, perhaps for a few centuries, perhaps for ever, like Sweden and Switzerland and more recently Austria? Who could be frightened by that? There would be no danger of Germany becoming the scene of an atomic war. It may be that this is inconceivable for a few people in Bonn. But I believe that the vast majority of the Germans in East and West would consider such a state an unheard-of advantage.

I want to stress expressly that the present draft peace treaty contains no provisions which restrict economic or scientific activity in Germany for peaceful purposes in any way. On the contrary, this is the real field for the ambition of the Germans. In these fields we Germans and both German states could give the world something which is far better than cold war and war cries and genocide, these specialties of the German militarists.

Naturally the plan to change the relation of forces in Europe and in the world in favour of militarism has failed. And even if the West German army were to be further armed the West German militarists would be unable to change the relation of forces. Thus the most reasonable thing would be for them to base themselves on facts. These gentlemen cannot prevent the construction of socialism in the GDR in any case. Naturally we for our part also do not intend to interfere with the social system of West Germany.

It is a commandment of reason immediately to prepare and conclude the peace treaty with the two German states and thus create a link between the two German states which makes easier their step-by-step rapprochement and peaceful competition between them. We are convinced that we shall win this peaceful competition. Let the representatives of the Bonn state calmly continue to believe that they could win it.

When we repeatedly propose that the two German states should negotiate with one another and reach understanding it is self-evident that negotiations on social systems would not be realistic. The social system in the German Democratic Republic is the subject neither of any negotiations nor of any electoral manoeuvres, just as it would likewise not be realistic to suppose that the representatives of the Bonn state would be ready to agree to the abolition of capitalism, the liquidation of the rule of the monopolies, etc., in negotiations or through elections.

If one approaches things realistically one therefore has to ask, on what are negotiations in fact possible?

Possible and necessary are negotiations on the safeguarding of peace, that is, on the removal of the vestiges of the Second World War and the conclusion of a peace treaty and the peaceful settlement of the West Berlin question and, naturally, on the normalization of relations. All Germans in East and West are likewise interested in peace—if they have not completely taken leave of their senses. Even a dyed-in-the-wool monopoly capitalist will not like to see his factories, his bank accounts and the labour power exploited by him perish in an atomic explosion in the course of the adventurist policy of the West German militarists.

Thus an understanding about peace should be possible. We therefore also address our appeal to the West German bourgeoisie. Let us jointly remove the vestiges of the Second World War! Let us remove everything which could again lead to a military conflict, to civil war and war. Let us conclude the peace treaty with the two German states and let us consider in the course of these negotiations and afterwards how the two German states can cooperate reasonably and matter-of-factly in the interest of peace and the German nation.

In the present great international discussion US President Kennedy, British Prime Minister Macmillan and other representatives of the western imperialist states like to speak frequently of alleged western rights, for example, that of the presence of troops and occupation authorities in West Berlin and of the use of the GDR's communication routes by land and air leading to West Berlin. It is alleged that these are original rights. Rights of the conqueror, rights granted by God personally, so to speak, valid for all times. Concerning rights there is but one legal claim based in international law, that of the provisions of the Potsdam Agreement corresponding to the United Nations Charter. And that is the legal claim to a peace treaty.

The right of the GDR and its citizens to be master in their own house, to make decisions for their own country and demand respect from everyone for the frontiers and sovereignty, this right of the GDR is at present still ignored by the western powers. And that is the reason for many differences, too. That is also a reason for the accumulation of ever new grounds for conflict.

I want to say quite clearly that the German Democratic Republic is no state of inferior rights. And the citizens of the German Democratic Republic are not people of inferior rights as the politicians of the imperialist western powers want to characterize them.

Naturally this conception of the western powers has absolutely nothing to do with international law. There is no original right to the occupation of another country. The western powers have violated the Potsdam Agreement by creating the separatist West German state and subordinating it to American imperialist policy. They have violated the Potsdam Agreement by creating and arming the West German army and putting fascist generals at the head of this army, promoting them and allowing the power of militarism to be restored in West Germany. The Potsdam Agreement is the fundamental charter for the aims of the occupation of Germany after 1945. There is no right to occupation detached from these aims. Valid democratic international law provides no right to the arbitrary occupation of a foreign territory for an incalculable period nor an "abstract right of the victor". With regard to Germany, too, the occupation could be legitimate only for the realization of the objectives of the Potsdam Agreement, that is, primarily for the destruction and elimination of the militarists and fascists for ever.

The present occupation regime in West Berlin in particular no longer has anything to do with the objectives of the anti-Hitler coalition, either legally or in fact. It has long since had no legal foundation because its aims are diametrically opposed to the original goals of the occupation of Germany. The western occupation troops came to West Berlin on the basis of the agreement of the anti-Hitler coalition, that is, on the basis of the Potsdam Agreement, and then took advantage of their presence to support the revanchist politicians in violation of the Potsdam Agreement.

The freedom and security of the West Berliners are to be protected according to our proposals and assured with the strongest conceivable international guarantees. However, for this it is also necessary that West German militarism and the revenge-seeking politicians of the Bonn government and their fascist extremists disappear from West Berlin. By concluding a peace treaty with the GDR the people of West Berlin would in any case be freed from the restrictions imposed on them by the separate occupation regime in West Berlin and would have the opportunity to decide their destiny for themselves within the framework of the demilitarized Free City of West Berlin.

Let no one allow himself to be argued into thinking that it is a question of the destiny of the West Berliners, in whose affairs we have no intention of interfering.

I repeat it here expressly before the world and I assure the citizens of West Berlin in the name of the Council of State and the government of the German Democratic Republic, in the name of the People's Chamber, in the name of the Socialist Unity Party of Germany and the other parties of the Democratic Bloc, that the right of the demilitarized Free City of West Berlin to determine its own system itself and the freedom to decide its affairs for itself will in no way be infringed upon, that no one intends to interfere in the affairs of their city and that we are prepared to guarantee the communications of the Free City with west and east, north and south.

We demand only one thing from you: West Berlin must cease to be a base of the cold war.

The German Democratic Republic is prepared to negotiate on how the questions arising out of the removal of the occupation regime by the conclusion of a peace treaty with the GDR can be settled–in so far as they affect the sovereignty of the GDR. That is a concession on the part of the GDR and the governments of the western powers should not fail to recognize that. They should be reasonable and not count on the German Democratic Republic putting up with a violation of its sovereignty. No state on earth would accept that–no African, no Asian, no Latin American and also no European state, including the GDR. Nor are the US representatives superior beings equipped with international privileges.

It seems the most reasonable to us to conduct the inevitable negotiations on the basis of facts and international law–in the spirit of the equality of rights and mutual benefit–and jointly seek for a solution which meets as far as possible the legitimate interests of all parties concerned.

Influential voices in the public opinion of Great Britain and the USA advocate such a reasonable solution. They proceed from the unquestionable fact that a large part of the present difficulties originates simply from the fact that the western powers think that they can ignore the existence of the German Democratic Republic and violate its rights and the rights of its population at will. A reasonable recognition of the facts which have developed historically in Germany would make it easier for the western powers to distinguish in their policy between questions of vital importance and propaganda theses which have grown on the soil of the Bonn militarists and are today already completely worthless and cannot stand the test of history.

The German people can prosper only in peace, they can live and work only in peace. Peace in Germany and for Germany is safeguarded, however, only when militarism and revanchism have been overcome everywhere in the country and have disappeared from Germany for all time. On this depends the future of the German people, on this depend the life and happiness of our children. Without the overcoming of militarism and the spirit of revenge in West Germany there is also no possibility of reunification. That is the iron logic of German history which today can be recognized by anyone who realistically assesses our historical situation.

The strongest bastion of peace in Germany is our German Democratic Republic. Here that force has developed in the last decade which strengthens and supports the German patriots and friends of peace in the West German Federal Republic and gives them decisive aid in their difficult struggle against militarism and the revanchist spirit in the interest of the great common national task–the safeguarding of the peaceful future of Germany by muzzling the forces of war.

The German Democratic Republic gives all friends of peace hope and confidence also in the West German Federal Republic. It is therefore of such extremely great importance that the German Democratic Republic should honourably fulfil its economic tasks, that its sciences and arts flourish and win prestige in the world, and that we stand at the top in the world in the field of science and technology.

That requires that our work must be constantly improved, that planning and organization function well.

We strengthen the GDR as bastion of peace to the degree that we fulfil these economic, scientific, technical and organizational tasks and prove the superiority of our social system in our daily work and in its results, thus making a decisive contribution to the safeguarding of peace in Germany and at the same time ensuring the approach of the day when the division of our country can be overcome.

Our German Peace Plan will encourage the peace-loving people in West Germany in their struggle and point out the common goal to them more clearly. I think that the time has now come for the peace-loving forces in West Germany to take the cause of peace firmly into their hands and together with us safeguard the peaceful future of Germany.

It is a matter of fact that socialism is the strongest force of peace in the 20th century. Even its bitterest enemies must admit that socialism prospers in peace and is itself peace in the last consequence.

I want to say quite frankly that only those friends of peace in West Germany who have a normal attitude to, and normal relations with the first German workers' and farmers' state, the first German peace state, the German Democratic Republic, can rightfully say of themselves that they consistently work for the safeguarding of peace in Germany.

This does not mean, of course, that the citizens of West Germany with whom we are at one in the passionate effort to overcome militarism and safeguard peace and thus the future of the German people must accept all details of the anti-fascist democratic and also the socialist revolution in the German Democratic Republic. It is quite understandable that many things may look different from the point of view of a West German friend of peace than from our point of view. He will see many things one-sidedly.

Nobody demands that in the course of overcoming militarism and the spirit of revenge in West Germany and the transformation of the West German Federal Republic into a peace-loving and democratic state everything which it was necessary to do in the German Democratic Republic should be copied. The workers of West Germany, the farmers, scientists, members of the middle classes, all peace-loving forces will use their own heads to find out how the peaceful and democratic transformation can best be carried through in West Germany and with the greatest benefit for the people and for peace.

I am convinced that our German Peace Plan will help the friends of peace in West Germany. It will encourage them, give them suggestions for their struggle which no one can fight for them. This, our German Peace Plan, can be signed with a good conscience by every West German citizen who values peace.

Dear members of the People's Chamber, dear friends, history takes its course. The world changes from year to year. The forces of peace are growing. And our road, too, leads forward into a bright and peaceful future. There is no turning back for us. It is a question of paving the way in West Germany, too, to a bright and peaceful future, thus also opening the way to a lasting peace and the unity of the nation.

The only legitimate representative of the German nation is the German Democratic Republic. Its People's Chamber, conscious of its great responsibility, will adopt the Peace Plan of the German people, the fulfilment of which is the affair of all Germans in East and West.

The Measures of Our Government
Saved Peace in Europe and the World

From the television address on 18 August 1961

Dear citizens of the German Democratic Republic and dear friends in West Germany and West Berlin.

Eventful days lie behind us. The workers and with them all honest working people of the German Democratic Republic can breathe a sigh of relief. They were fed up with the activities of those involved in the traffic in human beings and the revanchist politicians in West Berlin and Bonn. With growing anger they had seen how they were being made fools of and robbed by the militarist rabble. The Bonn militarists mistook our patience for weakness, however. An embarrassing mistake, as can now be seen.

You know that for years we have consistently proposed the solution of all questions through peaceful negotiations and through agreements.

But how have the incorrigible militarists and revanchists answered these proposals? The Bonn government rejected these as they have rejected more than one hundred proposals made in the past. War Minister Strauss ordered a speed-up in the atomic armament of the Bonn NATO army which is commanded by Hitler generals. He was even insolent enough to declare that the Second World War was not yet ended. In other words he directly connects his adventurous plans with those of Hitler and Himmler.

The German militarists increased their diversionist activities against the German Democratic Republic as a further step in the preparation of aggressive action. They used all means at their disposal to organize the traffic in human beings and diversionist activities. They were even capable of committing the most abominable crimes against humanity in order to undermine the GDR and make it ready to be attacked.

We know the plans of the Bonn government. They were aimed at creating conditions that would allow an open attack against the GDR, civil war and open military provocations after the West German elections.

It was clear that, in view of such adventurist plans and the speed-up of preparations to carry them out, a very dangerous situation had arisen for peace in Europe and in the world.

In order to remove this danger to the peace of our people and other peoples we contacted our friends at an early date and agreed to eliminate it. The measures taken by our government contribute to saving peace in Europe and the world which was endangered this August 1961 by western militarists and revanchist politicians. The citizens of West Germany and West Berlin should also understand that it is very possible that their lives were saved by these steps.

Many GDR citizens have asked us why we waited so long, why these necessary measures were not taken at an earlier date. I reply quite frankly that there was a time when we had hoped to exploit every possibility for understanding. We exposed the war preparations of the Bonn government in ample time. I wrote to Bonn Chancellor Adenauer and warned him. We appealed directly to the West German workers and explained just what was brewing in West Germany. We appealed to all West German citizens in an attempt to clarify to them what responsibilities they have for developments in their country.

For everyone who had eyes to see and ears to hear, it is obvious that West Berlin is in fact an extremely dangerous hotbed of war which can become a second Serajevo. An increasing number of people in Germany as in other countries have arrived at the opinion that it is no longer sufficient to speak of peace in general. It is much more important to see that the fire which is being kindled in West Berlin is brought under control before it spreads to neighbouring houses.

It was our task to do this. Even more so because West Berlin is located in the centre of our territory and within the frontiers of our state. Our house was the first which was to go up in flames. Thus we, too, were responsible for seeing that this danger point was brought under control. In addition, we as a part of the socialist camp, as a socialist state, have the great obligation to see that the policy of peaceful coexistence which is so desperately needed in the world is not disrupted by insane West German militarists or their West Berlin hangers-on.

We have, I believe, made an important contribution to peace by securing the frontiers of the German Democratic Republic with West Berlin and with West Germany. In carrying out the measures we lived up to the agreements with the Soviet Union and the other member states of the Warsaw Treaty which obligate us to protect effectively the borders of our state and to keep them under control.

Even the most obtuse politicians in West Berlin and Bonn must now realize that the disruptive activities originating in West Berlin have been stopped and there is no possibility of continuing them with any hope of success. Now, in many capitalist countries people are beginning to understand what a danger spot West Berlin was for peace in the entire world. I have the impression that people in many NATO countries, too, are pleased with our action.

Many citizens have asked if it was absolutely necessary to use tanks and guns in carrying out our protective measures which also had the character of a lesson.

I want to say quite unmistakably–yes, indeed, it was necessary! It contributed to the exact, rapid and smooth realization of the measures necessary to secure peace and protect the GDR borders. The provocateurs were thus warned against stirring up dangerous incidents.

Our measures also coincide with the stated and unstated interests of bourgeois circles in France, Britain, the United States, Belgium, Italy and other countries, which have in many ways prompted the GDR government to establish control over the trouble-making centre in West Berlin. The reaction of the NATO countries up to now clearly shows that many NATO politicians were obviously relieved when they received reports on 13 August that this dangerous situation for peace had been eliminated in a peaceful manner by the measures taken by the GDR government.

It must now be clear to everyone–and that was also the point of this lesson–that neither the Soviet Union nor the German Democratic Republic can be blackmailed.

Many West German politicians have answered our patience, our repeated proposals for negotiations and our unswerving search to safeguard peaceful coexistence by making threats against us, preparing acts of aggression against us, organizing diversionist activities, or in other words practising "non-peaceful coexistence".

I appeal today to the citizens of West Germany. I want to tell them that peace and order prevail in the capital of the German Democratic Republic. Nobody should allow himself to be confused by the hysterical cries of a few West Berlin politicians. The measures taken by the first German workers' and peasants' state and its allies serve the cause of peace. They help to guarantee that West Berlin will not become a second Sarajevo.

But I should like to say quite frankly to the workers, peasants and

all peace-loving people in West Germany that the further maintenance of peace depends to a very great extent upon them. For militarism and revanchism have their base in West Germany. The peace
of the world is threatened from West Germany. That is why it is
necessary for all reasonable citizens of West Germany and all good
Germans to unite to put an end to the insane policy pursued by the
incorrigible elements intent upon a drive to the east, by Hitler
generals thirsting for revenge, by old and new fascists. This is necessary in order to maintain peace, to bring about normal relations between the two German states, so that finally the unity of the nation
can be restored.

I addressed myself especially some time ago to members of the
West German bourgeoisie with a suggestion that they should, in
their own interests as well as in the interests of peace, renounce support of the adventurist policy of revenge and accept peaceful coexistence. I hold to this suggestion today. I believe that the West
German bourgeoisie has every reason to consider this seriously and
to accept it.

Everyone must realize that we now have a new situation. We are
not the only ones to see this—it is also felt by our enemies. It is in
fact a new situation in Germany. This must have certain effects.

Many of those who until now were not convinced will now find it
easier to understand that a peaceful solution of the German question
is only possible through the maximum strengthening of the workers'
and peasants' power in the GDR and by muzzling militarism in West
Germany. That is the prerequisite for overcoming the division of
our nation.

And now many who until now did not want to believe it will find
it easier to understand that since West Germany became affiliated
with NATO through the Paris Treaties it is senseless to hope for a
unified Germany under the command of NATO to be brought about
by some secret force of the western powers.

It must now be clear to everyone that the division of the German
nation can only be overcome by the great popular struggle to muzzle
militarism and imperialism. The workers and other working people
of the German Democratic Republic and their state power are in
the front rank of this movement. They are today more conscious of
their power than they were yesterday. They have dealt the militarists
a defeat and they know that they are backed by a thousand million
people of the socialist camp.

But no one should get the idea that the strict security measures on
our borders mean that we have written off the workers and peace-

loving people in West Germany. No, no one is written off. This is the situation: the consolidation and strengthening of the German Democratic Republic in all fields are necessary so that some remaining misunderstanding about the perspectives will be finally eliminated in West Germany and everyone will recognize the role of the German Democratic Republic.

Although we know the weaknesses and difficulties of the West German working class and are under no illusions, we are still counting on the West German working class as well as on the large number of reasonable people in West Germany; we are counting on their insight, their understanding, their intelligence and their love for our people. But they must all think about the situation anew and draw the necessary conclusions.

This new situation has led us to the following conclusion: the working people of the entire Republic, their sons and daughters in the armed forces, have helped the capital to protect its borders. Now they are also helping to speed up socialist construction in Berlin, so that the capital of the German Democratic Republic will once and for all be free of all disruptive manoeuvres and all the after-effects of the unhealthy atmosphere radiating from the West Berlin front-line city.

The Historic Task
of the German Democratic Republic
and the Future of Germany

From the speech at the 11th session of the
National Council of the National Front of Democratic Germany
on 25 March 1962

The draft of the document on the *The Historic Task of the GDR and the Future of Germany* has been submitted to the National Council of the National Front of Democratic Germany. This national document is of great significance. It was conceived as the political basis of the work of all citizens of our state over a long period of time.

A detailed analysis is made in the document of the development and situation of our national problem, and the way and aim are pointed out.

Important national documents, published by progressive personalities, groups or parties at turning points in the development of our nation are the landmarks of German history. I recall Fichte's speeches "To the German Nation" at the beginning of the last century, as well as other important documents issued in the course of the long years of struggle by the forces of progress among the German bourgeoisie for freedom and democracy.

When the working class stepped into the arena of history, Karl Marx and Friedrich Engels published the Communist Manifesto on the eve of the bourgeois-democratic revolution. In the abyss of Germany's national catastrophe during the First World War, Karl Liebknecht and the Spartakus Group in their appeal of 7 October 1918 pointed the way to the immediate ending of the war, to the overthrow of the imperial war government, and to the foundation of a new Germany of peace, democracy and socialism.

At that time the vanguard of the working class was still unable to put these great national and social ideas into effect. Reaction gained ground. The nazi party was spoon-fed with the aid of huge subsidies by the big bourgeoisie. In this situation Ernst Thälmann proclaimed the Program of National and Social Liberation of the German People on behalf of the Central Committee of the Communist Party of Germany (KPD) in August 1930. When German fascism enslaved our people and prepared the Second World War, the Bern Conference of the KPD at the beginning of 1939 announced the Program of Unification of all forces of labour, the peasants and the democratically-minded middle class within the Popular Front, and pointed the way to the overthrow of Hitler and the struggle for the new democratic republic.

In October 1941, when the Hitler armies had viciously attacked the Soviet Union–the world's first socialist state–German workers, peasants and other working people who were prisoners of war published a document in which the whole truth about the inevitability of the defeat of Hitler was told to all Germans, particularly to officers and soldiers. This appeal explained why the German people must break with Hitler and go their own way in order to attain peace and a free, independent Germany. When the Hitler government and army had surrendered in Berlin, the Communist Party of Germany in its appeal of 11 June 1945 pointed out the peaceful, anti-fascist, democratic way to the German nation. This was followed in 1949 by the document of the National Front on the democratic way to a united, peaceful, anti-fascist and democratic Germany.

In the meantime profound changes have taken place within the German nation as a result of the partition measures carried out by the western powers and by West German finance capital. Our people are threatened by the revival of German militarism and the NATO atomic war policy.

The National Document starts out from the fact that the German nation today is split into two states facing each other on German soil in hostility, a situation that we do not desire and that should not persist.

The document contains a historically substantiated, irrefutable accusation against the German big bourgeoisie which has forfeited all claims to leadership of Germany; it contains equally irrefutable evidence of the fact that only the working class, allied with all democratic forces can claim the right to lead Germany.

The historic mission, the way and the aim of the German Democratic Republic, socialism and peace, are today clear. It is just as obvious that the dream of the Adenauer government of annexing the GDR to the West German NATO state by means of rearmament and provocations has dissolved into thin air. Thus the struggle in Germany now is for the only possible peaceful solution of the German problem, by way of the peaceful coexistence and peaceful competition of the two German states, i.e., by peaceful coexistence and confederation. The development of our national problem since 1945 has amply proved that only the prevention of atomic armament in

Germany, renunciation of the use of force and disarmament in both German states can clear the road for a peaceful solution.

The national document clarifies the complicated problem of "Socialism–Imperialism and the National Question in Germany" and makes it easier for every German to take the clear stand inevitable in these days, towards this basic question of our national existence. The influence of this national document will not be confined to the German Democratic Republic. It will assist peace-loving and democratic forces in West Germany in their difficult and long struggle to overcome the rule of imperialism and militarism, in defence of the interests of the people and for the transition to a democratic and national policy.

This national document will finally help other peoples to understand what is going on at present in Germany and in the two German states, how this complicated situation came about, and where the German people will go.

Why was it so necessary to draw up the balance of the development of our national question at this particular moment, and to reformulate the principles of our national policy?

Various events of the past years have shown that the results of the Second World War are unalterable, and that there is no longer any unclarity as to the fundamentally different policy conducted by the two German states.

It is clear what the German Democratic Republic represents and what it wants. It is clear what the West German Federal Republic represents and what its ruling imperialist and militarist forces want.

The safeguarding of the state frontier on 13 August 1961 and related events have dispelled the fog which had still prevented many Germans from recognizing what was going on. Supported by the socialist camp, we frustrated all attempts to destroy the power of the German workers and farmers. This Adenauer policy has therefore failed. It has failed once and for all. This has been confirmed by the Bonn government by its renunciation of any kind of national policy and by its turning towards a West European confederation or even a confederation with the United States. It is proceeding to open betrayal of the nation.

What is to become of Germany under these conditions?

How shall relations between the two German states be shaped? Can they come to an understanding, and under what conditions? Is a new disaster already brewing again in Germany?

All these questions are today of concern to Germans. To answer them it was necessary to establish a national balance and draw the necessary conclusions. That is one of the tasks of the national document under discussion.

The time chosen for drawing up this balance has thus not been arbitrarily selected. Certain basic decisions have been made in both German states.

It is interesting to note that a national balance is being drawn up not only in the German Democratic Republic. In West Germany, too, we find an honest endeavour being made in all sections of the population to obtain clarity concerning the situation, the way and aim, and the necessary reorientation. Our document will advance this process. There is a growing awareness in every section of the West German population that the Adenauer policy is leading further and further away from reunification, that atomic armament and the revanchist policy are risking the continued existence of West Germany and its population. What are the main items of this national balance in this spring of the year 1962?

Like every balance sheet this one also has its assets and its liabilities. Let us begin with the latter. West Germany is once again under the domination of monopoly capital, clerical obscurantism, the Hitler war economy leaders, generals, judges and hangmen of the nazi regime. Supported by the United States these elements have split Germany. They have integrated West Germany into the NATO system and are taking other steps with a view to completing the withdrawal of West Germany from the German national community. The Christian Democratic Union (CDU), the German government party, wrote off peaceful reunification in calling for the inclusion of the whole of Germany in the NATO military alliance. The Bonn government openly defends the conception that there is no longer a national state policy for Germans, only the NATO policy. Representatives of the Bonn government are offering an aggressive confederation of the USA and West Germany to the US monopolies whereas they reject a peaceful national confederation of the GDR and West Germany as well as all other proposals for understanding and cooperation. Bonn is feverishly engaged in rearmament, insistently striving for control over atomic weapons. The democratic rights of the West German population are being systematically reduced.

These are a few—by no means all—items on the liability side of our national balance.

What about the assets?

In one part of Germany, in the German Democratic Republic, the conclusions have been drawn from historical developments, and the forces of imperialism and militarism have been deprived of power.

In the GDR the workers and farmers, allied with all anti-fascist and democratic elements have created the foundations for a peaceful and flourishing life for the German people. The German Democratic Republic has shown itself to be stable, and it has reliable and powerful friends. The alliance with the USSR, membership in the socialist camp, which embodies the future of the world, and the relation of forces in the world have deprived West German militarists and imperialists of every chance to undermine the foundation of the GDR. A process of rethinking and re-assessing the situation has begun in all sections of the West German population.

West German working people and other peace-loving and democratic forces are fighting against the obstinate policy of revenge pursued by the Bonn regime. The peace-policy of the GDR and its perspectives are clear. The principle of peaceful coexistence between the two German states and the formation of a German confederation propagated by the GDR with unswerving consistency, may also be approved by the overwhelming majority of the West German population. The German Democratic Republic is building socialism and advancing towards its triumphant achievement. In this way the superiority of the peaceful system of the people to the reactionary system of the old forces of exploitation and war is becoming increasingly evident. Finally the assets of our balance sheet also include our proposals on neutrality and disarmament in Germany, and on the creation of an atomic-weapon-free zone including the two German states, which also correspond to the conceptions of many West German citizens.

In comparing the assets and liabilities, in drawing up the balance sheet, it becomes apparent that the assets are more significant. The scales are weighted in favour of peace, peaceful coexistence and confederation. The policy conducted by Bonn can no longer be carried out.

Our national balance shows that our time has now come; that the overwhelming majority of Germans, also in the West German Federal Republic, may be won for a peaceful national policy, for peaceful coexistence in Germany and for a German confederation. The national document will also be of use in this respect.

Allow me a few words in this connection on a number of current questions of our own and the Bonn policy.

Even with a very cautious estimate of the situation we can see that certain advances have been made since 1958 in the struggle for a German peace treaty and for a demilitarized Free City of West Berlin.

The fact that, in view of the relation of forces in the world and the safeguarding of the socialist camp by the Soviet Union as an atomic world power, the revanchist plans of the West German extremists will not be supported by other states has become unmistakably clear. The western powers know this and in part openly admit that the situation brought about by the existence of two sovereign German states as well as the frontiers of these two states as they are at present, cannot be altered.

Even Herr Adenauer knows this in effect, even though he does not want it to be true and does not openly admit it. In a moment of discernment he publicly stated that the West German Federal Republic could not avoid the payment of accounts incurred by the Second World War. He is quite right.

Numerous small advances have been made, the sum total of which prepares the ground for a negotiated and peaceful solution of the West Berlin problem, i.e., for the removal of the hotbed of war in West Berlin and its transformation into a peaceful, neutral Free City.

A peculiar situation exists. Throughout the world the peoples are yearning for relaxation and the safeguarding of peace.

The state leadership of the GDR—in accordance with the wishes of the people—has submitted proposals to the government in Bonn for disarmament and for negotiations on normal relations so that military or other conflicts may be avoided. The Bonn government is well aware that it can do nothing to alter the fact of the existence of the sovereign GDR and that under the present conditions a normalization of relations is inevitable.

Nor does the West Berlin Senate believe in the possibility of maintaining the present state of affairs—the status quo—the source of continuous conflicts and dangers to peace. A peace settlement is therefore inevitable.

The draft of our national document contains a concrete guarantee of peaceful coexistence between the two German states by their cooperation within a German confederation.

We have reached the conclusion that the form of peaceful coexistence best suited to our specific historical conditions is that of a confederation of the two German states, in which a demilitarized, free and neutral West Berlin could also take part.

Such a confederation, of course, is not intended as a permanent solution. The division of the German nation will not last forever. In the same measure that the working class in West Germany, allied with the peasants, craftsmen and broad sections of the middle class, acquire the strength to overcome imperialism and militarism, the confederation will gradually develop into an organ of the progressive unification of the two German states and West Berlin.

On the other hand the peaceful coexistence between the socialist GDR and the capitalist West German state represents not merely a temporary and perhaps most insecure cease-fire. It should not only be a situation where there is no shooting.

Peaceful coexistence means rather that the two German states conduct normal economic, cultural and political relations, that they cooperate in the various fields, and that they respect each others' rights and reasonable interests on a basis of reciprocity and complete equality.

It would be particularly important that peace be assured for the German people throughout the entire period of transition within the framework of such a confederation. The two German states, united within a confederation, would require no armaments. The confederation could agree on total disarmament in Germany, on the prohibition of atomic and nuclear weapons on German soil and on the neutrality of the German states. A minimum of good, decent and firm relations could immediately be established between the two German states.

Liberal measures could be agreed upon in commerce, currency circulation, transport, goods traffic and cultural exchanges. Within the framework of such a general settlement—the national document further indicates—a reasonable settlement of travel between the two German states on the basis of the recognition as a matter of course of state-issued travel documents should hardly present any difficulties.

The cooperation of the two German states within a German confederation would soon show the complete absurdity of the stationing of foreign troops on German soil.

The joint effort of the two German states would probably succeed in persuading the US imperialists to withdraw from West Germany, and to abandon the intention of continuing the occupation of the Federal Republic up to 2005.

It is our opinion that nothing should dissuade the two German states from immediately setting out upon this way of peaceful coexistence and national confederation in the interest of peace in Germany and the future solution of the national question.

The policies of the two German states are fundamentally different and they obviously have no common denominator. But there are citizens on either side of our state frontiers who believe that the two German states should give in to a certain degree and somewhat readjust their policy in line with that of the other. Then some way of approach would be found.

Unfortunately the matter is not as simple as that. Let us stop to examine which policy–that of the German Democratic Republic or that of the West German Federal Republic has permanency and which must be changed.

Let us begin with the attitude of the two German states towards the problems of peace and armament.

The government of the West German Federal Republic is feverishly arming, calls for control over atomic and nuclear weapons and makes claims to the territories of neighbouring states. The government of the German Democratic Republic proposes the renunciation of atomic weapons for both German states and their complete disarmament and neutrality. Obviously peace and war may not be blended with each other. One of the two must change its policy. Could the German Democratic Republic be expected to adopt a war policy, calling for atomic weapons? I think not. The West German Federal Republic will have to change its policy. That alone would correspond to the interests of the peace-loving German nation.

Let us consider another question: The relations between the two German states.

The government of the West German Federal Republic rejects normal relations and an understanding on peaceful cooperation between the two German states. The government of the GDR has declared its readiness on more than one occasion to maintain normal, peaceful relations with the West German Federal Republic and to come to terms with it on various matters of national and international importance.

Which policy is to be changed? Which policy corresponds to the interests of the German nation? I think there can be no doubt. Only a policy of normal, peaceful relations and understanding between the two German states and their cooperation within the framework of a national confederation corresponds to the interests of the entire German people. The policy of the West German Federal Republic must also be changed in this respect. There is no other way.

Or let us consider the reunification of Germany. The CDU, the ruling West German government party, has written off the idea of peaceful reunification by calling for the integration of the whole of Germany into NATO. The German Democratic Republic has repeatedly made and is making attempts to prepare the way for a peaceful reunification. Now we again propose to clear the road for reunification by way of peaceful coexistence between the two German states and their gradually increasing cooperation within a German confederation. This is the only possible way still open.

Which policy corresponds to the interests of the German nation? Which policy will have to be changed? Obviously the West German Federal Republic will need to change its policy very radically.

Here is still another field: the composition of state power and the administration.

In West Germany many elements have returned to power which should be excluded from key positions in accordance with the provisions of the Potsdam Agreement for the exclusion of nazis and militarists from public functions; they include individuals who were sentenced at Nuremberg for their serious crimes against other peoples and against the German people.

In the German Democratic Republic fascist and militarist forces have been deprived of power. Imperialism and militarism were eliminated once and for all. Which policy corresponds to the interests of the German people? Which policy will have to be changed? Should we in the German Democratic Republic place Hitler generals and SS leaders at the head of our National People's Army, or entrust nazi hanging judges, stained with the blood of thousands of innocent victims, with the task of dispensing justice over peaceful and decent people in Germany? Should we start paying high pensions to Hitler's associates?

No one will assume that we could so violate the interests of the German nation. Nor can anyone assert that such things responded to the interests of the German people. It is therefore the policy of the West German state which must be changed—and very thoroughly.

Or, take still another field: education and culture.

In West Germany the educational privilege of the wealthy continues now as in the past. The large majority of working people have access neither to education nor to culture. In the German Democratic Republic the educational prerogative of the wealthy has been abolished. Every citizen of the German Democratic Republic may acquire an education in line with his abilities, regardless of position, income and origin. Every citizen of the GDR has access to the treasures of culture, regardless of position, origin or income.

Who then should change policy in this domain? Are we expected to do so? Should we reintroduce the educational privilege of the rich? Should we banish the large mass of workers, office employees and young farmers from our lecture halls and once again convert our universities into breeding grounds of arrogant young dandies, learning there how to dominate the people, how to deceive the people, how to despise the people and how best to avoid all contacts with ordinary folk?

It is quite clear that the West German Federal Republic will have to change its policy in this sphere, too. Its educational system and cultural policy are reactionary, those of the German Democratic Republic are progressive.

In this way we could continue considering every field of life and find the same thing:

The German Democratic Republic is on the right way. It is following a correct policy. Its policy is progressive and serves the interests of the whole people. It will continue to develop and improve this policy in the various fields. A fundamental turn, a radical change, however, is necessary in the West German Federal Republic where the forces of the past are throwing their weight about.

The German Democratic Republic, which has already advanced to a higher stage of historical development in regard to its social structure, will not return to the Middle Ages. The task of all peace-loving and democratic citizens of West Germany and of the whole West German population consists in finding the ways and means for West Germany finally to overcome the reactionary past and take the first steps into the new age, to a bright and happy future. This would remove the major obstacles still in the way of cooperation and mutual approach of the two German states.

The Program of Socialism and the Historic Task of the Socialist Unity Party of Germany

From the report at the
Sixth Congress of the Socialist Unity Party of Germany
from 15 to 21 January 1963

Dear Comrades,

Our great historic task is struggling with all our force, passionately and perseveringly, so that war is banned from the life of the German people once and for all. The path we are following leads to this goal.

The program states: "The Socialist Unity Party of Germany firmly adheres to its aim of restoring the unity of Germany and of overcoming the division effected by the imperialist western powers in complicity with West German monopoly capital."

Without disarmament and an ensured peace, however, it is not possible to overcome the division of Germany. In this sense peace and national unity are inseparably linked in the policy of the Socialist Unity Party of Germany. A peace-loving Germany needs neither nuclear weapons nor any other forced armament. On the contrary: armament—and in particular nuclear armament—is absolutely incompatible with a peaceful solution of the German problem and with reunification.

It was made clear already at the National Congress that the national question of the German people is the safeguarding of peace through the overcoming of militarism and imperialism. It was therefore of decisive national significance that in the German Democratic Republic the solid foundations for a consistent peace policy were created through the uprooting of imperialism. The struggle for the settlement of the national question is a question of social power because the revanchist and atomic war policy is conducted by the representatives of a certain class, monopoly capital, which have the state power in their hands in West Germany. Our principal point of view on the settlement of the national question is set forth in the party program and our reason for struggling so that in West Germany, too, the source of war is plugged up once and for all.

In the course of creating normal relations between the two German states we want to set up a confederation which shall prevent the people from leading even more separated lives and will clear the way for reunification. This presupposes the muzzling of the militarists through the struggle of the peace-loving forces in West Germany.

"The historic mission of the German Democratic Republic", states the program, "is creating the firm basis upon which the working class can take over leadership throughout Germany, the bourgeois monopolists can be deprived of power in West Germany and the national question be solved in the spirit of peace and social progress by means of a comprehensive realization of socialism in the first German workers' and peasants' state."

The GDR cannot wait with the completion of the construction of socialism, with the fulfilment of its historic mission until the peace-loving forces in Germany determine matters. It cannot and will not let its development depend on the lagging behind of the social system in West Germany, of which we in the GDR are in advance by a whole historical epoch, regardless of all our growing pains.

Time and again the opposite development of the two German states demonstrates to what degree peace and the national problem, the social system and democracy are inseparably linked in Germany. The unity of peace, national interests, democracy and the socialist system determine the historic function of our German Democratic Republic.

Hence the struggle of the German Democratic Republic against the aggressive policy of revenge implemented by the West German extremists is not only waged in the interests of the entire German people, but of all peace-loving peoples and states. Safeguarding the GDR state frontier at the same time safeguarded peace for our people as well as for the other peoples, including those living in the NATO states. By thus safeguarding the state frontiers of the GDR the West German militarists were prevented from involving their allies in the adventure of a nuclear war with incalculable consequences.

The consistent defence of peace against the aggressive policy of the West German extremists which imperils peace has strengthened the international authority of the German Democratic Republic. Ever more peoples, ever more people on all continents understand that the German Democratic Republic is *the* German peace state. We not only succeeded in barring the way to revanchist policies to the German militarists. In West Germany itself the peace-loving forces were encouraged to resist the militarist extremists by our success. These fruits of our peace policy must be highly valued. But in this struggle we also suffered losses and injury. The enemy had used the open frontier to wage an economic war with all available means and had made considerable economic difficulties for the GDR.

The GDR working people, who made a substantial contribution

to ensuring peace in Germany and in Europe by means of their peaceful work, did not let temporary economic difficulties keep them from actively supporting our correct policy. The fact that these feats were achieved under the difficult conditions of struggle against the West German imperialists shows the strength of our socialist system.

In connection with deliberations of this kind some citizens ask: "Why didn't we safeguard the GDR state frontier a few years ago and thus spare us these losses?" I would like to give the following answer: Above all we wanted to leave open all possibilities for developing normal relations with West Germany. However, the possibilities of the enemy to organize the cold war against us with the help of the open frontier were also underrated to a certain extent.

In our endeavours to promote and extend good relations between the two German states and their citizens we went to the utmost limits of the reason of state. Unfortunately the circles ruling in Bonn incorrectly assessed our patience and our willingness to negotiate. They multiplied their attempts to undermine the German Democratic Republic and forced us to take well-known effective measures to protect our frontiers.

Many things have become clearer now. And despite all these difficulties the GDR has developed well.

The German Democratic Republic strives for the very best for the workers, farmers, intellectuals and for all peace-loving West German citizens. For instance, in having unmasked Strauss, Lemmer and the active nazis we have complied with the peaceful interests of the West German citizens. But even much more: by our democratic example we have demonstrated how the workers should have greater rights in the whole of Germany, how the farmers can be protected from the effects of the Green Plan and from the extortion of finance capital. We are for the restoration of normal relations between the social organizations in the two German states. Especially we are for cooperation in the fields of sport and culture.

We have also done all we could to promote the cooperation of West German scientists with GDR scientists on a basis of equality. But unfortunately the West German government prevents this equal cooperation. According to their wish, we have submitted to West German teachers our experience concerning polytechnical instruction, and after we had introduced the ten-class school in the GDR the introduction of a nine-class school was discussed in West Germany. It is scarcely our fault that there are still 5,000 to 6,000 one and two-class schools in West Germany. One or two-class schools ceased to exist in the GDR years ago.

We are glad that progressive people in West Germany are so interested in achievements in the GDR. We think it is in compliance with the principles of humanity for us to help West German citizens along in as far as it is their wish. On the other hand we are also quite prepared to examine without prejudice anything progressive that has been achieved in science and technology in West Germany for its applicability in the German Democratic Republic.

We very much regret that the aggressive revanchist policy of the West German militarists and other extremists has brutally cut off or interrupted many family or friendly relationships between citizens of the two German states. Bonn has declined all the proposals which we have repeated for years to come to negotiations between the two German states in order to achieve a lessening of tension so that separation and alienation will be prevented. It has been proved that rearmament in West Germany and Bonn's policy of revenge have also increasingly restricted the relations between the citizens of the two German states. It is high time for this regrettable development to be stopped by ousting the revenge politicians and extremists in Bonn.

We are for the normalization of relations, for making relations between the two German states objective. This should be a first step. What are West German citizens interested in? Are they interested in the perpetuation of the cold war? Who, after all, needs the cold war and the smouldering vestiges of the Second World War? Is it perhaps the West German workers and farmers or the professors, craftsmen, merchants or artists who need them? No! It seems to me that they are interested in finally getting rid of the fear of war and no longer having to live in the shadow of the atomic bomb. So it is really better for West Germany's policy to be thoroughly revised. Then it will be possible to create peaceful conditions in Germany and to achieve at least a minimum of normal and reasonable relations between the German Democratic Republic and the West German Federal Republic.

But this also requires a minimum of truthfulness on the part of West Germany in presenting the situation in the German Democratic Republic. For years now—and I regret to have to say this—the West German people have been deceived and told nothing but lies about the situation in the GDR and our policy, and they are stuffed with the most obnoxious invention cooked up in the decades-old anti-communist manner.

The silly and fantastic lies that are put together there about the German Democratic Republic beat everything. West German citizens should insist on at least objective information. Or they must inform themselves about the situation directly in the German Democratic

Republic. The citizens of the Federal Republic should no longer tolerate the lying propaganda in the Goebbels style.

Therefore, let us make the relations between the two German states and their citizens more objective! It will then be easier to solve the existing problems in the different fields. This will also facilitate negotiations on cooperation between the two German states in a German confederation after the conclusion of a German peace treaty and an agreed settlement of the West Berlin question.

We are ready to make relations between the two German states objective. We are ready to examine objectively what is good and what is bad in West Germany. We know that in many fields there are a number of good accomplishments in West Germany. There are able men and women whose accomplishments we recognize. But the militarist-clerical rule and the steeping of millions in the slough of ignorance are a bad thing and unworthy of a great and able people.

For an Agreement of Reason and Good Will

We propose to create prerequisites step by step for matter-of-fact and normal relations between the two German states. For this purpose we propose an agreement of reason and good will, taking into account the existence of two German states with different social systems, an agreement which might be along the following lines:

1. Respect for the existence of the other German state and its political and social system. Solemn renunciation of the use of force in any form.

2. Respect for the frontiers of the other German state. Solemn renunciation of all attempts and endeavours to encroach upon or change these frontiers. To fix and to confirm, as well, the existing German frontiers with other countries.

3. Solemnly to renounce the testing, possession, production and acquisition of nuclear arms as well as control over such weapons.

4. Arms stop in both German states linked to the obligation not to increase expenditure for military purposes. Agreements on disarmament in both German states.

5. Mutual recognition of passports and the citizenship of both German states as a prerequisite for a normalization of travel. To omit all discrimination and unequal treatment of citizens of the two German states both in Germany and abroad.

6. Establishment of normal relations in the fields of sport and culture between the two German states. The Federal Republic, its representations abroad and its social organizations renounce all dis-

crimination against GDR citizens when representatives of the two German states participate in international conferences, congresses and sport events in West Germany and abroad, and vice versa, we assume the same obligations towards citizens of the Federal Republic. The government of the Federal Republic also renounces any kind of undignified practice so unworthy of the nation as enforcing in NATO descrimination against GDR citizens through the Travel Board in West Berlin.

7. Conclusion of a trade agreement between the governments of the two German states with the aim of extending and developing trade between them.

These are our proposals. Naturally we are also ready to negotiate on West German proposals serving the same purpose. We are of the opinion that after the conclusion of the German peace treaty it will be possible gradually to develop the cooperation of the two German states.

Where Germans Sit Down Together
They Can Come to an Agreement

From the speech on the occasion of the
45th anniversary of the founding of the Communist Party of Germany
on 3 January 1964

Our initiative for relaxation (meaning the Berlin Agreement between representatives of the government of the GDR and of the Senate of West Berlin–Editor) corresponded to the proposal of the Sixth Congress of the Socialist Unity Party of Germany (SED) of January 1963 on agreements of reason and good will between the GDR and the West German Federal Republic as well as between the GDR and the West Berlin Senate. The question repeatedly arises as to where the initiative came from. This is very easily answered. At the end of November 1963 I suggested in the Political Bureau of the Socialist Unity Party of Germany that the Council of Ministers of the GDR should approach Herr Brandt, Governing Mayor of West Berlin, and the West Berlin Senate to make a Christmas agreement to enable West Berliners to visit their relatives in the capital of the GDR. This proposal was unanimously approved by the Political Bureau as well as by the Council of Ministers.

We were guided by the thought of fulfilling the wishes of many West Berlin citizens and also GDR citizens and at the same time of creating an atmosphere of relaxation between the government of the GDR and the West Berlin Senate. Of course, only regular negotiations between competent organs, between plenipotentiary representatives of the GDR government and the West Berlin Senate could lead to a result.

We are glad that as a result of our initiative such negotiations finally came about in which it was agreed upon that GDR representatives would function temporarily in West Berlin to receive requests for entry permits and issue entry permits to cross the frontier into the capital of the GDR, and that they would carry on their activity with the support of the organs of the West Berlin Senate.

We are glad about the success that at least during the holidays the cold war could be repulsed and hundreds of thousands of West Berliners and many citizens of the GDR could be given great pleasure. It would be an exaggeration to call the agreed upon protocol on the

Berlin Agreement a state treaty. For West Berlin is still not a Free City, but a part of the city subject to the occupation regime. But still a bit of self-determination for West Berlin could be implemented in this case. And there were regular negotiations between legitimate representatives of the state power of the GDR and the West Berlin Senate which is the leading state organ there. Thus, negotiations proceeded from the actual facts which include the indisputable existence of the German Democratic Republic, in fact and in international law.

During the negotiations the Council of Ministers of the GDR considered the special position of West Berlin. West Berlin is in the middle of the German Democratic Republic. The population of West Berlin can live in peace and quiet only when they do not allow their territory to be used as a NATO or revanchist base. The West Berliners can live in peace only when the cold war ceases and normal relations are brought about between the government of the GDR and the Senate of West Berlin. Of course, there are differences of opinion between us about the social system. But these differences of opinion need not be decided in the form of the front-line policy and cold war.

It is the special situation of West Berlin that its position in the middle of the GDR induces the West German revanchist politicians and representatives of the so-called forward strategy to misuse West Berlin as a centre of provocation. It is therefore of decisive significance that West Berlin is not a part of the Federal Republic and cannot be a part of the Federal Republic.

As to security nobody is harming the West Berliners. However, the West Berliners would undoubtedly be able to live more tranquilly and peacefully if there were no longer an occupation statute, no occupation troops, no foreign and West German espionage centres and no foreign radio stations broadcasting incitement in West Berlin.

The normalization of relations between the GDR and West Berlin depends decisively on the overcoming and cessation of the cold war. West Berliners are right not to let themselves be intimidated by the screams of certain West Germans of the radical right. Up to now it has been repeatedly stressed precisely from Bonn that West Berlin should be an example. But now the West Berlin Senate and Mayor Brandt have really set a reasonable example for negotiations and understanding. This example will have still more significance in the relations between the two German states. Many of those who today still oppose it will see the time when the government of the West German Federal Republic and the government of the German Democratic Republic will achieve reasonable results in official negotiations on questions of common interest.

Many West Berlin and GDR citizens rightfully ask: How shall things go on? We think that a basis has been created through the Berlin Agreement on which further negotiations are possible. We continue to be ready for such negotiations. We think it useful in the sense of relaxation and the stopping of the cold war that agreements are made which serve the interests of both sides.

The governments of the two German states face a new situation. The German Democratic Republic has developed into a stable socialist state in the centre of Europe. It is secured through its own strength and the alliance with the Soviet Union and the peoples' democracies.

The West German Federal Republic has developed into an economically strong state with authoritarian ruling methods. It has the strongest military force among the West European capitalist states and struggles for equality of rights with the USA. It endeavours to make the alliance between West Germany and the USA the nucleus of the NATO. In this way it tries to harness the USA to the cart of its revanchist policy.

In the German Democratic Republic the population decided in favour of a socialist state on the basis of its right of self-determination. The workers, farmers and members of the intelligentsia in the German Democratic Republic have made good and reasonable use of their right of self-determination. They have taken power from the imperialist rulers, the monopoly capitalists, the big landowners and militarists and set up a democratic order in which the working people really have the power.

In West Germany the citizens decided in favour of a capitalist state and social system on the basis of a somewhat curtailed right of self-determination.

At present the two German states unfortunately have a basically different status. Whereas the Adenauer government delegated the right of West Germany to negotiate on reunification to the western powers, thus renouncing an essential part of its right of self-determination, the German Democratic Republic always preserved its right of self-determination and did not cede any such rights to the other signatory states of the Warsaw Treaty. The German Democratic Republic obviously cannot be expected to renounce its right of self-determination nineteen years after the end of the Second World War. Thus we can but direct the serious request and entreaty to the western powers to interpret the provisions of the Paris Treaties in a way that the West German federal government receives the freedom to regulate its relations with the German Democratic Republic itself.

The Bonn government should renounce the detours via Washington, Paris and London, as the West Berlin Senate finally renounced fulfilling the wish of the Bonn government to take up contact with the GDR only via the International Red Cross in Geneva or via some jurists who are responsible to no one. It should choose the normal, shorter way via the possibilities for contacts which exist in Germany. The representatives of the two governments could negotiate with each other in German and would need no interpreter.

The Berlin Agreement which is a German affair finally shows that Germans can reach understanding and find solutions for many problems when they sit down together and talk. The practice of carrying through the Berlin Agreement on the question of entry permits is an example showing that such matter-of-fact cooperation is possible.

Would it be so bad for the population of West Germany, after all, if the West German federal government would cease its cold war against the German Democratic Republic and its citizens and conclude an agreement of reason and good will on the basis of equality of rights with the GDR? I think that this would be nothing but good for the West German population. Thus the two German states would jointly set out on the way of relaxation. The citizens of the German Democratic Republic as well as the citizens of the West German Federal Republic could live in peace. Normal relations would develop in the fields of economy and culture and in other fields.

With such an agreement the citizens of West Germany could shape their social system as they please. Likewise the citizens of the German Democratic Republic would further build their socialist system in accordance with the laws of social development. As West Germany makes up two-thirds and the GDR but one-third of Germany, West Germany would really not need fear cooperation on an equal footing. Up to now Herr Erhard has not declared his readiness for negotiations with the government of the GDR because the extremists exert pressure on him and because he himself is not yet willing to negotiate on the basis of equal rights. But there is no other way. The attempt of a few ministers of the Bonn government to apply the so-called agent theory and reject negotiations by saying that the GDR is a Soviet occupation zone and that its government has nothing to say is not taken seriously by anyone.

We want to tell all West German citizens clearly and unmistakably: A peaceful settlement of the German question is possible only with a renunciation of multilateral nuclear armament, a renunciation of revenge, and with good will for disarmament. A policy of non-recognition of the German Democratic Republic excludes every possibility of reunification. We do not like the Bonn government, either. But we are ready for negotiations and recognition of the government of the West German Federal Republic, however, on the basis of reciprocity and equality of rights.

Neither the big powers nor the UN General Assembly can replace negotiations and certain steps to understanding between the two German states as well as between the GDR and West Berlin. And there can be a united Germany only when the two German states disarm and are militarily neutral.

The rigidity of the fronts was slackened by the Berlin Agreement. A movement for rapprochement through negotiations and understanding through negotiations has started in West Berlin as well as in West Germany.

Every West German citizen who is for relaxation and understanding only asks: Why can the West German federal government not negotiate with the government of the GDR as did the Senate of West Berlin? Both the government of the German Democratic Republic and Herr Brandt, the governing mayor of West Berlin, proceeded from the status quo. Up to now the Bonn government has refrained from doing this under the pressure of certain revanchist circles.

It is the joint task of the German Democratic Republic and the peace-loving people in West Germany to save the German people from war and especially from a nuclear war. Despite different political conceptions and world outlooks there nevertheless exists the great common concern of guaranteeing peace and security to the Germans in East and West through the lessening of tensions, through the normalization of relations between the German states, through a non-aggression pact, through disarmament measures and the removal of the vestiges of war.

The common interest of the working class of the GDR and the working class of the West German Federal Republic, the common interest of the citizens of the GDR and the peace-loving citizens of West Germany therefore especially requires the prevention of the multilateral nuclear armament of NATO and a share in the control over nuclear weapons by the ruling circles in Bonn.

For a Non-aggression Pact

Everyone who is concerned about the preservation of peace should welcome the coming into effect of a non-aggression pact. It would provide that both sides obligate themselves to settle questions at issue by means of negotiations and renounce the use of military force, the method of war. Obviously only those can be against a non-aggression pact who pursue a revanchist policy and want to change the frontiers in Europe. But in the whole of Europe such a policy is conducted only by the West German imperialist revanchist politicians who want to expand their power to the East.

Representatives of the Bonn government base their refusal of a non-aggression pact on the statement that it includes the recognition of the GDR. Naturally, such a non-aggression pact cannot protect only West Germany and other NATO states from an attack by the states of the Warsaw Treaty which, of course, do not at all threaten. Naturally, such a non-aggression pact must guarantee security also to the states of the Warsaw Treaty, including the GDR, People's Poland and Czechoslovakia, that they will not be attacked by West Germany and NATO. This is what the Bonn government dislikes in the non-aggression pact. It is thus not at all a question of any considerations in international law. The point is that in such a non-aggression pact the Bonn government would be forced to obligate itself to renounce its plans for the forcible inclusion of the German Democratic Republic in the NATO system and the revision of the existing frontiers through a revanchist war. This must be clearly seen.

Properly speaking a non-aggression pact is the expression of the will to peaceful coexistence.

That means that the existence and recognition of the GDR is a fact in international law which needs no confirmation by a non-aggression pact.

A non-aggression pact, however, means the recognition of the renunciation of revenge, i.e., the recognition of the fundamental provisions of the Potsdam Agreement.

A non-aggression pact means the self-obligation of every one of the participating states, including West Germany, to do everything to prevent a war from ever again starting from German soil.

A non-aggression pact means the recognition of the serious will of all participants to settle all questions of relations between the states and of all questions at issue by means of negotiations.

A non-aggression pact also means the self-obligation of every participating state to cease the cold war so that it cannot be transformed into a hot war, so that war agitation does not poison relations between peoples and states. The common interest in the preservation of peace should induce the states to see that an atmosphere of relaxation is provided and war agitation stopped.

The safeguarding of peace now depends primarily on the activity of the peace-loving citizens in West Germany. The majority of the working class and large sections of the farmers and bourgeois intellectuals already understand that the defence of peace requires the right to express one's opinion and the prevention of the emergency laws, as well as the stopping of war propaganda and revanchist agitation. If the West German citizens want to live in peace they can do this only through determined resistance to being molested by war propaganda, revanchist agitation, against intellectual blackmail, moral terror and the militarization of public life. I shall perhaps be answered that people first demand economic and social reforms. This is correct to a certain degree. But economic and social reforms are made impossible by the very pressure of militarism.

It must be frankly stated that Social Democracy bears the chief responsibility. One cannot expect Herr Erhard, who is under strong pressure from the Adenauer group, to go farther in the cause of peace than the Social Democratic Party of Germany.

A road of peace, disarmament, understanding and confederation will obviously only be entered upon in West Germany when the Social Democratic Party changes its previous course and stops its efforts to be considered a "better CDU". Many social democratic organizations are today making efforts to get out of the clenched embrace of the CDU and the Bonn government.

The Social Democratic Party in West Germany will be forced to make new decisions by the facts of life. The facts of life say that the internal contradictions are sharpening in West Germany through the accelerated armament. The antagonisms between the imperialist states are growing at the same time.

If the Social Democratic Party wants to win the next elections it must have the courage to stand up for the renunciation of atomic armament, for disarmament and for a policy of rapprochement and understanding of the German states. If the SPD wants to be elected by the working people it must advocate a policy of peace initiative and disarmament, for only such a policy meets the national interests of the German people. It cannot be disputed that the present atomic armament in West Germany bars any way to the peaceful settlement of the German question and even more so to reunification.

Our proposal to begin negotiations on an agreement of reason and good will between the GDR and the West German Federal Republic and on this basis solve several questions of interest to the German states and their citizens lies on the table. We maintain our proposals.

6 January and 26 May 1964

To the Federal Chancellor
of the Federal Republic of Germany
Professor Dr. L. Erhard

B o n n
Palais Schaumburg   6 January 1964

Dear Sir,

The prevention of nuclear war has become a life and death question
for the German nation. A German government cannot possibly con-
template how many people might survive such a holocaust. A nuclear
war would imperil the physical existence of the German nation.

The arms race continues unabated and more and more nuclear weapons are being stockpiled. The risk of a nuclear war breaking out because
of power-political interests, or even by accident, increases by leaps and
bounds as the number of states possessing nuclear weapons grows. For
this reason and in view of the dangers threatening our nation I consider it an urgent necessity to appeal to you to relegate to the background what separates you and me in our political views, and to take
joint steps to avert the danger of nuclear war. For the sake of the
security of the Germans in East and West, for the sake of the existence
and health of future German generations, with the object of preserving
the inestimable artistic and scientific values of the German past and
present, I hope you will realize that it is necessary to agree without
any delay on a total renunciation of nuclear weapons. Steps must be
taken to avoid the further piling up of inflammable matter for nuclear
war along the border of the world's two largest military alliances. The
present situation is that, in the event of a conflict, any country possessing nuclear weapons will automatically become the target for the
other side's nuclear weapons. That is why certain NATO powers
vigorously oppose the stationing of nuclear weapons on their territories. The best guarantee of security for the German territories would

313

be if we kept them free of nuclear weapons and if we could obtain guarantees from the member states of NATO and the Warsaw Treaty and from the United Nations to the effect that nuclear weapons of third states would never be used against the German territories.

This is first and foremost a matter of humanitarian concern which should not be affected by political or legal reservations. If you should wish to avoid prejudicing governmental relations between the Federal Republic of Germany and the German Democratic Republic, I am prepared, for the sake of the matter, to agree to a settlement which would take this point of view into account. In the question of war or peace we should not be governed by prestige interests or by questions of mutual recognition. All our action must rather be determined by the vital interests of the German nation. If one can speak here of recognition at all, it can only be the recognition of the necessity of eliminating the menace of the extermination of our nation in a nuclear war.

With this in mind, I am sending you the draft of a Treaty between the Government of the German Democratic Republic and the Government of the Federal Republic of Germany on the total renunciation of nuclear weapons.

Deeply concerned, I urge you to help relieve the German people of the fear of nuclear war and ensure that the gulf between the two German states is not further deepened as a result of nuclear armament in the Federal Republic of Germany.

Both in the interests of peace and of the unity of the German nation we should take action to bring about a relaxation of tension between the two German states. Obviously, there is no other way than a sincere attempt to reach agreement on at least the most burning issues of the present. To coordinate the ways and means and the subject of such an exchange of views I suggest that you and I nominate representatives to take up preliminary contacts as soon as possible.

With the assurance of my high consideration,

W. Ulbricht
Chairman of the Council of State
of the German Democratic Republic

Professor Dr. Ludwig Erhard
Chancellor of the Federal Republic of Germany

B o n n
Palais Schaumburg   26 May 1964

Dear Professor Erhard,

You reacted brusquely to my letter of 6 January 1964 with the proposal for an agreement on measures to prevent a nuclear war on German soil and a draft of an appropriate treaty.

The behaviour of you and your government on this matter as well as on other questions of relations between the German states and their governments is obviously inadequate to the great responsibility which you and I both bear for the destiny of the German nation. I can only interpret your reaction to my matter-of-fact, soundly based and very seriously meant proposals to mean that you and your government are still maintaining a course which further deepens and broadens the breach between the two German states, runs counter to international relaxation and endangers peace in Germany and Europe. You cannot deny that your government's demand that the frontiers of 1937 be restored is a revanchist demand. Moreover, you demand West Germany's participation in a NATO multilateral atomic force for the carrying out of your plans of expansion. You know very well that this aggravates the situation in Germany and Europe. With this course the West German government is consciously and intentionally barring any step to overcoming the division of Germany. I regret that you are steering this course.

The seriousness of the situation and the great responsibility for the destiny of the Germans induce me once again to appeal to your consciousness of national responsibility and to propose that you and your government re-examine your attitude and work together with us to overcome the division of Germany through the safeguarding of peace, and through understanding and cooperation between the two German states.

You have deemed it right to designate as your own and to take over Adenauer's frustrated, sterile and dangerous policy. You have rejected the idea of peace in Germany on the basis of disarmament and understanding between the two German states. Broad circles of the West German population which expected a policy of understanding from your taking over the government are disappointed by the way you have taken. Why do you insist on remaining in the blind alley to which Adenauer has led the German question?

You will perhaps reply that the elections which will be held in West Germany next year prevent you from examining the sterile Adenauer policy and making your own conceptions more strongly felt. You will perhaps also say that these impending elections force you to play the revanchist policy into the foreground in order to win the votes of extremists and the old and new fascists. That would be a very dangerous policy.

Assuming that you were right and really needed revanchist aims and an aggressive policy to win votes then West Germany would be in a very, very bad situation. For that would mean that the competition which has been conducted for years in West Germany by the government and all political parties represented in the parliament to outdo each other with the revanchist organizations with regard to chauvinism and the revanchist spirit has already conjured up a disastrous situation in West Germany which can change into open fascism one day soon.

It simply cannot be justified—especially in the historical situation in which we live today—that the peaceful vital interests of the nation are subordinated to any electoral interests of certain CDU/CSU groupings as well as to the vagaries of the leaders of the revanchist associations. You have already proceeded very far on this dangerous way. I seriously fear that you are on the point of sacrificing any possibility of a peaceful development and the overcoming of the division of Germany to your electoral contest and the irresponsible revanchist policy.

The way taken by you and your government is now as before the way of forced armament and conflict, the way of putting the Bundeswehr under the command of Hitler generals, the way of atomic armament, of participation in a NATO multilateral atomic force, of the stationing and storage of ever more foreign nuclear weapon systems on West German soil. But this way leads into the abyss and makes the overcoming of the German division impossible. This policy puts the existence of Germany and even the physical existence of the Germans and especially the West German population at stake.

Why do you want to continue this policy of revenge? Adenauer failed with it. Do you also want to fail ingloriously with this policy? And in addition conjure up the danger of the physical extermination of the people entrusted to you?

You say that you do not want war. I would like to believe you. But you identify yourself with revanchism. You demand the frontiers of 1937, poison the young generation with revanchist ideas and prepare for war, for nuclear war. Who is to believe you when you assert that you are striving for peace? You say—let's get to the bottom of the matter

–that you want to divide and conquer the GDR and other countries in a peaceful way. I can understand that only as a cruel mockery. And then you speak of your variation of the right of self-determination of the Germans. Now there can no longer be any doubt about what you and your government mean by the right of self-determination of the Germans. The shameful Munich treaty which divided Czechoslovakia and was extorted by Hitler Germany with the threat of war has been represented as a model of the right of self-determination of the Germans and as valid in international law with the responsible cooperation of a member of your government. You did not disassociate yourself from your minister!

But you know fully well, Professor Erhard, that any attempt to realize such or similar demands means war, nuclear war. Or do you have some idea that the People's Republic of Poland, the Czechoslovak Socialist Republic and the Soviet Union would dismember themselves voluntarily for your sake, for the sake of your government and your Hitler generals? Or do you think that the government and citizens of the German Democratic Republic who have made use of their right of self-determination in a good and reasonable manner are yearning to subject themselves to the Bonn and NATO military boots? I do not think that you are so foolish as to believe in such a possibility. But in that case all your protestations of peace are base coin!

Should you, however, really cling to the illusions described you and the policy of your government would be a no less great danger to peace. Have you not yet had enough from two wars? I want to admonish you and your government in all seriousness and with all emphasis to reverse your policy.

There can be no doubt that the many thousands of millions for armament and the revanchist policy are senselessly wasted. The results of the Second World War can no longer be revised even through war.

The results up to now of the 15-year-old cold war of the government of West Germany against the GDR have already shown that you and the circles which you allow to influence you have no prospect at all of achieving your objectives. The governments in Bonn have tried in vain for fifteen years to undermine the GDR and discriminate against its citizens. They succeeded in inflicting heavy material damage on the citizens of the GDR, it is true. They also succeeded in having renowned citizens of the GDR, including German scientists and artists of world-wide reputation, exposed to mean and degrading treatment by your NATO allies when they want to travel to one of the NATO countries. But you and your government have not been able to shake the GDR and its government, nor will you ever be able to do so. The result of this policy? The German Democratic Republic has become stronger from year to year and has strengthened its international position. And your government is today farther than ever from the goal of annexing the GDR. But for incomprehensible reasons you and your government cling to your policy which is as evil as it is foolish, detrimental to the nation and peace and completely hopeless.

You make an effort to persuade the West German population into believing that you have discovered a "new foreign policy". This allegedly new policy is that the Federal Republic establishes normal trade relations with the peoples' democracies. I can only say about this that the establishment of normal economic relations between all European countries and moreover with all countries of the world is to be welcomed, but it is not special or "new". What is new is that the Bonn government itself breaks the Hallstein doctrine by establishing normal relations with the peoples' democracies. You will have to take notice of the fact that the peoples' democracies have attained a solid stability and that cooperation in the Council of Mutual Economic Assistance is making quite good progress.

I urgently ask you to seriously examine my proposal of 6 January which is to serve to prevent a nuclear catastrophe in Germany. Give up your resistance to the attempts made by us and many West German citizens to eliminate the cold war in the relations between the two German states.

Many people in your surroundings put speculative hopes in the fact that West Germany's economic potential is greater than that of the German Democratic Republic. But that does not benefit you at all. For the GDR has a firm economic and political foundation and, in addition, good and strong economic partners and allies. And what is more important, the German Democratic Republic relies on a superior social system, the socialist system, whereas the West German Federal Republic clings to an outdated social system of the past which has been doomed by history.

Thus it would be better if you and your government gave up such speculations and renounced all attempts to exert pressure or extortion against the GDR by economic means. This leads to nothing and only poisons the atmosphere.

I am convinced that the deep chasm which today separates the two German states must lead to definitive and irrevocable separation, perhaps for a long historical period, if the German states and their governments do not learn to get along peacefully with each other, talk and deal with one another in a matter-of-fact and reasonable way and place the great national interests of the safeguarding of peace for our people, peaceful coexistence and the gradual overcoming of the division above prestige questions, party politics and personal antagonisms.

I want to state that this very responsible conception has always been represented and practised by the Council of State, the People's Chamber and the government of the GDR. The citizens of the GDR also stand firmly on the ground of this policy just as the majority of the citizens of West Germany, I am also convinced, would agree to such a policy of national responsibility, reason and good will if they only had an opportunity to decide.

You and other members of your government hold the view that foreign powers, namely, four of the victor powers of the Second World War, are responsible and competent for the settlement of the German question. You say that the two German states are not authorized to negotiate with one another and reach agreement if they are not ordered or charged to do so under the control of these foreign powers. Three of them, the USA, Great Britain and France are, as is well known, united with West Germany in the aggressive military NATO pact which is directed against the Soviet Union, the fourth of these victor powers, and against the German Democratic Republic. But these three powers allied with West Germany in the aggressive NATO are obviously not interested in a reunification of the Germans. At the most the USA is interested in enlarging NATO's military, industrial and human potential by incorporating the resources of the GDR. And since this can never happen the governments of all of these three states are, in the final analysis, for the maintenance and further deepening of the division.

The shaping of relations between the German Democratic Republic and the West German Federal Republic is solely the affair of the German states and their governments and parliaments. We do not recognize any competency on the part of foreign powers on this question and are especially not ready to accept any orders of such governments which, like the government of the USA, for example, show an outspoken prejudiced and even hostile and malicious attitude towards the first German workers' and peasants' state and its citizens and persistently refuse to conclude the long overdue peace treaty.

However, if your government, Professor Erhard, should hold the view, taking into consideration the "Treaty on the Relations between the Federal Republic of Germany and the Three Powers" of 1955 that it needs permission or an order from other states to negotiate with the government of the GDR or to cooperate in joint commissions of the German governments I must leave it to you to effect such a permission or order for West Germany. To support you the government of the GDR has addressed an appropriate call to the three western powers.

The German Democratic Republic for its part needs neither such a permission nor such an order. In accordance with Article 1 of the Moscow State Treaty of 1955 it decides freely and without foreign intervention on all questions of its relations with the West German Federal Republic.

The overcoming of the division of Germany requires the renunciation by the West German Federal Republic of a revanchist policy, atomic armament including participation in a NATO multilateral atomic armament, disarmament and understanding on a peace treaty on the basis of which West Berlin becomes a peaceful and neutral Free City. The way to the overcoming of the division of Germany leads via free negotiations with equal rights by the governments of the German states, free from foreign tutelage, and via the step-by-step extension of their practical cooperation for which all-German commissions composed of representatives of the two governments and deputies of the West Berlin Senate could be very useful in various important special fields of common interest.

Such commissions could do good and useful work in the fields of culture, education, legal aid, economic, scientific and technical cooperation, passenger, goods and monetary traffic, trade and sport. They could seek for solutions acceptable to both sides in matter-of-fact exchanges of opinion and submit appropriate proposals to the two governments.

The permit agreement between the government of the German Democratic Republic and the West Berlin Senate of December 1963 has proved that it is possible to reach results acceptable to both sides despite antagonistic political views. Here it became clear that existing differences of opinion can be overcome through patient and persistent negotiations. Especially it could be proved here with a practical example that representatives of two German state organs can reach agreement, that negotiations between German states can have positive results if they are guided by reason and good will.

These first successes of a policy of reason and good will which were achieved between the GDR and West Berlin at the end of 1963 should be exemplary for relations between the two German states, too. Your government, Professor Erhard, harmed the German cause when it prevented permit agreements for Easter and Whitsun 1964 through massive pressure on the West Berlin Senate for reasons arising out of the cold war. That was a policy against the understanding of the Germans, against the overcoming of the German division.

Your attitude is incomprehensible to me. Now and then you speak of your desire for reunification, it is true, but you reject negotiations between the two German states which alone can overcome the division. At the same time you make efforts to prevent new permit negotiations between the government of the GDR and the West Berlin Senate with the assertion that only the government of the West German Federal Republic is competent for such negotiations although the special territory of West Berlin in no way belongs to it. Do you also defend the principle of some of your political friends that West Berlin must be a "bleeding wound" in order to justify the revanchist policy? Such a wicked play with humanity and national interests is irresponsible!

Professor Erhard, we have both experienced how the First World War was prepared and how it ended, what sufferings it brought upon the German people and how Germany became smaller as a consequence of its rulers' desire for conquest.

And we also both experienced how the Second World War was prepared and unleashed by a deluded German government, what unheard-of sufferings it inflicted upon the German people, how it ended and what consequences the revanchist and conquest policy of the ruling circles had for Germany. Again Germany became smaller. Moreover, it was divided into two German states and a special territory of West Berlin by the forces which rule West Germany today, effectively supported by the imperialist western powers.

I do not insinuate that you have any personal blame for the First or Second World War. But the circles of German monopoly capital and German militarism which are behind you bear the full responsibility. And the policy of your government embraces the danger of the unleashing of a third world war which would endanger the life of the German people in particular. In all probability our people would not survive such a war.

This year it is fifty years since the beginning of the First World War and twenty-five years since the beginning of the Second World War. Should this not be an additional occasion for reflection, an occasion to make every effort so that the German states and the German nation finally become a firm factor of peace in Europe for ever? I believe that this is our obligation which makes us responsible for the German nation and which we must fulfil if our nation wants to live and have a happy future.

The People's Chamber, the Council of State, the government and citizens of the GDR are ready to enter upon the national road of peace, rapprochement and understanding together with West Germany.

I am convinced that the citizens of the GDR as well as the great majority of the citizens of the Federal Republic desire such a policy with all their heart. Since it is in the final analysis a question of the well-being and the future of all Germans, the citizens of the two German states and the special territory of West Berlin, I propose:

That the government of the Federal Republic of Germany and the government of the German Democratic Republic obligate themselves through independent declarations

– not to produce nuclear weapons on their own sovereign territory or on the territory of other states, themselves, or with foreign assistance;

– not to acquire or accept nuclear weapons or relevant production and research data;

– not to seek control over nuclear weapons in any form, directly or indirectly through third states or power groupings, alone or in alliance with other states;

– not to participate in nuclear weapon tests in any form;

– not to station nuclear weapons of any kind on their own sovereign territory or allow them to be stationed by third states or power groupings;

– never to employ nuclear weapons themselves or in conjunction with third states or power groupings.

We are ready to examine any other such draft declaration.

I request that the government of the Federal Republic of Germany, the deputies of the Bundestag and the provincial parliaments, the leaderships of the political parties, the trade unions, the women's organizations, the farmers' and youth associations express their attitude to the following three questions:

First question: Are you for a renunciation of atomic armament in any form, for step-by-step disarmament including appropriate control measures and for a reduction in armament expenditures in the two German states?

Second question: Are you for understanding and cooperation on a basis of equality between the two German states and West Berlin with the aim of overcoming the division of the nation and the creation of a united peace-loving Germany?

Third question: Do you favour cooperation and the gradual growing together of the two German states and West Berlin, in the interest of overcoming the division, by means of the establishment of a German Council composed of an equal number of representatives of the People's Chamber of the German Democratic Republic and the Bundestag of the Federal Republic?

Say Yes, Herr Erhard, to peaceful understanding and No to atomic armament!

I am convinced that the Council of Ministers, the deputies, the National Front, the political parties and the leaderships of the social organizations in the German Democratic Republic are ready to answer the same questions or submit them to their members for decision.

I am convinced that the majority of citizens of the two German states and also of the special territory of West Berlin take a positive attitude to these questions. The victor powers, too, as well as the governments of all other states also have a good reason to take a positive attitude to them for they have an interest in the reduction of tensions in Germany.

The citizens of the German Democratic Republic await a careful examination of these proposals and a reply of reason and good will.

Respectfully yours,
Walter Ulbricht

The German-Soviet Friendship Agreement
and the German Peace Doctrine

From the speech delivered at the friendship meeting in the
Kremlin Congress Palace on the occasion of the conclusion of the
Agreement on Friendship, Mutual Assistance and Cooperation
between the German Democratic Republic and the
Union of Soviet Socialist Republics on 12 June 1964

For a Stable Peace

The safeguarding of peace has become a question of to be or not to be for the German people. That is, here, the vital national interests of the GDR and of the entire German people meet the vital interests of the Soviet Union in the decisive question of our time.

The same also applies in regard to the need to replace the post-war period with its cold war and its dangerous tensions by a secure system of peace in Europe. The German people therefore need the peace treaty which, 20 years after the end of the Second World War, is still being denied to us today by the imperialist western powers at the instigation of the Bonn government.

The Soviet Union is also striving for the conclusion of a German peace treaty. For it is in its interest that the vestiges of the Second World War, artificially kept smouldering during the post-war era should be removed and that the road should be cleared for the lasting and ensured peaceful coexistence of the peoples and states with different social systems.

The German people are interested in a stable economic, cultural and scientific development in the interest of their welfare. This development in turn calls for varied cooperation and the division of labour with the Soviet Union in every sphere, to the advantage of both states. The Soviet Union is just as interested in this as we are. The German people are interested in the economic and cultural upsurge of the Soviet Union just as the Soviet Union is interested in the economic and cultural flourishing of a peace-loving and democratic Germany. Here, too, we therefore see the agreement of the national interests of the German people with the interests of the Soviet Union.

The same applies to the questions of world-wide disarmament, the agreement on measures for the prevention of a nuclear war, the conclusion of international treaties to economic exchange free of all restrictions and obstructions imposed by the cold war and a policy of discrimination, and so on.

The Soviet Union has always made a careful distinction between the German imperialists, militarists and all false leaders of the people and the peace-loving German people themselves. This is also reflected in the Potsdam Agreement which unmistakably establishes that the German people can have no future under the leadership of imperialists, militarists and fascists.

After the western powers, in the interest of their self-preservation, had entered into an alliance with the Soviet Union for the overthrow of the Hitler rule they sought after the overthrow of Hitler to preserve the domination of reactionary forces in West Germany. They allied themselves with the representatives of monopoly capital and the most reactionary elements in West Germany with a view to splitting Germany. This was intended to prevent the unification of the German working class and workers, and to make West Germany the main basis of struggle against socialism in Europe. The splitters of Germany were guided by their capitalist class interests.

Now that the division of Germany has been deepened by the Bonn government and by NATO in spite of our resistance and in spite of our proposals for the conclusion of a peace treaty and for reunification, there now remains no other way to safeguard peace than the normalization of relations between the two German states, disarmament and the conclusion of a peace treaty between the victorious powers and the governments of the two German states.

I recently addressed a letter to the head of the West German government, Professor Erhard. In this letter I started from the consideration that we were obviously approaching the end of the post-war period, and that we must draw the necessary conclusions from this fact for the policy of the two German states. On that occasion I urgently warned Herr Erhard against the continuation of the policy of revenge. Adenauer failed with that policy. Erhard, too, must fail with it. This would be only natural. But this policy of revenge is conjuring up the danger of a nuclear war on German soil.

The peoples, including the citizens of both German states, do not want the post-war period, which is drawing to a close, to become a new pre-war period. The peoples, including the citizens of both German states, want stable peace and stable security, in conformity with the aspirations of the whole of mankind.

I called Herr Erhard's attention to the fact that the new historical era required the open-hearted and honest participation and cooperation of both German states and their governments in bringing about peaceful coexistence.

A West German state and a West German government which

resisted this development and insisted on a course of militarism and a policy of revenge would be putting themselves in the pillory of world history as perpetual disturbers of the peace.

In this connection I submitted a number of constructive proposals for the safeguarding of peace in Germany and for the rapprochement and understanding of the German states on the basis of reason and good will. I regret to have to state today that the Bonn government has once again rejected all ideas of a rapprochement of the two German states and their citizens. Bonn is thus interested in the maintenance and sharpening of tension in Germany and Europe. The policy conducted by the Bonn government can be described only as a fundamental policy of tension and conflicts, hostile to mutual understanding and the reunification of Germany.

The West German ruling class of the monopoly capitalists, supported by militarists and other revanchist politicians responsible for having plunged Germany into two world wars, is also proving at the present turning point of history its inability to represent the interests of the German people. The only hope and at the same time the only guarantee of a peaceful development in Germany is and remains the rule of the working class in alliance with the peasants, progressive intellectuals and the other sections of the working population.

This, our memorable journey of friendship through the Soviet Union, and the negotiations conducted in this connection have been crowned by the conclusion of the

"Agreement on Friendship, Mutual Assistance and Cooperation between the German Democratic Republic and the Union of Soviet Socialist Republics".

This Agreement has a great national and international significance. It extends and consolidates the fraternal friendship and cooperation between our states and at the same time it expressly lays down the inviolability of the frontiers of the German Democratic Republic as being one of the basic factors of European security. It obligates the partners to consider and treat West Berlin as an independent political entity which is in no way part of the West German Federal Republic and which does not come under the authority of the West German Federal Republic. The Agreement envisages immediate mutual assistance in conformity with the Warsaw Treaty in the event of an attack on either of the partners of the Agreement in Europe by any other state or group of states. The Security Council of the United Nations will be informed about measures taken in such an event.

The Agreement envisages the further development and reinforcement of economic, scientific and technical relations between the two states in conformity wich the principles of the Council for Mutual Economic Assistance. National economic plans are being coordinated and specialization and cooperation are being developed in production in accordance with the principles of the international socialist division of labour. The coming together and coordination of the national economies of the two states are to ensure the highest possible labour productivity.

The validity of the Agreement has to begin with been fixed at 20 years, with an envisaged extension of another ten years after the end of that period, unless notice has been given of its cancellation one year before it expires. This means that this Agreement on Friendship and Mutual Assistance contains the framework of relations and cooperation between the German Democratic Republic and the Union of Soviet Socialist Republics up to the year 1984 or 1994. It corresponds to both our national policy and also to the great understanding of the government of the Soviet Union for the specific situation of the Germans, living as they are in two independent states with antagonistic social systems, that in the event of the formation of a united, democratic and peace-loving German state or the conclusion of a German peace treaty the Friendship Agreement can be re-examined even before the end of the 20-year period, at the request of either of the signatories.

In this connection it is important to stress that the Agreement expressly stipulates that a peace-loving, democratic, united German state can only be established by way of negotiations on a basis of equality and an understanding between the two sovereign German states.

This Agreement on Friendship and Assistance serves the safeguarding of peace in Germany and Europe. It offers greater security for a peaceful life not only to citizens of the GDR and the USSR but also to citizens of the West German state. For they are especially endangered by the adventurous revanchist policy of the Bonn government.

The Agreement is in accord with the provisions of the Warsaw Treaty and constitutes an additional factor of the stability and effectiveness of the jointly adopted policy.

The Agreement is also of great significance for the peaceful co-existence of the German states and for the safeguarding of peaceful coexistence in Germany and Europe. It will contribute towards overcoming the revanchist policy of the West German imperialists and to normalizing relations between the German states.

This Agreement deprives all those West German revanchist politicians of hope, who, contrary to reason and hard historical facts, insist on nurturing the illusion that they could isolate the German Democratic Republic from the socialist states and in particular that they would succeed in driving a wedge between the first German workers' and peasants' state and the Soviet Union.

The Agreement also forces those West Germans who up to the present have refused to consider rapprochement and understanding in Germany to reflect on the inevitability of establishing normal relations with the GDR. In this connection the Friendship and Assistance Agreement with the Soviet Union is also suited to promoting the rapprochement of the two German states and efforts for the step-by-step overcoming of German division—after a certain time has elapsed for the adoption of a more sober attitude on the part of the responsible German politicians. Every advance in the direction of reunification presupposes that the two German states should come closer together, reaching agreement on a basis of complete equality on the questions of the peace of the nation, and finally coming to an understanding about the first steps for overcoming the division of Germany.

In this connection I should like to renew my appeal to the governments of the USA, Great Britain and France to release the West German Federal Republic from those provisions of the Paris Treaties which prevent the federal government from negotiating on its relations with the GDR and on steps to be taken for overcoming the division of Germany. These provisions of the Paris Treaties obviously do not fit in with our present time. They are a very vile vestige of the cold war and they should disappear as quickly as possible with the transition from the post-war period to a secure system of peace in Europe.

I appeal to the governments of the three western powers no longer to stand in the way of the aspirations of the GDR and of numerous West German citizens jointly to find the way, through negotiations on a basis of equality, towards a peace-loving and democratic, united Germany! Release West Germany from these disgraceful provisions of the Paris Treaties.

The Friendship and Assistance Agreement between the GDR and the Soviet Union promotes stabilization and world peace. It thus corresponds to the interests of all peoples. Not least it also corresponds to the interests of the allies of the West German Federal Republic who obviously do not place too great value on becoming involved by the West German revenge politicians in their policy of conflicts and perhaps even in a nuclear world war.

The peaceful nature of the Agreement also favours the development of good relations between the Federal Republic and the USSR. The

German Democratic Republic is particularly interested in good relations between the Federal Republic and the USSR because this is a condition for peace in Europe. The development of good relations is only possible if neither of the two sides makes demands concerning the internal affairs of other states. The more thoroughly the essence of the Agreement between the GDR and the USSR on Friendship, Mutual Assistance and Cooperation is known to ruling circles in Bonn, the better will it be for the development of relations between the Federal Republic and the USSR.

Finally, the Agreement is also in accord with the spirit of the United Nations Charter, to which it makes express reference. The Agreement takes fully into account the fact that the post-war period is drawing to a close. The Agreement itself becomes an essential part of the stable system of peace which follows the post-war period.

The western powers have so far prevented the conclusion of a German peace treaty on the insistence of their West German NATO partner; such a peace treaty could, under existing conditions, only be conceived as a peace treaty to be concluded with both German states. In contrast to the powerful peace trend of our time Bonn is striving unduly to prolong the post-war period. That is why the peoples are increasingly speaking of the disturbers of the peace in Bonn. Bonn would like to preserve the dangerous atmosphere of the post-war period as long as possible in the interest of its policy of revenge.

Yet the West German government is thereby coming into ever greater opposition to the interests of the peoples. In the great majority they are ardently interested in the stabilization of peace and security. The peoples ardently desire that the post-war period should not be followed by a new pre-war period but by a stable peace settlement. The Agreement on Friendship and Mutual Assistance between the GDR and the Soviet Union corresponds to this striving of the peace-loving peoples, for it is making an effective contribution to the stabilization of peace and security at one of the most critical points in Europe, namely along the line dividing the two German states with opposed social systems.

How can we assess the situation of the two German states and how are the relations between them to develop in the future?

The German Democratic Republic, which celebrates its 15th anniversary this year, has passed through important stages of development within this historically short space of time. A firm workers' and peasants' power has evolved out of the anti-fascist–democratic order of the immediate post-war period–a socialist state which plays an important part in the struggle for the safeguarding of peace in Europe.

The stability of our state arises from the triumph of the socialist mode of production.

How then are the future relations between the German Democratic Republic and the West German Federal Republic to develop? Obviously the establishment of normal relations is by no means a simple matter since the present West German government rejects any rapprochement, negotiations or understanding with the GDR. Bonn insists on a theory which is as foolish as it is untenable and according to which the power to negotiate and determine the relations between the two German states does not lie with the governments or parliaments of the German states but with the four victor powers of the Second World War. In addition, as is known, Bonn asserts that the GDR does not exist. Thus the responsible politicians in Bonn have obviously entangled themselves in such a web of nonsensical assertions and theories that it is hard to imagine how they will ever get out of it.

It will therefore become inevitable that first some basic prerequisites for the establishment of normal relations between the German states are established. The most serious obstacle in this connection is atomic armament. Therefore in my above-mentioned letter to the Bonn head of government Herr Erhard I proposed the following: The West German government and the government of the GDR pledge themselves in independent declarations

not to produce nuclear weapons either on their own sovereign territory or on the territory of other states, themselves, or with foreign assistance;

not to acquire or accept nuclear weapons or relevant production and research data;

not to seek control over nuclear weapons in any form, directly or indirectly through third states or power groupings, alone or in alliance with other states;

not to participate in nuclear weapon tests in any form;

not to station nuclear weapons of any kind on their own sovereign territory or to allow them to be stationed by third states or power groupings;

never to employ nuclear weapons themselves or in conjunction with third states or power groupings.

On the basis of the consideration that it is first a question of guarding the German people and their neighbours against a nuclear war, I promised Herr Erhard to accept and examine any other draft of such a declaration.

In view of the fact that the policy of the West German government directed towards obtaining control over nuclear weapons is undoubtedly not in accord with the aspirations of the majority of the West German population I further demanded that the West German government, members of the West German Bundestag and the provincial parliaments, the leaders of the political parties, the trade unions, women's organizations, farm and youth associations should express their opinion on the following three questions:

First question: Are you for a renunciation of atomic armament in any form, for step-by-step disarmament including appropriate control measures and for a reduction in armament expenditures in the two German states?

Second question: Are you for understanding and cooperation on a basis of equality between the two German states and West Berlin with the aim of overcoming the division of the nation and creating a united, peace-loving Germany?

Third question: Do you favour cooperation and the gradual growing together of the two German states and West Berlin, in the interest of overcoming the division, by means of the establishment of a German Council composed of an equal number of representatives of the People's Chamber of the German Democratic Republic and the Bundestag of the Federal Republic?

These three questions are being discussed among the population of both German states.

The government in Bonn, however, is intensifying its revanchist policy which is expressed among other things in the arrogant pretension that it is exclusively entitled to speak for the German people. This exclusive rights pretension by Bonn has two aspects: in the form of the Hallstein doctrine it is directed against the German Democratic Republic; as non-recognition of the territorial changes brought about as a result of the Second World War it is directed not only against the GDR but also against the Soviet Union, the People's Republic of Poland and—as shown by the attempt by representatives of the Bonn government to justify the Munich Agreement—also against the Czechoslovak Socialist Republic. It thus clearly expresses the revanchist territorial claims of the West German Federal Republic.

In this connection I should like to point out the following: these revanchist territorial claims not only form the subject of chauvinistic speeches by West German ministers and parliamentarians; they have also been included in West German legislation.

Thus, for example, the West German customs law which came into force on 1 January 1962 and its official justification contain territorial claims not only against the GDR and West Berlin, but also against the western territories of the People's Republic of Poland and the Soviet Union. An even more brazen expression is given to the policy of revenge in the new West German Penal Code. In fixing the jurisdiction of this new West German Penal Code the following official explanation is given of the term "inland", i. e., in the final analysis, for the term "Federal Republic"–I quote verbatim:

"According to the present status of international law the 'inland' comprises, in addition to those regions belonging to the territorial jurisdiction of the Penal Code, also such regions which are situated outside that area. These include the Soviet Occupation Zone of Germany, the Soviet Sector of Berlin and the other regions of the German Reich within the frontiers of 31 December 1937 at present under foreign administration."

Which way remains to Germany? I think it is necessary for both German states first to recognize each other's existence on a basis of equality without reservation and seek for ways for their peaceful co-existence and for the settlement of as many problems as possible of interest and concern to both German states and their citizens in negotiations on a basis of equality.

I believe that it is urgently necessary that the two German states and their citizens should recognize their right of self-determination and the situation brought about through the exercise of that right in the 20 years since the end of the Second World War, seeking rapprochement and understanding on that basis.

Those willing to do something for the peaceful solution of the German question and for the unification of the German states into a peace-loving, democratic and united Germany should maintain and develop normal relations with both German states, avoiding all discrimination against one of the German states in favour of the other.

In view of the dangerous consequences of the Bonn policy against relaxation and understanding it seems necessary to me to indicate the way to replace the post-war period by a stable peace settlement and the peaceful solution of the German question by means of a peace doctrine to all those peoples and governments interested in peace and relaxation. The fundamental principle is always the recognition of realities as they have developed since the end of the Second World War.

This is the German Peace Doctrine:

Recognition of the existing German frontiers gives greater security in Europe.

Recognition of the equal rights of both German states and respect for their right of self-determination safeguard peace in Germany and

Europe and pave the way for reunification into a peace-loving Germany.

The normalization of the relations of the states of Europe, Asia, Africa and America with the two German states promotes security in Europe and understanding among the Germans.

It is necessary to carry through the German Peace Doctrine because it corresponds to the requirement that the post-war atmosphere, poisoned by the cold war in the heart of Europe and affecting the entire world be replaced by an atmosphere of peace, respect for the sovereign rights of states and matter-of-fact cooperation between them;

because it contributes towards neutralizing one of the most dangerous centres of tension in the world, thus effectively promoting international relaxation;

because it contributes towards overcoming the policy of revenge and atomic armament of the West German Federal Republic, thus corresponding to the interests of the German nation as well as those of all peoples;

because it supports the establishment of a stable system of peace in Europe, facilitating the way towards universal and complete disarmament;

because it takes into account the fact that the unity of the German nation can be re-established only if the revanchist policy and atomic armament are ended in West Germany, if negotiations are brought about on a basis of equality and without foreign tutelage between the two German states. The West German exclusive rights pretension is no foundation for the re-establishment of the nation's unity;

because it leads to the establishment of normal relations between all states of the world and the two German states, thus removing a factor disturbing matter-of-fact international relations.

Such a German Peace Doctrine corresponds to the interests not only of the citizens of the GDR, but also to those of the citizens of the West German state and of the special territory of West Berlin. It can make a decisive contribution to the removal of the smouldering vestiges of the Second World War. It can contribute towards facilitating decisions regarding the re-establishment of the principles of international law by the various states which today are still giving way to West German pressure in the form of the peace-endangering Hallstein doctrine.

Our Just Cause Will Win

*From the speech on the occasion of the
fifteenth anniversary of the founding of the
German Democratic Republic,
on 6 October 1964*

After 15 years it is customary to strike a balance. How does this balance stand in the two German states?

The favourable side shows that the great opportunity which arose when Hitler fascism was defeated has been made good use of in the eastern part of Germany. The unity of the working class was created. The alliance with the peasantry, the intelligentsia and other sections of working people was concluded. It was not merely a question of settling with the past, but a new anti-fascist democratic state order and later a socialist order were created. The working people themselves under the leadership of the party of the working class brought order in their own house. They swept away the remains of militarism and deprived the war criminals, monopolists and militarists of power.

All citizens of the German Democratic Republic can be proud of the fact that in their German state the socialist revolution has been carried out, the exploitation of man by man has been abolished, a powerful nationally-owned industry has been created and in agriculture the union of farmers into agricultural production cooperatives has taken place. Thus the basis for the development of our beautiful community of man was created, the humanistic content of which is a commandment for all our actions. The scientific teachings of Marxism-Leninism, the program and resolutions of our Socialist Unity Party guarantee the development of the community of the people and the cooperation of the bloc parties in the National Front of Democratic Germany.

The unfavourable side of the balance shows that in West Germany the great opportunity was thrown away. West German finance capital and the imperialist organs of occupation prevented the unity of the working class. The splitting of the working class, the prevention of the alliance with the peasantry and the illusions about the way being made easier with the Marshall Plan made it possible for finance capital to restore the big monopolies and German militarism to power. The progressive forces in West Germany were unable to overcome the past.

The ruling circles in the imperialistic West created the West German separatist state as a part of their NATO alliance. They invented the Hallstein doctrine to the high honour of the profits of monopoly capital and to guard its areas of domination against the socialist countries and they prevented the establishment and development of normal relations between the German states.

If the ruling circles in West Germany maintain that they are for the unity of Germany then it is necessary to ask them over and over again: What sort of unity do you want? For what purpose do you want unity? As is known Germany was a unified country when it began two world wars.

The West German monopolies, who want to continue on this way, have therefore split Germany. We, however, want a peace-loving, democratic and progressive Germany. Only in this way is unity conceivable. This time we want unity for a lasting peace. We want a unity where the peace-loving, democratic forces of the people make the decisions in the state and the economy under the leadership of the working class. We want all guarantees to be created so that a war will never again be started from German soil.

In the consciousness of our national responsibility I declare: After 15 years of a divided Germany the time is more than ripe to tread the path to understanding through mutual recognition of the German states. It is now time to come to an understanding on armament in both German states and on the safeguarding of peace.

All peoples await such steps to understanding from both German states for they serve the relaxation of tension and the safeguarding of peace in the world.

Even the clearest and most far-sighted persons cannot predict today when and under what circumstances the German states will be reunited. But it is clear that preparations for reunification begin with negotiations on equal terms between the two German governments and the mutual recognition of the two German states.

For our part, we have struggled with all our strength against the splitting of Germany, we want reunification, and we will do all that we can to smooth the path for it, to make it possible, and to complete it.

We know, however, the conditions under which the reunification can under no circumstances take place. Reunification is quite impossible under the sign of the rule of monopoly capital, the revenge-seeking policy, and militarism. It can and will take place peacefully and democratically or not at all. The alternative to peaceful and democratic reunification would be a frightful civil war, probably within the framework of a world war. And such a war would not reunite Germany but wipe it out biologically.

Reunification is also out of the question the way some incorrigible fools seem to imagine by buying up the GDR from someone or other. The German Democratic Republic is a sovereign state. It belongs to its citizens, and they are not prepared to sell themselves or their republic to the imperialist western powers.

In West Germany they really should give up speculating on such idiotic ideas and rather turn to life as it is. Real life demands that the two German states negotiate with each other sensibly and work out steps towards the relaxation of tension and ways of working together.

I repeat:

We want reunification. The class-conscious German workers have always been the truest sons of the German nation. They have never sold their country as separatists, as the feudal lords and monopoly capitalists have done more than once. They have never made their country the vassal of another state. They have always known how to combine the social interests of their class with the national interests of their country and the real peaceful international interests of the nation. That is still our policy.

Why do we want reunification?

Here I must first say: Reunification is not a prerequisite to assure a happy life for the people, to assure the continued economic, social, and cultural advancement of the German Democratic Republic. We will complete the construction of socialism and proceed to the building of communism even without reunification.

If we are asked with reference to our long-range plans up to 1970 or 1980 if we have written off the reunification of Germany for this period, the answer is NO! The first place was and still is taken by the need to safeguard peace and understanding about the moulding of the new, peace-loving, disarmed, democratic, progressive Germany. The most important thing is that there should be no war. War would make any progress, for Germans in East and West alike, impossible.

All other questions, especially the improvement of the material position, the achievement of general prosperity, can be completely solved within the framework of the German Democratic Republic. This is all the more possible since our close friendship and cooperation with the Soviet Union and other fraternal socialist countries eases the solution of our economic problems.

That applies, moreover, to West Germany as well. All the economic and social problems can and must be solved in one's own country. It requires only that the workers join with the peasants, intellectuals and all other peace-loving strata of society to weaken or eliminate the influence of those circles which are driving West Germany into war-like adventures or social crises.

What, then, is the heart of the national question of Germany?

The reunification of the German states must serve to the greatest measure possible the safeguarding of peace, never revanchism and war.

The reunification of the German states must strengthen the peace potential of the German nation, never its war potential.

The reunification of the German states can and must serve the welfare of the citizens of both German states. It must not be abused to detract from their welfare. Thus, the reunification of Germany calls for no sacrifices on the part of the people. Reunification must coincide in every respect with the national interests.

What are these national interests?

The big capitalist and monopolist gentlemen are always telling us that their profit interest is identical with the national interests. But in a frightful past we have experienced just how homicidal such so-called national interests of the monopolists are. They are anti-national in the highest degree.

For us, however, for the vast majority of the nation, the national interest means the preservation of peace, justice and freedom for the working people, the avoidance of economic and social crises, social security, and the development of democracy and culture. If, then, the reunification of the German states is to serve the national interest of the Germans, those conditions must be fulfilled that make national reunification worth striving for to 95 per cent of all Germans.

Yes, indeed: We are in favour of a national reunification that will guarantee that never again will war be unleashed from German soil, that causes no disquiet in Europe and the rest of the world, that does not encroach upon the borders of other countries, that does away with the atomic bomb, that limits armament and guarantees general and complete disarmament.

We are in favour of a reunited Germany where the principle holds good that what the people's hands have created shall belong to the people, where the great talent of the united German working class, the engineers, the farmers and craftsmen, the scientists creates prosperity for all the Germans still more rapidly than is possible today and makes of the whole of Germany that rich, cultured, and peaceful land that we Marxists have always visualized.

That is the reunification that we are struggling for in building up the German Democratic Republic. That is our decisive historical contribution to the reunification of the German states. The quicker and the more successfully we achieve our work of construction the better will be the chances for reunification in West Germany. Providing, of course, that, fired by our example, the working people of West Germany finally make a peaceful democratic state out of the Federal Republic of Germany.

We endeavour to take up contact talks and negotiations with every West German government. Anyone can understand that without such official contacts, talks, and negotiations between the governments of the German states no reunification can result.

It is inconceivable that, without the mutual recognition of the two German states, even a first serious step towards reunification can be made.

I ask the gentlemen in the government and in the Bundestag in Bonn: how much longer are you going to stubbornly behave like sectarians and close your ears to reason? How much longer are you going to hold off doing what in the end is inevitable? How much longer do you propose to confuse reactionary obstinacy with national pride and make the situation between the German states more complicated than it is already?

A few days ago the West German head of government, Herr Erhard declared and had declared that the German Democratic Republic is not a subject of international law, that it is not subject to international law. That is the way Hitler always talked when he was about to attack peoples. Herr Erhard, you do not determine what is international law and who is a subject of international law. You do not even decisively determine Bonn policy. Leave such Hitlerian tones aside. And should you want to excuse yourself for such madness by saying you had to talk like that because you had a Franz Josef Strauss, a Baron von und zu Guttenberg, and an Adenauer behind you, let me remind you that pressure and coercion can never excuse a crime.

Further, Professor Erhard, you should finally stop demanding a Germany with the frontiers of 1937. You know as well as I do that that is an impossibility. It is possible that you will no longer be chancellor after a time, that is possible. But no one will change the frontiers of 1964. Anyone who might try to do so would hardly survive the first step.

Also, Professor Erhard, you should finally give up the political folly you took over from your predecessor. You should finally take a step towards understanding with the German Democratic Republic. Instead of remaining a very minor, completely unfruitful episode of German history you could achieve something significant for the whole

German nation. You could clear away the prohibitions which are to prevent you and your government from showing common sense in relation to the other German state.

There are not a few voices in West Germany itself that try to make clear to you, Herr Erhard, that the enormous sums that you put into armaments, aside from enriching the arms millionaires, are otherwise completely senseless. No one wants anything from the West German Federal Republic. No one is planning to take anything away from it, not the factories, not one piece of land, nor its right to settle its own affairs.

We have very often made proposals to Herr Adenauer and to you on joint disarmament, on the joint undertaking not to strive for atomic and hydrogen bombs or to allow anyone to stock them on German soil.

We have repeatedly laid before your predecessor and you yourself proposals that on various questions joint committees with equal representation should be established so that we might reach understanding on such matters as economic, cultural, and sports questions. We have repeatedly proposed to you that we should set the whole of Europe at rest by concluding a peace treaty that would not cost West Germany a penny but would at last bring about a state of peace in Europe and could be a factor in the relaxation of tension in the whole world.

We have often proposed to you much that is useful and necessary, and we shall continue to do so, also to your successor and, if need be, also to his successor. No one will find it easy to disturb our patience. If we did not have this patience, the new agreement on visitors' permits between the government of the German Democratic Republic and the Senate of West Berlin would not have been concluded, and the policy of those forces in the West German government which were trying to prevent agreement from being reached would have been victorious. As it is, the West German government has suffered a political defeat. And that will always be the case when it acts against the interests of the people. The results of the local elections in North Rhine-Westphalia and in Lower Saxony speak pretty unambiguously.

We are not influenced and led by big capitalist interests or by revanchists and generals, specialists in lost wars who would like to win a war for once. For us the real interests of the people and of the nation are our lodestar.

So it was in the past, so it is now, and so will it be in the future. Why? Because we were socialists, because we are socialists, and because we shall remain socialists.

Of course, for us the Erhard government and the circles it represents are not the whole of West Germany. Workers, peasants, craftsmen, technicians, scientists—all those who live by the honest toil of their hands and brains form the great majority. And in the end what they want, what corresponds to their interests will happen in West Germany.

What force is able to deflect the threat to peace, to security, and to democracy, what force is able to save the German people from a third world war, which they in all probability would not survive? What force is able to safeguard peaceful development and create the prerequisites for the reunification of Germany?

If anyone knows another, more convincing answer, let him give it. We know, however, that there is only one force in Germany that can do that:

That is the working class in alliance with the peasants and the other democratic and peace-loving forces of the people in both German states and in the special territory of West Berlin.

Under the conditions of the existence of two German states and a special territory of West Berlin the safeguarding of peace in Germany and for the German people is therefore to a decisive degree dependent on an understanding between the Socialist Unity Party of Germany, the Communist Party of Germany, and the Social Democratic Party in West Germany, on an understanding and on cooperation between the trade unions of the German Democratic Republic and the trade unions in West Germany. I see no other possibility of safeguarding the national, peaceful, vital interests of the entire German people.

As long as the working class parties and trade unions of the two German states and the special territory of West Berlin do not go along with each other but stand against each other there can be no definitive safeguarding of peace for Germany. Anyone who claims to want the reunification of Germany but rejects an understanding between the working class parties and trade unions of the two German states and the special territory of West Berlin cannot reconcile his words with his deeds. He seems to me like a man who takes two steps backwards after each step forward and then wonders why he is not making any progress.

The working class parties and the trade unions in Germany will have to come to an understanding with each other or there can be no reunification of Germany. Every social democrat, every trade unionist, every social democratic official and leader must know that. In the vital interests of the nation the working class parties and the trade unions must pursue a policy of their own. The leaders and officials of the Social Democratic Party (SPD) and the German Trade Union Federation (DGB) will have to realize as a body, and this realization has already begun, that the rejection by the Adenauer government and the present Erhard government of our proposals cannot be the policy of the West German and West Berlin working class. Or will anyone maintain that the social democratic leaders and the West German trade union leaders are obligated to follow the Erhard government up the blind alley and to stay in a blind alley with them?

I have several times pointed out the consequences. The West German big bourgeoisie, which rules the state over there, does not want any reunification if it means even the least possibility of the restriction of its rule, its profit economy. But no god, no kaiser, no tribune can guarantee the continuation of the capitalist social system, condemned as it is by history to fall.

What then are we waiting for in Germany? Are we to wait another five years and then another five years and then another five years before we make the slightest serious move towards the reuniting of the German states? The time would come when the vast majority of German citizens would know no other condition, and perhaps even could imagine no other condition. But that means we are approaching the critical limit, beyond which, in all probability, the division will be for an unforseeable period. In view of the opposite directions that development in the German states is taking it is obvious that reunification grows more difficult from decade to decade.

Only the state of the German workers and farmers, together with the working people of the West German Federal Republic and West Berlin and their political and trade union organizations together can save peace and the national unity of Germany.

A state of understanding and peace between the SED and the SPD in West Germany with the participation of the trade unions in both German states is, as things are today, the only possibility which will allow the gradual overcoming of the division of Germany. It is the key to the solution of the national question.

I proceed from the fact that West German Social Democracy and the West German trade union movement also reject the idea of military conquest. If I am wrong on this point, and time will show, then the threat of the inferno of a nuclear war would be considerably greater than we see it today. In that case the possibility of reaching an understanding and of reunification would really have to be written off for a long time, perhaps even for ever.

Peace in Germany and the possibility of the reunification of Germany depend, then, on understanding and peace between the Socialist Unity Party of Germany and the Social Democratic Party of West Germany.

There is no place here for tactical manoeuvres or a petty seeking for advantage. All ulterior motives of one party perhaps eliminating and liquidating the other must be rooted out. After all, the question is that of the vital interests of Germany, nothing more and nothing less.

If would be tragic for the German people if old antagonisms, old distrusts, and the memory of controversy and argument should prevent the necessary rapprochement of those forces in Germany whose co-operation is historically necessary and indispensable for the future of Germany. The burdensome responsibility for the fate of the German nation bears down upon the working class and its organizations here and over there.

Dear West German workers,

We are waiting for your answer in the spirit of reason and good will.

We can only hope that it will not come when it is already too late.

A Thaw in Europe Is Possible

From a television interview with Professor Gerhart Eisler,
chairman of the State Broadcasting Committee,
on 24 January 1965

Gerhart Eisler: Mr. Ulbricht, as leader of the delegation from the German Democratic Republic you took part in the meeting of the Political Advisory Committee of the Warsaw Treaty states.

What was in fact the reason for this Warsaw meeting which aroused so much attention and interest throughout the world?

Walter Ulbricht: A meeting of the representatives of the Warsaw Treaty states was necessary because a new situation has developed in Europe. It is characterized by a serious threat to the peace and security of the European peoples and states.

Typical of the new situation is, for example, the fact that the policy of the government of the West German Federal Republic is becoming ever more adventurous. Nuclear armament, persistent striving for control over atomic weapons, plans to create a zone of atomic mines along the eastern frontier of the West German Federal Republic, the aggressive so-called forward strategy, threats of "undercover warfare" and civil war directed against the German Democratic Republic by responsible representatives of the West German government, the unlimited arming of West Germany and the intensification of the policy of revenge—all these are essential, even if they are not all the elements by far of this new situation.

The government of the West German Federal Republic, which is itself a product of international tension and which expects to gain advantages for its revanchist policy from the perpetuation and sharpening of tension, is playing the role of an international centre of disturbance with stubbornness and cold contempt for humanity, against peace, security and the understanding of the peoples.

Gerhart Eisler: Talk of an atomic mine belt undoubtedly alarmed many people but in West Germany as well as in other countries there are still many people who do not want to recognize the danger. They are of the opinion—and want to persuade us to believe—that all this is not intended to be malicious and take the standpoint that things are never as bad as they sound.

Walter Ulbricht: Our people have had to pay dearly for under-estimating the aggressiveness and adventurousness of its ruling imperialist forces in two world wars. The German people cannot afford at any time to disregard the experiences of history.

You see, plans for a war to be fought on German soil with traditional as well as with atomic weapons are being openly discussed by people in responsible government positions and are already being practised in manoeuvres. West German Vice-Chancellor Mende, member of the government and also of the defence committee of the West German Bundestag, a man therefore who must be fairly accurately informed of Bonn's plans and intentions, has openly threatened us with "sub-limited warfare" and civil war. Heinz Hoffmann, Minister of National Defence in the German Democratic Republic, found it necessary to tell him clearly and simply at a press conference what every individual participant in an aggression against the German Democratic Republic could expect.

It is certainly a fact that the preparations of the NATO multilateral nuclear forces have led to West German military personnel having the closest access to atomic war-heads and carrier rockets and to them being intensively trained to use these weapons. At least one atomic missile ship with a crew consisting partly of West Germans is already at sea. With the coming into existence of the MLF, whether in the American or British or any other form, a part of the atomic missile ships would be under the command of West German generals and admirals who have already shown in the Second World War what they were capable of.

In West Germany as well as abroad the West German government has made preparations to produce its own atomic weapons. Rockets are already being produced in West Germany. The commanding positions and higher staffs in NATO are already occupied by so many West German military personnel that one can scarcely talk of the West German militarists being under the control of their NATO allies.

It would be more correct to put it the other way around.

Whoever closes his eyes to these and many other no less convincing facts is in danger of building his policies on illusions. We, however, are used to taking facts into account and not the idle talk of wolves on high holidays. That means that we precisely evaluate the new situation on the basis of the facts and draw the necessary conclusions even if it is unpleasant for the wolves.

Gerhart Eisler: What did the allied socialist states want to achieve in Warsaw?

Walter Ulbricht: It can be seen from the communiqué of the meeting that the Political Advisory Committee had to assess the new situation, examine the possible effects on peace and the security of our states and peoples and prepare joint action and the necessary measures.

Here, too, the fact that the heightening of the danger of a war in Europe is, finally, a result of the continual breach of the basic agreements of the Potsdam Agreement by the government of the Federal Republic encouraged by western imperialist powers must, of course, also play a part. Thus it was necessary to discuss how respect for international treaties can be restored.

We also discussed, of course, measures which would be taken in the most widely differing fields and in part confirmed those which the participating countries of the Warsaw Treaty and their united supreme command considered necessary to guarantee peace and security and the peaceful work in our countries. Thus it was the task of the meeting in Warsaw to set limits on the potential aggressors and introduce effective measures and steps to encourage peace and security.

We regard the results of the meeting of the Political Advisory Committee as a success for the cause of peace and security in Europe. A new stage in the struggle against the West German Federal Republic having joint control of nuclear weapons, no matter in what form, has been introduced.

Gerhart Eisler: Mr. Chairman, it is quite natural that such an important meeting should begin with the participants first of all agreeing on the assessment of the situation. You mentioned at the beginning some elements of the new situation, especially in so far as they concern the aggressive policy of the government in Bonn. How did the delegations in Warsaw judge the present situation?

Walter Ulbricht: This can be seen from the joint communiqué. The delegation from the German Democratic Republic handed to all delegates a memorandum containing plain facts on the atomic arming, the aggressive "forward strategy" and on the preparation of a "sublimited war" by the West German Federal Republic. In this memorandum, among other things, the military, strategic conception of the West German government as an expression of its revanchist intention towards the socialist states, the continually growing influence of the West German government on the atomic aims and plans for the use of the nuclear weapons in the possession of its NATO allies and the gradual progress by the West German government towards demanding control over nuclear weapons are set out in detail convincingly and quite openly.

I would like to point out that there was general agreement in assessing the present situation. This concerns especially the role played by the government of the West German Federal Republic as an international centre of disturbance against peace and understanding among the peoples. Of course, the new situation is not influenced only by the development of the policy of the West German government which is negative in every respect. The historical development trends throughout the world are taking quite a different course.

They are also characterized in the present stage by an increase in the forces which support the maintenance and consolidation of peace. The power of the socialist countries which pursue a consistent policy of peace is steadily growing. The communist parties and the popular masses of the European states and other countries resolutely favour a healing of the international situation. The independent states of Asia, Africa and Latin America are actively contributing towards the consolidation of peace.

At the same time the imperialist powers which are striving to intensify the international situation in various parts of the world and to provoke differences between the states are being very active and are showing great stubbornness. I recall here the US aggression in South Vietnam, the policy of intervention in the Congo and the colonial methods used against the peoples of Malaysia. The imperialist forces are interfering in the internal affairs of independent states and are using methods of economic and military pressure. They are using their military groupings to suppress the national liberation movements.

Agreement was also reached in estimating the special role played by a NATO multilateral nuclear force in which West Germany is to have a share. These plans were unanimously denounced as a serious threat to peace in Europe and in the whole world.

But there was also clarity that the military technology available to the armed forces of the Warsaw Treaty countries guarantees that every aggressor will have to reckon with his destruction.

I would like to point out with satisfaction that the Soviet delegation led by Mr. Brezhnev, first secretary of the Central Committee of the Communist Party of the Soviet Union, the Polish delegation, the delegation from the Czechoslovak Socialist Republic and the delegations of other fraternal countries agreed with us in assessing the present situation.

Gerhart Eisler: How do you, Mr. Ulbricht, judge the role of the Erhard government whose ministers have developed the initiative for multilateral nuclear armament?

Walter Ulbricht: The present West German Federal Chancellor Erhard declared on entering the government that he intended to follow a middle course, i.e., an equalization policy. But in the meantime it has become quite clear that his policy in fact is anything but an equalization policy. He has even committed himself to an intensified revanchist policy. In his actual policy Erhard differs from Adenauer mainly in that he is striving for an atomic pact with the US which will give him joint access to atomic weapons, whereby France and England are rated more as helpers. Adenauer, in contrast, placed the main emphasis on the alliance with France so as, relying on France and its atomic weapons, to force the USA to grant the West German demand for atomic armament and support the policy of revenge.

Gerhart Eisler: Could you outline in the simplest possible formulation the essence and aim of the policy of multilateral nuclear armament? The problem has become extremely complicated.

Walter Ulbricht: What is the essence and aim of the atomic armament policy of the Bonn government? The essence of the matter is the striving of the ruling circles in West Germany to blackmail the Soviet Union and other socialist states through the linking of their revanchist demands with joint control of the use of atomic weapons and war provocations.

Unfortunately, the view that this nuclear war policy is the way to incorporate the German Democratic Republic into the West German Federal Republic also prevails among leaders of Social Democracy.

Gerhart Eisler: What was said at the Warsaw meeting about limiting the further spreading of nuclear weapons?

Walter Ulbricht: The member states of the Warsaw Treaty are against the further spreading of nuclear weapons, especially against any handing over of such weapons to the West German militarists. The communiqué expressly states—and I would like to quote from it: "The member states of the Warsaw Treaty decisively declare that they are opposed to the passing on of nuclear weapons to the German Federal Republic, in whatever form—directly or indirectly through state groupings—and against it finally controlling or having joint control in any way over these weapons."

Thus the Warsaw Treaty states regard the establishment of a NATO multilateral nuclear force in any desired variation as incompatible with the ban on the spreading of nuclear weapons.

This seems particularly important to us because the US government is obviously reckoning on the socialist states agreeing to a ban on the further spreading of nuclear weapons being made after a multilateral nuclear force has been established. We are convinced that in this question of a ban on the further spreading of nuclear weapons an international cooperation on a broad basis can be created against the atomic arming of West Germany. There are indeed already a few UN resolutions which demand that the further spreading of nuclear weapons should not be permitted, but that is not enough. We consider it necessary to incorporate this demand in an international treaty.

Gerhart Eisler: The Bonn government suffered a defeat in Paris at the meeting of the NATO Council. There are people who now claim that this has also reduced the danger of the MLF. What do you think of this?

Walter Ulbricht: In Paris the Bonn government suffered a defeat because it linked its so-called Germany initiative with the direct demand for the right of joint control over atomic weapons. France, Britain and also the US were justifiably afraid that with such a policy being pursued by the West German leaders they would be drawn into a nuclear war. In addition, neither France, Britain nor the US want a reunification.

Yet the US as usual would like to force West Germany to have nuclear arms but under the guidance and command of the USA. Thus the US supports the policy of atomic blackmail against the socialist countries but wants to retain control of this policy for itself.

Therefore it is not correct to think the danger of the MLF is not as great as before. This danger will exist as long as a West German government strives to obtain atomic weapons, so long as disarming has not begun and so long as revanchism has not been abolished.

Gerhart Eisler: Some West Germans think the plans for atomic armament and atomic mines by the Bonn government are too venturesome and too mad to fear that they may be realized. What do you think of this view?

Walter Ulbricht: Historical experience contradicts this view. I believe we all deserve a thrashing if we forget the experiences of history.

You see, when German imperialism and its Hitler generals, some of whom hold commanding positions in the Bundeswehr and leading positions in NATO, decided during the Second World War—it was in 1940—to attack the Soviet Union, many a responsible politician did not want to believe it. The war in the west after all had not ended and so responsible statesmen regarded such a—right from the outset—suicidal plan for the aggressor as highly unlikely.

This underestimation of the traditional venturesomeness of the policy of the German imperialists and their generals and their likewise traditional inability to assess the relation of forces in the world realistically had to be paid for with great sacrifices by the peoples including the German people. From these historical experiences we must draw the conclusion that for the present West German government, for its revanchist politicians and its Hitler generals no plan of aggression is too venturesome.

Gerhart Eisler: Some NATO governments claim the MLF would prevent the West German Federal Republic from gaining control over atomic weapons. Is that true?

Walter Ulbricht: I regard this point of view as an attempt at conscious deception or at best a sign of remarkable naïveté. Furthermore certain ruling circles in England, France and the US have long been characterized by such naïveté in their relations with German imperialists.

I would like only to recall here Munich or the famous naval agreement between Great Britain and Hitler Germany. In the one case the western powers granted Hitler aid in his aggressive acts, falsely reckoning that they would thereby secure peace for themselves and divert aggression to the east.

In the other case the British government gave its contractual agreement to a limited naval arming of Hitler Germany in the hope that it could bind Germany contractually and that it could keep the Hitler German naval armaments within the limits which were still just tolerable to England. But in reality the western powers made the way clear for German militarism to aggression and the Second World War at Munich and with the naval agreement Great Britain merely legalized the previous illegal and somewhat slower working, unlimited naval arming of Hitler Germany which had certain inconveniences.

Gerhart Eisler: Do you, Mr. Ulbricht, see any connection between the revanchist policy of the Bonn government, the striving for a NATO multilateral nuclear force and the claims by the Bonn government on Berlin?

Walter Ulbricht: There can be no doubt that a connection does exist. The pretensions of the Bonn government concerning West Berlin as for example the illegal and provocative practice of holding committee meetings of the West German Bundestag and the provocative appearances of the West German federal president in West Berlin are an essential part of the revanchist policy just as the forward strategy, the atomic mine belt and participation in a multilateral atomic armament.

I would like to leave no doubt about this question: West Berlin does not belong to the West German Federal Republic and will never belong to it. Problems of vital importance for the German Democratic Republic are involved in the West Berlin question.

This problem is for us of somewhat similar importance as the question of the Oder-Neisse peace frontier is for the People's Republic of Poland. Bonn's pretension that West Berlin is part of the West German Federal Republic will be categorically rejected by us and also by the other countries of the Warsaw Treaty.

Gerhart Eisler: What path did the Warsaw meeting indicate for the safeguarding of peace in Europe?

Walter Ulbricht: Starting from the consideration that peace on our continent is indivisible the meeting of the Political Advisory Committee has made a whole series of proposals the realization of which would be suitable for creating step by step an effective collective security for all states and peoples of Europe.

This aim is served by the proposals to freeze atomic armament, to create a nuclear-weapon-free zone in Central Europe as well as the already mentioned Polish proposal for the calling of a conference of European states to discuss measures to guarantee collective security in Europe. This aim is also served, now as before, by the valid and timely proposal for a non-aggression pact between the states of the Warsaw Treaty and the member states of NATO, to abolish the vestiges of the Second World War and to bring about a German peace settlement.

The participating states of the Warsaw Treaty support the proposal of the German Democratic Republic, as emphasized in the communiqué, for a renunciation by the two German states of nuclear weapons. I am convinced that such a renunciation would be a worthy contribution by the Germans towards safeguarding peace in Europe. The meeting of the Political Advisory Committee moreover supported every initiative which aims at a complete ban on and the complete destruction of all nuclear weapons in the world and which also leads to world-wide disarmament.

Gerhart Eisler: What conceptions do the Warsaw Treaty states have for the cooperation of the peoples and states of Europe?

Walter Ulbricht: At the meeting in Warsaw all the delegations expressed the desire that efforts should be made to bring about good cooperation of all the peoples and states of Europe. The German Democratic Republic supports these efforts. The GDR finds itself in a special position among the states of Europe. As a result of historical developments since the Second World War the main problems of the living together of the peoples of Europe have concentrated themselves as in a burning glass. In certain respects the paths towards safeguarding the peace and towards an understanding of the whole of Europe lead through an agreement with the German Democratic Republic.

In view of the fact that we are the German state of peace which has mastered the past, it is only natural that the great initiative for the safeguarding of peace for the German people has come from the German Democratic Republic.

Is a thaw in Europe possible? I believe it is! The ice of the cold war which has obstructed cooperation in Europe for so long can be made to melt. Our policy serves the purpose of a thaw in Europe. We are willing to work together with all European states and peoples irrespective of their social system, political aims and world outlook as well as with all Europeans of good will.

To start with we should effect a true relaxation of tension through the normalization of relations between all the European states and peoples. In order to achieve this the good will of all those taking part and the willingness to work in confidence together are above all necessary.

We are convinced that such a thaw would be in the interests of all the peoples of Europe.

We are in favour of a European system of security which guarantees security to all European countries and which relieves all Europeans of the strain of the danger of war. In connection with measures for disarmament we are also in favour of agreements on the control of armament production and the implementation of measures of control in the two German states to prevent surprise attacks.

We take the view that a common history and a culture which has grown up over centuries to which all European peoples have made lasting contributions as well as joint interests in the safeguarding of peace should offer good prerequisites for peaceful coexistence and cooperation regardless of all ideological opposition and political differences.

We socialist states feel a special responsibility for the humanistic and cultural heritage of the peoples of Europe. Two thirds of the territory of Europe constitute the territories of socialist states. And every second inhabitant of our continent is the citizen of a socialist state.

Gerhart Eisler: What tasks do you see for the citizens of the GDR and for the peace-loving people in West Germany in connection with the new situation and the necessity of leading the struggle for the safeguarding of peace and against every form of NATO multilateral nuclear armament?

Walter Ulbricht: You are quite right when you take the standpoint that the struggle for the safeguarding of peace and against the nuclear arming of the West German Federal Republic in any form whatsoever

351

is today more than ever a vital necessity for Germans in the two German states. For the atomic arming of the West German Federal Republic not only prevents every serious step in the direction of reunification but also gambles with the physical existence of all Germans in the west and in the east.

We see the main task of the government of the German Democratic Republic and its citizens in this historic situation as that of preventing another war from beginning on German soil. To prevent another European war starting from the centre of disturbance of West Germany will be possible only if, through the cooperation of the consistent peace policy of the Union of Soviet Socialist Republics, the German Democratic Republic and the other socialist states with the struggle against the atomic arming of West Germany and with international actions against West German revanchism and its striving for atomic weapons, the present oppressive influence of the extremists on West Germany is decisively repressed.

Of course, I cannot speak in detail here about the tasks which the citizens of the GDR and the citizens of West Germany must fulfil in view of the new situation if they want to live, if they want to work and live in peace. I would like to say this much: Since the government of the GDR pursues a consistent policy of peace and security and since the GDR is the German state of peace it must be the main task of all the citizens to see to it that their state develops effectively in every field, that the force and efficiency of our state are constantly and persistently strengthened in all fields, that the prestige of the GDR in international life is constantly raised.

The peace-loving citizens of West Germany, above all the workers, farmers, office employees and tradespeople, in whose lives peace and security similarly play an essential part, will indeed not be able to refrain from overcoming their present disunion and come together in a great resistance movement against atomic armament, against making the split in Germany permanent, against war and revanchist policies and the dismantling of democratic rights. Of course it is a difficult task but no one can relieve the West Germans of it.

I would like to confess that I see the coming together of all West Germans of good will in such a broad resistance movement as the only possibility at the moment of stopping the insane march into the devastating abyss of a nuclear war by the West German Federal Republic and of preparing our joint way towards a peaceful and happy future.

I wish our West German fellow countrymen strength, perseverance and courage to make small sacrifices now for the sake of the life and happy future of our people.

For Cooperation of the Peoples and States of Europe

From the speech at the session of the
National Council of the National Front of Democratic Germany
on 15 February 1965

The proposal of the government of the People's Republic of Poland for the calling of a Conference on European Security was welcomed at the Warsaw Consultation.*)

As representatives of the German Democratic Republic we declared on that occasion: "We are in favour of the socialist states of Europe extending their hand to all nations of our continent, so as jointly to safeguard peace in Europe, to guard and continue the humanist traditions."

We are for the cooperation of all, from communists to bourgeois opponents of multilateral atomic armament and French supporters of de Gaulle who were opponents of Hitler and who reject the hegemony of West German militarism in Western Europe.

In the sphere of culture we are for the cooperation of all peace-loving and humanistic minded people–from the admirers of Becher, Brecht and Kuba to those of Sartre or Enzensberger or other humanist writers of Western Europe.

Our policy of understanding among the peoples is most clearly expressed in our endeavour to consolidate economic relations with the socialist countries of Europe and also to develop economic relations with the capitalist countries of Europe.

This endeavour on our part will become particularly evident at the Leipzig Spring Fair. We are in favour of expanding economic and trade relations, of course without political conditions or political dependence. We are in favour of an even closer cooperation between the socialist countries, of the further strengthening and development of cooperation by the states of the Council for Mutual Economic Assistance, accomplishing certain production tasks in cooperation. But we are also in favour of concluding cooperation agreements with certain firms in capitalist countries, to the advantage of both sides and for reciprocal purchases and sales of licences. This economic policy

*) Session of the Political Consultative Committee of the Member States of the Warsaw Treaty from 18 to 20 January 1965 in Warsaw

and these trade relations are at present being conducted with France and Great Britain; relations of this kind have even been established with firms in the USA. We are in favour of extending these economic relations.

To be sure, that is only possible if economic relations are separated from all political controversies or from any political so-called expectations or, to put it more plainly, conditions.

As regards West Germany we have made efforts to normalize relations. We have made proposals as to how a step-by-step rapprochement could be brought about. We have concluded the permit agreement between the GDR government and the Senate of West Berlin. This was to serve the normalization of relations and at the same time be a model for the development of relations between the government of the German Democratic Republic and the government of the West German Federal Republic.

These proposals and this policy have unfortunately been answered by the Bonn government with speeded up atomic armament, with the agreement on the right to share control over atomic weapons and with the planning of the forward strategy. Everyone understands that these measures obstructed the normalization of relations between the two German states. A situation has thus been brought about in which we shall have to start again at the beginning as far as Germany is concerned, with the gradual development of economic relations. The repeated attempts to link economic negotiations with political "expectations"–this is the more polite form for political extortion, in diplomatic circles one speaks of "expectations" and carries out extortion–these attempts at political extortion have failed.

We think that the time is approaching when the Bonn government, too, will understand that it will have to adapt itself to the real situation and proceed to the developing of normal economic relations between the two German states to the advantage of both, without political extortion. We are convinced that the extension of economic relations between the two German states is possible. The political problems existing between the two German states should be discussed by the representatives of the governments of the two German states, the representatives of the government of the German Democratic Republic and of other European states. At the Warsaw Consultation I stated that we, the GDR delegation, consider an atmosphere of thaw in Europe to be possible. The ice of the cold war which for so long obstructed cooperation in Europe can be made to melt. In the television interview I repeated that part of my speech. We consider that the time has come to raise the question of the establishment of peaceful relations between the European states quite openly because the situation in the peoples' democracies has further stabilized, because the authority of the GDR has grown and because in West Germany as well the forces which are starting to form a realistic judgment of the situation are gradually increasing. That is why the time has arrived to speak openly of bringing about a thaw in the relations between the states and peoples of Europe.

We consider that the formation of an atomic-weapon-free zone in Europe, including the two German states, and the conclusion of a non-aggression pact between the Warsaw Treaty and NATO states would be especially appropriate for promoting the relaxation of tension in Europe and cooperation between the European states. We are for good cooperation with all states of Europe. We are for a European security system as a guarantee of the security of all European countries and as a means of relieving all Europeans of the pressure of the danger of war. In connection with the disarmament measures we are also in favour of agreements on the control of the arms production and of enforcing control measures in both German states for the prevention of surprise attacks.

We believe that a joint history and a culture evolved in the course of centuries and to which all European peoples have made lasting contributions as well as the common interest in the safeguarding of peace should offer favourable conditions for peaceful coexistence and fruitful cooperation—regardless of all differences in world outlook and political differences.

We socialist states feel particularly responsible for the humanist and cultural heritage of the peoples of Europe; for two-thirds of the territory of Europe are territories of socialist states; and every second inhabitant of our continent is the citizen of a socialist state. We are in favour of the socialist states extending their hand to all the nations of our continent with a view to jointly safeguarding peace in Europe, guarding and continuing humanist traditions. We are in favour of striving, jointly with all other European states, to enrich the cultural heritage of the peoples of Europe by cultural achievements and creations of our day and above all to ensure that this heritage be handed down to future generations intact.

The peaceful creative competition between equal and free European nations, not threatened by any hegemony or fury of war, will decide which social system will ultimately triumph throughout the whole of Europe. Divergencies of opinion and different political systems need be no obstacle to fruitful cooperation and a great creative competition between the peoples of Europe. We thus desire the consistent establishment of peaceful coexistence in the life of the states and peoples with different social systems in Europe.

The German Democratic Republic has a special position among the states of Europe. As a result of the historical development since the Second World War the main problems of the coexistence of the peoples are concentrated in the GDR as in a burning glass. In a certain respect the ways to the safeguarding of peace and understanding throughout the whole of Europe involve the problem of reaching an understanding with the German Democratic Republic. In view of the fact that we are the German peace state which has overcome the past it is natural that the great initiative for the safeguarding of peace for the whole German people should have come from the German Democratic Republic.

If the question is raised as to how developments are to continue, I should like to reply that one must proceed from the real situation in Germany, Europe and the world. There are two social systems in the world, a world socialist system and a capitalist system. Their point of contact runs right through Germany. In Germany two states exist with fundamentally different social systems. When one proceeds from this real situation there is but one way. It is the way indicated by our Peace Doctrine. This maintains that normal, peaceful relations should be established between the two German states, that all peoples should establish normal, peaceful relations with the German Democratic Republic and that the German Democratic Republic should establish normal, peaceful relations with all peoples. In a certain respect the ways to the safeguarding of peace in Europe involve peaceful understanding with the German Democratic Republic. Every step taken by the states towards normalizing relations with the German Democratic Republic serves relaxation in Germany and strengthens the elements in West Germany which are ready for understanding. The content of the Germany question is in effect the safeguarding of peace.

In the interest of such understanding and the safeguarding of peace it is necessary and desirable that a European security conference be held. A non-aggression pact should be concluded between the Warsaw Treaty and NATO states. The conclusion of an agreement between the states on the non-proliferation of atomic weapons should be brought about, in whatever form. Such a policy of understanding would in West Germany call for the renunciation of the forward strategy, the renunciation of atomic armament, the renunciation of the application of the statute of limitations to nazi crimes and of the emergency legislation which is equivalent to military dictatorship. That is, it is necessary to establish normal relations on a basis of equality between the two German states, to develop cooperation up to the time when a German Council can be formed.

In the public discussion on the peaceful solution of the German question the problem of the price to be paid for reunification played an important role in West Germany. You may recall that in recent years entire caravans of politicians from various countries flocked to Moscow in order to find out the price there for which the West German rulers could advance up to the Oder-Neisse line and up to the frontiers of 1937.

To the question as to the price of reunification we answer quite clearly. The price of reunification is disarmament, the renunciation of revanchism, the establishment of a democratic system in West Germany which expects no one to live under the threat of the atomic bomb and together with murderers. The price is the establishment of normal relations between the two German states and with the states and peoples of Europe. This price corresponds exactly to the provisions of the Potsdam Agreement on the elimination of nazism and militarism. The German peace settlement would then clear the road to reunification.

The interest of the European peoples in peace and security will be fulfilled to the extent to which they support the German Democratic Republic in the struggle against the anti-peace policy of West German imperialism. Understanding in Europe involves understanding with the German Democratic Republic.

The German Democratic Republic possesses the only constructive program for the shaping of the future Germany because it is setting the example for the future of the whole of Germany in the present.

Speech at the Reception in the Abdin Palace (UAR)

24 February 1965

Mr. President,
Dear Mrs. Nasser,
Dear Egyptian Friends,

Our visit to the United Arab Republic and the friendly meeting of leading representatives of our two peoples and states is being watched by the German people, the citizens of the German Democratic Republic, and also by the peace-loving and progressive citizens of the West German state with joyful approval and great interest, for these meetings correspond to the sympathy and the friendly feelings which our German people have for the United Arab Republic, liberated from feudal and imperialist exploitation.

This friendship visit is a continuation of the traditions of great humanist Germans of the past who, as Egyptologists or outstanding representatives of other sciences, were active in your country and who, after their return to their German homeland, stood up for friendship with the great Egyptian people.

The liberating action of the courageous Arab people who under the leadership of Gamal Abdel Nasser and his closest comrades-in-struggle nationalized the Suez Canal Company and in a heroic battle repulsed the tripartite imperialist aggression, roused the solidarity of the German people and especially that of the citizens of the German Democratic Republic.

Since then there has been a constantly growing sympathy for, and a continuous vivid interest in your country's development, the development of socialism which is going on here and also the development within the community of states of the Arab nation.

This is not to say that it has always been easy for everybody in Germany to understand the road of the Arab peoples and states. In the course of a long history and on the basis of a culture which is thousands of years old, conditions have grown in your country which make many problems appear in a light different from what we are used to under our historic conditions.

But we have always made an effort to see and appreciate the common features in the interests of our states and peoples. There were and there are many such communities of interests. They are rooted in our common struggle for the safeguarding of peace, for the freedom, equality of rights and sovereignty of all peoples and states; and we regard imperialism, colonial rule and neo-colonialism as our common enemies.

Unfortunately, we Germans have so far overthrown the exploitative rule of the imperialists, monopoly capitalists and big landowners, have deprived it, once and for all, of its foundations and established the power of the working people only in one part of Germany, in the German Democratic Republic. On the basis of the firm alliance of the workers and peasants with the intelligentsia and other patriotic sections we are building the socialist state whose image will one day stamp the whole of Germany. For more than fifty years I have been standing in the ranks of the German working class which looks back on a long tradition. For more than half a century I have thus been engaged in the struggle against imperialism, and I can understand that the imperialists in Bonn and other capitals of imperialist countries do not exactly love me, just as they do not precisely appear to love our esteemed friend Gamal Abdel Nasser excessively.

During these more than fifty years of struggle against German imperialism we have scored victories. But, we have also experienced the bitterness of defeats. Finally, however, the German people were victorious in one part of Germany, in the GDR. And we do not doubt that some day the banner of the victorious people will be flying over all Germany. You, dear Egyptian friends, have dealt heavy blows at the imperialists, our common enemies. You have carried through social transformations of historic magnitude and are devoting yourselves to the construction of socialism.

I am very glad to witness—and I think I may say this also in the name of my friends—how the glorious people of the United Arab Republic—in a way that corresponds with their historic conditions—are working for the same goal that we are striving for. Its name is peace, freedom and socialism, happiness and prosperity for the people who will never again let the power slip from their strong hands.

Permit me to raise my glass to the welfare, the glory, the happiness and prosperity of the great Egyptian people and to the health of its great son, President Gamal Abdel Nasser, and his esteemed wife, to the well-being of all Arab friends.

Friendship!

The National Mission of the German Democratic Republic and the Peace Forces of West Germany

From the statement to the 13th session
of the People's Chamber of the German Democratic Republic
on 5 May 1965

Members of the People's Chamber,
Dear Friends, Dear Comrades,
Dear Guests,

Twenty years ago, on 2 May 1945, Berlin was conquered by the victorious Soviet Army. On 8 May 1945, the anti-Hitler coalition accomplished the liberation of the peoples which were subjugated, tortured and plundered by Hitler Germany.

It is understandable that in these days when we are crossing the threshold to the third post-war decade not only the German people ask themselves: "Where do we stand?" And the other peoples are still more justified in asking: What have you Germans done to ensure that a war never again starts from German soil?—What have you Germans done to eliminate the vestiges of nazism and war?—What guarantees have you Germans created for peace, humanism and progress to prosper in Germany?

We citizens of the German Democratic Republic can answer these questions with a clear conscience. For we have created the first German peace state in our Germany in the sovereign exercise of our right of self-determination and have overcome the imperialist war ideology here for all time.

We have implemented human rights and the basic rights of the citizens for which the German workers and farmers, the majority of the German people stood already before the First World War. In the German Democratic Republic, it is the people who are the sovereign ruler, thanks to the elimination of the exploitation of man by man and the development of socialist democracy. Not just a few hundred millionaires, but the millions themselves govern. Everyone who co-operates sincerely can also take a share in planning and governing. The people themselves are the owner of the economy. And all riches created by them belong to the millions and not to a handful of millionaires. The people have realized their right to education and to participation in the development of culture. The people have fixed the policy of peace and friendship with other peoples and implement it through the government elected by them.

The citizens of the German Democratic Republic can thus tell the other peoples with a clear conscience on this 20th anniversary of liberation: We have made good use of our time. We have made a clean sweep of the German warmongers and militarists, of the corrupters of our people and of so many other peoples. Humanism and democracy have been victorious in our part of Germany. In the German Democratic Republic, the National Front and the government and the people have overcome the past. The life of the present time is filled by the ideas of humanism. The organs of the democratic and socialist state promote the spirit of humanity.

But the citizens of West Germany must answer the question "What have you done and achieved?" as follows: "We have been fettered by the western powers and the foundation of a separate West German state has been forced upon us. They and the millionaires have split Germany. They deceived us when they told us that this would be the easier way. But now we know that the Marshall Plan and the so-called aid of the western occupation powers in reality only served to restore the power of the millionaires."

The great deception once made by the millionaires and their Hitler party against our people is continued in many ways, through the policy of the government as well as through the opinion factories of the big press trusts, such as the Springer trust and others. What was achieved twenty years ago on the day of liberation from the fascist terror regime and in the first years afterwards in democratic rights has since then been in the process of abolition. A great uneasiness is spreading over West Germany because ever more people feel that the past is not overcome and yet this is the responsibility of all.

It is a fact that everything has been done in West Germany which can serve to increase the trust profits. And at the same time revanchism has again been stirred up. West Germany has been discredited in the eyes of the nations because it identifies itself with the most reactionary forces in the world, with Tshombe in Congo, with the Salazar colonialists and with the US mercenaries in Vietnam. This is why the conscience of so many West Germans is in a turmoil. For more and more West Germans are beginning to understand that people in the West German state are about to be involved again in a crime by the millionaires and their revanchist politicians through their great deception.

The millionaires and their revanchist politicians thwart a lasting peace settlement with the German states and for Europe with the help of the imperialist western powers. And they are striving to change

361

the post-war period into a new pre-war period. This is the reason for their mad military armament and their greed for control over atomic weapons, for their aggressive revanchist policy, the poisoning of the young West German generation with the evil spirit of chauvinism, for their continued provocations for which they like to choose West Berlin because they think that thus they can most certainly involve the imperialist western powers in their adventures.

What is the real danger for the population of West Berlin and for the entire German people? The great danger results from the fact that the West German revanchist policy is coupled with atomic war plans. The Bonn government is striving for joint control of nuclear weapons within the NATO command which has already been interspersed by it with its men in all authoritative posts. And West Berlin is to be won as a bridgehead for this aggressive revanchist policy so that thus the western powers can be hitched to the chariot of their adventurous revanchist policy and precipitated into a serious conflict.

The German State Doctrine of the GDR

The German peace state, the German Democratic Republic, has stabilized itself and is energetically and methodically pursuing its great historic task as the representative of the national and social interests of the entire German nation.

It is the supreme law of the state doctrine of the German Democratic Republic to ensure that never again shall a war start from German soil.

Because the imperialist and militarist system has been abolished with all consistency in the German Democratic Republic, this Republic has become a secure factor of peace in Europe and throughout the world.

The character of the GDR and its state doctrine are determined by the rule of the people under the leadership of the working class allied with the farmers, the members of the intelligentsia and the working middle classes. Peace, democracy, social and cultural progress, international cooperation and understanding among peoples, these are the great aims for which the German peace state is striving, these are the fundamentals of the German state doctrine of the German Democratic Republic.

German state doctrine—that is the consistent policy of peace in Europe, in Germany and for Germany through agreement between the two German states on general and complete disarmament and on the renunciation of any participation at all in atomic armament. The foundation of the foreign policy of the GDR is thereby firm friendship with the Soviet Union and the other socialist countries.

German state doctrine—that is the untiring struggle for the overcoming of the splitting of the German nation, the striving for closer relations between and cooperation on a basis of equality by the German states after creating the basic conditions for a step-by-step rapprochement on the way to a German confederation. The path to the union of the German states is by way of disarmament and a peace treaty, by abolishing the remnants of the Second World War and by the completion of the great task of liberation from militarism, imperialism and fascism also in West Germany. In this, an all-German council, formed of the same number of representatives from both German governments, could play a useful part. It could be authorized to set up commissions for the preparation of the solving of special questions.

German state doctrine—that is the striving for peace and security for all peoples and all states of Europe by an agreement on peaceful coexistence and cooperation on the basis of equality and mutual respect.

German state doctrine—that is also the fostering of friendship and cooperation with the countries which have liberated themselves from colonial rule and with those peoples who are still engaged in the anti-imperialist liberation struggle.

The policy of the West German Federal Republic, however, is basically the old, only slightly modified policy of monarchist and nazi imperialist Germany.

Also West German imperialism—similar to its predecessors in imperial Germany and under Hitler—is beginning with the struggle for predominance over Western Europe. Here the direct action of the big monopolies, which are expanding their influence on the European Common Market and on the Coal and Steel Union, is playing an increasing part.

The nuclear weapon plot of West Germany and the USA is a new factor in the situation. The extraordinarily close connection of the US monopolies with West German monopoly capital and the fixing of joint imperialist aims has greatly accelerated the process of the relinquishing of all national connections of West German monopoly capital with the German people and their vital interests.

In the home policy of the Bonn state, twenty years after the liberation, there dominates once more the spirit of the war economy leaders, the Hitler officers in the army and the SS experts in the police force and the Hitlerite hanging judges in the judiciary organs. Apart from a few exceptions, a mass press, politically and morally of low quality, speculating on the basest human instincts, is systematically poisoning public opinion. Instead of the Hugenberg trust which did its share in delivering up the Weimar Republic to the Hitler gangsters and paving the path to war for them, the Springer trust has taken its place in the West Germany of today and does the same dirty work against peace and the nation. A reactionary internal political system of emergency dictatorship, undermining the last democratic rights, is only with difficulty disguised by parliamentary procedures.

A new factor in the situation results also from the fact that at present West German imperialism is not yet compelled to use military force for the establishment of its hegemony over Western Europe. With the aid of the ever-increasing influence of the West German militarists in the leading bodies of NATO, Bonn in many respects has achieved a result similar to that which Hitler attempted to attain by way of forcible military occupation.

In this connection there is also the fact that the West German government is making the greatest efforts—and at the same time filling the operational staffs of NATO with West German militarists—to obtain for it and thus for itself control over nuclear weapons.

The extreme imperialist and reactionary character of Bonn policy is also expressed in the attitude of the West German Federal Republic to the Arab and African countries. The participation of Bonn in a major way in the construction of bases of aggression directed against the Arab countries, for instance, and the endeavours to obtain influence and points of attack for political extortion through so-called military aid in other African states are evidence of the neo-colonialist approach and aims of the ruling imperialist circles in West Germany.

It is ominous that the Bonn government is the only government of Europe which is making demands for changes in its borders. And it is precisely to these adventurist forward strategists that the USA, with the support to some extent of the British Labour government, wants to give access to control over atomic weapons. The control of atomic weapons in the hands of imperialist gamblers of the Bonn type is a matter of life and death for the whole of Europe. This is especially so since there still prevails in Bonn the criminal Hitlerite ideology by which the entire German people and other peoples can go to the devil in a nuclear war when the attempt to gain revanchist aims by atomic extortion meets with another and inevitable defeat.

This is why it is only the German peace forces which can speak for the German people. Only we, the representatives of the German Democratic Republic, with its state doctrine serving the cause of peace, the German nation and also the forces of peace in West Germany, have the right to speak in the name of all peace-loving Germans. In fact, we represent the interests of the great German nation as a whole. The government in Bonn, on the other hand, is at most entitled to speak in the name of a handful of monopolies, multimillionaires, Hitler generals, hanging judges and—apart from this—also of a few US concerns. But that is not the voice of the German people. The voice of the great German nation is to be heard here, at this session of the People's Chamber of the German Democratic Republic.

Anti-communism Is No Substitute for a Policy

In Europe and Asia, in Africa and South America, the peoples of those continents connect the name of the German Democratic Republic with the conception of a consistent policy for the safeguarding of peace and a determined struggle for the elimination of any and all colonial domination and neo-colonialism. All the attempts to slander and discriminate against the GDR have not been able to change the fact that the German peace state is gradually and irresistibly taking its place in international life.

When, nevertheless, the representatives of certain imperialist western powers give free rein to their hostile attitude to the German Democratic Republic, I can only understand this as the expression of very narrow class-thinking, which thrusts aside the interests of peace and the national interests of the peoples of Europe.

The interests of peace in Europe require the normalization of relations between all European states, including the German Democratic Republic which, as is well known, is neither the smallest, nor the least, nor the weakest.

What I am saying is that anyone who is really interested in the stabilization of peace in Europe and in closer relations and good cooperation in the European family of nations cannot avoid admitting the fact that a peaceful order in Europe can only be negotiated and established with the German Democratic Republic as an equal member and can never be possible without the participation of the GDR.

German Unity for War or for Peace?

We are the most stubborn champions of the unity of the peace-loving German nation. And we are certain that a unified, peace-loving and democratic Germany will one day be a reality.

In the German Democratic Republic, it is the peace-loving forces of the people, the workers, the farmers, the members of the intelligentsia and of the middle classes, who are in power. And this guarantees a peaceful policy, peace and security for neighbouring countries, also for those who do not yet like socialism at present.

In the West German Federal Republic, however, the old imperialist and militarist forces, the old imperialist corrupters of Germany and Europe are in the saddle.

To continue supporting them and to assist them in the attempt to expand their power over the GDR is—objectively speaking—an adventurist policy, one of destruction and atomic war.

Only a united Germany in which the peace-loving forces of the German people, the workers and farmers and members of the intelligentsia and the middle classes have the power in their own hands, only such a united Germany can guarantee itself and its neighbours peace and security.

The Policy of Peaceful Coexistence Cannot Be a One-sided Affair

People rightly ask: How are things to go on in Germany in view of the existence of two German states with so fundamentally different social orders?

The recognition is gaining ground that the path must be pegged out by a mutual policy of peaceful coexistence. This means that both German states must endeavour to live with each other in peace.

On the basis of the resolutions of the People's Chamber, the government of the German Democratic Republic has in recent years been attempting to a quite exceptional extent to avoid everything which could in any way impair the relaxation of tension in Europe and in the world and the process of rapprochement and peaceful cooperation of states with different social orders.

We have done everything possible to contribute to a lessening of the danger of military conflicts, to disarmament and the safeguarding of peace and the establishment of an atmosphere of confidence.

With this consistent policy of peace, of rapprochement and tolerance, we have gone to the utmost limits possible and, often enough on this account, we have postponed our own important and legitimate interests.

This was made a little easier for us by the circumstance that a policy of peaceful coexistence and the status quo in Europe—whether it was expressed or not—was also recognized as an obligation by the governments of the western powers.

The starting-point for a policy of peaceful coexistence in Europe must in every case be the respecting of the status quo, that means, the respecting and recognition of the historical facts as they emerged in Europe as a consequence of the Second World War.

This is not at all intended to maintain the division of Germany. Quite the contrary! The recognition of the historical fact of the existence of two German states and a special territory of West Berlin and the respecting of the status quo are the prerequisite for overcoming the division which can only take place by a rapprochement and agreement between the two German states—after the completion of the task of liberation also in West Germany—and by taking into consideration the vital interests of Germany's neighbours.

Peaceful coexistence, respect for the status quo and understanding between the German states are, therefore, the prerequisite for a peaceful solution of the German question as well as the stabilizing of peace by the conclusion of a peace treaty with both German states. By peaceful coexistence and the respecting of the status quo the time essential for preparing disarmament and a peace treaty is also won.

Also the policy of the USA towards Europe should finally—so it seems to me—be based on the principles of peaceful coexistence, i.e., also the recognition of the status quo in Europe, which not least includes also the fact of the existence of two sovereign German states and the fact of the character of West Berlin as a special territory which is not part of the West German Federal Republic. To the policy of peaceful coexistence belongs furthermore the recognition of the borders of the European states and their inviolability, naturally including the borders of the German Democratic Republic in East and West, in North and South.

The support of the revanchist policy of the West German imperialists is incompatible with the good cause of rapprochement and peace in Europe, the emergence of a new community of European states, which can work together with confidence and develop a policy which guarantees peace to our old continent.

The USA practises an anti-European policy when it arms the West German revanchist politicians and militarists to the teeth and even wants to give them control over atomic weapons within the NATO leadership. Europe does not need a West German military base of US imperialists.

Obviously it would be easier to reach a European peace settlement if the US government would give up its policy of constantly interfering in this part of the world as up to now. Nobody recognizes the USA as the world's gendarme. Nobody grants the USA the right to interfere in the internal affairs of other countries and in the relations of the European countries among each other and to disturb these relations.

The Germany Initiative for Peace, Humanity and Happiness of the Nation

Twenty years have gone by since the end of the Second World War. And as yet the work of the liberation from the evil nazi spirit, militarism and imperialism has not been completed in the West of Germany, in the West German Federal Republic. There is not yet a lasting peace settlement for Europe. There is not yet a peace treaty for the German states. The forces of imperialism and militarism are still stirring up hostility between the Germans and the German states and are preventing them from reaching an understanding on a happy and peaceful future for the nation.

The facts are that never before was an honest Germany initiative for peace, humanity and the happiness of the nation, a Germany initiative with a national substance, which not only serves the peace of our people but also the peace and security of Europe, as urgent as it is today.

All peace-loving Germans in East and West are called upon to unite in a Germany initiative which completes the work of the liberation, begun twenty years ago, which bans the poisonous fumes of the insane arms race and the atomic mines in West Germany, which once and for all keeps from the Hitler generals and other militarists of the Bonn government the control of atomic weapons and thus paves the way for an understanding on the safeguarding of peace.

The liberation of the German nation from the barbaric Hitlerite rule of the German imperialists twenty years ago could only be a beginning, the start for a new beginning. The process of liberation had to be continued and completed by a spiritual, moral and political rebirth of the German nation.

That is also how it was stipulated in the Potsdam Agreement. This was also the will of the peoples of the anti-Hitler coalition and naturally, even more so, the will of the fighters of the German resistance.

Now there is no doubt that in the German Democratic Republic the work of the liberation, including the creation of the intellectual foundations of a moral and political rebirth of the German nation has been consistently completed. In West Germany, however, in the occupation zones of the imperialist western powers, the process of liberation remained in its initial phase. Instead of it being continued, remilitarization and even already to some extent a rebirth of fascism has taken place.

A lot must therefore be done to catch up in West Germany. Here liberation has still to be carried out. Here it is essential to arouse the conscience of the people. Here much is still to be done before this part of Germany, too, alienated from the vital interests of the nation, meets the fundamental demands of the Potsdam agreements of the anti-Hitler coalition, until here also the liberation begun twenty years ago is completed by the establishment of the foundations of a moral and political rebirth of the German nation.

Nazism was a swampy offspring of German imperialism. Nazism and militarism and imperialism belong together. The West German imperialists cannot say today that they had nothing in common with nazism. For it was they who brought up the nazi party. They brought it to power. They set up the concentration camps and the gas chambers. They produced the poison gas. They fixed the conception for the conquest of foreign countries, for domination over Europe, the conception of their world supremacy. They followed on the heels of the fascist armies and plundered the foreign countries. They exploited the concentration camp slaves in their factories and works and had them tortured to death. From here and from the exploitation of the West German working people originate their fantastic riches.

The West German monopolies, the big industrialists and bankers have the power in the Bonn state, that means, the same forces which are fully responsible for the Hitler regime and its outrages are again in power in West Germany.

The citizens of the German Democratic Republic and the fighters for peace and the peace friends in West Germany have—I think—one way and one common next aim. This is the safeguarding of peace for our people and for Europe. Never again shall war begin from German soil.

The German Democratic Republic alone cannot guarantee the attainment of this aim. You, West German peace friends, cannot do it alone, either.

But when we go together and stick together, then we shall certainly accomplish it in a joint effort.

The community of the peace forces of the German Democratic Republic and of West Germany is able to safeguard peace for our people.

And once we have reached this one aim we can also hope to jointly find the road to a peace-loving, democratic and united Germany.

The decision on the road which will be taken by West Germany can be made only by the West Germans themselves. Only they themselves can carry out the decision in West Germany. But we shall give you all help by imparting to you our experiences and knowledge. You can always and in every situation rely upon the fraternal aid of the

369

German Democratic Republic, as we hope to be able to rely upon the solidarity of the West German working people.

But the accomplishment of the urgently necessary liberation of West Germany from militarism and imperialism, nazism and neo-nazism can only be the work of the West Germans themselves.

On the threshold of the third post-war decade we address ourselves to all Germans and to the peoples and governments of the anti-Hitler coalition:

Help us to implement the Germany initiative for peace, humanity and the happiness of the nation!

Accomplish the great work of the liberation from war, nazism, militarism and imperialism for which millions of citizens of the Soviet Union, the other countries of the anti-Hitler coalition and tens of thousands of German resistance fighters died, in the sense of the Potsdam Agreement, also in the West German Federal Republic! Create there, too, the basis for the rebirth of the German nation and the overcoming of its division!

Let us enforce an agreement of the German states on their disarmament, on the renunciation of atomic weapons or participation in the control of atomic weapons in any form so that the 20th anniversary of liberation is honoured through an adequate contribution of the Germans to peace and security in Europe.

Let us finally, on the threshold of the third post-war decade, enforce the long due peace treaty with the two German states so that the still glimmering vestiges of the Second World War are removed and cleared away, so that no one can kindle the torch of war with them.

Let us provide for a European peace settlement, with the participation of the German states on a basis of equality, which gives our continent security and promotes the coexistence and the cooperation in confidence of the European peoples on a basis of equality regardless of the differences in their social systems and government systems.

Let us promote a rapprochement and understanding of the European peoples and states which eliminate all discrimination and promote the common interests in the development and future of Europe.

It must be possible in the third decade after the day of liberation to reach a rapprochement and understanding of the two German states on decisive steps to overcome the German division within the framework of this Germany initiative for peace, humanity and the happiness of the nation.

The accomplishment of the work of liberation in West Germany, too, a secure German and European peace system and the cooperation of the European peoples on the basis of equal rights would indeed guarantee that the rebirth of the entire German nation and the overcoming of its division can become reality. Then the historic mission of all peace-loving Germans in east and west would also be near fulfilment. Then Germany would never again threaten peace in Europe and the world.

We turn to all Germans: Support the Germany initiative for peace, humanity and the happiness of the nation! May everyone make his sincere contribution!

For the sake of peace and the happy future of our German people!

Security and Disarmament
Could Become the Prologue to Reunification

From the Sunday Talk
of the Deutschlandsender (German Broadcasting Station)
on 1 August 1965

Gerhart Eisler, Chairman of the State Broadcasting Committee:
We would like to talk about the elections to the West German Bundestag which will be held on 19 September. Will these Bundestag elections bring something good for the West Germans and, moreover, to the whole German nation, or will they further worsen the situation?

Walter Ulbricht: If a West German government favouring disarmament and peace in Germany as well as an understanding between the two German states resulted from these elections, then that would be a good thing for the West Germans and for the citizens of the German Democratic Republic. This would further our national concern.

You see, today is the first of August. Fifty-one years ago today the First World War broke out. I recall it very well. Big crowds of people cheered the soldiers who were going to the front. But that day was nevertheless one of the blackest in German history.

What mischief this First World War, this attempt by German imperialism to conquer and carve up foreign countries, brought to the German nation! I lived through that day.

Twenty-five years later I went through another black day of German history – the day of the outbreak of the Second World War, another attempt by the German imperialists to conquer and carve up foreign countries.

When I see today how Bonn is grasping for nuclear weapons and rushing through emergency laws, how a new pre-war period is being prepared in West Germany, when I see how the West German government, its newspapers and politicians engage themselves for the dirty and revolting US war of aggression in Vietnam and how they act as if it were their greatest hope to transform our Germany, too, into a Vietnam, then I am, as are all reasonable people, very concerned about the future of our German people. Those who thus commit themselves to the US war policy cannot be regarded as representatives of the national interests of our German people.

The situation is very serious and it would probably already be hopeless if there were no warning conscience in Germany, if there were no German Democratic Republic and if there were no warning conscience of the forces of peace.

I consider the carelessness and the blind confidence of so many people in West Germany to be especially serious. They see the Bonn government's armament and its striving for nuclear weapons. They see the rallies, they hear the revenge-seeking speeches and know of the emergency laws but still believe that all this is not so tragic. Nothing will happen to us. Nobody wants war, after all. Everyone wants peace, for everyone speaks about peace. It is especially during the election campaign in West Germany that every candidate of the war party, the CDU, talks about peace.

Gerhart Eisler: The more they scream for nuclear weapons, the more they say that that also belongs to peace.

Walter Ulbricht: This is part of the psychological preparations for war. Experience shows, however, that this goes on only for a certain time, until it happens one fine day all the same.

We have experienced it. The elections for the West German Bundestag are being held in the 21st year after the end of the Second World War. The danger has increased and is still growing. Almost half the people of West Germany did not themselves consciously experience the preparation of the Second World War, the cruel nazi rule and the war. It was almost the same in the period between the two world wars.

The Second World War was launched by the German imperialists some twenty years after the end of the First World War at a time when Germany had rearmed. They took advantage of the fact that a whole generation had grown up in the meantime that could not recall the First World War and which they could drive into the second great war because it did not know the secret of the war preparation and the secret for the outbreak of war.

The atomic war armament staged by the Bonn government at present and the danger threatening peace is, not least, so great because the CDU/CSU, the ruling party, and the West German militarists are reckoning on the fact that now the younger West German generations who do not know the Second World War from their own experience and who also do not know the secret of how wars are prepared and launched have grown up.

We, the members of the older generation, must reveal this secret to the younger generation. All who have experienced this once already should give us a helping hand. We, the older generation of the two German states, owe this to German youth in East and West, to the women and mothers of our nation. The present generation must have the strength to restrain the atomic war politicians in time to prevent a war.

Gerhart Eisler: Perhaps we can say something about the Geneva Disarmament Conference in this connection. Or perhaps we should talk about which national interest the Germans have in the development and progress of the Geneva Conference.

Walter Ulbricht: The fundamental national interest of the Germans in East and West, however, requires serious disarmament measures. May every German answer the question for himself: can the Germans gain anything if one of the two German states or both German states possess nuclear weapons or if they participate in the control of nuclear weapons in any way? The careful examination of this question must make every German in East and West understand that the German nation and every German personally can only lose by it. It is sheer madness to play with nuclear weapons in the heart of Europe.

Albert Norden, member of the Political Bureau of the Central Committee of the Socialist Unity Party of Germany: May I interrupt you, Comrade Ulbricht. The pretext, the alibi used by the Bonn government to torpedo the success of the Geneva negotiations—even if it is folly and madness—is the alleged threat from the East. But it is known that nobody is threatening to attack the Federal Republic. It is also known that this allegation about an attack from the East is simply a plagiarism of the speeches of Hitler and Goebbels. They always substantiated their aggression by talking about an alleged threat from the East. This bears evidence of the fact that nuclear weapons do not guarantee the security of the Federal Republic, but are fraught with insecurity and the danger of a nuclear adventure. They are a means of self-destruction.

Walter Ulbricht: The Bonn government cites still another argument. It says that it wants equal rights in nuclear armament. But the whole world knows that the West German government is the only government which makes territorial claims and which thus has the intention of moving against other states aggressively. And this of all states shall be given nuclear weapons? They say: We just want to have the little finger on the trigger as far as the use of nuclear weapons is concerned. But everybody understands that every additional finger on the trigger increases the danger of a nuclear war, especially if it is a West German finger.

Nuclear weapons in divided Germany would extremely aggravate the danger of war. A nuclear war on German soil would have the most frightful consequences. Only a person who is completely bent on war can suppose that a West Germany equipped with nuclear weapons can force success for the West German policy of conquest. The only result of such a war provocation would be destruction.

Walter Ulbricht: Nuclear weapons in the possession of the West German Federal Republic, the right of co-determination by the West German government over nuclear weapons would also mean that the reunification of Germany would be completely blocked and that rapprochement of the two German states and joint steps towards reunification would be made impossible. Those who, like the West German government, are striving for control over nuclear weapons are indeed writing reunification off, the national concern of us Germans, the national interest of the Germans in East and West thus requires a renunciation of nuclear weapons and any form of participation of one German state in the control of nuclear weapons.

A prohibition of the proliferation of nuclear weapons makes sense only if any possibility of a West German share in control over nuclear weapons is excluded. The national interest of our German people requires that the two German states give their unconditional consent to an eventual international agreement on the non-proliferation of nuclear weapons or on a prohibition of underground nuclear tests as well. Thus you are quite right in stressing the significance of the Geneva Conference of 17 states. The national interest of our German people requires us to do everything possible to make this Conference a success. We have a national interest in the success of the Conference.

Gerhard Kegel, Envoy: A success would be useful for the cause of German reunification.

Walter Ulbricht: That's right, that's right. It would be very useful for reunification for it would serve the relaxation of tension. A successful Geneva Disarmament Conference would also promote understanding between the governments of the two German states. The security of the citizens of the two German states would only gain thereby. And I believe that security and disarmament could become the prologue for reunification, for the restoration of the unity of Germany, and this is what the Germans in the western part of our country also want.

Gerhart Eisler: Comrade Ulbricht, it would probably be good if we could—briefly and in summary—outline the policy of the German Democratic Republic regarding nuclear weapons and disarmament.

Walter Ulbricht: I will put it this way: The national interest of the Germans requires hands off nuclear weapons, participation of the two German states in an atomic-weapon-free zone in Europe, no nuclear weapons but a peace treaty with the two German states.

It would be good if the Germans would this time develop a peace initiative and not—as up to now every twenty or twenty-five years—take the initiative in starting a world war.

Gerhart Eisler: Sometimes one thinks that madmen govern in West Germany. All the details for a total, nuclear war are worked out there with identity disks, gas masks, etc. Would it be too much to expect them to be reasonable there and consider how the two German states could come to an understanding instead of killing each other?

Walter Ulbricht: We advocate, above all, that the two German states reach an understanding as to how peace for the German people and in Germany can be safeguarded. That is why the German Democratic Republic favours an agreement on the non-proliferation of nuclear weapons. The GDR supports the prohibition of underground nuclear tests. In addition, our Republic is working for an immediate freezing of nuclear armaments and for an atomic-weapon-free zone in Europe, including the two German states and the special territory of West Berlin. We are for an agreement between the two German states on an armament stop.

When you say we should take the initiative, then this initiative is very simple. The two German governments need only sit down together and begin with the renunciation of nuclear weapons and an armament stop.

Gerhard Kegel: Would the German Democratic Republic participate in such international conventions as might be agreed upon in Geneva now?

Walter Ulbricht: We would participate in international agreements or conventions on the prohibition of underground nuclear tests and on the prohibition of the proliferation of nuclear weapons. Of course, on condition that these prohibition provisions also apply to the West German Federal Republic.

Gerhart Eisler: May I ask a question, Comrade Chairman of the Council of State? It is not without intention that I mention now your state function. Suppose you were to receive a letter from Federal Chancellor Erhard proposing that you meet him and confer with him on the possibilities of joint action for the prohibition of nuclear weapons. Or if Erhard does not do that, then perhaps the next federal chancellor. In any case, suppose you were to receive such a letter. What would be your reply?

Walter Ulbricht: Let us suppose that the next federal chancellor were to write such a letter. We would answer this letter positively. We would inform him that we are ready for such negotiations. We would suggest that we agree on the place where the talks were to be held. We are realistically thinking people. We take the government in Bonn as it is, and we pose no prior conditions. We are in fact ready to negotiate.

I just hope that the position against nuclear weapons, in any form, will also be further developed within the leading circles of Social Democracy and that as broad a circle of leading social democrats as possible will arrive at a reasonable position, i.e., at a well-considered attitude against any nuclear armament of West Germany.

The CDU/CSU has been in power for sixteen years. Everyone can judge what has happened in these sixteen years. Has there been a step ahead during these sixteen years as far as the safeguarding of peace or reunification are concerned? The contrary is the case. Reunification has been completely blocked. The insecurity for the West Germans is bigger than ever before since the end of the Second World War. The danger of a nuclear adventure, armaments and emergency dictatorship cast a shadow over the life of the West German people.

They are gradually coming to realize it. If the West Germans are given the identity disks—or as we called them during the First World War— the death disks, they will start thinking it over. We thought things over in the First World War when we were given the death disks.

During the sixteen years that the CDU has been in power it has in fact impeded the national concern of the German people, the over-coming of the division of Germany, deepened and widened the gulf between the two German states. Those who want security against war and against the loss of all that has been so laboriously acquired, who wish progress in the direction of a reconciliation in Germany, who are striving for a normalization of relations between the two German states, their rapprochement and the overcoming of the division of Germany can under no circumstance cast their vote for the CDU. Sixteen years show that the CDU is a party of the deepening of the division. Every West German should be clear about the new policy necessary in the interest of the nation and also demand from the candidates campaigning for his vote an avowal to its basic concepts.

Gerhart Eisler: But how do we formulate the basic concepts of a new West German policy, for example?

Walter Ulbricht: We are thinking it over. But we also hope that the West German voters will confront their candidates with this question. Every West German voter must make up his mind: if he wants peace and security, if he wants to preserve and increase what he has acquired through his labour then he must contribute so that a new policy will be carried through.

What are our ideas about a new policy in West Germany? Of course, we cannot expect a socialist policy from a capitalist government in West Germany. We have no illusions in this respect. But the Germans and the whole German nation still have common interests. What policy would correspond to these common interests of the Germans in East and West? What must come out of the forthcoming West German elections?

I would like to put it this way. The election result in West Germany would only correspond to the national interests of all Germans if it would make possible the formation of a new West German government which will steadfastly and consistently pursue a policy of peace and understanding, a policy of disarmament. For only peace, understanding and disarmament can be the prelude to German reunification. Without safeguarding peace and without reaching an agreement on disarmament reunification will not be realistic. Reunification can result only in a democratic Germany. (Acclamation: Not so that it can again wage war!)

Not so that it can wage a war and not so that the nazi generals command in this Germany. That is certainly not what the Germans want, also not what West German citizens want.

This new West German government should, in our opinion, oppose all armament, especially all nuclear armament and the striving for control over nuclear weapons. It should provide guarantees that a policy of real security through the relaxation of tension and understanding replaces the so ruinous and so harmful CDU policy of marching into a new adventure.

The election should result in a new West German government which would lift the sixteen-year-old CDU blockade on German reunification. (Gerhard Kegel: This is quite true: An actual blockade has been imposed upon reunification during the last two decades.)

Every militaristic step by the Bonn government will aggravate the blockade imposed upon reunification. This is the historical fact. We want a new West German government to strive for a policy of reconciliation in Germany directed towards the rapprochement of the German states and the normalization of their relations as an indispensable prerequisite for a peaceful solution of the national question of our people.

A new West German government should emerge from the election that will promote step by step the cooperation between the German states in various fields and which will also free the trade between the German states and their economic cooperation, which I think can be developed, from the fetters of the cold war.

basis of equality. That means that we are really for a genuine and peaceful competition that would benefit the whole German nation.

And, not least, we should apply for the admission of the two German states, at first, as observers to and later as members of, the United Nations.

Certainly it will also be possible to agree on some other steps that seem suitable for bringing us closer to the aim of overcoming the division of Germany.

Thus I would like to emphasise that we are very serious about these ideas and proposals. And we would very much welcome it if an open discussion were held in West Germany during and after the elections.

Gerhart Eisler: Comrade Chairman of the Council of State! At the end of our talk I would like to ask a question on the issue of passes.

Walter Ulbricht: We still consider the permit agreement to be useful, otherwise we would not have taken the initiative. We regret, however, that the permit agreement between the government of the German Democratic Republic and the Senate of West Berlin did not yield the results the two parties had expected because of the pressure and intervention by the Bonn government.

We still favour permits. There is certainly also the possibility of a new agreement. It is up to the negotiators of the government of the German Democratic Republic and the West Berlin Senate to conduct the negotiations correctly and in a business-like manner. I, personally, can only hope that they will achieve a result which will help us to move forward in the normalization of relations between the German Democratic Republic and West Berlin and at the same time contribute to the relaxation of tension.

The German Democratic Republic Has Prepared the Ground for Friendship of the Whole of Germany with Its Great Neighbour in the East

From the Sunday Talk
of the Deutschlandsender (German Broadcasting Station)
on 7 November 1965

Gerhart Eisler, chairman of the State Broadcasting Committee:
Today is the 7th of November. Today, nearly half a century or, to be exact, forty-eight years ago, began the triumphant advance of the Great October Socialist Revolution.

Can you still recall your impressions, Comrade Walter Ulbricht, when you heard the news of the Revolution in Russia and its call–To All, All, All–for the first time?

Walter Ulbricht: I was a German soldier in a transport company in the Balkans, i.e., at one of the fronts of the first imperialist world war. For years already I had been a member of a group of young Leipzig socialists which had connections with Karl Liebknecht and Franz Mehring. We were struggling to end the war and overthrow the monarchy.

When we received the news of the October Revolution I was filled with enthusiasm. Most of my comrades said: Now, the war will finally end. Lenin's call To All had been joyfully hailed by the German soldiers.

Gerhart Eisler: Were there many Germans who realized already at that time the close connection of the national destiny of the Germans with their attitude towards the Great October Socialist Revolution and the Soviet Union?

Walter Ulbricht: You are right, Comrade Eisler, when you see the national destiny and–let me add–the vital interests of the German nation in close connection with their relationship to the October Revolution and to the Soviet Union which emerged from it.

What do the historic experiences of these forty-eight years imply? It was precisely the German people who had to learn some bitter lessons. Karl Liebknecht, the great fighter against war, had proved to be a German patriot, a genuine hero of the German nation. And it was also Karl Liebknecht who, in 1918, was the first to demand the establishment of normal diplomatic and friendly relations between Germany and the young Soviet state.

Let us proceed from the situation in Germany: Our German father-land situated in the heart of Europe could and can develop only in peace, can win international reputation by the acievements of its science, by high-quality work and humanistic works if it lives in peace and friendship with the continent's biggest country. Bismarck already understood that one has to live in peace with Russia. But the ruling circles in Germany, from Wilhelm II to Adenauer and Erhard, have not grasped that to this day.

What Bismarck had already recognized was, of course, true for the German nation to an even greater extent after the great turning point inaugurated in the world by the October Revolution. Nobody can any longer argue that Russia was a reactionary tsarist empire, for now it was a question of having relations with the first country in the world where the workers and peasants governed, where the exploitation of man by man had been abolished and where all human progress was welcomed.

I think that the mortal sin which the German bourgeoisie committed was to maintain hostile relations between Germany and the Soviet Union. From this followed, in the final analysis, the disaster of the Second World War.

Let nobody say that there were not people in Germany at that time who recognized the importance and the necessity of friendly relations with the Soviet Union. There were such forces, even within the bourgeoisie. But they had been gagged and were unable to assert themselves.

There can be no doubt that the most harmful thing German governments have done since 1917 to the German people and to the cause of the German nation was and is the hostile policy towards the Soviet Union, the policy of anti-Sovietism and anti-communism. At the same time this policy served to justify the preservation and continuation of aggressive German imperialism and militarism.

We, the Socialist Unity Party of Germany and the National Front of Democratic Germany, have learned the lessons of history. Since May 1945 we have been consistently and constantly developing relations of lasting friendship and good cooperation with the Soviet Union.

What is the foundation of the policy of friendship and cooperation based on equal rights between the German Democratic Republic and the Soviet Union?

It rests, first of all, on the national vital interests of our German people.

The Soviet Union was the only country among the victor powers of the Second World War that opposed the division of Germany and advocated the democratic development of a united Germany liberated from nazism and militarism.

The cooperation between the progressive and peace-loving forces in Germany and the Soviet Union rests on the fact that here the workers and farmers are in power and that the policy of the Soviet power is inseparably linked with the struggle for peace, freedom and the independence of the peoples. In addition we are linked with the Soviet Union by the great common interest we have in the victory of socialism, the best social system mankind ever brought forth.

It must be added that the Soviet Union is a continent, a huge country, with enormous material resources and reserves. Friendship and good cooperation with his great neighbour are a vital necessity for a country like Germany. It goes without saying that this does not prevent us from cooperating with other countries, including the USA. West Germany's unilateral orientation towards the interests of US monopoly capital, however, cannot in the long run serve the national concern and the national interests of the Germans well.

With whom shall the German people, above all, establish bonds of friendship?

I think that the history of these forty-eight years has shown that the national question of the German people can only be solved satisfactorily if it is linked by friendship and good cooperation with the Soviet Union, with all neighbours and the other European states. A solution serving the interests of our entire nation is possible.

Where are those, the imperialists, who wanted to destroy the Soviet Union at that time? Imperialist Germany tried it for the second time under the Hitler regime. It failed and had to fail. The German nation still has to pay for it today. Or let us have a look at British imperialism. In the first years after the October Revolution Winston Churchill —undoubtedly a prominent British statesman—held the view that the capitalist powers should strangle the young socialist system in the Soviet Union in its cradle. He organized wars of intervention against the Soviet Union; he organized a starvation blockade, an economic boycott and sabotage. But in the Second World War he nevertheless felt compelled to form an alliance with the same Soviet Union, because Great Britain had been threatened by German imperialism and he was up to his neck in difficulties.

They were right who, as we communists had already done in 1917, held the view that the young bearing the future within itself will gain the upper hand. For people want to be free from the danger of war and free from capitalist exploitation and oppression. The future belongs to the young which bears the future within itself, even if at the beginning it looks weak and insignificant. The old, historically out-lived, on the other hand, dies away and must step off the stage of history sooner or later, even though it may still look strong and impos-ing and even if it still possesses considerable power potentialities. We see how this law is effective also in Germany and also increasingly on the relations between the fundamentally different social systems. The rule of the German imperialists and militarists over West Germany still seems to be firm, but it is nevertheless historically outlived and is in contradiction to the vital interests of the German nation.

Gerhart Eisler: As is well known, imperialist forces of the USA and West Germany firmly re-established German imperialism after 1945 under the slogan of defence against communism.

Walter Ulbricht: It was around 1950 when Adenauer, the then West German head of government, appealed to the American govern-ment for the green light to establish a West German army under old nazi generals. In this connection Adenauer deliberately rode the old anti-communist nag. His arguments were the old lie that the Soviet Union wanted to attack West Germany and conquer it. But if it suc-ceeded, Adenauer told the US politicians, the West German industrial potential would be lost to the capitalist world and the USA would be defeated by communism in the economic field. The US politicians were very receptive to these anti-communist arguments. The more so as Adenauer's revenge-seeking plans and his policy of restoring German imperialism coincided with their own interests to a large extent. It was the intention of the USA to use West Germany's in-dustrial and human potential for its own aggressive policy directed against the Soviet Union and the other socialist countries.

The revenge-seeking policy of the Adenauer government, however, proceeded from the false conception that only the USA would possess nuclear weapons. In addition, the Adenauer government did not take into consideration the rapid tempo in the overcoming of the war damage and the further development of the national economy of the Soviet Union. In peaceful economic competition alone, without war and without conquest, the socialist camp achieved much larger increases through the rapid economic growth of the Soviet Union, than would have corresponded to the addition of a state like West Germany with all its economic potential.

Gerhart Eisler: In the years after 1917, when many people in the capitalist countries still regarded the young socialist state as weak, susceptible and non-viable, it was customary among bourgeois politi-cians to use all possible insulting and abusive words against the Soviet Union and undeviatingly to predict its early downfall.

That reminds me somewhat of the desperate efforts of our "dear German brothers" in the Bonn government to slander our German Democratic Republic and its citizens and even to deny our existence as a state.

As the latest variation of this degenerate manifestation of brotherly love the government of Mr. Erhard in Bonn published a language regulation to be uniformly used by all authorities and other official agencies. This regulation prescribes, for instance, that it is not allowed to speak or write of the German Democratic Republic or GDR but only as "Soffyetzone" or–abbreviated–simply "zone" or "SBZ". Furthermore, one shall not speak of the Federal Republic if one means West Germany, but shall say Germany, because thus the pretension is at the same time raised that the West German Federal Republic is the only German state.

Walter Ulbricht: I regard these efforts to replace matter-of-fact policy and business-like discussions between the German states and between the Germans in East and West by a tirade of abusive words decreed from the top as an admission of weakness and, finally, even as an admission of the political-moral inferiority of the positions of the Bonn government and its so-called Germany policy.

What actually do they want to achieve with it? Are Mr. Erhard or any of his ministers so foolish as to suppose that they can obliterate or upset the German Democratic Republic with such a list of abusive words to be applied as a binding language regulation? Or is it to improve the atmosphere in Germany? Or shall perhaps the officially decreed use of defamatory words against the GDR and its citizens be a preliminary alternative for acts of violence that appear too risky in view of the real relation of forces?

Let this nonsense be stopped. It does not benefit anybody and only harms the efforts aimed at overcoming the division of Germany. It promotes the further alienation of the Germans in East and West and deepens the antagonisms between them and between the German states. But perhaps precisely that is the intention?

We citizens of the German Democratic Republic are not only interested in maintaining and developing good friendly relations between us and the Soviet Union. We are likewise interested in the West German Federal Republic, the workers and peasants, West German intellectuals and the realistically-thinking representatives of the bourgeoisie having good relations with the Soviet Union.

The Bonn government maintains that the existence of the German Democratic Republic makes relations between the West German Federal Republic and the Soviet Union difficult. Just the contrary is true. For we are setting the example for the whole of Germany by our friendly relations with the Soviet Union. We have prepared the ground for friendship between the whole of Germany and its great neighbour in the East.

At present relations between the Federal Republic and the Soviet Union are being disturbed by the demand for the restoration of the frontiers of 1937 and the efforts of conquest made by the West German rulers towards the GDR and other socialist countries.

There can, of course, be good relations with the socialist countries if the Federal Republic renounces revanchism and nuclear war armament that is only directed against the Soviet Union and the other socialist countries. The West German Federal Republic will have good relations with the Soviet Union if it proceeds from the real situation in Central Europe. Such an improvement in relations between the West German government and the government of the Soviet Union can also contribute to the relaxation of tension in Germany and would be in the interests of the entire German people.

As far as we are concerned, we, the representatives of the German Democratic Republic, are prepared to do everything in our power to promote the development of friendly relations between the West German Federal Republic and the Soviet Union.

I would like to say in this spirit how good it would really be if political forces pursuing a policy based on realistic perceptions and serving the interests of the German nation—as in France—gained the upper hand in West Germany.

West Germany must become independent of the special interests of the USA so that Germany can be Germany again. I should like to say to all social democrats, all trade unionists, all citizens of West Germany: Strive for a realistic assessment, above all, of developments in the Soviet Union. Visit the Soviet Union and also the GDR and try to examine everything without prejudices and without blinkers in a matter-of-fact way and form a realistic opinion. But then please have the courage to correct former wrong or outdated impressions. It is no disgrace to disavow an error. The interests of the German nation demand that you not become hardened in a policy of hostility to a country like the Soviet Union. It is not only three times as big as the USA. Friendship with the Soviet Union is vital and indispensable for the German nation, for its happiness and for its peaceful future.

But how can West Germany arrive at a reasonable policy of friendship with the Soviet Union? I am convinced that it is not so difficult. The West German Federal Republic need only throw overboard the policy of hostility to the Soviet Union as well as the revenge-seeking policy. The West German Federal Republic need only recognize the realities which, in any case, it is not able to change. It need only cooperate honestly on disarmament and the prevention of a nuclear war as well as on understanding on peace and security in Europe. All this is of vital interest for the German nation the welfare and woe of which we are concerned about and which, dear viewers and listeners, all of us love.

With Optimism into the New Year!

New Year's Message for 1966

Dear Fellow Citizens, Comrades and Friends,
Citizens of West Germany,

The year 1965 was again a year of peace for Germany and Europe. And it is the wish of us all that in 1966 the efforts of the peoples may not only preserve peace but lead to advances in the establishment of an enduring European peace system.

It would be flippant to ignore the fact that the dangers threatening our peace have also grown. The dirty war of the United States of America against the Democratic Republic of Vietnam and against the brave, freedom-loving people of South Vietnam casts its shadow over the whole world.

The West German federal chancellor and his government have made it understood that in 1966 they will wage the struggle for hegemony in NATO and Western Europe and for joint control over nuclear weapons. At the same time they declared their solidarity with the USA's barbaric war against the Vietnamese people.

The napalm incendiaries who with their crimes have burdened themselves with the hatred and contempt of all peace-loving people are friends and allies of the West German armament billionaires and their Bonn government.

The declaration of sympathy for murderers and the emergency plans for the suppression of the West German citizens are two sides of a uniform Bonn policy. It endangers world peace, peace in Europe and peace in Germany. The Bonn government, allied with the USA's war of aggression does not want a German policy in 1966, either, but a policy against the vital interests of the Germans in East and West.

This situation requires that these war dangers be overcome through the persistent work and the persistent struggle of the citizens of the German Democratic Republic and the peace-loving majority of the West Germans. Let us all give our best so that 1966 may become the year of the joint concern for security and peace.

Dear Fellow Citizens, Comrades and Friends,

For the German Democratic Republic 1966 will be a year of continued socialist construction and thus of further social progress.

The 11th plenary session of the Central Committee of the Socialist Unity Party of Germany had the character of a great democratic deliberation. The citizens of the GDR and the entire German people received a clear report on the situation, on what has been achieved, on our next tasks and on the perspectives up to 1970 and beyond. 1965 was a good year for us because the German Democratic Republic has again come a good step forward.

Our industrial production grew by about seven thousand million marks in 1965. The plan for the production of commodities was fulfilled and even somewhat overfulfilled. Labour productivity was some six per cent higher than in 1964. The yields of our agriculture in field husbandry as well as in cattle farming increased considerably. Progress was also made in the building industry, in trade and in transport. Good progress in the development of the socialist educational system can be recorded, and outstanding performances were made in the field of culture.

Even our enemies are forced to recognize that the GDR, the first socialist German state, has further consolidated itself internally and externally.

The state visit to the United Arab Republic in the spring of this year was a significant national and international event. The visit of the party and government delegation this year to the Soviet Union and its far-reaching results have again clearly shown that we are linked with this great country by firm friendship, solidarity and relations of fruitful cooperation on the basis of equal rights for the benefit of our peoples and countries. The growing prestige of the GDR and its role in international life have made widely evident the justification of our claim to be the legitimate representative and authorized speaker of the entire German nation.

The capable and diligent workers and office employees, cooperative farmers and agricultural workers of the German Democratic Republic, our engineers and technicians, scientists and intellectual workers, our teachers and artists, economic and state officials, the tradesmen, the members of our armed forces who protect our peaceful work of construction—they have all contributed to the advances of 1965.

I would like to use this message at the end of the year to thank very cordially all who contributed to the successes of 1965 with their work, their abilities and their intelligent advice.

Are we content with what has been achieved? Of course not! We know that much remains to be done. We make ever higher claims on life. But developments, too, put ever new questions on the agenda and make new solutions necessary. We are far from self-satisfaction. Nevertheless, we know our way—and we know the objective! It is a great pleasure for us that—thanks to the good work results of our people in the last years—we can introduce in 1966 the five-day week every second week. In addition for those working people for whom the weekly hours of work could not yet be reduced to 45 hours and for those working people who regularly work in the three-shift or the continuous shift system there is a shorter work week. Moreover, the working people can participate financially in the good economic results of their enterprise through the introduction of a year-end bonus.

I believe, dear fellow citizens, friends and comrades that what we are doing is right. We first concern ourselves with good work, and when the results have been obtained we examine and decide how the living standard of the working people can be further improved, and we do that after thorough reflection. We do not make leaps. We advance step by step, solidly and continuously.

Naturally we shall never be content with what we have achieved. We strive for high prosperity for all and in addition comprehensive social security. We strive for a united, peace-loving, democratic Germany. We strive to be at the top in the intellectual and cultural development of mankind. We want all citizens of the GDR to be highly developed people, professionally and culturally. We wish to have the best scientists and engineers, outstanding physicians and architects, teachers, writers and artists, people who enrich the culture of mankind.

That is what our national ambition is aimed at, and it would be good if we could say already today that both German states try to fulfil their national ambition exclusively in those peaceful aims which at the same time serve the progress of mankind.

The great national mission of the German Democratic Republic is becoming ever more evident. In Germany only the GDR has a clear conception of a progressive democratic society which respects the freedom and human dignity of the individual and preserves the interests of the entire society. Only the GDR has a long-term plan for the social development of the German people. It is in accord with the trend of development of human society as well as with the vital national and social interests of the Germans. The GDR is the only German state which has a realistic conception of a democratic and peaceful solution of the German problem which is based on the facts of history, a realistic conception of the unification of the German states into a peace-loving and democratic Germany.

The Socialist Unity Party of Germany and the National Front clearly answered the question of the perspective of Germany. This perspective takes the social changes resulting from the growing anatagonistic contradictions in state monopoly capitalism into consideration. Herr Erhard's "formed society" is nothing but the dictatorship of state monopoly capitalism. His statement in the USA that his "formed society" is identical with the conceptions of rule of US monopoly capital again confirm this.

We, however, orient ourselves on the rule of the people, on the rule of human dignity and freedom from misery and exploitation, on the co-determination and shared responsibility of all who do or have done something for society. The perspective worked out by us which has validity for the entire German people at the same time takes into consideration those fundamental changes the carrying through of which is the most urgent task set to our entire nation by history with its hard lessons. I am deeply convinced that the German Democratic Republic, its working citizens and especially its young people will prove worthy of the great national mission.

Dear citizens of the West German Federal Republic,

It distresses us that the government in Bonn is pushing the national ambition of the West Germans in a direction which repeatedly brought disaster to our German people, in the direction, that is, of the striving for economic, political and military supremacy over other peoples, for changes in the frontiers, for control over nuclear weapons. This policy discredits the name of Germany throughout the world. This policy especially threatens your lives, dear West German friends.

Many West Germans believe that in fact the situation is not as dangerous as we see it. But I tell you that he who demands territories of other states and does not recognize existing frontiers can declare a thousand times that he wants peace. He lies! For he wants to swallow and dismember other states. No one should believe such a government with such goals.

I tell you that the West German government in Bonn is pursuing a policy of escalation similar to that of the USA. It aggravates the situation step by step. But he who in West Germany eases his mind with the fact that there is no war yet makes the same serious mistake that was made by a large part of the German people at the time of Hitler. That is criminally irresponsible.

We appeal to the workers and office employees, to the farmers, the intellectual workers, to all German patriots in the West German Federal Republic: Do you want peace as we want it? Then you ought to do more so that it will finally be victorious. When the workers, farmers and intellectuals, when the social democratic voters, the members and friends of the trade unions stand up against atomic armament and emergency dictatorship no Bonn government will be able to realize the plans directed against peace, democracy and the freedom of the people.

There was talk recently in the West German Bundestag of a NATO target file for the employment of nuclear weapons against German towns from West German territory. We think that what the Germans in East and West really need and what they can only obtain through joint struggle for peace is a target card file which banishs all atomic weapons from Germany and prevents by means of international agreements German towns from ever becoming the targets of nuclear weapons.

The West German government is in the process of selling the right of self-determination of the West Germans for the mess of pottage of a questionable co-determination over nuclear weapons. Bonn thereby makes the division of Germany irrevocable for a long historical period. In doing so the government in Bonn knows as well as we do that its participation in the control over nuclear weapons is rejected by the majority of all states and peoples, no matter how it is camouflaged.

If the government in Bonn should absolutely have the need to completely isolate itself in Europe then the maintenance of its frontier demands is obviously an infallible way to attain this goal. But all West Germans should realize that neither the frontiers nor the course of world history will be changed thereby, for there exist two German states, as is well known, and Bonn is not the navel of the world. He who wants peace must recognize the existing frontiers.

The recognition of the existing frontiers would be a positive step on the way to a European security system which protects all European states against intervention from outside and against acts of aggression. Moreover, such an official renunciation by the Bonn government of its hitherto existing revanchist policy could facilitate the economic activity of the West German industrial enterprises both in the East as well as in the West.

We welcome and support the initiatives of the government of the Soviet Union in the United Nations for the security of the peoples and states and the promotion of world peace. We welcome and support the declaration against interference in the internal affairs of foreign states and on the protection of their independence and sovereignty. We welcome the initiatives for the promotion of international cooperation, the preparation and holding of a world disarmament conference.

The common interest of the citizens of the German Democratic Republic and the citizens of the West German Federal Republic requires working jointly for the good cause of the safeguarding of peace. This community of interests of the Germans in the East and West on the fundamental questions of vital interest could be expressed, for example, in solidarity declarations of the two German states with the United Nations decisions promoting peace.

Especially at the end of this year we Germans from the GDR, from the West German Federal Republic and from West Berlin should seriously reflect on what we can and must do together to put a final stop to the calamitous escalation into adventure and to win the victory for peace in 1966.

I am convinced that all peoples of Europe would draw a deep sigh of relief if the German states took the initiative for steps in favour of an enduring European peace system. I assure you that the German Democratic Republic will make every effort to reach this goal.

The Council of State of the German Democratic Republic makes the following proposals to the newly elected Bundestag of the West German Federal Republic:

● Both German states renounce nuclear armament and participation in the control over nuclear weapons in any form;

● the two German states recognize the existing frontiers in Europe;

● the German Democratic Republic and the West German Federal Republic take up diplomatic relations with all NATO states and Warsaw Pact states in the interest of European peace and European security;

● the two German states declare their readiness for negotiations on disarmament in Germany;

● the two German states solemnly renounce measures, laws and decrees which block the way to the overcoming of the division and to reunification as, for example, atomic armament, emergency legislation, etc.;

● the governments of the two German states begin negotiations with the aim of normalizing the relations between the German states and their citizens.

We should begin with disarmament in Germany. There should be no difference of opinion between us Germans in East and West that relaxation in Germany and a normalization of the relations between the two German states is impossible without disarmament. I think that the Germans in East and West should be interested in the membership of the two German states in the United Nations to serve disarmament and peace. The successful relaxation of the situation in Europe through disarmament in Germany would at the same time be a good contribution to security and peace in the whole of Europe. It would provide conditions under which the great concern for the reunification of the Germans could receive a new, strong impetus.

Certainly it would then also be easier to normalize the relations between the German states and their citizens. We think that the right of the two German states to membership in the United Nations must not be impaired by the fact that up to now there is no German peace treaty.

Let us seek new ways together to solve our national problems.

Properly speaking, it should not be so difficult—despite the differences of opinion on many questions—to transform the common vital interest of the citizens of the GDR and the citizens of West Germany and West Berlin in the preservation and safeguarding of peace into joint first steps to a stable European peace system in the new year 1966. Let me state that a common way could be found if there were at least good will on the West German side.

At the end of this year 1965 I address the cordial and urgent request to all citizens of West Germany and West Berlin: Do not close your mind to our call for joint steps which are to serve the safeguarding of peace for Germany and for Europe.

Dear Fellow Citizens, Friends and Comrades,
Citizens of the West German Federal Republic,

I am convinced that we can and shall jointly master the problems of our peace-loving nation. Let us enter the new year with joy of life and optimism! But let us also think that in 1966 we must do something decisive for the victory of peace, so that in years to come we can celebrate the turn of the year in safeguarded peace, without worries and free from the fear of war.

In this spirit I wish you and your families success in the struggle for peace, health, success and happiness!

To a very happy and healthy New Year 1966!

Friendship!

The Road to the Future Fatherland of the Germans

Speech in the Dynamo Sports Hall
in Berlin on 21 April 1966

Dear Comrades, Dear Guests and Friends,

I welcome you most cordially in the name of the Central Committee of our party. I extend my special greeting to the old comrades throughout the Republic, the companions-in-struggle in the founding of our successful Socialist Unity Party of Germany.

To many of the comrades gathered here—former members of the Communist Party of Germany (KPD) or the Social Democratic Party (SPD)—the notable events of twenty years ago which found their climax in the unification of the two working-class parties into the Socialist Unity Party of Germany (SED) are still vivid, as if it happened but yesterday.

The two decades which have passed since then were filled to the brim with epoch-making events and revolutionary transformations which fundamentally changed the face and the destiny of Germany. Two revolutionary transformations took place in this period whose significance is also felt well beyond the frontiers of the German Democratic Republic, the anti-fascist, democratic revolution and the socialist revolution.

The social democrats and communists who joined in the Socialist Unity Party of Germany and hundreds of thousands of young comrades who gathered around them have accomplished a tremendous work in these twenty years, a work which has the recognition of the peace-loving peoples. Often working under the most difficult circumstances, our comrades have worked miracles in self-sacrificing, even heroic work. I want to thank all these comrades in the name of the Central Committee of the Socialist Unity Party of Germany for their loyalty, for the great work they have accomplished in these two decades and at the same time congratulate them on their successes. What did our country look like in 1945–46? And what has been created under the leadership of the party! We can be proud of what we have achieved!

Very many members of our party do not know the division of the German working class from personal experience. But these younger comrades for whom the unity of the working class in the German Democratic Republic is a matter of course should always remember:

This unity is and remains the pledge of the victory of peace and humanity, of democracy and socialism in the whole of Germany.

On the mountains of rubble left to us as a heritage of the German imperialists after their Second World War the idea grew in our people that only the German working class is entitled to make the historical claim to the leadership of the nation, that only under the leadership of the united working class in alliance with the other working people can a peaceful and happy future of the German people be secured.

The national task long since put on the agenda by history could also be solved only under the leadership of the party of the united working class, the task of taking up relations of friendship and trustful cooperation with the most progressive country in the world, with the socialist world power of the Soviet Union. With enormous sacrifices the Soviet Union had saved Europe and its humanist culture from the barbaric enslavement of the misanthropic German imperialists and their Hitlers and Himmlers. It had become clear to many Germans that Germany can prosper only in sincere friendship with this country of the highest social progress. The 23rd Congress of the Communist Party of the Soviet Union (CPSU) has demonstrated to the entire people the purposeful peace policy and the systematic and planned character of communist construction in the Soviet Union. We are proud of having tied the link of firm friendship with the glorious Soviet people.

The victory of the peoples of the anti-Hitler coalition over German fascism obliged the German working class and the people to learn the lessons of history and make use of the great opportunity to construct a peace-loving and progressive Germany.

The memorable fusion of the Communist Party and the Social Democratic Party was not only the decisive turning-point in the eventful history of class struggles in Germany but at the same time a national event of the first rank. The basis for the peaceful and happy future of the German people was laid twenty years ago.

The unification of the parties of the working class was the decisive prerequisite for all the achievements and successes of the working people of our Republic since then. It is the source of the force which mastered the immense difficulties of our construction. With the unification of the two working-class parties twenty years ago the foundation was created on which in this part of Germany a strong, flourishing socialist state came into existence in a historically short period out of the rubble and ruins of war, a state whose economic, scientific and cultural potentials and political significance and international authority are constantly growing.

Thus the German people have realized their right of self-determination in the German Democratic Republic.

We can say with full right that the overcoming of the split in the working class and the establishment of its unity on a revolutionary basis is the hitherto greatest achievement in the now almost 120 years of the history of the German working-class movement since the Communist Manifesto and the establishment of the KPD.

The revolutionary theory of the two greatest sons of the German people, Karl Marx and Friedrich Engels, a long common way in the old revolutionary German Social Democracy as well as the progressive and humanist traditions of the German workers' movement were undoubtedly strong unifying links between communists and social democrats. With their merger a genuine amalgamation of the two streams of the working-class movement was introduced and the road taken to a united Marxist-Leninist party of the German working class.

The unification of the two parties gave and gives the working class the strength to play the leading role in the shaping of the new system and in the fulfilment of the national mission.

Under the leadership of the SED a firm alliance of the working class with the peasantry, the intelligentsia, the craftsmen and tradesmen as well as with broad circles of the bourgeoisie was created and a cooperation borne by mutual confidence with the other anti-fascist democratic parties was brought about.

Balance-sheet of the Amalgamation of the Workers' Parties

In these twenty years our Socialist Unity Party of Germany has become the strongest of the German parties, a powerful force. It has swept the idlers aside and it shapes the future of Germany in a disciplined, united, conscious manner, always ready to take up the fight, guided by the scientific theory of Marxism-Leninism.

Our party enjoys the confidence of the people. It is based not least on the fact that the German Marxists have correctly foreseen developments and always told the truth to the German working class and the entire people, even when large sections of the people did not want to hear an unpleasant truth. We always assessed developments realistically and never built up our policy on illusions.

It was social democrats, revolutionary social democrats, old social democrats such as Karl Liebknecht, Rosa Luxemburg, Franz Mehring, Clara Zetkin, Wilhelm Pieck and many others who at the outbreak of the First World War stormed against the policy of the social democratic leaders when these politicians became an appendage of the Kaiser's imperialist war policy. Let us not forget that the unity of the SPD was broken as a result of the reactionary pro-imperialist policy of its leaders at that time and that the real social democrats then had no other opportunity than to rally all social democrats who did not want to submit to this fateful policy.

At the end of the First World War we warningly pointed out that the maintenance of the rule of the armament trusts, the big banks and their militarists, that the policy of revenge for the military defeat and the change in the frontiers which had come into existence after the war would lead to new crises and wars.

We perceived in good time and also stated that Hitler meant war, although large sections of the people did not want to believe us then. And when Hitler began his wars we proved that his defeat was certain. We swam against the stream of public opinion fabricated by the big bourgeoisie with their press trusts, but we always told the truth to the German working class and our German people. We also told the truth to the German working class and the German people when after the defeat of Hitler the imperialist occupation powers together with the German monopolists and bankers set about splitting Germany and restoring the power of the old corrupters of our fatherland in the western occupation zones under the mask of economic reconstruction.

We appealed to the responsibility of the German workers and all working people and struggled against the division of Germany. Our efforts to create the united front of the working class in the whole of Germany, which corresponded with the longing of the majority of the German working class, also served the liberation of Germany from the vestiges of fascism as well as the preservation of the unity of Germany. Finally we developed a German policy together with all forces of good will possessed of a sense of responsibility, a policy which is based on the vital interests of the great majority of our peace-loving people.

We Have Paved the Way for Humanity

The attempt is often made, also in the reply of the Social Democratic Party executive to our Open Letter to separate the German question from humanity. That cannot be done.

Anyone who really wants to do something human for the German people pursues a policy which makes all wars impossible in the future.

Anyone who really wants to do something for humanity shows and enters upon a road which leads to disarmament and social security and to the end of the national division.

Anyone who really wants to do something for humanity shows and pursues a policy which leads to a Germany which is not governed by reaction and does not become a scene of action for the big capitalist trusts and banks, for militarists, reaction and the unleashing of dangerous international crises up to and including war.

Anyone who really wants to do something for humanity pursues a policy which leads to understanding between the two German states, which puts an end once and for all to the cold and sub-limited war against the GDR.

We must have learned from the history of Germany how to struggle for humanity and how not. Only he who struggled against German imperialism in the imperial period, who opposed the unleashing of war and issued the slogan in the war to turn the weapons against one's own imperialists, only he really did something for humanity.

Only he did something for humanity in Germany who proposed to defeat national socialism through a joint big anti-fascist front of the working class and the democratic forces of the bourgeoisie.

Only he really did something for true humanity who during the war did everything possible to liquidate the Hitler regime. And only he did something for humanity who after 1945 directed every effort to ensuring that a Germany does not come into existence again in which the old warmongers and reactionaries seize power anew.

Only he did and does something for humanity who directs every effort of the people to finally expelling from the life of the people the reactionary rulers in West Germany, the continuers of the Hitler policy in new forms.

This is the real struggle for humanity!

Mere phrases about humanity which do not mitigate the danger of the West German militarist reaction are of no use whatever. It is necessary to say this frankly to our social democratic friends so that nobody allows himself to be duped by those false friends who in the name of humanity do the traditional business of German imperialist reaction and the US imperialists.

By the way, who dares in West Germany or West Berlin to utter the word humanity when at the same time he supports the cruel war of the US imperialists against the Vietnamese people?

In our part of Germany, in the German Democratic Republic, we have realized in the sense of true humanity what had been striven for by social democrats and trade unionists in the militant period of German Social Democracy, what had been fixed in their programs and what was demanded by progressive citizens for the completion of the bourgeois revolution.

Our goal was and is a really human Germany, a Germany of peace and peaceful work in which only the interests of the people and not the interests of armament industrialists and other war profiteers decide.

In realizing this goal we have studied and taken to heart the lessons of the unfortunate Weimar Republic. We have learned that after the war it could not be enough simply to remove the rubble, get the economy going again, but postpone the complicated problems of the reorganization of society for an indefinite period. Such a policy benefits the restoration of the old pernicious forces of monopoly capital. This was proved by Weimar, and this is proved by the development of the West German Federal Republic in the last two decades.

The task was rather to create the guarantees for the rule of the anti-fascist democratic forces along with removing the rubble and getting the economy going. The power of German imperialism, the rule of the big monopolies and the feudal big landowners, the power of militarism had to be uprooted. Along with reconstruction the property of the people in the enterprises of the big war profiteers and war criminals was safeguarded, and thereby the possibility was taken from the feudal and big capitalist forces of reoccupying their power positions at a later date. The working class set about taking into its own hands not only the administration of the state and economy, but also and especially the conscious shaping of social production. We did the most difficult things first. We understood that the working people must erect their house on solid foundations. Thus the German working people became masters of their country and of their own destinies.

Thus we see that the working people of the GDR and the working people of West Germany took different roads. Both here and there they cleared away the rubble and built up the enterprises. But in West Germany the rule of reaction was restored because of the split in the working class and the dictatorship of the imperialist occupation powers. In the GDR, however, the working people rule and are building their socialist system. Can there be any doubt as to which way was better?

The leadership of West German Social Democracy repeated the mistake of Weimar. It persisted in the illusion that it was possible to

401

grow into democracy and socialism on a "third way" by way of the restoration of the rule of monopoly capital and the big banks. In reality the deeper causes of exploitation, the crises remained in existence. With its "third way" the SPD leadership only supplies German reaction with the "democratic" facade behind which the multimillionaires, their war economy leaders and Hitler generals again extended their old power apparatus and made anti-communism the ruling state doctrine. The Hitler war economy leaders at the head of the big trusts, the Hitlerite Gestapo officials in the West German Office for the Protection of the Constitution, the Hitler hanging judges in the judiciary and the Hitler generals at the head of the army, that is the result of this "third way".

In view of such relations of power, which can only be characterized as the dictatorship of monopoly capital and its militarists, it is illusory to expect the urgently necessary transformation of society and the securing of a real co-determination of the working people only from elections.

The attempt of the SPD leadership to change the majority situation by outdoing the revanchist big bourgeoisie in nationalism and pushing back the CDU with a policy of adaptation, has finally brought the SPD policy into the same blind alley in which CDU/CSU policy hopelessly sits.

Our balance-sheet of the last two decades shows the victory of two revolutions—the anti-fascist democratic and the socialist transformation. It was a continuous revolutionary process. The only successful revolution in German history was carried through in a democratic way on the territory of the GDR.

On the occasion of the 20th anniversary of the Socialist Unity Party of Germany we present the working class in the two German states with the *History of the German Working-Class Movement* in eight volumes. This work contains the lessons acquired by the older generation in decades of hard struggles and in thorough scientific study. It is not enough to know on the basis of the laws of social development that the working class is called upon to replace the decaying class of the bourgeoisie. Guided by the scientific theory of Marxism-Leninism, the revolutionary party of the working class has worked out the strategy and tactics of the struggle for political power in our period. The historical work ends with chapter XV, with the decision on the program of socialism. The present speech contains the syllabus for chapter XVI. It shows the way of the struggle and the unification of the working class and the peace-loving democratic forces of the GDR and the West German Federal Republic.

Our party can proudly state, together with the bloc parties and mass organizations in the National Front, that it has paved the way for humanity.

It was in the sense of humanity that under the leadership of the SED the working people not only extirpated fascism and militarism but also the exploitation of man by man. This was the greatest deed for humanity and freedom.

Through the overcoming of the power of the monopolies and the transfer of the enterprises and banks into national property as well as through the purging of the administrations of war criminals and lackeys of the monopolists, the workers and working people for the first time received possibilities of developing their creative forces. They proved their abilities, their sense of responsibility and their initiative in the democratic reorganization of political and economic conditions. They learned to manage the state and economy. A democratic school system came into existence on a humanist basis with the school reform. Democratic conditions were introduced in the villages with the land reform. Freed from Junker and capitalist exploitation, the former farm-hands, agricultural labourers and working peasants learned to run farms themselves and govern with the support of the working class.

A growing number of workers, farmers, engineers, scientists and other members of the intelligentsia as well as craftsmen and forces of the bourgeoisie ready for construction took an active part in setting up the anti-fascist, democratic system. They did self-sacrificing work in the solution of the complicated political, economic and cultural tasks of that time. The equality of rights of women was realized step by step as well as the basic rights of the young generation.

Under the leadership of our party the working class won the decisive positions in the state, economy and cultural life and enjoyed the trust and cooperation of all working people. The restoration of the old reactionary forces was made impossible. The conditions were created for the socialist development in a peaceful and democratic manner.

This peaceful transition from the anti-fascist democratic to the socialist transformation had already been contained in the "Principles and Aims of the SED" adopted at the unification congress. We have creatively applied the theory worked out by Lenin in his work *Two Tactics of Social Democracy in the Democratic Revolution* on the transition from the bourgeois-democratic to the socialist revolution under the specific conditions of development in Germany.

In the process of the deep-going socialist revolution which took place with an open frontier with the imperialist camp hard conflicts were sometimes necessary. In their course the reactionary forces were defeated and the forces of democracy and socialism increasingly asserted themselves.

In the construction of socialist economy and culture new socialist relations between the people developed and are developing. A socialist community of people is maturing which masters the complicated problems of the technical revolution in the period of the all-round construction of socialism. We consider this development of people in the process of the revolutionary transformation of social reality as the greatest success of the last two decades.

What a difference between people in the former Soviet occupation zone of 1946 and the conscious and self-confident citizens of the socialist GDR in 1966. Let us not forget that most of them are still the same people.

We are happy to be able to state that the majority of those millions of people who believed the mendacious slogans of the fascist leadership, are today educated, self-confident co-shapers of the new socialist life. Our party was in a position to change the consciousness of the people because it had the strength to change life, because it had the strength to destroy the economic foundations of imperialist policy and ideology.

A straight road leads from the historic appeal of the Communist Party of Germany of 11 June, 1945 via the "Principles and Aims of the Socialist Unity Party of Germany" adopted by the unification congress to the program of the all-round construction of socialism in the GDR which was adopted at the Sixth Congress. The working out and realization of the economic system of socialism has led to a remarkable upswing in industry and agriculture, in trade and the crafts. The further way of socialist construction in the period of the long-range plan up to 1970 was fixed at the 11th session of the Central Committee. The strength and the certainty of further successes lie in the community of the work of our people for the shaping of a new social system.

Great Tasks Still Lie Ahead

Together with all forces united in the National Front, our party has fulfilled the basic tasks concerning the GDR. As regards the basic solution of the national question, we have created solid foundations for this in the GDR. Yet big and difficult tasks still lie ahead. They can only be accomplished in a way conforming to the interests of the

German working class and with the national and social interests of the entire nation if the working-class parties in the east and west come to an understanding and come together on at least a minimum of common conceptions and joint action.

I am convinced that I will meet with the approval of West German workers when I say that the CDU/CSU leadership can continue its revanchist policy and its demands for a share in the control of atomic weapons only as long as it can count on tolerance or support from among the ranks of Social Democracy. Those wishing to prevent the CDU/CSU from plunging West Germany into a catastrophe must help to bring about the community of the Social Democratic and the Socialist Unity Parties, the community of the working class of the West German Federal Republic and the GDR. All workers consider the fact that representatives of trusts should conduct negotiations with representatives of the GDR, whereas trade union officials are prohibited from conducting joint consultations, to be a contradiction.

In view of the barbaric war of the US against the Vietnamese liberation movement and the Democratic Republic of Vietnam and in view of the moral and material support of the brutal aggression of the US imperialists by the ruling circles in Bonn, it is high time to rally the forces of peace, democracy and progress.

West Germany has become the second centre of war provocation in the world and the main disturber of the peace in Europe.

Precisely for this reason we addressed our Open Letter to the delegates of the forthcoming Dortmund Congress of the Social Democratic Party and to all members and friends of Social Democracy in West Germany.

We put to the SPD delegates and members the question:

1) Are you in favour of negotiations and an understanding between the governments of the two German states with the aim of relaxation and the creation of the prerequisites for their cooperation and step-by-step unification?

What do we mean by an understanding with a view to relaxation?

We have openly stated that relaxation can only be considered once both German states have renounced atomic armament and all claims to sharing control over atomic weapons. All men and women who are neither willing to live under the threat of the atomic bomb nor under the martial law of emergency regulations must be mobilized in the spirit of the Easter March movement.

Unfortunately we have not yet received a clear answer to our clear question. Atomic armament in West Germany and the revanchist policy of Hitler generals are inhuman. This inhumanity cannot be

405

reduced by the GDR opening its frontiers so that the Hitler generals can march in. This was what happened once in Austria and Czechoslovakia. It is a good thing that these matters are openly discussed.

Of course this discussion serves the aim of finding common ways to the normalization of relations between the two German states. These include the normalization and extension of economic relations not only between West German enterprises and representatives of the GDR Ministry of Foreign and Inter-German Trade, but also of the direct relations between the economic ministries of both German states. The decisive point is that the normalization of relations must serve the safeguarding of peace. It must not be useful to the revanchists and atomic war politicians.

The exchange of opinions and arguments and the discussion to bring about a clarification of mutual interests and a community of views have begun. Thousands of social democratic comrades and trade unionists in West Germany are already participating in the dialogue between the SPD and SED. They have recognized that the conception of the Bonn government, striving for a military alliance with the most aggressive of imperialist states, the USA, is internationally discrediting the West German Federal Republic and isolating it also from those countries of Western Europe not interested in military adventures and taking a more realistic view of the situation than is being done in Bonn.

A great fear still prevails among the leaders of the West German social democrats of being reproved by the CDU/CSU for having started a discussion with us. But the time of the divine right of kings is long past and we should like to encourage the members of the SPD leadership to refrain from making the way in which they continue their discussion with us dependent upon the divine right of the CDU/CSU.

Fear of the reactionary party of the bourgeoisie is a bad counsellor and has always been fatal for the working class, as the course of history has proved. Despite the pressure and the anti-communist campaign of the state power in Bonn, a growing number of West German social democrats are becoming aware that all attempts of the Bonn government to implement the aggressive forward strategy would find a terrible end in the fire of atomic war. Many have convinced themselves that no success could be attained by the undercover war against the GDR and that the extremely extensive plans of the so called Research Advisory Council of the Bonn government are only good enough to be collected by the rag-picker and to be taken to a paper-mill.

The awareness, which has become unpleasant to many social democrats, that they are stuck in a blind alley together with the CDU, and the need to find a way out of that blind alley are at the root of the discussion at present in progress in West Germany on the reality of the frontiers which have existed for the past 20 years; certain circles of the Evangelical Church have recently joined this discussion.

We see a remarkable parallel development in the struggle waged by the intellectuals, the trade unions and social democracy against the continued curtailment of democracy coupled with emergency regulations. The fact that prominent scientists and other intellectuals have made contact with the trade unions in order to discuss joint measures to be taken against the emergency dictatorship of the property-owning bourgeoisie shows that important democratic forces have become active in the Federal Republic.

On the other hand we do not fail to recognize the fact that fascist forces are forming inside and outside the CDU/CSU. This has become evident in several recent elections in West Germany and was emphasized by the increased arrogance and aggressiveness of West German policy. Under the slogan of the "formed society" a group of CDU leaders is about to develop the immediate and totalitarian claims to power of the big bourgeoisie into a firm system with the aim of restraining the democratic movement of the people and, if need be, to suppress it with force.

On the Way to the Future Fatherland of the Germans

The key to the safeguarding of peace, to European security and a peaceful solution of the German question—as far as West Germany is concerned—thus lies in the hands of the working class and its allies, in the hands of the social democrats, socialists, communists, trade unionists and non-party workers, with intellectuals also playing an important part.

Without guarantees that a war shall never again start from German soil a solution of the German question is absolutely impossible. Such guarantees are demanded by the vital interests of the German people themselves. And they are with justification being demanded by Germany's neighbours who were attacked by German militarists twice in the first half of this century.

The transformations effected in the GDR and the complete deprivation of power of the imperialist and militarist forces interested in war and conquest and the corresponding consistent peace policy of the GDR provide the German people and their neighbours with such guarantees, as far as this lies within our power.

In West Germany an entirely different situation prevails. The basic provisions of the Potsdam Agreement were not carried out there, although the majority of the population was in favour of an anti-fascist democratic development. Therefore a peaceful solution of the German question and a unification of the German states are not possible before the prerequisites for a peaceful policy as laid down within the Potsdam Agreement have been created in West Germany by means of basic internal changes.

We cannot omit including the position of Germany in the world of today and in the world of tomorrow in our considerations.

The world has undergone considerable changes since the time when the unified German state, usurped by the fascist lackeys of the German imperialists, suffered an annihilating defeat in the rapacious war which it had organized. The German people in both German states must acknowledge these changes and act accordingly if they wish to open the road to a unified Germany. The peoples have drawn their conclusions from the fact that German imperialists twice plunged the world into devastating wars.

Along with the Soviet Union a number of states have emerged whose policy is directed towards the safeguarding of peace and combating the aggressive imperialist policy, that source of war danger. Those states are vigilant and ward off the danger resulting from the policy of the West German partial state, which claims to be the successor of the Hitler Reich and which increases world tensions by its striving for atomic weapons and its territorial claims.

The story spread by West German anti-communists about the possibility of inciting the socialist countries of Europe against each other has burst like a soap bubble. The 23rd Congress of the CPSU demonstrated the internal firmness, the creative power and resoluteness of the party of Lenin and of the peoples of the Soviet Union. No one with all five senses intact could believe that in this present period, when the majority of the peoples of Europe live in the Soviet Union and in socialist states, the Soviet Union could be willing to encourage the dismantling of socialism in the GDR. At the 23rd Congress 86 communist and working-class parties of the whole world proclaimed their fraternal sympathy with the Soviet Union, the heroically fighting people of Vietnam and with the workers' and peasants' state in Germany, the German Democratic Republic. The peoples are against the adventurers in West Germany.

The peoples of not a few capitalist states of Europe and the world are heedful of the lesson taught by two wars and are defending themselves against having their lives and future put at stake as a result of the actions of West German revanchist politicians.

Finding the way towards a future united Germany in the world of today and tomorrow means respecting the demands of the peoples for peace and security.

These demands are in conformity with the vital interests of the German working people. In this spirit we consider it urgently necessary for the Federal Republic also to take the road of a consistent peace policy.

A realistic estimate of the international situation and the position of the German states in Europe shows that there never can be a united Germany belonging to one of the two opposed military alliances. Anyone who calls for a united Germany within the alliance of US imperialism, NATO or as a part of a Bonn-Washington axis—as the Bonn government does—has in fact abandoned the idea of the unification of the German states.

I cannot consider the present rulers in Bonn to be so foolish as not to know that their so-called "legal claims" to the frontiers of 1937 virtually mean war. But a war starting in West Germany—with or without a Bonn-Washington axis—would mean the certain annihilation of the West German Federal Republic.

The talk about the frontiers of 1937 is therefore a dangerous game of war and testifies to very limited political thinking. The West Germans should at last recognize that in 1945 a full stop was set to mark the ultimate end of an entire period of German history. The present frontiers are the result of the criminal rapacious wars of the German imperialists and their monstrous misdeeds. To the West Germans I can only say: it will make no difference if you cling ten times to the apron strings of the USA. You will attain nothing! Do stop pitying yourselves at last and moaning over the frontiers forfeited by the German imperialists and over the frontier between the two German states and between the GDR and West Berlin. It would be more sensible finally to carry out such democratic transformations in West Germany as would make possible the fusion of the two German states and West Berlin into a German confederation. That would ensure the German people a peaceful life. That would serve to ensure a peaceful and happy future for Germany. And it would at the same time allow the solution of human problems at present without a possible solution, and the elimination of burdens.

By developing its relations with other peoples in a spirit of peace and good neighbourliness the German people are serving their own interests and beginning to solve their national problem in the only realistic way.

During the elections to the Bundestag the SPD brought up the question of the German peace treaty. Since nothing was said in detail about the content of such a peace treaty we asked the question in our Open Letter:

2) What is your attitude towards the peace treaty?
What are the ideas of the SPD about the preparation and content of a peace treaty?

Unfortunately the SPD Executive failed to reply to this question as well in its answer. The GDR government had submitted a proposal for the drafting of a peace treaty to the four powers on 4 September 1958. The Soviet government declared that it would do everything in its power to bring about the conclusion of a peace treaty with Germany. In January 1959 the USSR submitted the draft of a peace treaty to all states which had participated with their armed forces in the war against Hitler. This draft contained the proposal that the allied powers should conclude a peace treaty with Germany, which was at present being represented by the German Democratic Republic and the German Federal Republic, or in the case of the existence of a German confederation with the latter.

The characteristic feature of this draft was the formulation of the conditions to guarantee a peaceful German state. The treaty should not only close the books on the war unleashed by Hitler Germany. It should also provide the guarantees that a war would never again start from German soil. The possibility of a peaceful and democratic development and fruitful cooperation with other states as an equal member of the family of nations should be guaranteed to Germany. The SPD leaders are fully familiar with the Soviet Union's draft of a peace treaty and with the proposal of the German Democratic Republic. They are also familiar with the proposals of the western powers which mean a non-peaceful solution of the German question. It is generally recognized that the attitude towards atomic armament and disarmament shows whether a peaceful or a military solution of the German question is desired. The questions raised in the letter of the SED to the delegates of the SPD Congress were not only addressed to all members and friends of Social Democracy, but to all citizens of West Germany.

We should start with disarmament in Germany. The Bonn government has unfortunately taken no steps whatsoever up to the present with a view to developing a policy of peace, disarmament and military neutrality or to join such a policy. On the contrary, its real political interest is expressed by revanchist policy, accelerated armament, in particular the drive for control of atomic weapons and the striving for a society shaped according to the dictate of the monopolies. The conception of a "formed society" has taken over a great deal from Hitler. That is dictatorship in the service of the big monopolies with Hitlerite methods, as for example reflected by the emergency legislation.

The recently published so-called peace note of the Bonn government was described even by some of its allies as being no more than a scanty fig-leaf for the policy conducted up to the present and which is to be continued in the old spirit. The world very soon recognized that here the old aggressive policy of revenge has been wrapped up in non-committal peace phrases. Some said that this note had a very American flavour.

Every West German citizen should stop once to think about the reasons why quite a few Western European allies of Bonn will have absolutely nothing to do with the revanchist policy of that government and are moving away from it? How should one explain the fact that French President de Gaulle, who obviously is not a communist, should wish at this particular moment to take France out of the danger zone of war provocation? Is he not doing so because he knows the details of Bonn's aggressive "forward strategy" and its axis with Washington, including the plans for the escalation of war, and because he considers these intentions to be adventurous and suicidal?

De Gaulle certainly knows more about these things than the citizens of the West German Federal Republic, who are being deceived by their government. Obviously de Gaulle takes a more realistic viewpoint of the situation.

The West Germans should draw the objective conclusion from his action that it is also high time for them at last to conduct a German policy instead of following that of the USA and finally to advance a West German contribution to stabilizing European security. It can become mortally dangerous to stare as though hypnotized at the Bonn-Washington axis and to insist on revanchist plans which in any case have no prospects of ever being implemented. If the security of the European peoples and that of the Germans is to be ensured, the West Germans must at last make a real contribution, putting a stop to the doings of the adventurers in Bonn.

The first prerequisite for peaceful coexistence of the two German states and of a peaceful solution of the German question is the creation of an atmosphere of relaxation in Europe by the renunciation of revanchist plans and atomic armament by the Bonn government. The governments of the USSR, the People's Republic of Poland and the GDR have submitted to the European states proposals for a treaty on European security. We propose that negotiations should be conducted on this proposal by all European states.

411

To the West German Federal Republic we propose a peaceful understanding. We propose serving the cause of humanity by disarmament. The proposals for a peaceful understanding proclaimed by us on 1 January 1966 can be accepted by all men of good will as a basis for negotiations:

both German states renounce atomic armament and every form of control over atomic weapons;

the two German states recognize the existing frontiers in Europe;

the German Democratic Republic and the West German Federal Republic open diplomatic relations with all states of NATO and the Warsaw Treaty in the interests of peace and European security;

the two German states declare their readiness for negotiations on disarmament in Germany;

the two German states solemnly renounce all measures, laws and regulations which block the road towards overcoming the division and reunification, such as atomic armament, emergency legislation, etc.;

the governments of both German states open negotiations with the aim of normalizing relations between the two states and their citizens.

If the Bonn government demands first moves, then we can only say that it is now the turn of those who have up till now failed to fulfil the terms of the Potsdam Agreement.

The question is sometimes raised as to how things will go on if the attempt of the Socialist Unity Party and the government of the German Democratic Republic to bring about an understanding with the West German state should not lead to results for an extended period.

I shall reply to this question so that no one in West Germany may remain under any illusion.

The German Democratic Republic has everything necessary to complete socialist construction out of its own resources, through its economic agreements with the Soviet Union, the socialist and other countries. Our military alliances guarantee a firm protection of our frontiers, which, as everyone knows, would be defended by the Warsaw Treaty alliance in a joint military action in the event of an attack.

Therefore an understanding with the West German state is not essential for the further construction of our socialist democracy and our socialist economy. We desire such an understanding as quickly as possible. But we emphasize that our construction of socialism in no way depends on our relationship with the West German state. The time is past when we were obliged to build up socialism while having our pockets continuously picked from outside. The firm and well protected frontiers of the German Democratic Republic set an end once and for all to this plundering and disruption of our construction work.

As concerns the preservation of peace, we can do a great deal, together with the entire socialist camp and with all peace-loving forces in the world, to prevent a new world war. And we hope that it will be prevented despite the dangerous policy of US imperialism and its West German imperialist supporters. I should like to observe in this connection that the struggle for the preservation of peace would be more or less hopeless without the rapidly increasing economic, political and not least the military strength of the Soviet Union. Our efforts alone will not suffice to transform the existing aggressive, monopoly West German state into a peaceful, democratic state ready to reach an understanding. For this it is necessary above all to bring about an understanding between the workers and the organizations of the workers of both German states. That is why we have taken the initiative in an effort to bring about a dialogue with the West German social democrats, the members and friends of the Social Democratic Party on questions on which we will have to come to a common point of view in order to advance at all.

On the Preparation of a German Confederation

We consider that the most important aim must be an exchange of opinions between the two great German parties, the SPD and the SED, about the way of a peaceful settlement of the German question. In the letter to the delegates of the Dortmund Congress of the SPD and to all members and friends of Social Democracy in West Germany, we raised the question:

3) What should the united Germany you are striving for look like?

Is it to be a German state in which the people take the final decision, or shall the tune be called by multimillionaires and Hitler generals?

As the SPD Executive has as yet failed to reply to this essential question as well, I should like to go into the position of the SED somewhat more closely, in order to animate the dialogue on a constructive basis.

The SPD leaders will know that the so-called "Research Advisory Council of the All-German Ministry in Bonn", which also includes representatives of the SPD, drew up a comprehensive documentation for "X Day". This documentation states that German unity should serve the purpose of extending the domain of the big West German monopolies and of militarism to the German Democratic Republic, too. The "formed society" of state monopoly capitalism in West Germany is to be extended to the GDR. The whole of that documentation is not worth the paper on which it is written.

The Bonn government thus intends to implement its "exclusive representation claim" in the spirit of extending the rule of the big monopolies, big landowners and Hitler generals to the east. It would like to export militarism.

We, on the other hand, are realistically thinking people. We have no intention simply to export our socialist system of society to West Germany. We have no model such as that drawn up by the so-called research council. We base our considerations on the interests and the will of the people. The working class of West Germany and peace-loving, democratic-minded sections of the population should conceive reunification as a means of liberating themselves from the strait-jacket of the formed society. We will certainly meet with the agreement of the working class, the social democrats and trade unionists in that we consider the road to reunification to be a long struggle between the peaceful and democratic forces and those of reaction and militarism.

Our proposal for the formation of a confederation serves the aim of facilitating the transition by the people without injury by virtue of their own strength.

We are convinced that peace-loving Germans will be supported by the peoples of Europe fighting for European security.

Our statements on reunited Germany are meant as proposals and as a basis of discussion between the working class of the two German states, between the two strongest German political parties, the SED and the SPD, between the trade unions, between Christian circles of the population and between all democratic forces of the parties existing in Germany.

Any solution of the German question including the unification of the German states must be based on their rapprochement and understanding and their cooperation in the sense of a German confederation. There is no other way.

The conclusion of a peaceful understanding, above all between the two German working-class parties of the east and west, and also between the two German states is thus indispensable.

This will give their governments an opportunity to come to an agreement on the specific details of the preparation of their cooperation within the framework of the German confederation.

In this connection I should like to recall that some time ago a representative of the Adenauer government and a representative of the GDR government discussed the formation of a German confederation. If at that time agreement had been reached, as we had desired, we should have been spared the constant deepening of the gulf of division since that time. The People's Chamber and the government of the German Democratic Republic have not only on one occasion advanced the proposal of this only remaining way to overcome the split. In case the SPD leaders should support the CDU opinion that reunification is a matter of concern of the four powers, they are faced with the fact that as a result of the specific interests of US finance capital during these past 20 years the four powers have not advanced a single step. Peace-loving forces in Germany will thus first have to reach an understanding themselves.

We renew our offer today. We are preparing to turn the idea of a German confederation into reality and for a new, united homeland of the Germans to arise one day out of the cooperation and assembly within the framework of that confederation.

It is comparatively simple for us to say what the GDR should and will do in order to prepare that way and to provide for a respected position for the future Germany in the world of tomorrow.

The German Democratic Republic will unswervingly continue its peace policy and its socialist construction, so that the power of its ideas may exert an even greater effect on the workers and all peace-loving forces in the other German state. The strength of our system arises from the agreement of the interests of the citizens with the well understood interests of society and its state. The Socialist Unity Party of Germany and the government of our workers' and farmers' state will make every endeavour to ensure that the interests of individual citizens and those of work collectives correspond even better and more harmoniously with the interests of society. As regards the basic political problems, such as for instance the struggle for peace, these interests have always been in agreement.

In the economic sphere we have a complicated phase of development behind us. It was difficult to give shape to the new after the catastrophe of the war. Since we experienced these things ourselves, we are taking such a resolute stand in favour of imposing the historically necessary social transformations in peace through the struggle of the forces of democracy.

During the first years our state had to demand a great effort from individual citizens and from work collectives; these efforts hardly appeared to harmonize with their interests. Yet they were absolutely necessary for making possible higher living standards, even though slow at first but still continuous and certain. I recall the slogan: First work more and then live better! In the meantime we have achieved a great deal. Today every citizen of the GDR who does honest work is aware that doing good work is to his own advantage.

The safeguarding of our state frontier in Berlin made sure that we should no longer be deprived of the fruits of our labour. Only after this step had been taken did it become possible to bring the laws of socialist economics to full effectiveness. The new system of economic planning and management released new impulses for creative work. As a result of self-sacrificing work in the past, the fruits of joint labour at present are ripening much faster than previously.

We have firm ground under our feet on our way, which to begin with demanded much sweat and toil from the working people. We have begun the construction of our new house with the laying of solid foundations, not with the carpet for the living room or the refrigerator in the kitchen.

In West Germany the inevitable new construction of the foundations of society has so far been prevented by the CSU/CDU, the party of West German monopoly capital, and the US occupation authorities. In an effort to divert the attention of the West German working class and of all working people from this inevitable necessity, a so-called state of prosperity was conjured up with the aid of the Marshall Plan and other anaesthetics.

We have always held the opinion that a high living standard presupposes the safeguarding of life itself. In West Germany, however, the majority of the workers allow themselves to be hypnotized by a refrigerator and television set, electric washing machines and motorcars. In this way they allowed themselves to be misled into confiding their destiny once again to the same old imperialist wreckers of the German people, grossly neglecting the foundations of their house and the safeguarding of their own lives and of the life of their people.

At times many West German workers nurtured the illusion that they were better off than workers of the GDR. Yet today it has already become clear that workers of the GDR, led by the united party of the working class and by the establishment of their workers' and farmers' state and the construction of socialism have gone the better and safer way. We have laid the solid foundations of the rule of the people, the foundations of socialism. That was the hard start. Television sets, refrigerators and washing machines are coming into the fore today, and the number of motorcars will also increase.

In West Germany, on the other hand, the Ruhr miners have to recognize today, for example, that their "prosperous society", their "social market economy" have kept them from the main thing, namely, from laying the foundations of society. They see today what their much-praised "social partnership" is worth. And the "formed society", headed by the dictatorship of a small clique of the big bourgeoisie, with their emergency regulations and their militarism is to prevent them from drawing the correct conclusions from these correct perceptions.

The good results of previous work allow us to implement a new long-term plan in the GDR, which has set bold goals to all workers. As a modern socialist industrial state with an intensive agriculture, the GDR will receive and consolidate a good place within the group of advanced industrial states of the world. It will make further advances in the field of science by making considerable progress in the technical revolution.

Great tasks can also be set to socialist agriculture, as the material interest of cooperative farmers in modern agricultural production has proved to be a powerful driving force. Farmers are living in security for the first time in German history.

In accordance with the requirements of the modern socialist state we shall implement our great plan for a unified system of education and for a socialist national culture step by step.

The living standard of the citizens of our Republic will be determined by the results of their own work, in other words, it will constantly rise.

During the coming years socialist democracy in the GDR will be experiencing an even more successful development.

These perspectives are all the more important in the light of the fact that even a man such as the bourgeois philosopher Jaspers felt obliged to note the process of continuous deterioration and decadence of formal bourgeois democracy in West Germany and to warn against the danger of renewed fascism linked with the so-called "formed society" of the big arms monopolies and militarism. It is noteworthy to us Marxists that such a scholar, who has no sympathy for our policy and world outlook should come to conclusions similar to ours in an unprejudiced analysis of West German facts.

West German and foreign observers of our country cannot fail to confirm that the people of the GDR are increasingly clearly and firmly identifying themselves with their state and society, and that the citizens of this workers' and peasants' state in Germany are increasingly being guided in their actions by the interests of society. They have no differences with that society. They feel profoundly linked with it.

We are certain that the gradually growing socialist community of the citizens of our Republic will not fail to exert an effect on West Germany, and that they are making an essential contribution towards shaping the face of the future fatherland of the Germans.

In this way we are preparing for the formation of a German confederation.

Undoubtedly much must be changed in the West German Federal Republic before the process of the joining of the two German states and the special territory of West Berlin can begin. The West German working class and all West German working people are faced with the task of making up for much that should have been done or at least begun energetically already twenty years ago. This is difficult, of course.

On the other hand, the West German working people and other patriots have it much easier today than the people of the GDR. For the people of the GDR have successfully carried through two historical transformations in the past twenty years. Thus experiences are available as to how the historical tasks can be solved, what is suitable and what is not suitable. The West German working class with its allies, the farmers, intellectuals and the middle classes and all peace-loving and democratic forces can thus more easily find and enter the way which corresponds to the specific conditions of West Germany.

The West German monopolists and their politicians know but one conception of a future united Germany. With regard to the power conditions it does not essentially differ from the Germany of 1914 and the Germany of 1939.

We openly declare that such a united, but aggressive and war-thirsty German state in which the monopolists and militarists exercise power will never exist again. It will not exist because the people of the GDR who have built up an up-to-date peace state for themselves do not want it. It will not exist because a growing part of the West German population does not want it, either. It will not exist because the progressive states and the peoples of Europe, especially the Soviet people and even influential circles in most imperialist countries do not want it, either.

In order to advance the next important steps it is therefore necessary for those patriotic forces in West Germany which have a genuine interest in a peaceful settlement of the German question to gain in political influence.

The solid core of this great movement for peace, democracy and progress should be formed by the trade unions, the Social Democratic Party, the Communist Party, progressive intellectuals and the working peasants around which all democratic and peaceful forces could group themselves.

We are not of the opinion that first a kind of a second GDR should be created on West German territory so that later a uniform

German peace state could be erected. But we share the view of many West Germans that the common road to the great aim can only be found when the policy of the West German state is based on the vital interests of the working people.

In the decisions and discussions of West German trade union organizations, of organizations of the Social Democratic Party, the Communist Party, the Socialist Youth, the young trade unionists, the teachers' associations, etc., there are many demands, proposals and ideas which all aim at the necessary social reorganization of the West German Federal Republic. They make allowance for the present state of development in West Germany.

In the following are summarized the most important of these demands, proposals and ideas which are contained in the decisions of the Easter March movement of the opponents of atomic armament, the decisions of trade union organizations and of socialist organizations, of circles of intellectuals and the decisions of peasant organizations. Naturally no claim is made here to completeness, of a fully rounded-off picture of the necessary social transformation. This can only be a sketchy compilation of important spheres which, however, make the aim and the way clearly visible, seen as a whole.

The point is the realization of the most elementary demands of humanity and the safeguarding of peace. The movement for peace, democracy and progress developing in West Germany is based on the most elementary general democratic demands. Progressive members of the Bundestag demand a reform of parliament which restores the full rights of the deputies. These progressive parliamentarians demand the right to check on the enforcement of the laws and to report back to the population.

In the letter to the social democratic comrades we referred to the fact that the concentration of capital and the technical revolution imperatively demand the struggle for co-determination and the trade unions' right of control in the economy and in the enterprises.

Important trade union forces rightfully demand a change in the relations of power in West German big industry, above all. This is necessary in order to create lasting foundations for the livelihood of the working people and their future policy.

Recently the social democratic scientist Vilmar proved that with the now attained high level of the concentration of capital and production, armament economy is an essential and bearing element of late capitalism which secures the basis of the economic and political existence of the ruling circles and at the same time determines its political action. Vilmar proves that the co-determination of the working people in the economy, the democratic control of the large enterprises and the planning of the national economy compellingly result from the political and economic interests of the working people—and naturally he earns for it the sharp attacks of the trusts and their press.

It is of special significance to bring the newspaper trusts such as the Springer trust, etc., under control so as to end the cold war agitation and warmongering.

A democratic land reform ensuring peasant property is also opportune. Naturally such a land reform must not be an imitation of the measures which were necessary in the GDR and stood the test here. In West Germany different conditions have developed under state monopoly capitalism. The working peasants in West Germany increasingly seek for ways, through mutual help, joint and cooperative work, to utilize the advantages of modern agricultural methods—as far as this is possible at all under capitalist conditions.

Through repulsing the influence of the big banks and trusts it would be possible at once to make the Raiffeisen cooperatives democratic organs of the peasants again. They would play a major part in the development of mutual help and joint work, in buying and selling and the processing of agricultural products.

Tenant farming plays a big role in West Germany. All farmers who have leased land from the state or from big landowners could continue to cultivate it if they want to. Exorbitant rents would be reduced to a normal rate immediately. Land from the land reserve should also be made available to interested agricultural labourers, peasants with little land and especially peasant communities. Rents for land from big landed property could be used to finance peasant communities, the joint purchase of large machines, for the erection of cooperative buildings, etc. Naturally tenure agreements between farm enterprises would be untouched by these measures.

We ask the West German population: Is it not high time to realize the equality of rights for women in West Germany, too? It is not enough to talk about it, it must be forced through with the help of the trade unions so that equal pay for the same work is paid to women and men alike, so that women are given leading positions in the state, economy and the educational system on a basis of equality. Naturally this requires special measures for the advancement of women and support for their social rise.

Young people rightfully demand the guarantee of the basic rights of the young generation. This is the right to learn a vocation, the right to an education, the same right for the youth of the working class to go to college and receive material support during study. A law for the protection of working youth is urgently needed. The trade unions have made many good proposals on this, but their realization is still lacking.

One of the most important measures of the democratic forces in West Germany would be the removal from the state apparatus, the police, the administration of justice and especially the army of the militarist, revanchist and extreme reactionary forces which bear a heavy guilt for the past and today again brutally represent the interests and claims to power of the big monopolies and realize their aggressive policy which is hostile to the people. What is needed is not a repetition of the denazification comedy which thrashed the little ones and let the big ones escape unmolested.

Democracy is impossible as long as war and nazi criminals and their like-minded friends sit at the levers of power. A stop must finally be put to the pernicious development in which the constitution is systematically undermined by the misuse of the law, where people are persecuted for the views they hold and the emergency dictatorship is prepared step by step.

The basic constitutional rights of the citizens must be restored. In the parliaments and in all executive organs and other state administrative bodies such citizens should have decisive influence upon state leadership who stand up resolutely for these elementary rights of the people, who sincerely work for peace, disarmament and understanding.

Upright state officials may continue to be employed and their pension right will be guaranteed. But above all those forces of the working people who up to now have been largely excluded from co-determination in the Bonn state, the workers, peasants, progressive intellectuals and democratically minded forces of the bourgeoisie will have to take over important functions. In many cases outstanding social democratic specialists in the communities and provinces could be made good use of. All the good traditions existing in this respect in the history of our people, especially in the history of the working-class movement should be brought to life again.

The burden of the state monopoly redistribution of the national income in favour of armament and the profits of the monopolies has been placed on the West German provinces and communities. The share of the provinces and communities in the tax revenues could be essentially increased. The provinces and especially the communities could thus be put into a position to fulfil those state tasks which are in the interest of the working people. The educational system, road and bridge construction, the health service and the various communal facilities and institutions could be sufficiently promoted financially. Thus 3,000 dwellings alone could be built for the price of one destroyer with missile weapons. A sum of 360 million marks which is wasted by Bonn for armament in a few days would suffice to build 260 central schools in rural areas.

It is urgently necessary to democratize the educational system and modernize it, enforce the right to education for all and purge the entire instructional material from the evil spirit of militarism, the policy of revenge and war propaganda. An educational system must be created which guarantees all children the right to education and gives them a general knowledge-irrespective of the social position of the parents–which by far exceeds the level of the present eight-class school (compulsory nine or ten-class school). It has to guarantee that the children are educated in the spirit of humanism, democracy, peace and understanding among the peoples. It is furthermore necessary to provide an up-to-date vocational training corresponding to the development of the scientific-technical revolution, varied opportunities to acquire college entrance standard and attend colleges and universities, independent of the social position of the family.

Such an educational system corresponds to the action program of the German Trade Union Federation (DGB), the demands of the 7th youth conference of the Metalworkers' Industrial Union at its meeting in May last year, the demands of the progressive student organizations and also the educational policy principles of the SPD.

In the field of culture and art the democratic demands of the intellectual and cultural workers must be realized and the influence of those forces which today try to force their reactionary stamp on West German intellectual life repulsed. We greatly esteem the humanist scientists and artists of the Federal Republic who raise their voice for relaxation and peace in Germany under conditions which are very complicated for them, who courageously oppose armament and the atomic equipment of the Bundeswehr, who stand up against emergency legislation and other methods of war preparation and call the war of the USA in Vietnam what it is, a dirty crime.

Relations between State and Church

In West Germany the perception is growing that here, too, the relations between state and church should be regulated in a democratic way, i.e., on the basis of freedom of religious belief for all citizens, tolerance and the protection of the undisturbed exercise of religion as is the case in the modern states of Europe.

Such a regulation excludes the imperialist misuse of the church for alien interests contradicting the tasks of the church and the love for peace of religious citizens. The churches and the Christians do not need a military ministration agreement, for example, which leads them to the side of fascist generals but they do need the cooperation with all people of good will for the safeguarding of peace.

During the Second Vatican Council the head of the Catholic church declared that reason, the readiness for negotiation and understanding, confidence and treaties are principles for the regulation of relations between the peoples. And in his speech to the UN General Assembly Pope Paul VI announced:

"You propose an extremely simple and fruitful kind of coexistence to the multitude of states which can no longer ignore each other: You recognize and differentiate among each other."

Similar declarations also became known from the side of oecumenical bodies of the protestant and orthodox churches. The realization of such principles and their observance by the church leaders in the two German states could undoubtedly have a positive effect on the normalization of relations between them. This is also in the well-understood interest of the churches, for then and only then are normal relations between the churches in the two German states guaranteed.

In the development of relations of confidence borne by the spirit of mutual respect between the state authorities and the representatives of the churches, use should be made of those good experiences which dignitaries of the churches in the two German states have been able to gather in standing up for peace and understanding during the past two decades, in their cooperation with the authorities of socialist and anti-imperialist states. Dignitaries of the churches who in past years supported the peaceful solution of the national question as patriots will enjoy honour and recognition today and in the future.

What is the question at issue then?

It is a question of shifting from the rule of the millionaires over the millions to a system in which the basic rights of people have a firm material economic and political basis.

It is a question of transforming the seeming democracy in which the electors can vote every fourth year, it is true, but in which they have nothing to determine in fact, into a genuine democracy in which the citizens actively shape their social life, in which they make active use of their rights and fulfil their duties.

That will be the democracy which is necessary in West Germany so that the road to peace and understanding of the two German states, the road to the fatherland of the Germans can be entered.

This would also be the right way to prepare the first concrete step to this aim, the German confederation!

West Berlin and the German Confederation

Occasionally the question arises as to what position will be occupied by West Berlin within a German confederation and what kind of relations will then exist between the German Democratic Republic and West Berlin.

Firstly I want to state that West Berlin, which is located on the territory of the GDR, does not belong to the West German Federal Republic and moreover will never belong to it. On the other hand I do not doubt that West Berlin, too, will be a part of the German confederation. The position of West Berlin and its position with respect to the GDR within a confederation will depend to a great extent on the behaviour of the West Berliners and especially of the West Berlin Senate up to this time.

The continuation of a front-line city policy from which the cold war against the GDR is conducted would certainly not contribute very much to strengthening the future position of West Berlin in a German confederation. And every attempt to bring about complications through provocations of this or that kind will cost the West Berliners dearly.

Therefore, it would be most reasonable and for the West Berliners the most beneficial if West Berlin would not allow itself to be involved in any adventures by the Bonn revanchist politicians. The West Berliners should be quite satisfied with the status quo. Everything that worries many West Berliners at present will be settled in a reasonable way after the formation of a German confederation and the conclusion of a German peace treaty.

I want to tell the West Berliners as well as the West Germans that all measures which are necessary for the security of the GDR, its peaceful life and construction will be carried through. Nothing can be changed on this score. But when a German confederation will have come into existence, when West Germany will have finally renounced revanchist policy and armament, its striving to share control over atomic weapons, then we shall be able to give up many measures which are today necessary not only in the interest of the people of the GDR, but also in the interest of the population of West Germany and West Berlin.

On the Possibilities of the Confederated German States in the Transitional Period until Unification

A peaceful solution must be found and realized for the national and political questions of vital importance, and the two German states must approach each other and reach understanding. This would provide the foundations for realizing those ideas which deal with the economic and social development of the Germans in the last third of our century.

We Marxist-Leninists consider it our duty to set forth this order of priority unmistakably. We do not want the illusion to arise that the people of West Germany could solve the great problems of the social and educational system, of culture and the humanist sciences as long as reactionary forces rule there. We also cannot agree that social democratic leaders speak about the vistas of technical development and at the same time evade the burning social and political questions.

Although the confederation of the two German states will not yet settle the national question completely it will create important democratic foundations which make it easier than hitherto for the Germans to play an important role in the world as a power of peace and progress. We frankly say that in the age of the scientific-technical revolution the social transformation in the sense of the new shaping of social life is an inevitable commandment of the time. The growing together of the two German states in the period of the confederation is a struggle for the creative development of democracy in the state, in the economy and in the field of culture.

It should be self-evident that in the period of the confederation all cold war agitation and war propaganda are stopped. The freedom of opinion and world outlook is ensured only when the people free themselves from the pressure of war-greedy forces. It is therefore necessary to break the power of the masters of such opinion monopolies as the Springer trust. As long as the Springer trust and similar opinion factories rule there can be no freedom to form one's own opinion.

The interests of democratic development necessitate the transfer of the big trusts into national property with the indemnification of the shareholders in the period of the confederation. The participation of small shareholders shall be secured to the fullest extent.

We are certain that our people will highly appreciate the deeds of all those, among them also the members of the capitalist class, who have served the nation well, who have worked and are working for understanding and a peaceful and democratic development in Germany.

All those managers, directors, leading scientists and technicians who are connected with the people and their democratic system would certainly take an important place in society on which they could exercise all their abilities and talents for the benefit of the whole whereby they would receive adequate remuneration for their work.

425

Also the members of the liberal professions, the doctors, lawyers, writers, artists, etc., will experience new strong impulses under the new system for their creative activity in the spirit of humanism.

Instead of the dictatorship of the big banks which in economic life force their will upon the small and medium enterprises and make them dependent, which manipulates the so-called free market economy according to its profit interests, modern methods of national economic programming will prove to be useful and help to secure full employment, stability of the currency and social progress.

The social development would pave the way for an agrarian policy proceeding in the farmers' interests in West Germany, too. In West Germany the monopoly capitalist state, the feudal lords, finance capital, private big landed property, the banks, insurance companies and other capitalist companies—i.e., 1.4 per cent of all owners—possess one-third of the entire real estate. The peasant farmsteads of up to 20 hectares, however, i.e., some 88 per cent of all owners, must do with 37 per cent of the landed property. It is obvious that a land reform is necessary in West Germany.

The land of the feudal lords, the trusts, banks and insurance companies should be made available for cooperative use by those who cultivate it today. The state would grant them the necessary material and other aid during this transition.

If the people are in agreement, the feudal lords who in any case will forfeit their land, could keep a few castles and palaces and amuse themselves there with illusionary alliances of "reigning dynasties" and similar amusements as long as their bank account allows it. Indemnifications for private big landed property could be granted from armament funds saved. Naturally no farmer would understand it if those big landowners who are known as war criminals were also indemnified.

Private big landowners who after 1945 have served the German nation, the safeguarding of peace, the rapprochement and understanding of the Germans and reunification especially well should be allowed to keep landed property up to 150 hectares if they want it. Furthermore they would be enabled to exercise functions in the new system according to their capabilities which correspond with their experiences in the management of large agricultural enterprises.

Such a democratic land reform would also pave the way for a generous program for the improvement of the school system in the village, the placing of the village school on an equal footing with the city school, for tuition and teaching materials free of charge, no fees at agricultural schools and adequate grants at agricultural colleges.

Much could be done immediately to lighten the work of woman farmers, too, through communal institutions.

The progressive traditions of foreign policy, the consistent peace policy of the German Democratic Republic will be for the benefit of the German confederation and its external effectiveness.

With regard to their economic potentials the two confederated German states taken together would be the world's third economic power with a big lead over the fourth. The confederation would have available a considerable industrial, agricultural and scientific potential. Pledged to the policy of peace and disarmament the two member states of the German confederation would be able to guarantee their citizens a secure existence in prosperity which is based on the certainty that war will never again start from German soil.

But we have a different picture of the future life of the Germans in mind than that on which the present rulers in Bonn try to fix the mass of our contemporaries in West Germany. Philistine satiety, the stupid race for prestige consumption and desire for prominence as well as political passivity, coupled with nationalist arrogance and political ignorance do not fit into our conceptions. We reject all that. That is out of the question for us. We believe rather that it is important and will also be possible then to do much more than fully satisfy the material needs of all citizens including those who cannot fully care for themselves with their own strength. Only when the working people and their allies are in power will more resources, strength and time be avaibable to give all citizens a modern education and make accessible to them the treasures of knowledge, culture and art. Not limited by private property and the concentration of power, the rights and liberties of the citizens will fully develop.

To the extent to which working hours can be further shortened, active artistic creation, continued vocational education and the acquisition of knowledge in which people are personally interested will assume an increasingly larger share of personal life. But the participation of the citizens in public life will also grow. They will discuss, decide and solve their political and other social problems in the communities and towns ever more independently. Democratic activity and political responsibility will become genuine virtues of the Germans.

The two confederated German states will make use of their great economic power for peaceful performances in the fields of research and technology, art and welfare and an exemplary domestic system in the service of man and mankind.

The economic relations between the two confederated German states will be essentially intensified and brought to a level which corresponds with the requirements of the technical revolution. Practical West German economic circles already emphasize that in six to eight years a considerable part of the trade between the two states will consist of industrial plant. It is self-evident that the close scientific-technical and economic cooperation in such transactions will continue favourably to influence the development of normal state and other relations.

In a confederation the GDR can be of considerable help to the Federal Republic in opening up large new markets in the socialist states for its products, especially for industrial plants. The industry of the confederated German states will effect big sales which secure its full employment for a long time and which offer a close cooperation between enterprises in the two German states. In this sense the confederated German states will become an important factor of the increasing economic interdependence in the whole of Europe.

The confederated German states will be able to grant all peoples in the world who have entered upon the road of the construction of independent, sovereign national economies large material, cultural and organizational assistance. The German people will then be in an essentially better position than up to now to remove the scourge of hunger from millions of people in the Asian, African and Latin American countries by supplying them with the means of production and granting them other assistance which allows the peoples concerned rapidly to increase their own agricultural production.

Further important steps can be taken to make the citizens of the two German states benefit from the advantages resulting from the policy of peace underlying the confederation treaty. Thus tourist traffic between the two German states could be considerably extended and normalized. The security installations at the frontiers between the two German states and between the GDR and West Berlin can then be adapted to the conditions of peaceful coexistence.

Another big opportunity would be to complete the integrated educational system and make it effective for the entire nation; at present we are laying its foundation stone in the GDR. It will provide all prerequisites for reaching a new blossoming of the sciences in Germany on this basis. Research and teaching will be so promoted with a part of the means made available from disarmament that German science can once again achieve its world-wide reputation. Colleges and universities will be so extended and modernized that the democratic demand for "the same opportunities for all gifted young people, irrespective of the social position of their parents" can be fully realized in the whole of Germany.

The social system and public institutions could be shaped to meet the demands of coming decades. Instead of concentrating the creative forces on the construction of complicated weapons systems which in case of war would lead to the mass destruction of human life and the foundations of life, all resources will be available to combat on a large scale with the combined effort of medical scientists, biologists, physicists, cyberneticists, technicians, etc., cancer and other diseases menacing mankind today. Much could be done to arrange the work places at which the working people spend a large part of their life according to the modern conceptions of industrial hygiene.

Large resources become free to create a modern structure for modernizing the towns and villages, raising dwelling conditions and extending an up-to-date traffic system which will cope with the great burdens. Such expensive projects as the purification of the air and the waterways in the industrial areas and noise abatement in factories and traffic centres could then be realized successfully.

Older people who have a long life full of labour behind them could be given back a considerable part of what they achieved for society in their working years. All modern possibilities of social policy, medicine and psychology would be used to give the evening of life of aged working people purpose and content.

Thus out of the democratic development of the confederation will grow the peaceful reunification of Germany.

Dear Comrades,

Twenty years ago today one great aim stood in the foreground at the joining of the KPD and SPD into the Socialist Unity Party of Germany: The leading role of the German working class in state and society which was long demanded by historical and social development had to be realized, the destroyed country bleeding from thousands of wounds had to be led out of the greatest catastrophe of its history, and the destiny of the German people had to be turned to the good.

Today, on the 20th anniversary of the unification of the German working class we can state with pride that we have honourably fulfilled the historical and social tasks in that part of Germany for which we are responsible, in the German Democratic Republic.

But nevertheless on this 20th anniversary we must again deal, out of national responsibility and in view of conditions in West Germany, with quite similar questions which were already on the agenda two decades ago.

And what day would be more appropriate than this one to call into the consciousness of the working class and all progressive forces in the West German Federal Republic that the necessary changes will be impossible without a great movement for peace, democracy and progress in West Germany grouped around the working class. Likewise the overcoming of the division and the unification of the German states into a peace-loving, democratic Germany cannot be realized without a rapprochement and understanding of the SED and SPD on the basic questions of the future of the nation.

On the 20th anniversary of the unification of the two working-class parties into the Socialist Unity Party of Germany we again stand on the threshold of decisive historical developments. The future way of the whole of Germany must be fixed. The German working class in the east and west is faced with the task of maintaining its good name in the face of history and concluding the great work of national rebirth.

The Socialist Unity Party of Germany will exert all its forces to realize this great social and national aim.

Long live the Socialist Unity Party of Germany!

Friendship!

30 June 1893	Walter Ulbricht was born in Leipzig, the son of a working-class family.
1907–1912	Apprenticed as cabinet maker; travelled as journeyman through Austria, Italy, Switzerland, West Germany, North Germany, Belgium and Holland.
1908	Joined the Socialist Workers' Youth Organization.
1910	Joined the German Woodworkers' Association.
1912	Transferred from the Socialist Workers' Youth Organization to the Social Democratic Party of Germany.
1913	Attended the party school of the Social Democratic Party of Germany in Leipzig.
1914–1918	First World War. Walter Ulbricht opposed the granting of war credits as a member of the Liebknecht Group in Leipzig. During his military service he distributed leaflets of the Spartakus Group among the soldiers.
1918	November Revolution. Walter Ulbricht worked in the Education and Press Department of the Workers' and Soldiers' Council in Leipzig.
January 1919	Walter Ulbricht was among the founders of the Communist Party of Germany (KPD) in Leipzig.
End of 1919	Member of the KPD District Committee of Central Germany.
13–20 March 1920	Member of the combat leadership against the Kapp putsch in Leipzig.
December 1920	Walter Ulbricht became a member of the District Committee of the United Communist Party of Germany for West Saxony (Leipzig).
1921–1923	District Secretary of the KPD of Greater Thuringia.
5 November–5 December 1922	Walter Ulbricht met V. I. Lenin in Petrograd and Moscow as a member of the German delegation to the Fourth World Congress of the Communist International.
28 January–1 February 1923	Walter Ulbricht was elected member of the KPD Central Committee at the Eighth KPD Congress.
January–February 1923	Participation in the struggle of the Ruhr workers against the occupation of the Ruhr area.
3 November 1923	Arrest warrant issued against Walter Ulbricht who had to go underground until 26 October 1926.

1926–1928	Member of the Saxon Provincial Diet.
20 May 1928	Walter Ulbricht was elected to the Reichstag from constituency 18–Westphalia-South.
June 1929	Walter Ulbricht became political leader of the KPD in the district of Berlin-Brandenburg–Lausitz–Grenzmark.
1930–1933	At all Reichstag elections during these years Walter Ulbricht was elected to the Reichstag from constituency 3–Potsdam II.
26 September 1931	Sentenced to two years imprisonment by the Reich Court on the charge of "preparation for high treason"; his immunity as deputy of the Reichstag protected him against the execution of the sentence.
26 May 1932	The KPD proclaimed the Anti-fascist Action in the face of the threatening fascist dictatorship.
June 1932	Walter Ulbricht organized cooperation with the District Committee of the Social Democratic Party of Greater Berlin in the resistance to fascism.
3–8 November 1932	Participated in organizing the strike of Berlin transport workers.
1933	After the establishment of the fascist dictatorship Walter Ulbricht was among the KPD leaders who directed the anti-fascist resistance struggle. The Gestapo issued a warrant for his arrest.
1934–1935	Under the direction of Wilhelm Pieck and Walter Ulbricht the Political Bureau of the KPD worked out the Popular Front policy for Germany as a national policy of the unification of all forces against Hitler.
25 July– 20 August 1935	Seventh World Congress of the Communist International. Walter Ulbricht spoke about winning the majority of the working class.
3–15 October 1935	The Brussels Party Conference of the KPD developed the program for the establishment of the united action of the German working class and for the establishment of a Popular Front of all German opponents of Hitler. Walter Ulbricht reported on the trade union struggle in Germany.
23 November 1935	Walter Ulbricht and Franz Dahlem negotiated in Prague with members of the Executive of the Socialist Party of Germany on the establishment of a united front of communists and social democrats.
1936–1937	Together with Wilhelm Pieck, Rudolf Breitscheid, Heinrich Mann and other German patriots, Walter Ulbricht struggled for the establishment of a German Popular Front.
15 December 1936	Walter Ulbricht went to Spain to support the liberation struggle of the Spanish people.
1 September 1939	Outbreak of the Second World War.
22 June 1941	Hitler Germany attacked the Soviet Union.
1941–1945	Walter Ulbricht engaged in political enlightenment work among German prisoners of war in Soviet prisoner of war camps. He appealed to the German people to end the

criminal Hitler war. At the front, for example, during the battle on the Volga, he called on German officers and soldiers to save their lives and fight for a new democratic Germany.

12–13 July 1943	Foundation of the "Free Germany" National Committee with Walter Ulbricht among the leading members.

1945

February	The Political Bureau of the KPD formed a commission headed by Walter Ulbricht to draw up the guiding principles for the work of anti-fascists in the German regions occupied by the Soviet Army.
30 April	A group of German communists flew to Germany. The "Ulbricht Group" started to build up an anti-fascist, democratic administration in Berlin.
8 May	Unconditional surrender of Hitler Germany.
11 June	Appeal of the Central Committee of the KPD to the German people. In the Central Committee of the KPD Walter Ulbricht was responsible for directing economic and political construction.
19 June	Formation of a joint working group by the Central Committee of the KPD and the Central Executive of the Social Democratic Party of Germany, with Walter Ulbricht among its members.
25 June	First conference of KPD officials of Greater Berlin. Walter Ulbricht reported on the program of the anti-fascist, democratic order.
14 July	Formation of the Bloc of Anti-fascist, Democratic Parties. German central administrative bodies were formed in the Soviet occupation zone, the democratic land reform was carried out, enterprises were purged of active nazis and war criminals and the democratic school reform was introduced.
20–21 December	Joint Conference of the Central Committee of the KPD and the Central Executive of the SPD to prepare the merger of the two parties.

1946

9–11 February	First Congress of the Confederation of Free German Trade Unions (FDGB) in the Soviet occupation zone. Walter Ulbricht was elected to the National Executive, of which he was a member until 1963.
21–22 April	Unification Congress of the Communist Party of Germany and the Social Democratic Party of Germany. Walter Ulbricht was elected to the Executive of the newly founded Socialist Unity Party of Germany (SED) and at its first meeting he was elected member of the Central Secretariat and one of the two deputy chairmen of the party.
30 June	Plebiscite in Saxony on the expropriation of war and nazi criminals and on the abolition of the power of the trusts.

	After the plebiscite regulations were also issued in the other provinces of the Soviet occupation zone on the expropriation of war criminals and active nazis.
28 July–4 August	Walter Ulbricht spoke at numerous meetings and gatherings in Bavaria (West Germany) on the need for the establishment of the unity of the working class and for the development of a democratic life in the whole of Germany.
September–October	Walter Ulbricht spoke at numerous election meetings on the significance of the first democratic elections in the Soviet occupation zone.
20 October	Walter Ulbricht was elected to the Provincial Diet of Sachsen/Anhalt.

1947

January	Walter Ulbricht denounced the unification of the American and British occupation zones into Bi-zone as a step towards the division of Germany. He called for the creation of a central German administration with its seat in Berlin.
August–September	Walter Ulbricht opposed the separation of the Saar area from Germany and the Marshall Plan.
20–24 September	Second SED Congress. Walter Ulbricht reported on the construction of a new democratic economy and administration.
6–7 December	First German People's Congress for Unity and a Just Peace in Berlin. Walter Ulbricht was elected to the Standing Committee of the German People's Congress and the Permanent Secretariat.

1948

17–18 March	Second Meeting of the German People's Congress. Walter Ulbricht spoke about the program of democratic reconstruction of the economy. He was elected to the German People's Council and its Presidium.
15 April	Walter Ulbricht was elected chairman of the Economic Committee of the German People's Council.
2 July	Third Meeting of the German People's Council. Walter Ulbricht spoke on the two-year plan for the re-establishment and development of the peace economy.
23 July	First State Policy Conference in Werder. Walter Ulbricht spoke on the nature of the new state order.

1949

25–28 January	First SED Conference. Walter Ulbricht spoke on the economic policy of the party and the tasks in connection with the fulfilment of the two-year plan.
29–30 May	Third German People's Congress. In preparation for the elections to the People's Congress Walter Ulbricht spoke about the need to create a National Front of Democratic Germany.

4 October	The SED Party Executive adopted the document "The National Front of Democratic Germany and the Socialist Unity Party of Germany".
7 October	Foundation of the German Democratic Republic. Wilhelm Pieck was elected President of the GDR.
12 October	The Provisional People's Chamber of the GDR confirmed the Provisional Government of the GDR formed by Prime Minister Otto Grotewohl, with Walter Ulbricht as Deputy Prime Minister.

1950

3 February	Constitution of the National Council of the National Front of Democratic Germany. Walter Ulbricht became a member of the Presidium of the National Council of the National Front.
8 February	Walter Ulbricht justified the Law on the Participation of Young People in the Construction of the GDR and on the Advancement of Young People at School and at Work, in Sports and Recreation (Youth Advancement Law) before the Provisional People's Chamber.
6 June	A delegation of the Provisional Government of the GDR headed by Walter Ulbricht agreed in Warsaw on the joint declaration about the demarcation of the Oder-Neisse Line.
20–25 July	Third Congress of the SED. Walter Ulbricht reported on the five-year plan and the perspectives of the national economy. Walter Ulbricht was elected general secretary of the Central Committee of the SED.
4 November	Walter Ulbricht participated in the first German Peace Congress in Berlin.

1951

9 May	After a government declaration delivered by Walter Ulbricht the GDR People's Chamber decided to conduct a plebiscite against remilitarization and for a peace treaty with Germany.
30 October–1 November	The GDR People's Chamber adopted the Law on the Five-Year Plan for the Development of the National Economy of the GDR from 1951 to 1955, after a government declaration made by Walter Ulbricht.

1952

9–12 July	Second SED Conference. Walter Ulbricht reported on the present situation and the tasks of the SED. The Party Conference decided to start the planned construction of the foundations of socialism in the GDR.
5–6 December	First conference of chairmen and activists of agricultural production cooperatives (LPG). Wilhelm Pieck and Walter Ulbricht spoke about the new development of agriculture and the perspectives of the LPGs.

1953

8 May	Walter Ulbricht was awarded the Karl Marx Medal.
30 June	Walter Ulbricht was awarded the title "Hero of Labour" on the occasion of his 60th birthday.
24–26 July	Fifteenth session of the Central Committee of the SED. Walter Ulbricht was elected First Secretary of the Central Committee.

1954

30 March–6 April	Fourth SED Congress. Walter Ulbricht delivered the report of the Central Committee on the present situation and the struggle for the new Germany.
6 October	Walter Ulbricht was awarded the Distinguished Service Medal in Gold.

1955

14 May	Conclusion of the Treaty on Friendship, Cooperation and Mutual Assistance between the socialist countries of Europe (Warsaw Treaty).
20 September	Conclusion of the State Treaty on Relations between the USSR and the GDR, by which the GDR acquired full sovereignty.

1956

24–30 March	Third Conference of the SED. Walter Ulbricht explained the second five-year plan for the development of the national economy of the GDR.

1957

30 January–1 February	Thirtieth session of the Central Committee of the SED. Walter Ulbricht proposed a confederation of the two German states as the only real way to reunification. He explained why the laws of social development in Germany made a socialist perspective for the whole of Germany certain.
14–16 November	Consultation of representatives of communist and working-class parties of the socialist countries in Moscow. Adoption of a declaration by the communist and working-class parties of the socialist countries.
16–19 November	Consultation of 68 communist and working-class parties. Adoption of the Peace Manifesto of Communist and Working-class Parties. The SED delegation was headed by Walter Ulbricht.

1958

10–16 July	Fifth Congress of the SED. Walter Ulbricht reported on the struggle for peace, for the victory of socialism and for the national rebirth of Germany as a peace-loving state.

	1959
24 April	Bitterfeld Conference. Basic remarks of Walter Ulbricht on questions of the development of socialist literature and culture.
30 September	Walter Ulbricht presented the Law on the Seven-Year Plan on the Development of the National Economy in the GDR to the People's Chamber.
	1960
25 April	After all peasants had joined agricultural production co-operatives, Walter Ulbricht made a government declaration in the People's Chamber on the completion of the liberation of the peasants in the GDR.
7 September	Death of Wilhelm Pieck, President of the German Democratic Republic.
12 September	The People's Chamber decided to form the Council of State of the German Democratic Republic. Walter Ulbricht was elected Chairman of the Council of State.
4 October	Programmatic Declaration of the newly elected Chairman of the Council of State in the People's Chamber.
November	Consultation of communist and working-class parties in Moscow. Adoption of a declaration and an appeal to all peoples of the world. The SED delegation was headed by Walter Ulbricht.
	1961
17 April	Meeting of the Council of State of the GDR at which Walter Ulbricht presented the drafts on the tasks and working methods of the local organs of popular representation.
6 July	Walter Ulbricht spoke on the German Peace Plan before the People's Chamber.
13 August	Erection of the anti-fascist protective wall at the GDR state frontier with West Berlin.
	1962
6 January	On the occasion of the tenth anniversary of women's committees in the GDR Walter Ulbricht spoke to representatives of these committees on the subject "Women–Active Builders of our Socialist Life".
15 May	During the visit of a party and government delegation to the Czechoslovak Socialist Republic Walter Ulbricht spoke before the Czechoslovak National Assembly.
16–17 June	The National Congress discussed and adopted the National Document "The Historic Task of the German Democratic Republic and the Future of Germany" presented by Walter Ulbricht.
15–20 September	A party and government delegation headed by Walter Ulbricht visited the Rumanian People's Republic.
12 November	Walter Ulbricht spoke to the Research Council of the GDR

on the national responsibility of scientists and the struggle for the highest scientific and technical standards.

1963

15–21 January	Sixth Congress of the SED. Walter Ulbricht reported on the subject "The Program of Socialism and the Historic Task of the Socialist Unity Party of Germany." The Congress adopted the new Program and Statute of the SED.
10–12 April	Second session of the Central Committee of the SED. Walter Ulbricht reported on the "Past and Future of the German Working-class Movement".
24–25 June	Economic Conference of the SED Central Committee. Walter Ulbricht spoke on the "New Economic System of the Planning and Management of the National Economy in Practice".
30 June	On the occasion of his 70th birthday Walter Ulbricht was awarded the highest decoration of the USSR–the title of honour "Hero of the Soviet Union" together with the Order of Lenin and the Medal of the Golden Star, as well as the highest state award of the People's Republic of Bulgaria, the Georgi Dimitrov Order.
25–30 September	A GDR party and government delegation headed by Walter Ulbricht and Bruno Leuschner visited the People's Republic of Poland.
13 November	At the constituent session of the GDR People's Chamber after the election on 20 October, Walter Ulbricht was reelected Chairman of the Council of State of the GDR.
18 December	The taking into operation of the "Friendship" mineral oil pipeline, attended by Walter Ulbricht at the Petroleum Processing Works in Schwedt, marked a new phase in the development of the GDR chemical industry.

1964

6 January	Letter by Walter Ulbricht to West German Federal Chancellor Dr. Ludwig Erhard, proposing a joint agreement on the comprehensive renunciation of nuclear weapons.
3–7 February	Fifth session of the Central Committee of the SED. Walter Ulbricht reported on the "Implementation of Economic Policy in the 1964 Plan Year with Special Consideration of the Chemical Industry".
5 February	Walter Ulbricht received a group of deputies of the French National Assembly for friendly talks.
5 March	Walter Ulbricht received a delegation of Belgian parliamentarians.
11 March	Walter Ulbricht received a group of Italian parliamentarians.
12 March	Walter Ulbricht's reply to the Finnish "Appeal for the Peaceful Coexistence of All Peoples" was handed over in Helsinki.
22–23 April	Walter Ulbricht took part in the commemoration in Wei-

	mar of the 400th anniversary of the death of William Shakespeare.
6–12 May	A GDR party and government delegation headed by Walter Ulbricht and Dr. Lothar Bolz visited the Hungarian People's Republic.
26 May	Letter by Walter Ulbricht to West German Federal Chancellor Dr. Ludwig Erhard with renewed proposals for peaceful understanding between the two German states and for a bilateral renunciation of nuclear weapons.
29 May–13 June	A GDR delegation headed by Walter Ulbricht visited the Soviet Union for a great friendship trip, as a result of which the Agreement on Friendship, Mutual Assistance and Cooperation between the GDR and the USSR was concluded on June 12th.
18 August	Talks between Walter Ulbricht and the Bishop of the Evangelical Lutheran Church of Thuringia, D. Dr. Moritz Mitzenheim at the Wartburg on problems of the maintenance and safeguarding of peace.
1 September	Seventh session of the People's Chamber of the GDR. Statement by Walter Ulbricht on the occasion of the 25th anniversary of the outbreak of the Second World War and the 50th anniversary of the outbreak of the First World War.
11–19 September	A party and government delegation of the GDR headed by Walter Ulbricht and Max Sefrin visited the People's Republic of Bulgaria.
19–20 September	Talks between Walter Ulbricht and President Josip Broz-Tito of the Socialist Federative Republic of Yugoslavia during an intermediate stop in Belgrade.
21 September	Death of GDR Prime Minister Otto Grotewohl.
5 October	Walter Ulbricht was awarded the Great Star of Friendship Among the Peoples in Gold on the occasion of the 15th anniversary of the foundation of the GDR.
2–5 December	Seventh session of the Central Committee of the SED. In his concluding remarks Walter Ulbricht replied to current political and economic questions.

1965

15 February	Walter Ulbricht reported on the "National Mission of the GDR" at the session of the National Council of the National Front of Democratic Germany.
24 February	State visit of Walter Ulbricht to the United Arab Republic.
2 March	Walter Ulbricht was awarded the highest decoration of the UAR for heads of foreign states, the "Necklace of the Nile".
13 July	At the festive meeting on the occasion of the 20th anniversary of the Democratic Bloc Walter Ulbricht spoke on the theme "What We Vowed 20 Years Ago We Have Fulfilled".
1 August	In the Sunday Talk of the Deutschlandsender (radio sta-

	tion) Walter Ulbricht spoke on current problems in connection with the forthcoming elections to the West German Bundestag.
17–28 October	A GDR party and government delegation headed by Walter Ulbricht paid a friendship visit to the USSR.
15–18 December	Eleventh session of the Central Committee of the SED. Walter Ulbricht reported on "Problems of the Long-range Plan up to 1970".
31 December	In his New Year's message Walter Ulbricht again submitted proposals of the GDR Council of State to the West German Bundestag for the safeguarding of a lasting peace in Europe.

Zeit im Bild Publishing House, Dresden
First Edition, 1966
Printed in the German Democratic Republic
All rights reserved
Layout: Fred Brückner
Photograph: Gerhard Murza
Production: Grafischer Grossbetrieb Völkerfreundschaft Dresden

802/66 (2/3/4/5)